V.B. Rose™

Volume 2

Banri Hidaka

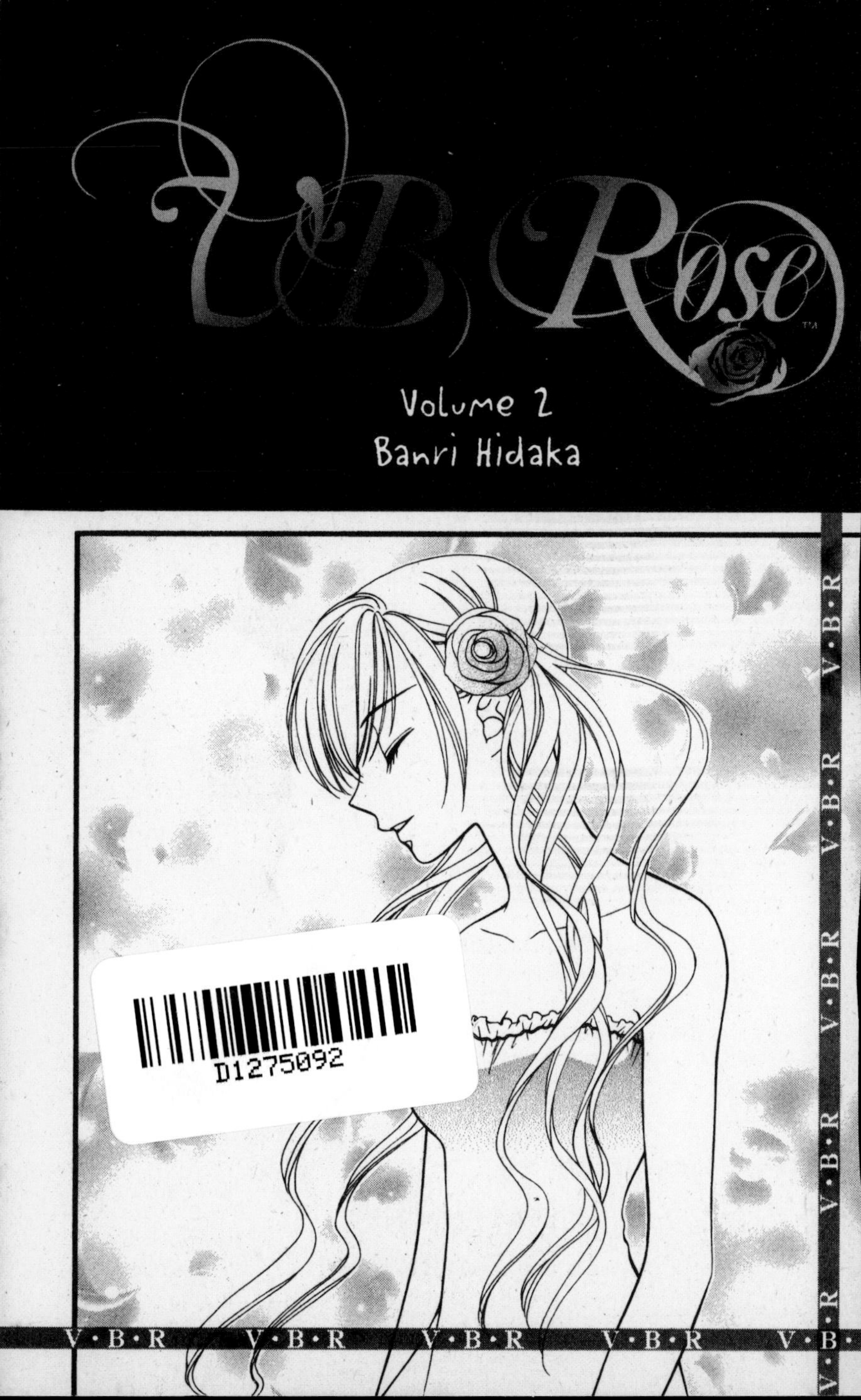

V.B. Rose Volume 2
Created by Banri Hidaka

Translation - Yuya Otake
English Adaptation - Rachel Brown
Retouch and Lettering - Star Print Brokers
Production Artist - Lauren O'Connell
Graphic Designer - James Lee

Editor - Lillian Diaz-Przybyl
Digital Imaging Manager - Chris Buford
Pre-Production Supervisor - Lucas Rivera
Production Manager - Elisabeth Brizzi
Managing Editor - Vy Nguyen
Creative Director - Anne Marie Horne
Editor-in-Chief - Rob Tokar
Publisher - Mike Kiley
President and C.O.O. - John Parker
C.E.O. and Chief Creative Officer - Stu Levy

A  Manga

TOKYOPOP Inc.
5900 Wilshire Blvd. Suite 2000
Los Angeles, CA 90036

E-mail: info@TOKYOPOP.com
Come visit us online at www.TOKYOPOP.com

V. B. ROSE by Banri Hidaka © 2004 Banri Hidaka
All rights reserved. First published in Japan in 2004 by
HAKUSENSHA, INC., Tokyo English language translation
rights in the United States of America, Canada and the
United Kingdom arranged with HAKUSENSHA, INC., Tokyo
through Tuttle-Mori Agency Inc., Tokyo
English text copyright © 2008 TOKYOPOP Inc.

ISBN: 978-1-4278-0331-3

First TOKYOPOP printing: May 2008
10 9 8 7 6 5 4 3
Printed in the USA

Volume 2

By Banri Hidaka

HAMBURG // LONDON // LOS ANGELES // TOKYO

Contents

Instructions to Velvet V・4

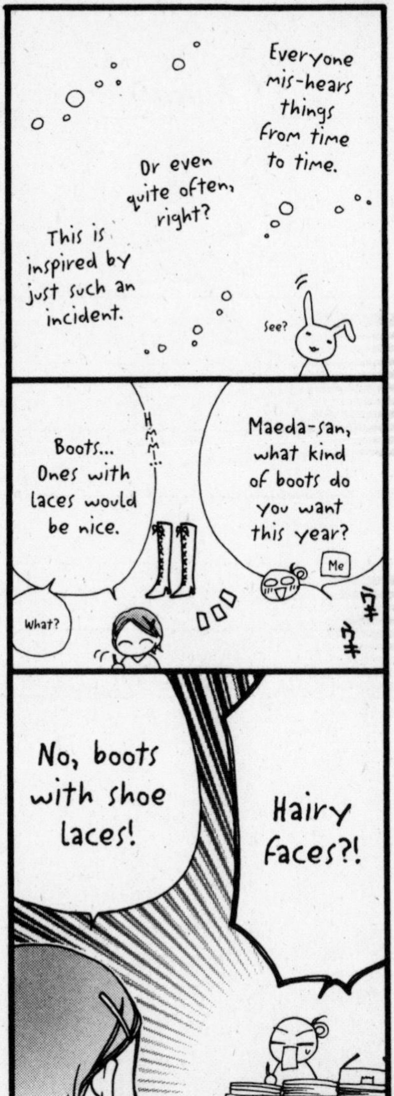
Everyone mis-hears things from time to time.
Or even quite often, right?
This is inspired by just such an incident.
See?
Maeda-san, what kind of boots do you want this year?
Me
ウキ ウキ
HMM...
Boots... Ones with laces would be nice.
What?
Hairy faces?!
No, boots with shoe laces!

I love Maeda-san's deadpan responses.

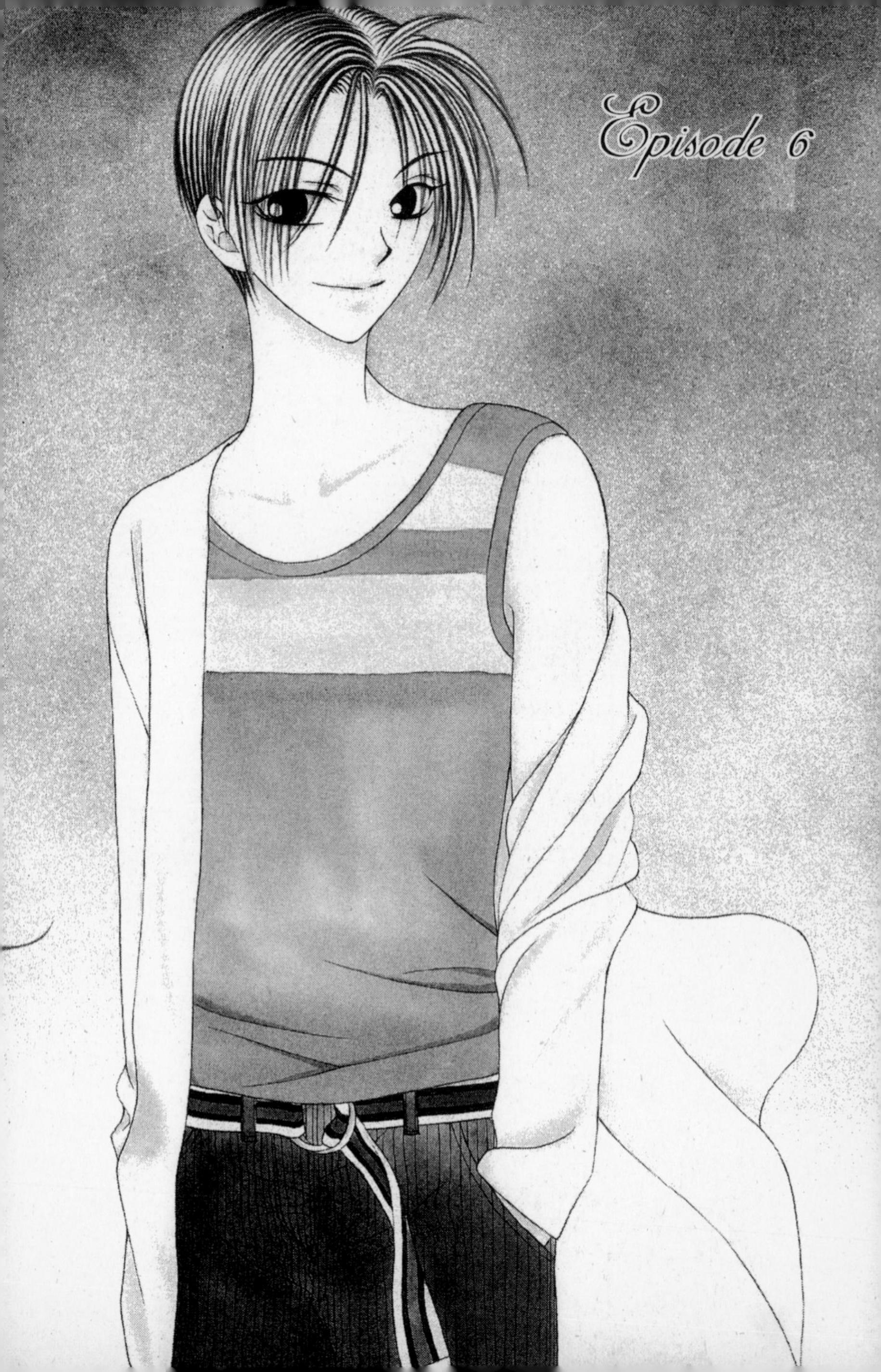
Episode 6

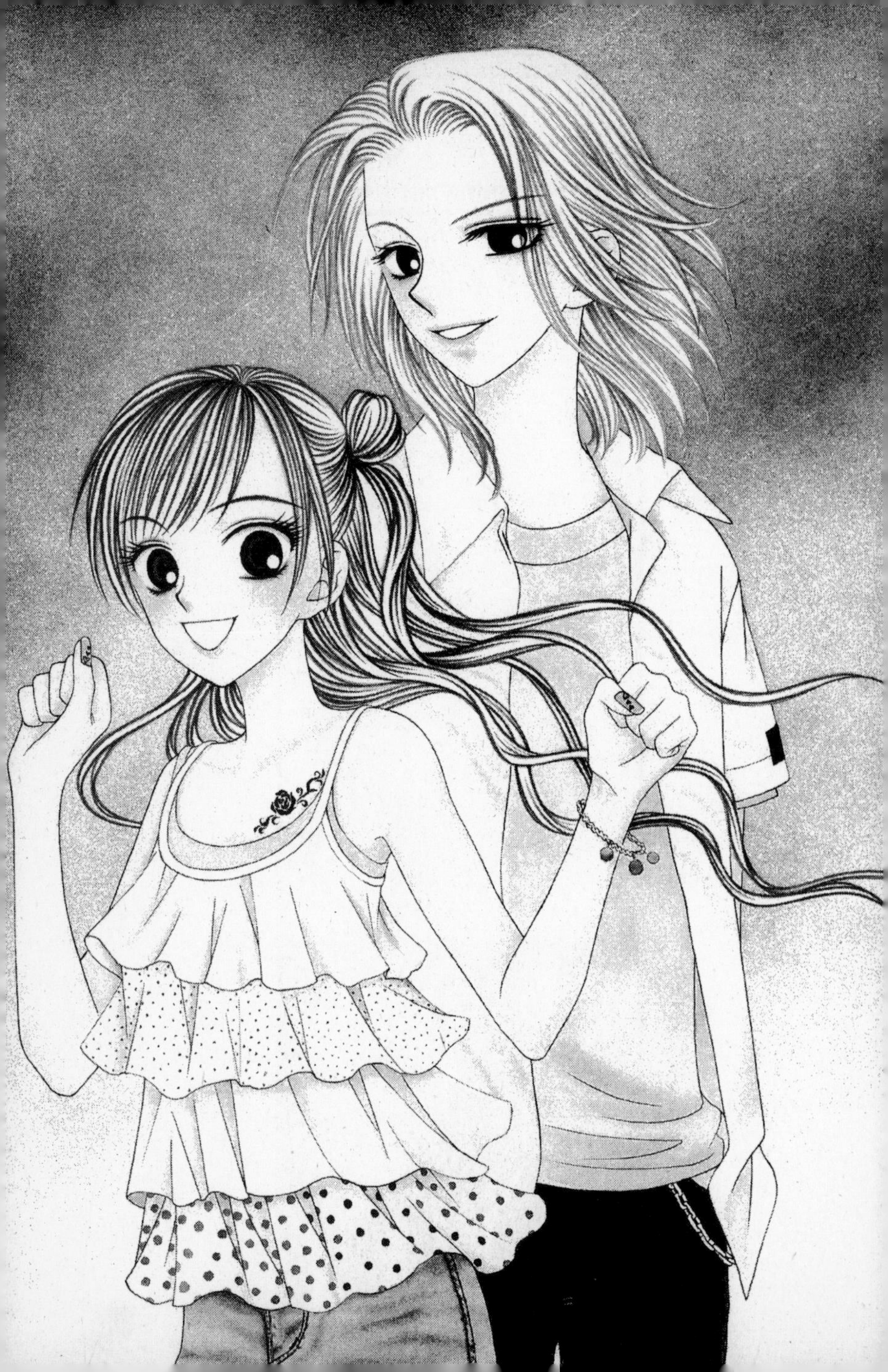

Instructions to Velvet V•5

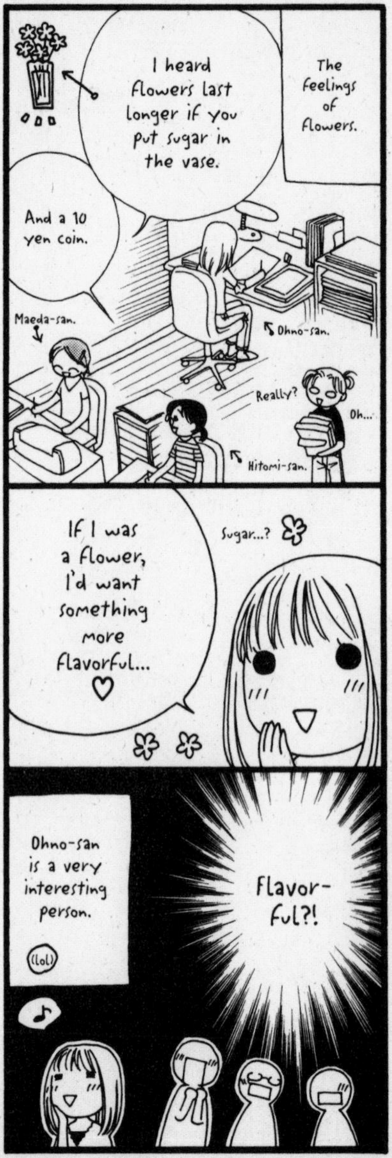
The feelings of flowers.
I heard flowers last longer if you put sugar in the vase.
And a 10 yen coin.
Ohno-san.
Really?
Oh...
Maeda-san.
Hitomi-san.
Sugar...?
If I was a flower, I'd want something more flavorful...
Flavor-ful?!
Ohno-san is a very interesting person.
(lol)

It was hilarious.

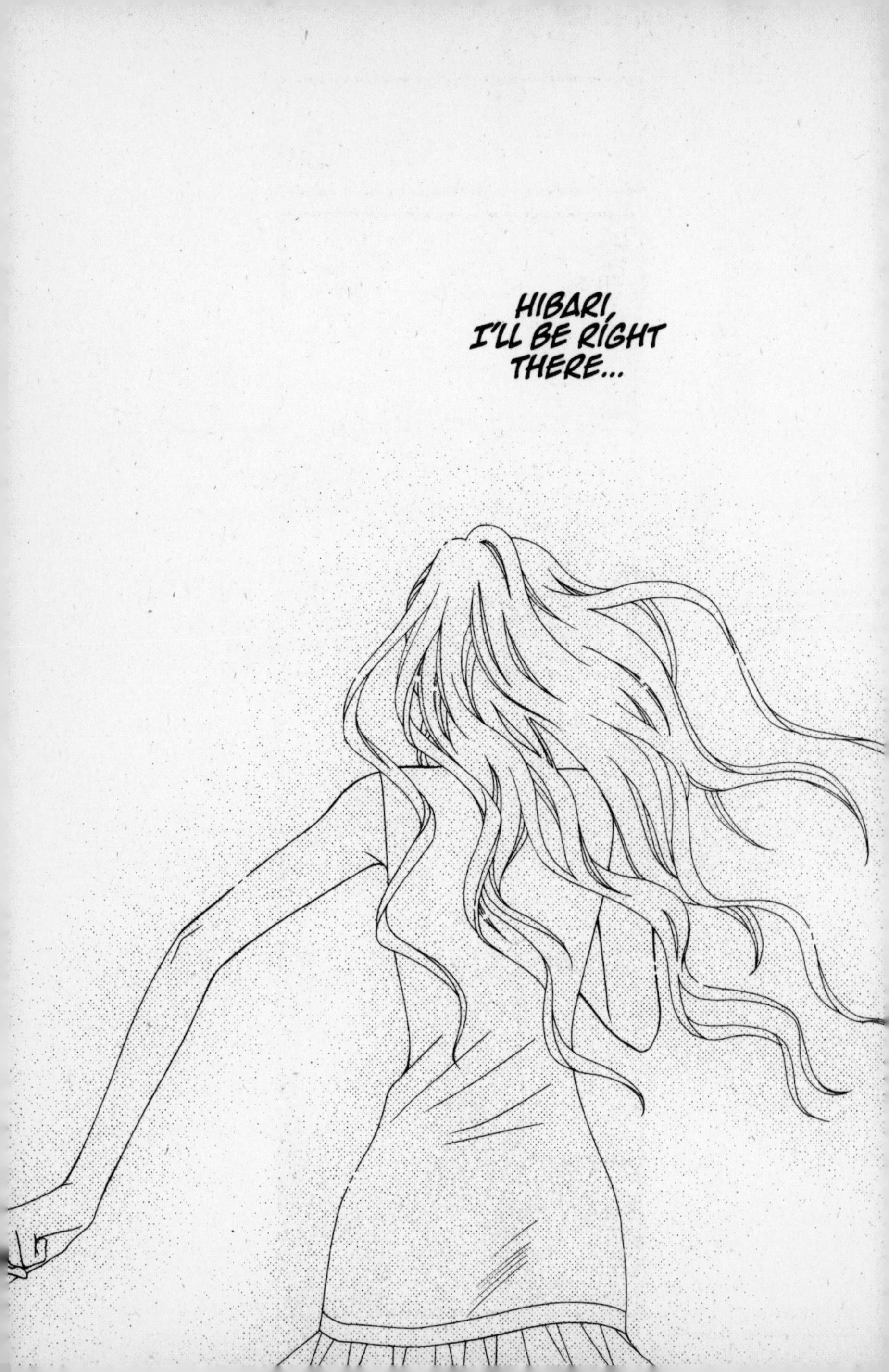
HIBARI, I'LL BE RIGHT THERE...

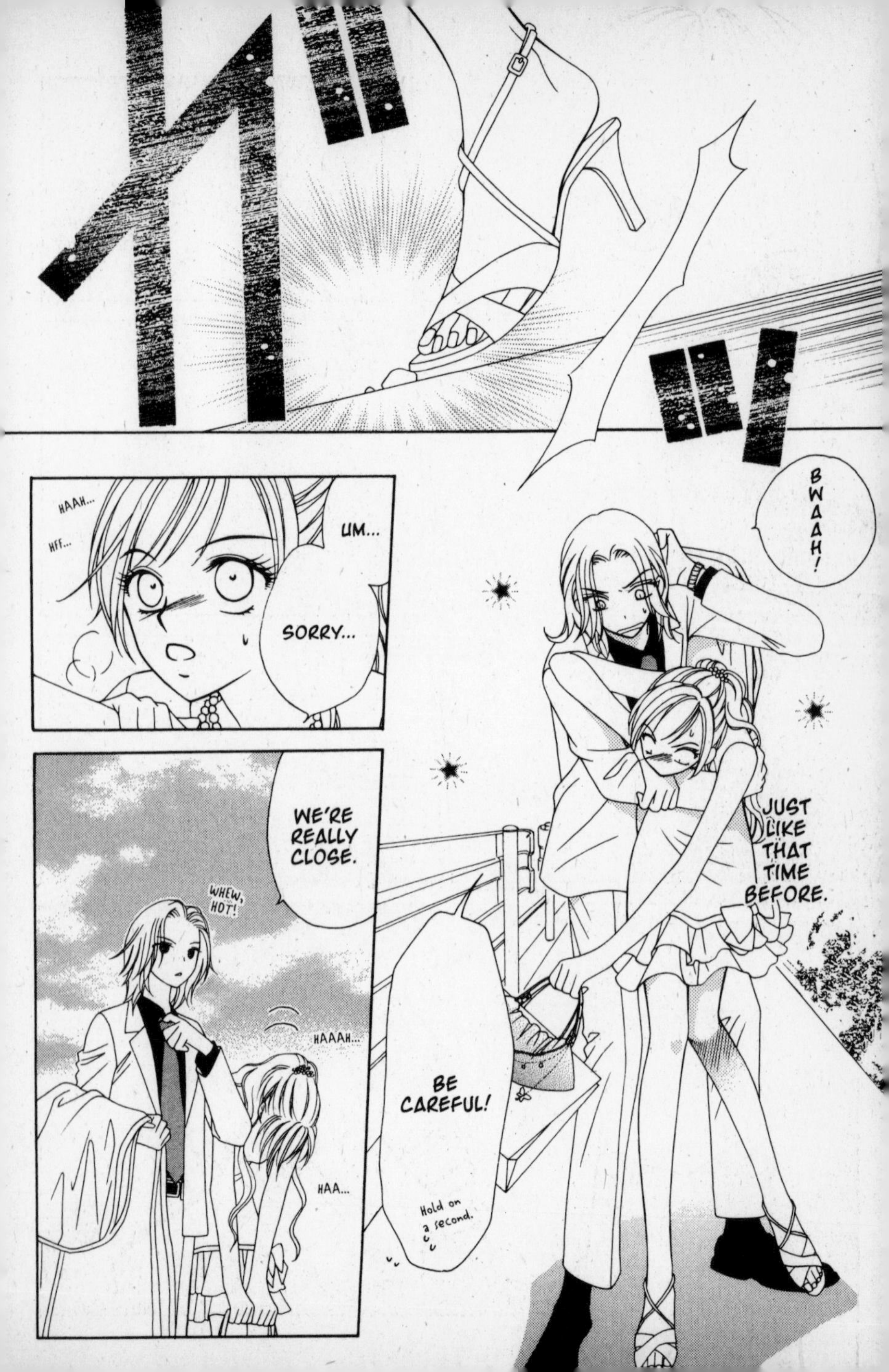
BWAAAH!
JUST LIKE THAT TIME BEFORE.
BE CAREFUL!
Hold on a second.
HAAH...
HFF...
UM...
SORRY...
WE'RE REALLY CLOSE.
WHEW, HOT!
HAAAH...
HAA...

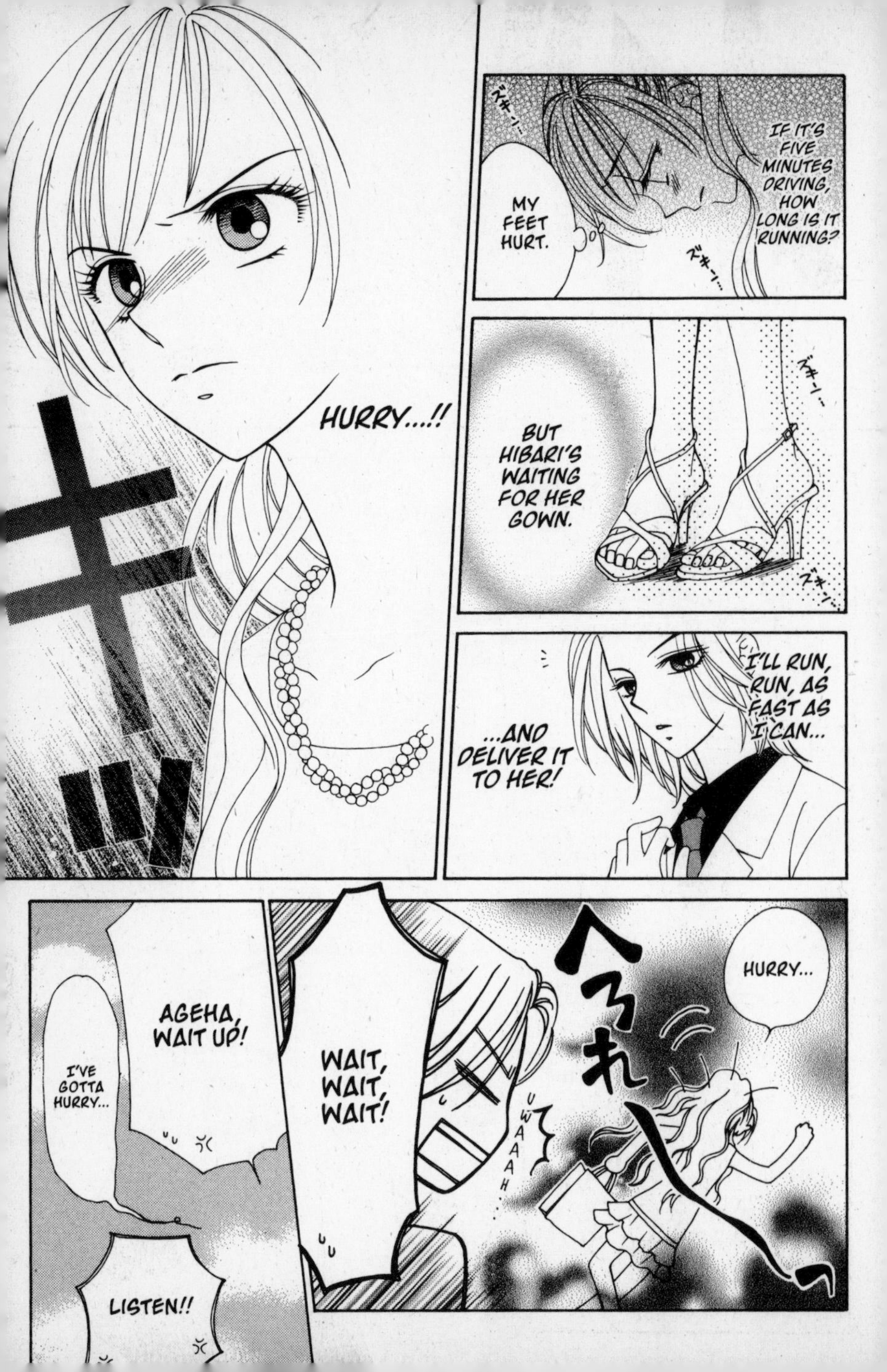
ズキー…
IF IT'S FIVE MINUTES DRIVING, HOW LONG IS IT RUNNING?
MY FEET HURT.
ズキー…
ズキー…
BUT HIBARI'S WAITING FOR HER GOWN.
ズキー…
I'LL RUN, RUN, AS FAST AS I CAN...
...AND DELIVER IT TO HER!
HURRY...!!
キッ
HURRY...
へろれ
UWAAAAH...
WAIT, WAIT, WAIT!
AGEHA, WAIT UP!
I'VE GOTTA HURRY...
LISTEN!!

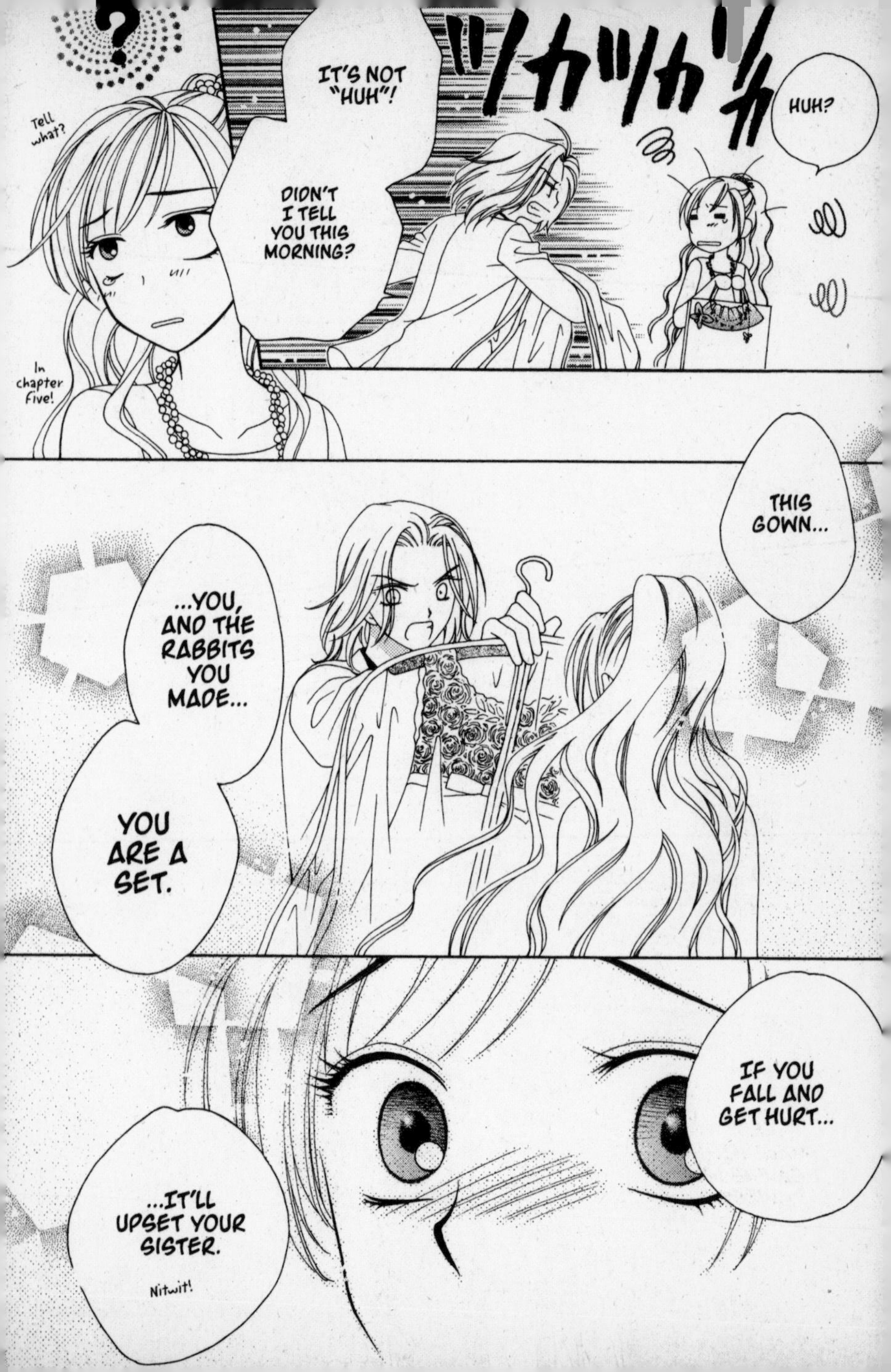
HUH?
ツカツカ
IT'S NOT "HUH"!
DIDN'T I TELL YOU THIS MORNING?
Tell what?
In chapter five!
THIS GOWN...
...YOU, AND THE RABBITS YOU MADE...
YOU ARE A SET.
IF YOU FALL AND GET HURT...
...IT'LL UPSET YOUR SISTER.
Nitwit!

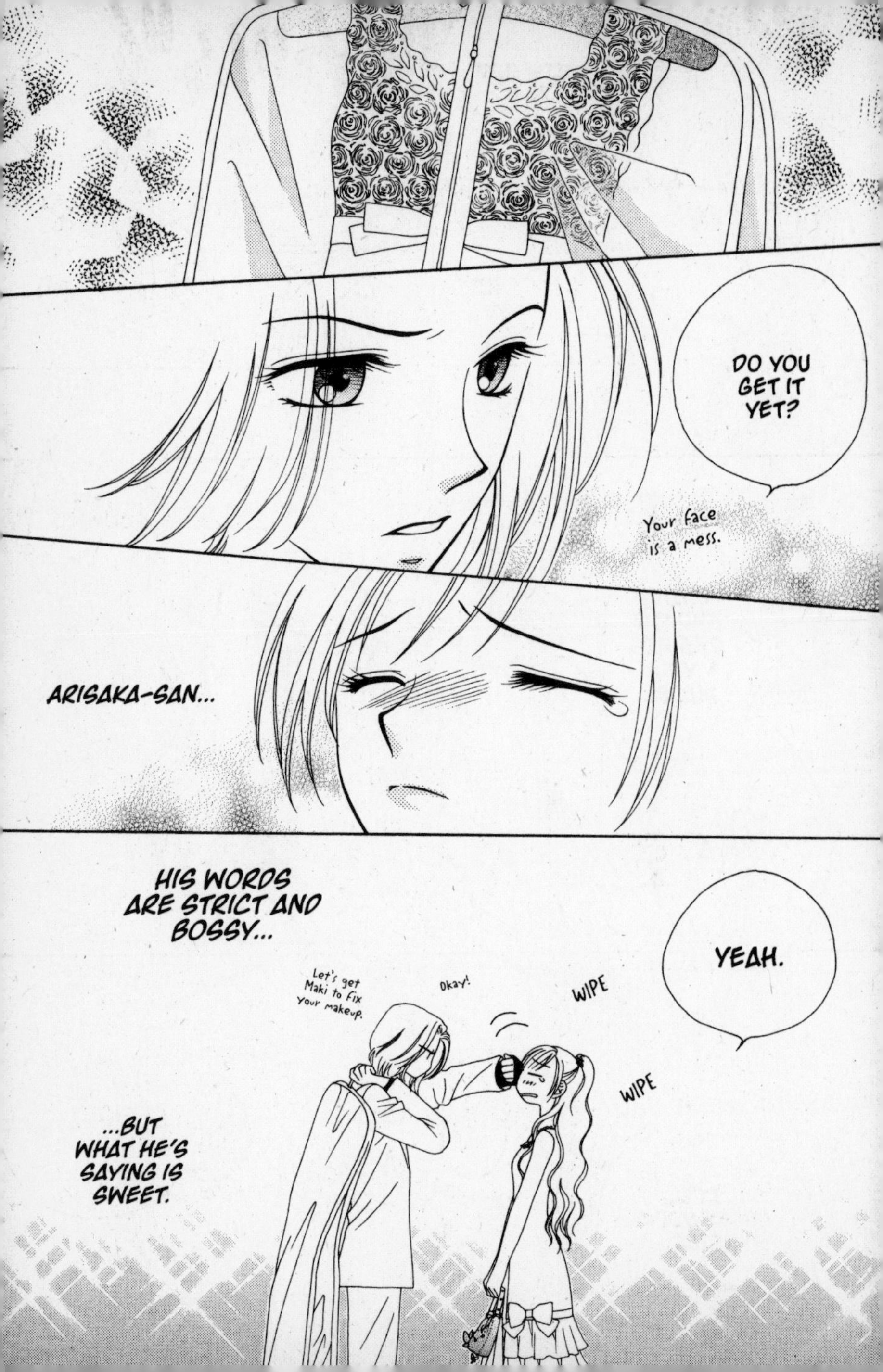
DO YOU GET IT YET?
Your face is a mess.
ARISAKA-SAN...
YEAH.
HIS WORDS ARE STRICT AND BOSSY...
WIPE
Okay!
Let's get Maki to fix your makeup.
WIPE
...BUT WHAT HE'S SAYING IS SWEET.

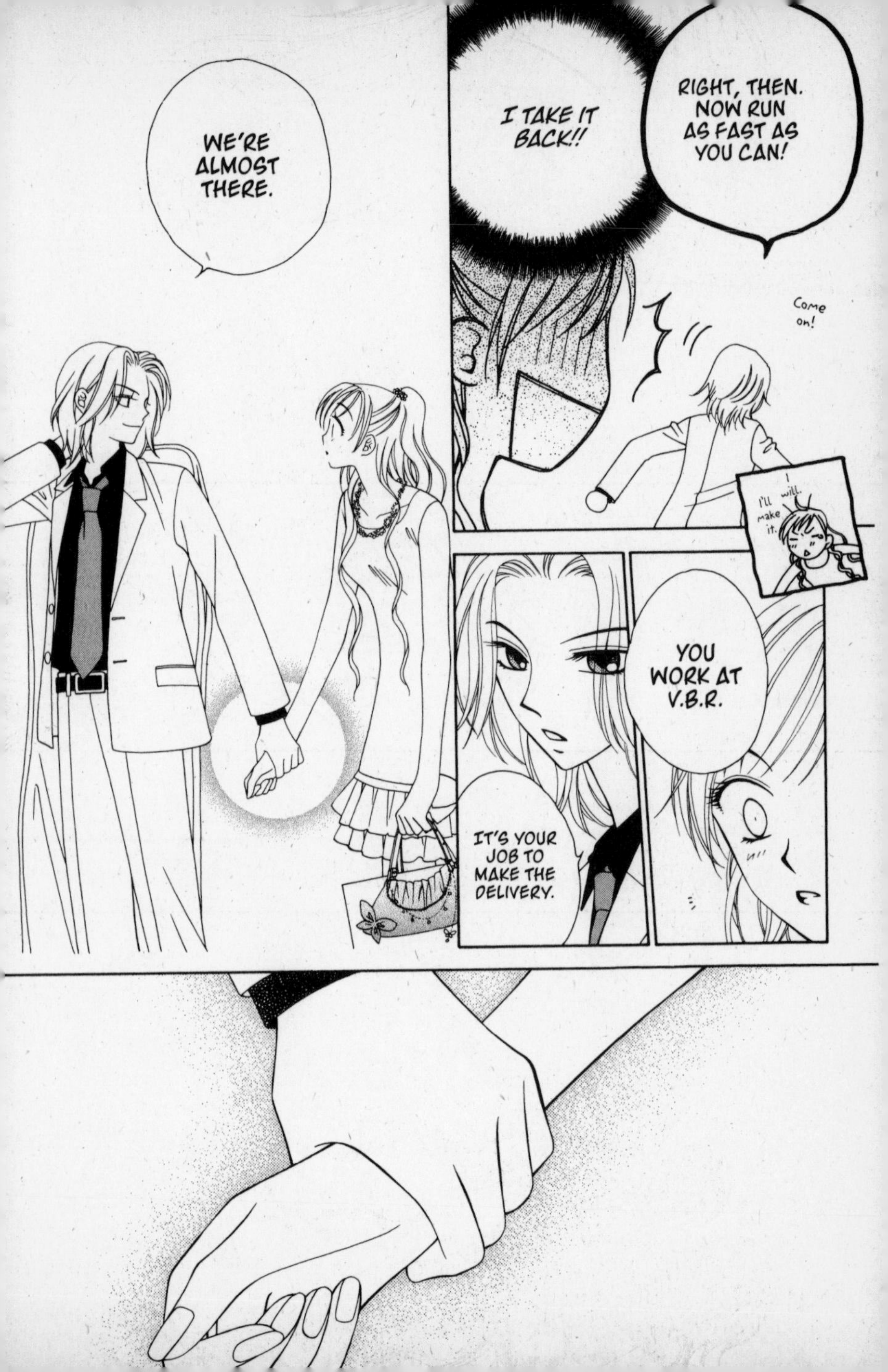
RIGHT, THEN. NOW RUN AS FAST AS YOU CAN!
I TAKE IT BACK!!
Come on!
I will.
I'll make it.
YOU WORK AT V.B.R.
IT'S YOUR JOB TO MAKE THE DELIVERY.
WE'RE ALMOST THERE.

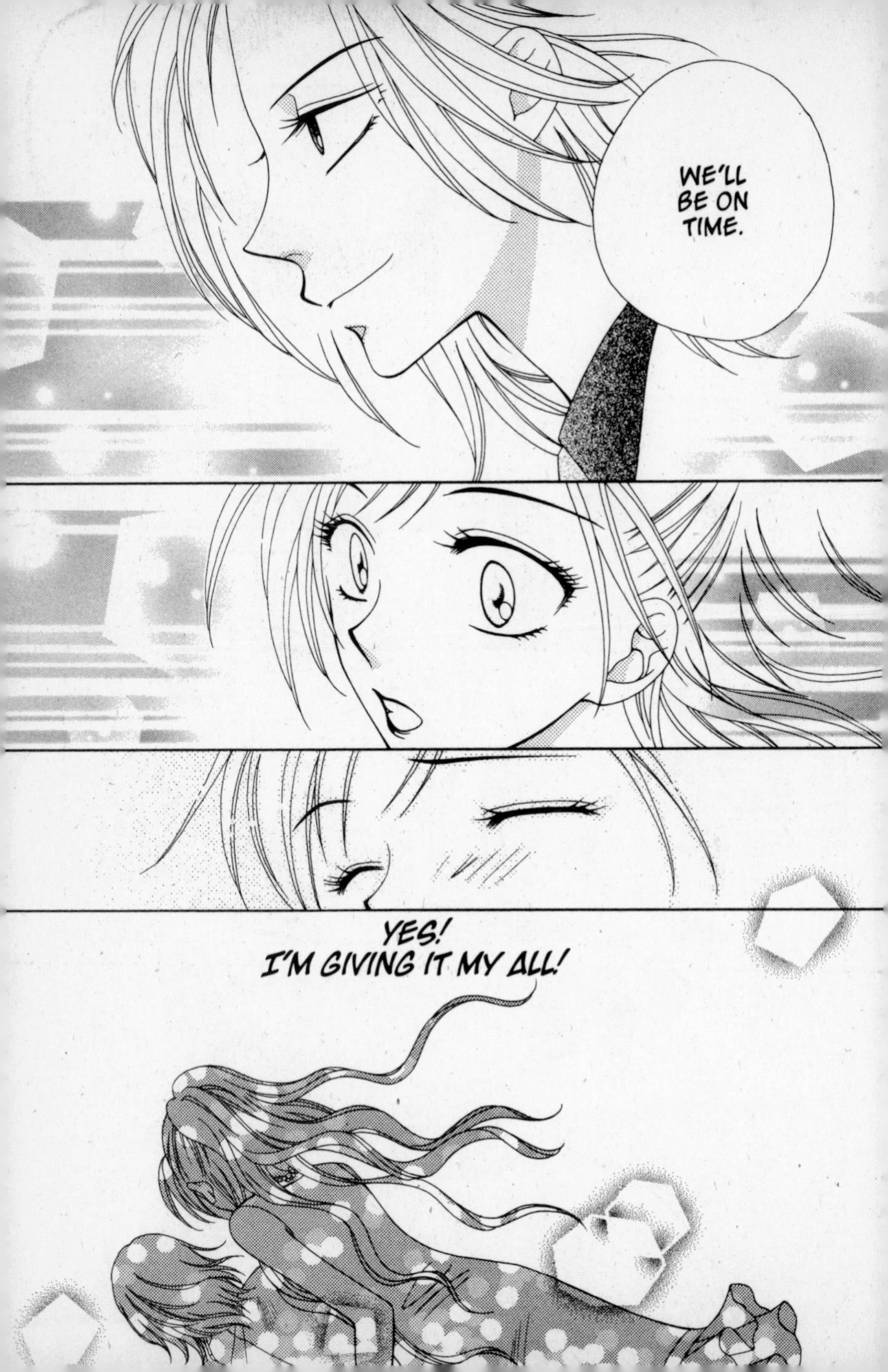
WE'LL BE ON TIME.
YES! I'M GIVING IT MY ALL!

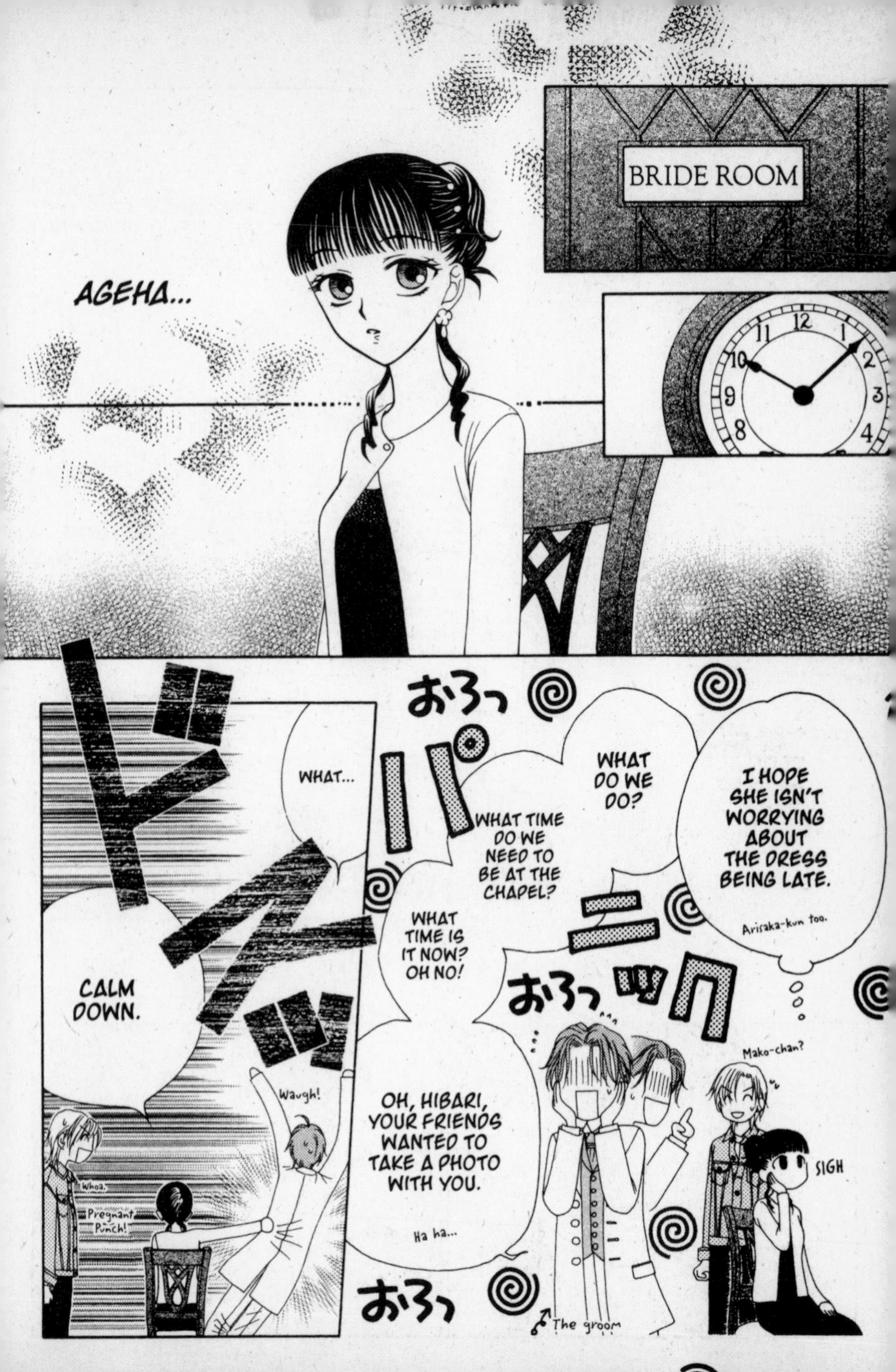
BRIDE ROOM
AGEHA...
I HOPE SHE ISN'T WORRYING ABOUT THE DRESS BEING LATE.
Arisaka-kun too.
Mako-chan?
SIGH
WHAT DO WE DO?
WHAT TIME DO WE NEED TO BE AT THE CHAPEL?
WHAT TIME IS IT NOW? OH NO!
おろっ
パニック
おろっ...
OH, HIBARI, YOUR FRIENDS WANTED TO TAKE A PHOTO WITH YOU.
Ha ha...
おろっ
The groom
ドンッ
WHAT...
CALM DOWN.
Waugh!
Whoa.
Pregnant Punch!

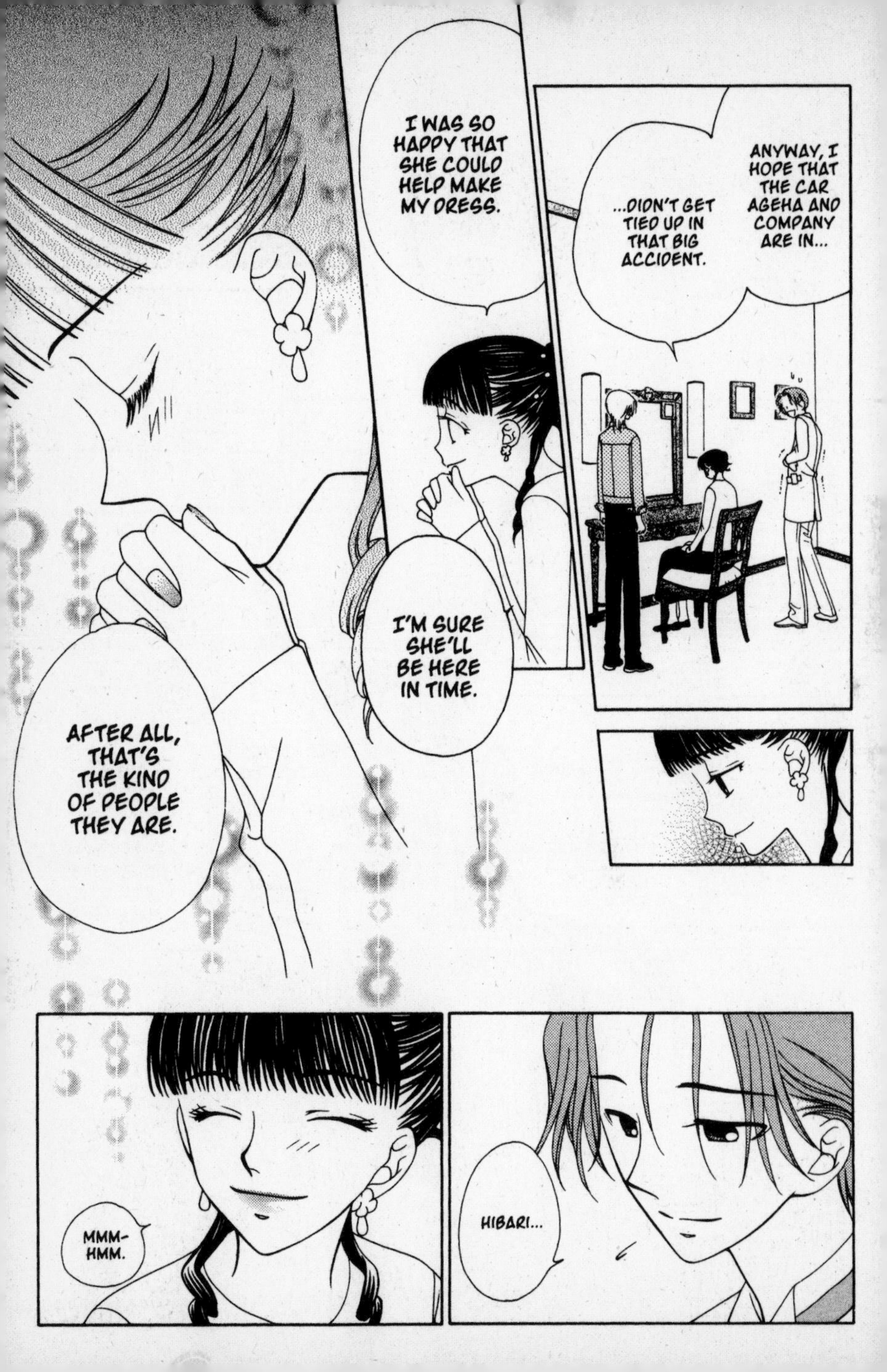
ANYWAY, I HOPE THAT THE CAR AGEHA AND COMPANY ARE IN...
...DIDN'T GET TIED UP IN THAT BIG ACCIDENT.
I WAS SO HAPPY THAT SHE COULD HELP MAKE MY DRESS.
I'M SURE SHE'LL BE HERE IN TIME.
AFTER ALL, THAT'S THE KIND OF PEOPLE THEY ARE.
HIBARI...
MMM-HMM.

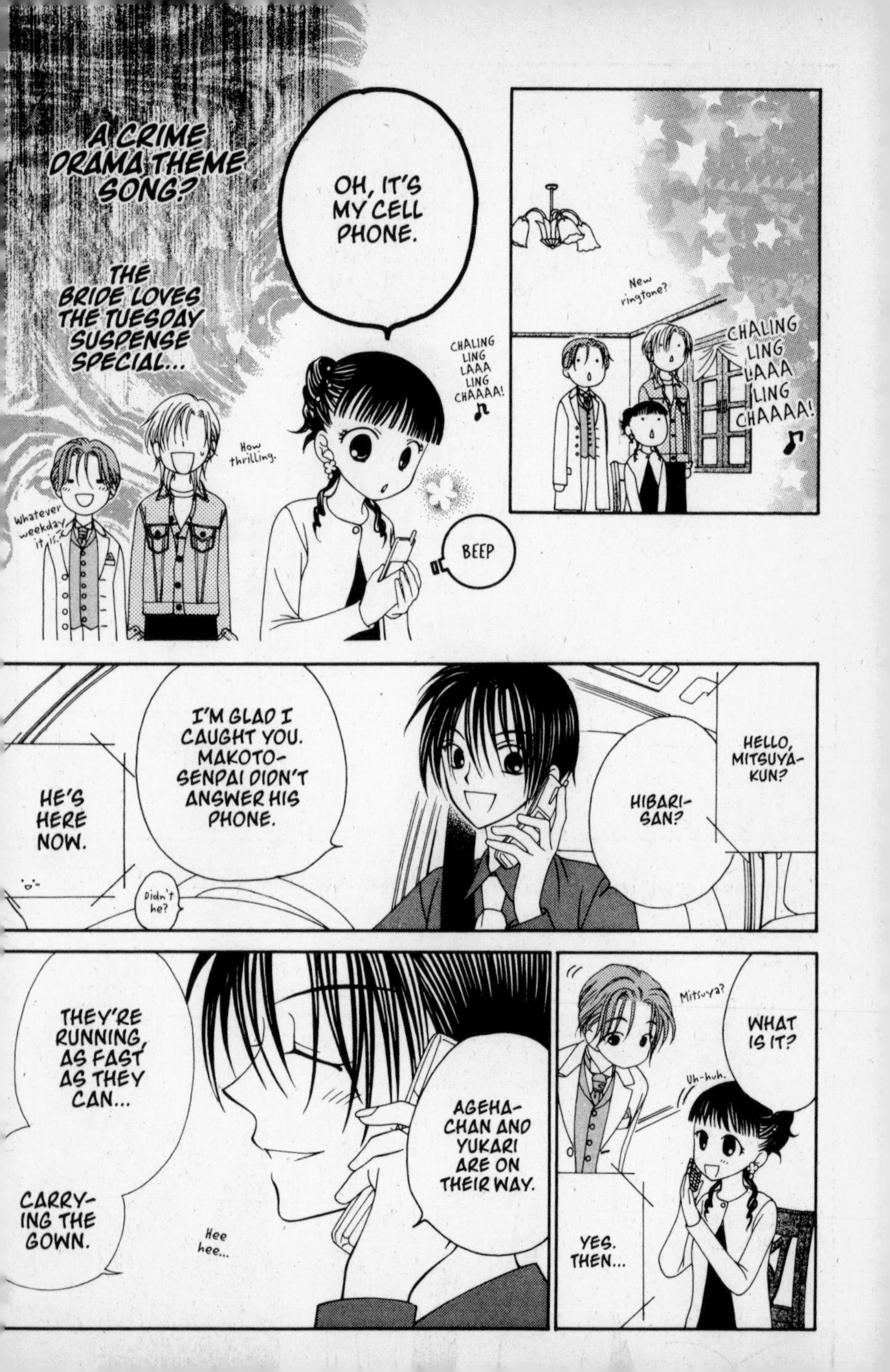
New ringtone?
CHALING LING LAAA LING CHAAAA!
CHALING LING LAAA LING CHAAAA!
OH, IT'S MY CELL PHONE.
A CRIME DRAMA THEME SONG?
THE BRIDE LOVES THE TUESDAY SUSPENSE SPECIAL...
How thrilling.
Whatever weekday it is.
BEEP
HELLO, MITSUYA-KUN?
HIBARI-SAN?
I'M GLAD I CAUGHT YOU. MAKOTO-SENPAI DIDN'T ANSWER HIS PHONE.
HE'S HERE NOW.
Didn't he?
WHAT IS IT?
Mitsuya?
Uh-huh.
YES. THEN...
AGEHA-CHAN AND YUKARI ARE ON THEIR WAY.
THEY'RE RUNNING, AS FAST AS THEY CAN...
CARRY-ING THE GOWN.
Hee hee...

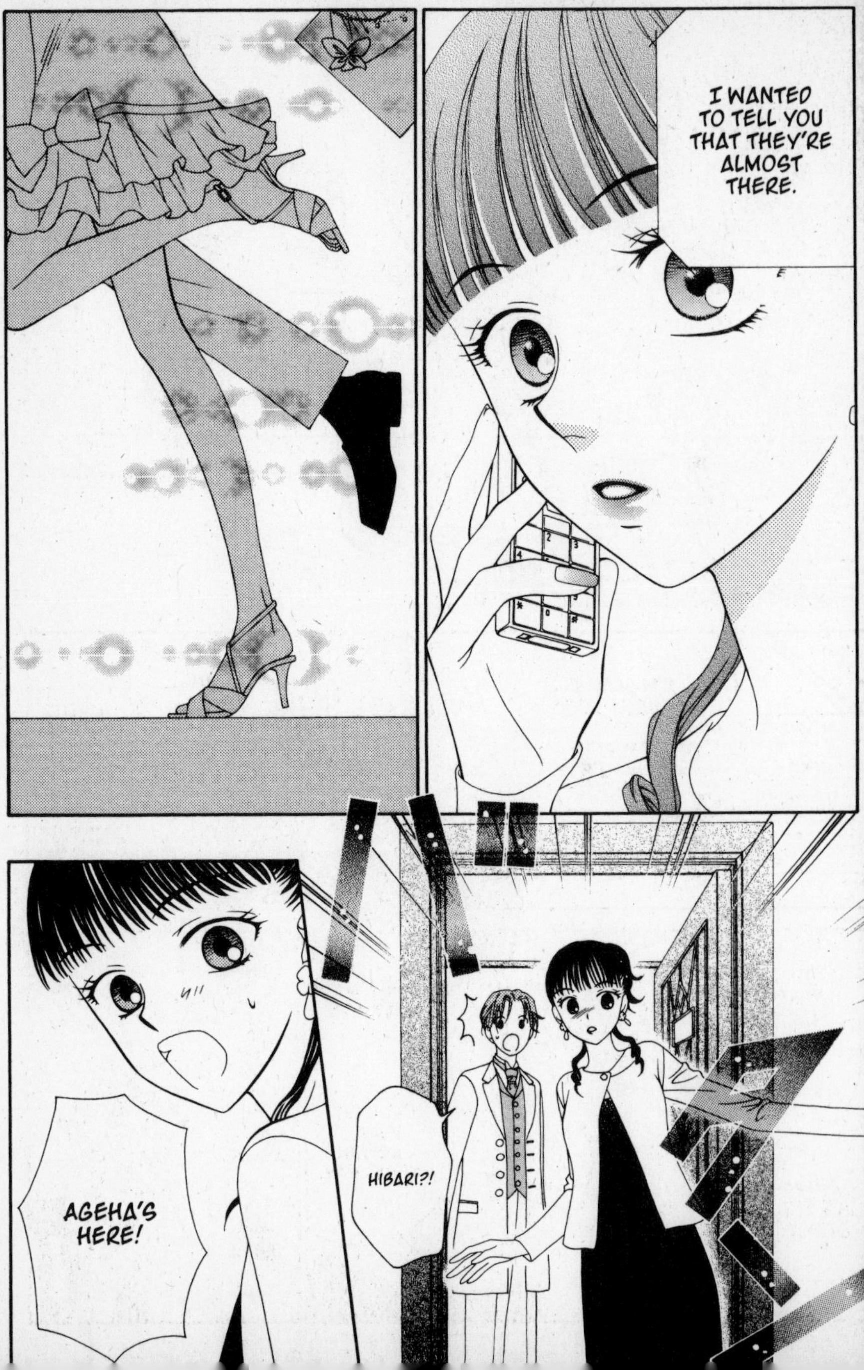
I WANTED TO TELL YOU THAT THEY'RE ALMOST THERE.
HIBARI?!
AGEHA'S HERE!

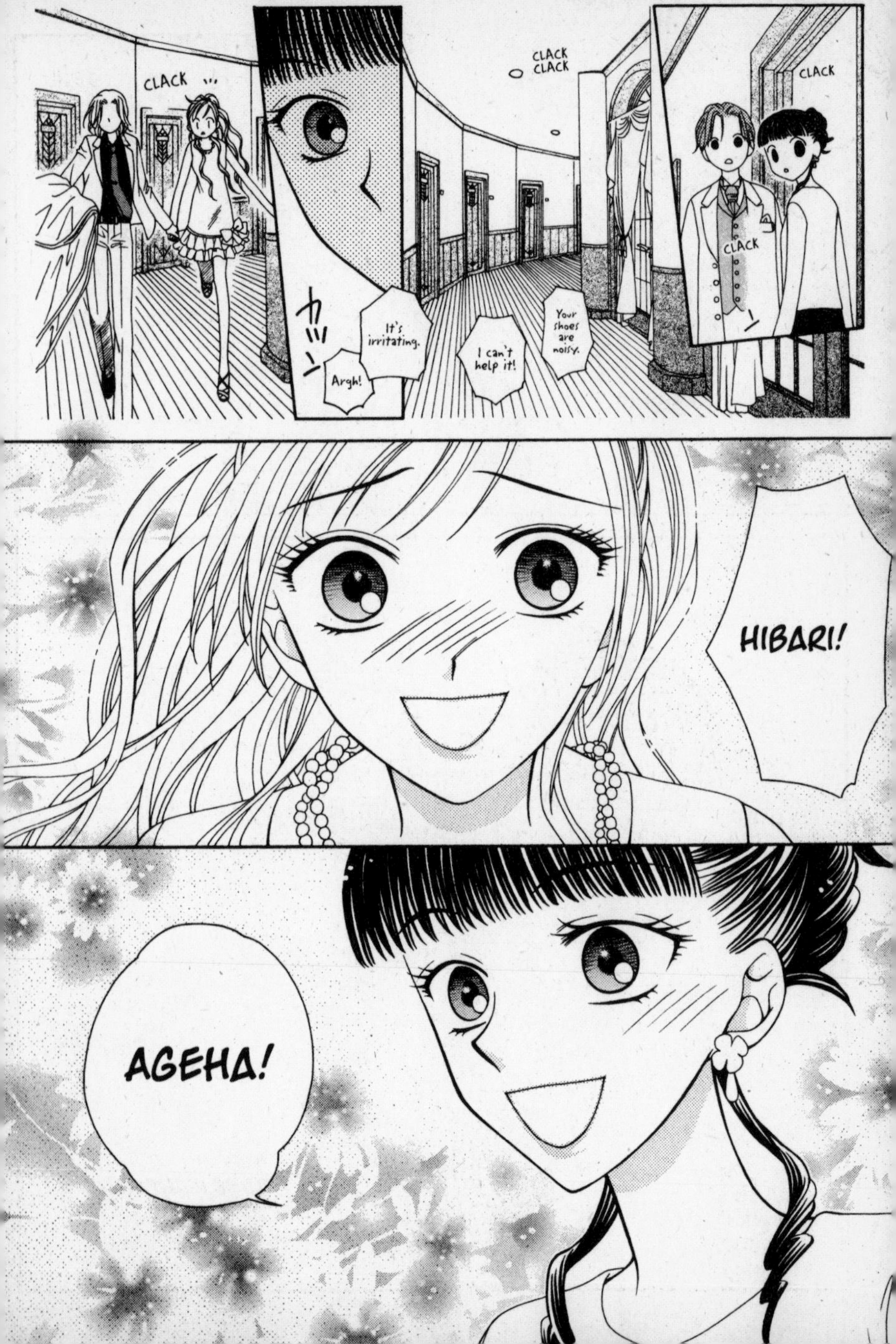
CLACK
CLACK
CLACK
CLACK CLACK
Your shoes are noisy.
I can't help it!
It's irritating.
Argh!
カツン
CLACK
HIBARI!
AGEHA!

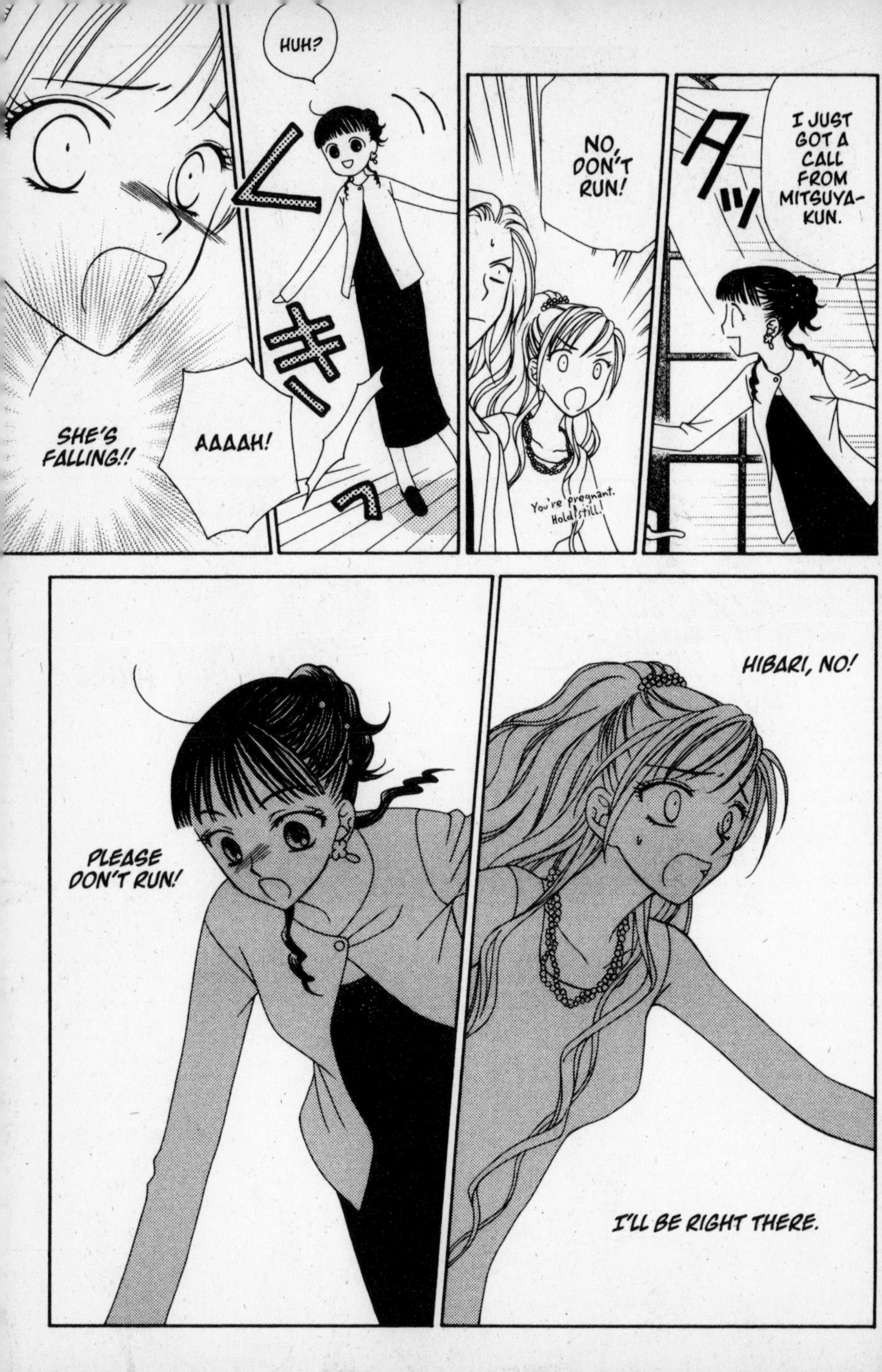
I JUST GOT A CALL FROM MITSUYA-KUN.
ダッ
NO, DON'T RUN!
You're pregnant. Hold still!
HUH?
AAAAH!
SHE'S FALLING!!
HIBARI, NO!
I'LL BE RIGHT THERE.
PLEASE DON'T RUN!

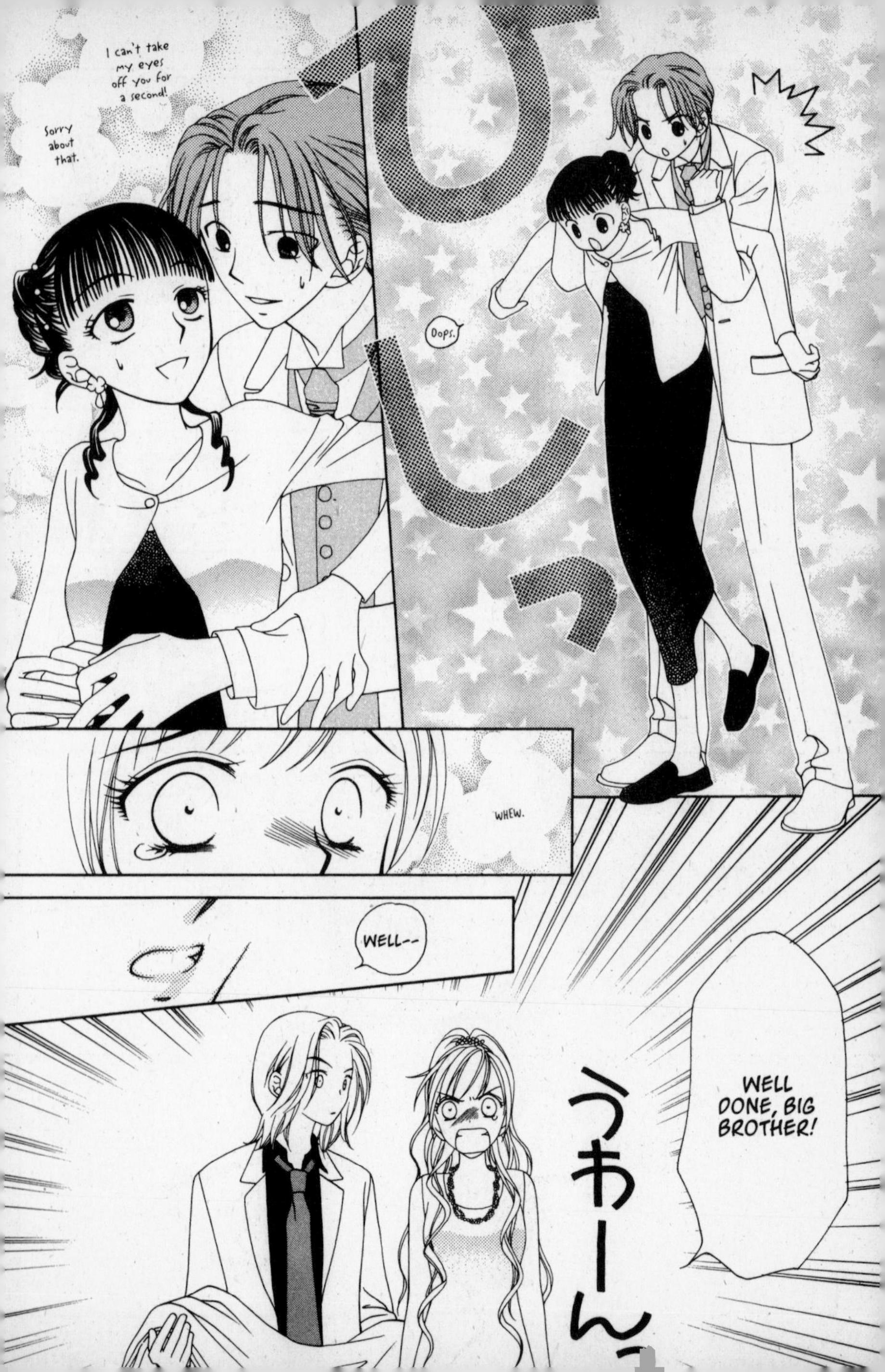

ぴしっ
Oops.
I can't take my eyes off you for a second!
Sorry about that.
WHEW.
WELL--
WELL DONE, BIG BROTHER!
うわーん

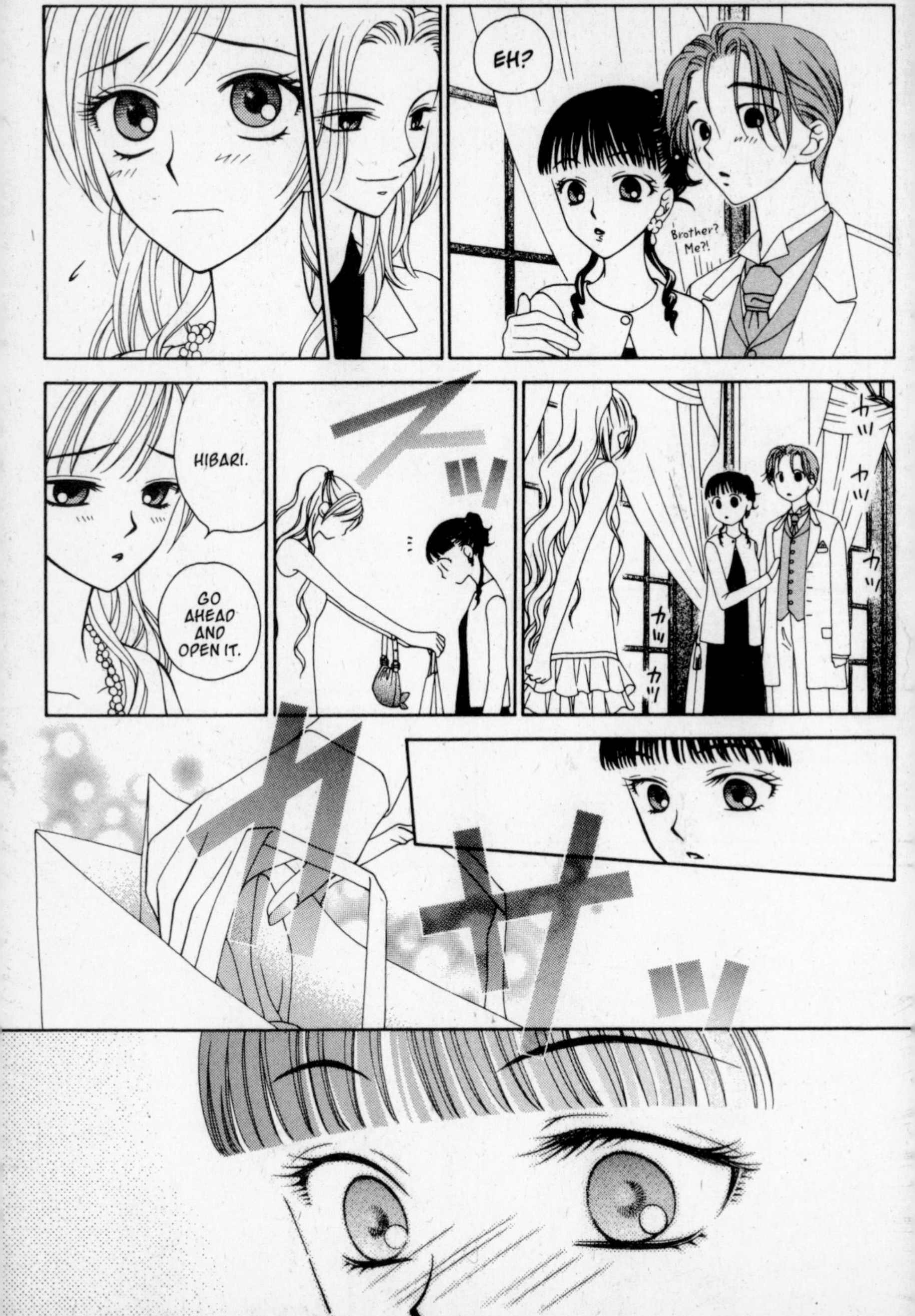
EH?
Brother? Me?!
カッ
カッ
カッ
カッ
カッ
カッ
スッ
HIBARI.
GO AHEAD AND OPEN IT.
カサッ

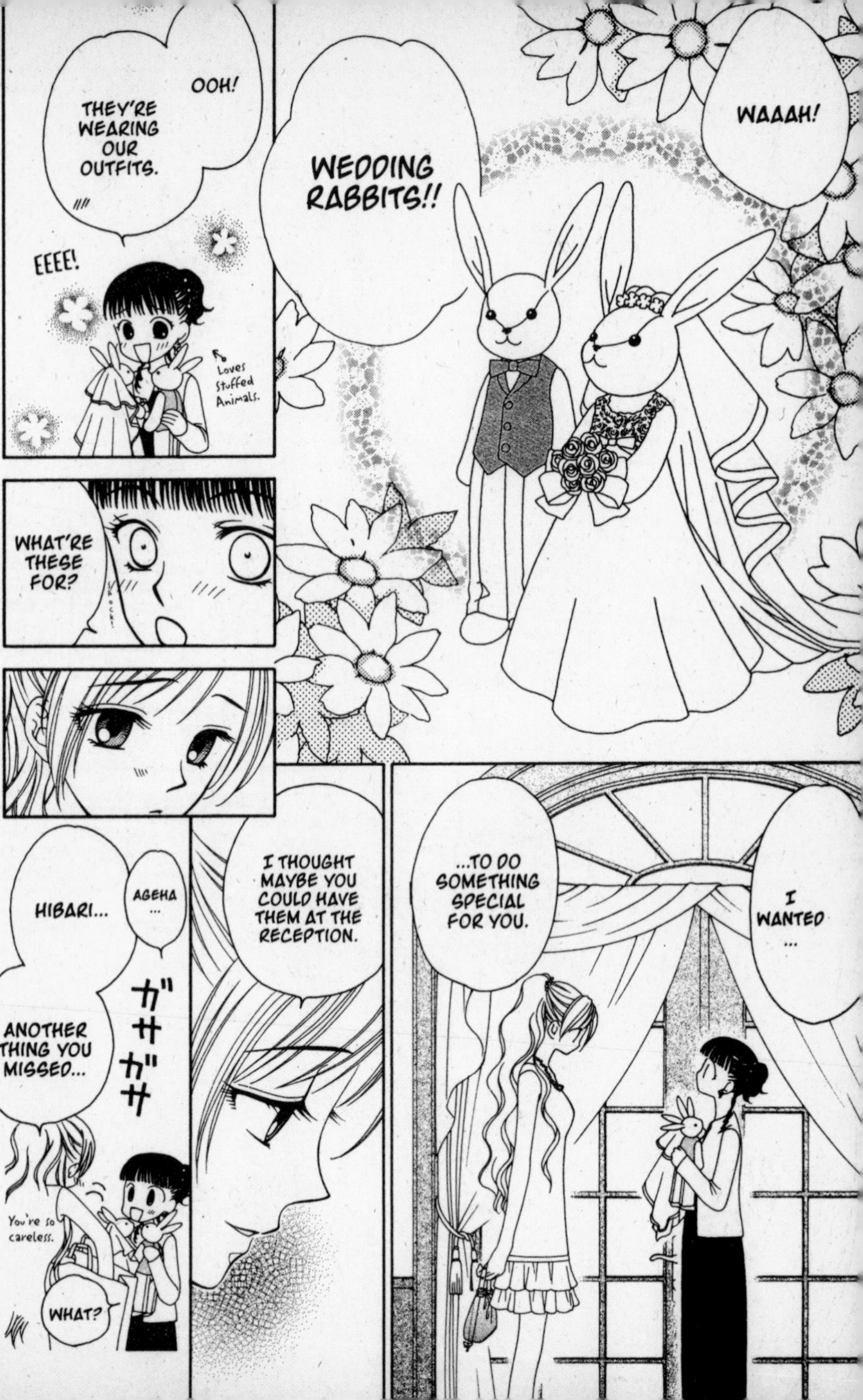
WAAAH!
WEDDING RABBITS!!
OOH!
THEY'RE WEARING OUR OUTFITS.
EEEE!
Loves Stuffed Animals.
WHAT'RE THESE FOR?
I WANTED ...
...TO DO SOMETHING SPECIAL FOR YOU.
I THOUGHT MAYBE YOU COULD HAVE THEM AT THE RECEPTION.
AGEHA ...
HIBARI...
ANOTHER THING YOU MISSED...
ガサガサ
You're so careless.
WHAT?

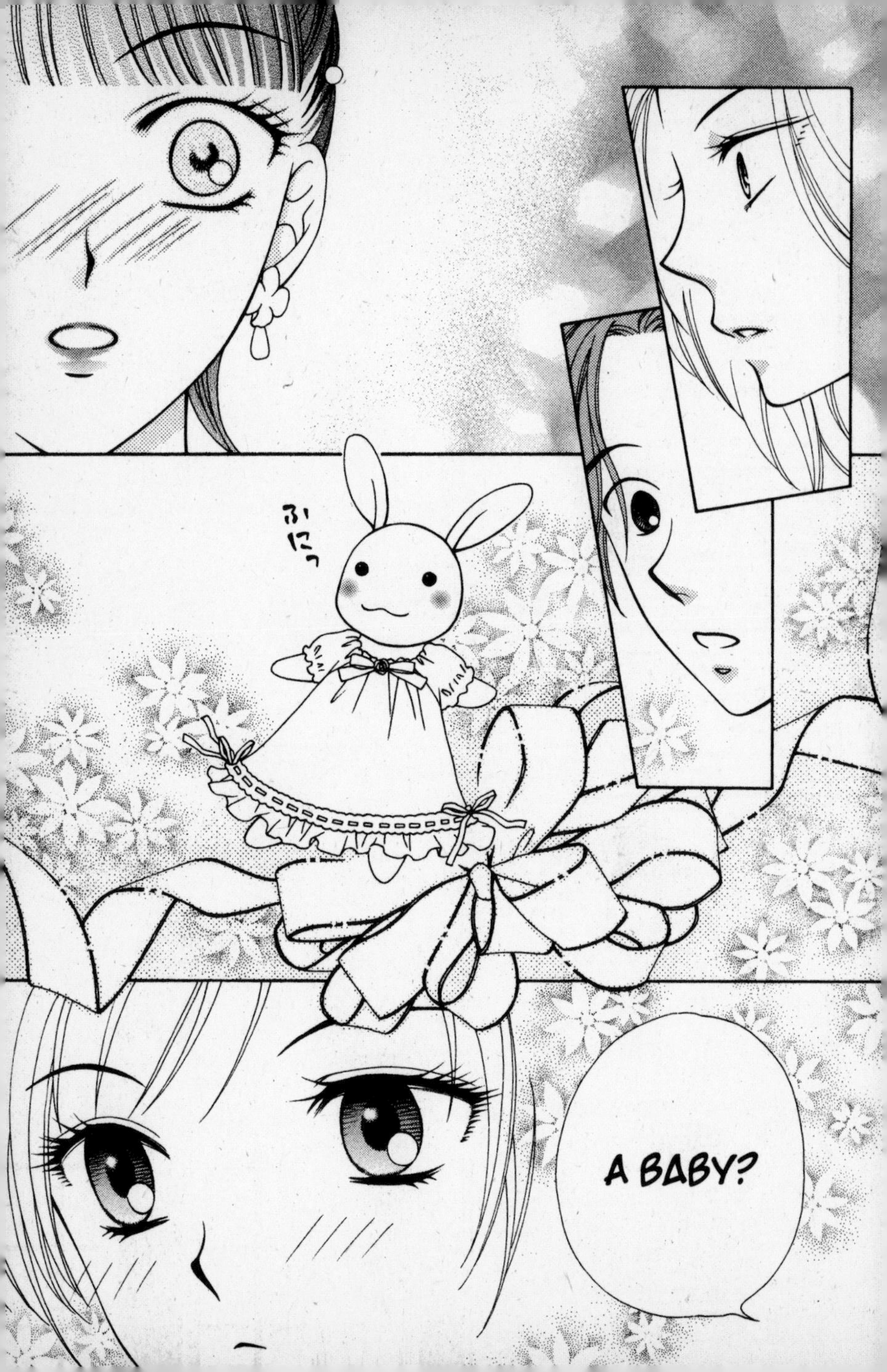
ふにっ
A BABY?

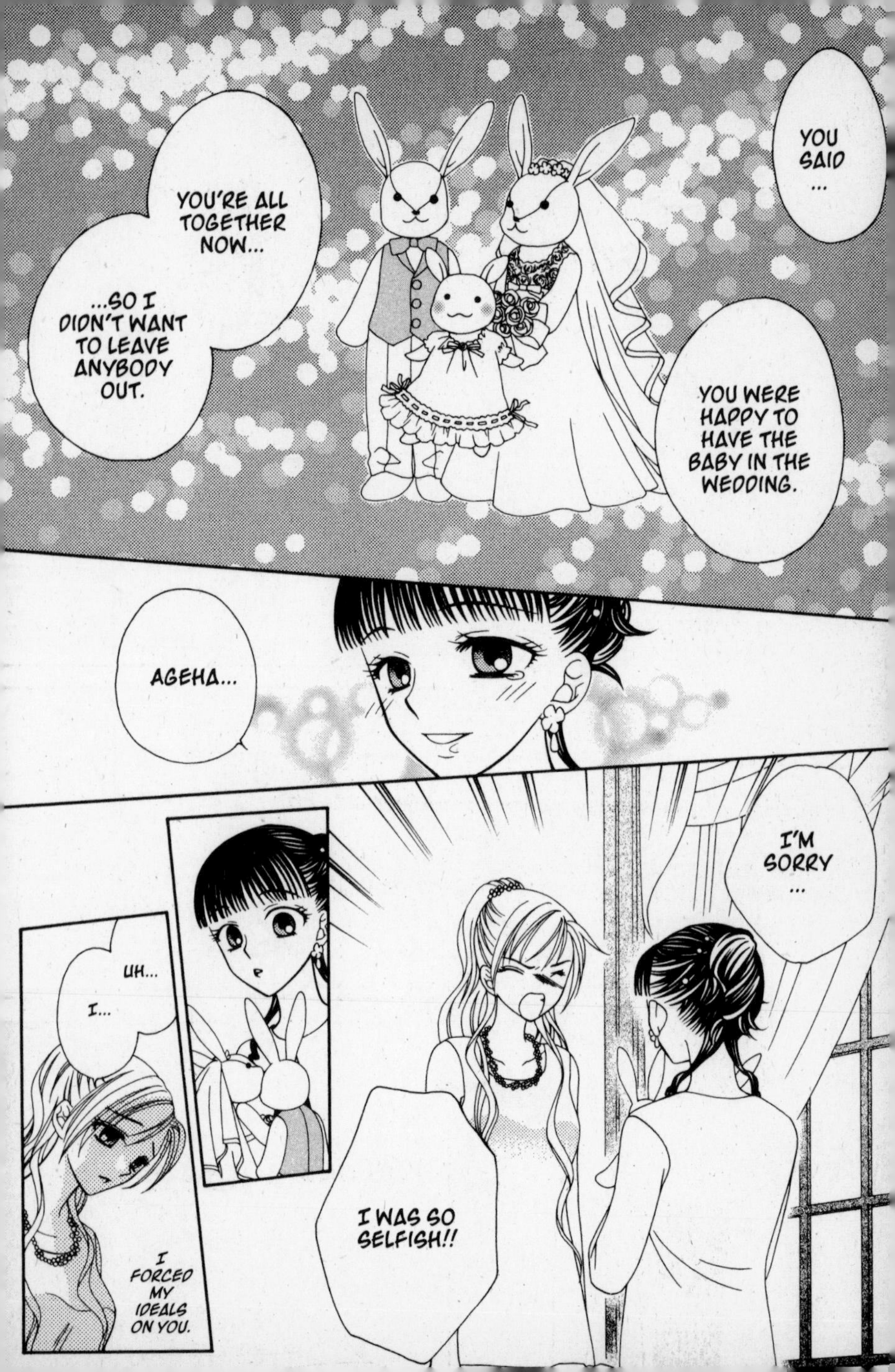
YOU SAID ...
YOU WERE HAPPY TO HAVE THE BABY IN THE WEDDING.
YOU'RE ALL TOGETHER NOW...
...SO I DIDN'T WANT TO LEAVE ANYBODY OUT.
AGEHA...
I'M SORRY ...
I WAS SO SELFISH!!
UH... I...
I FORCED MY IDEALS ON YOU.

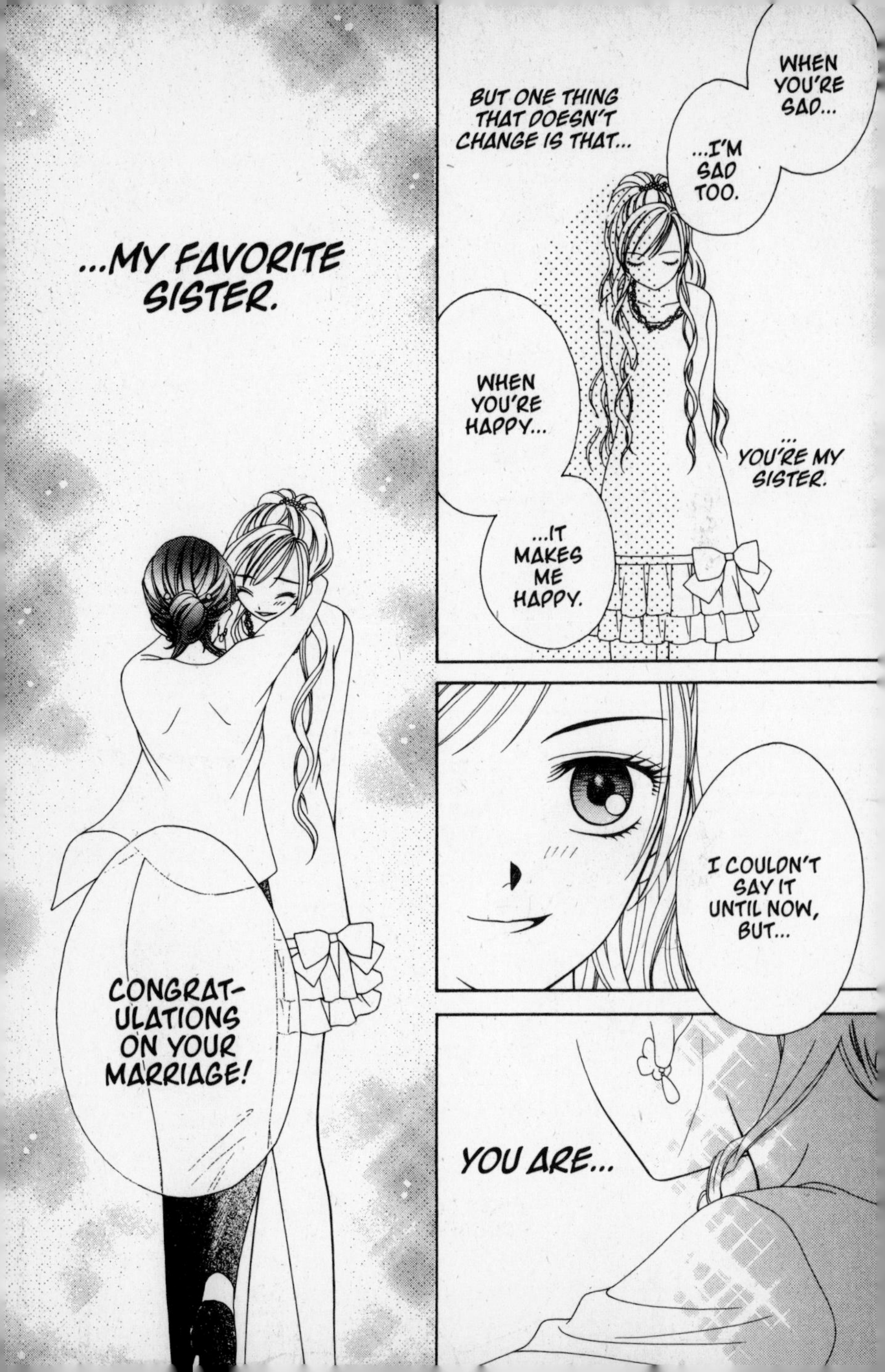
WHEN YOU'RE SAD...
...I'M SAD TOO.
BUT ONE THING THAT DOESN'T CHANGE IS THAT...
... YOU'RE MY SISTER.
WHEN YOU'RE HAPPY...
...IT MAKES ME HAPPY.
I COULDN'T SAY IT UNTIL NOW, BUT...
YOU ARE...
...MY FAVORITE SISTER.
CONGRAT-ULATIONS ON YOUR MARRIAGE!

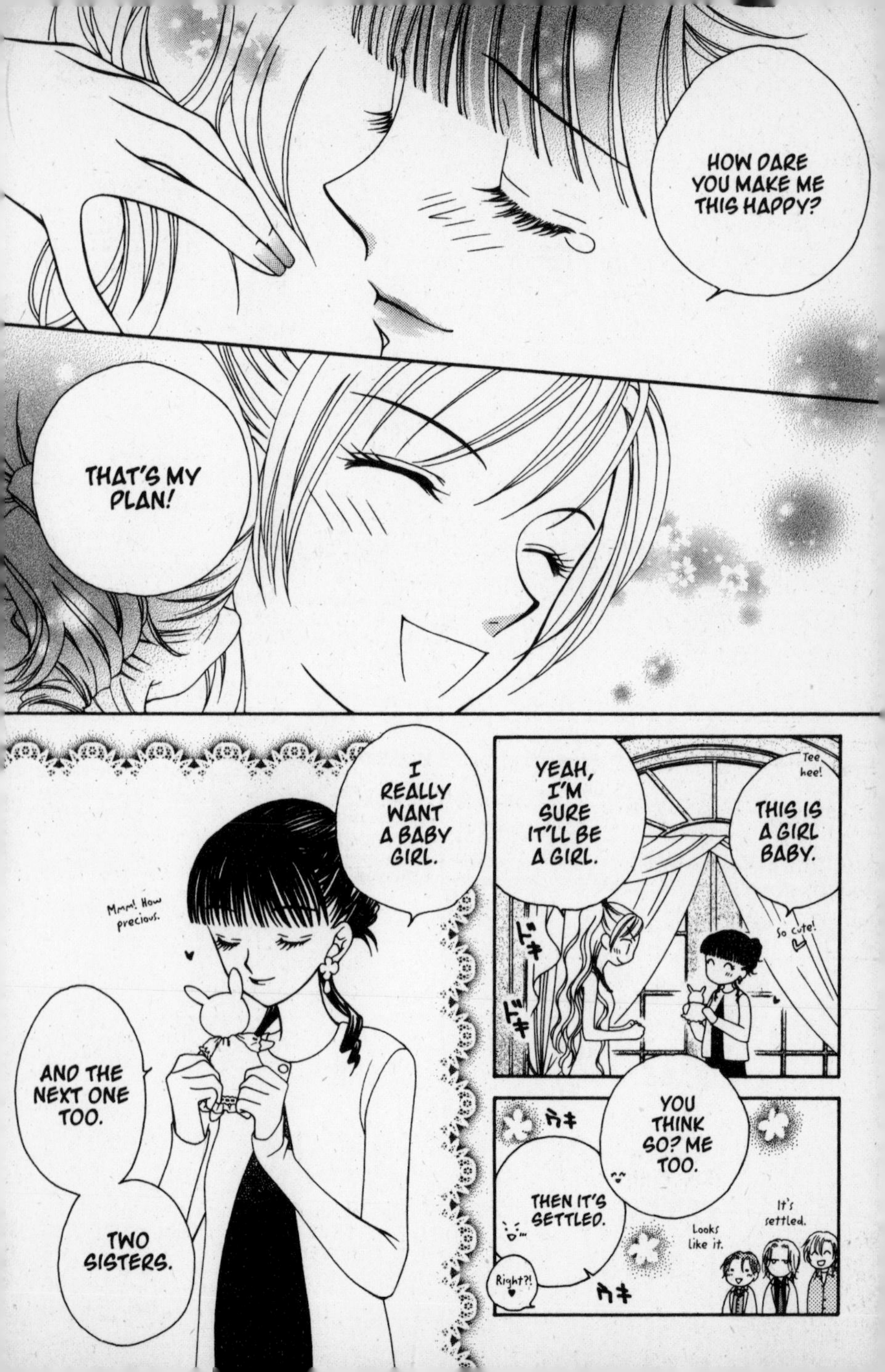

HOW DARE YOU MAKE ME THIS HAPPY?
THAT'S MY PLAN!
Tee hee!
THIS IS A GIRL BABY.
So cute!
YEAH, I'M SURE IT'LL BE A GIRL.
ドキ
ドキ
YOU THINK SO? ME TOO.
ウキ
It's settled.
Looks like it.
THEN IT'S SETTLED.
Right?!
ウキ
I REALLY WANT A BABY GIRL.
Mmm! How precious.
AND THE NEXT ONE TOO.
TWO SISTERS.

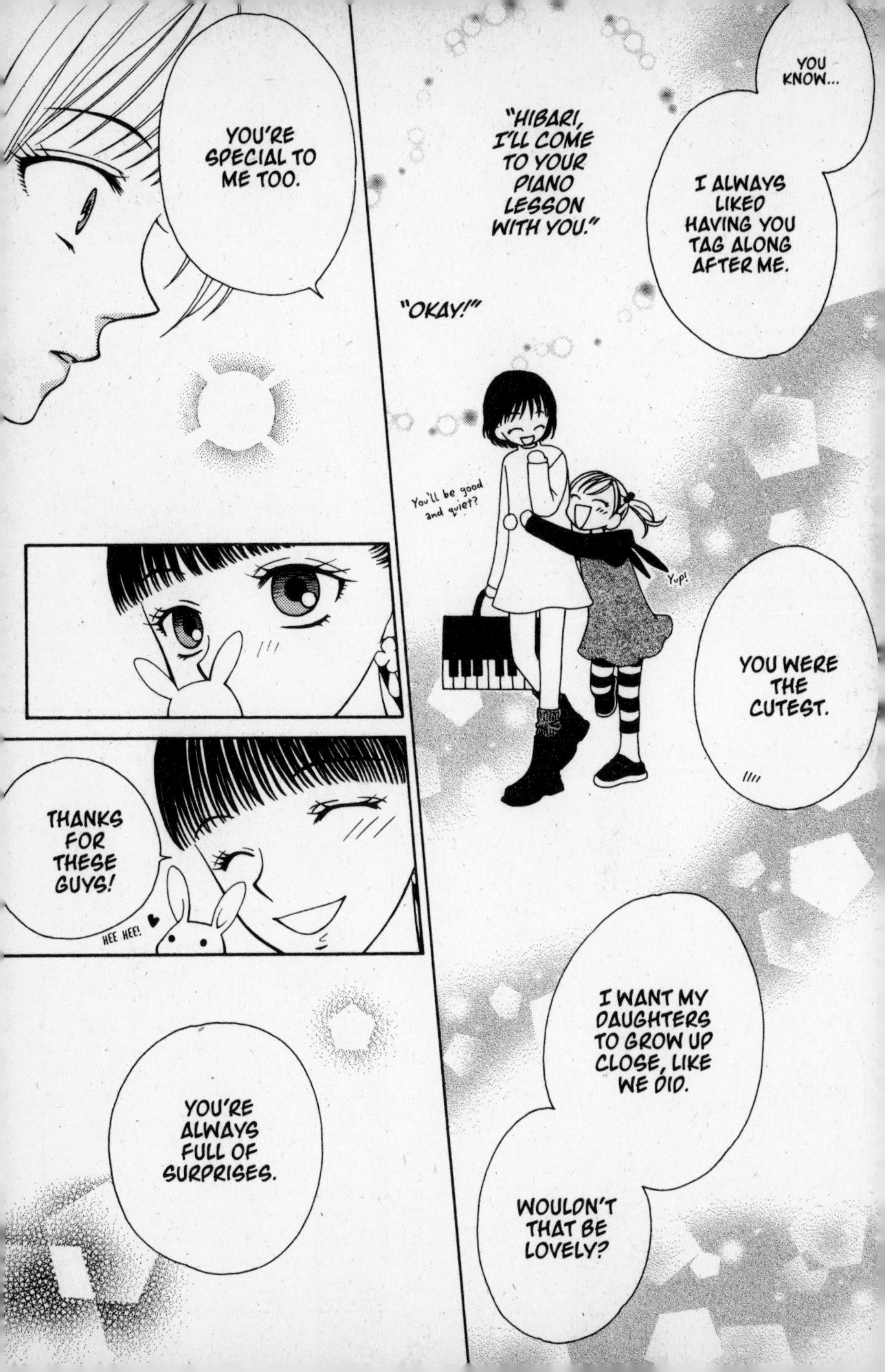
YOU KNOW...
I ALWAYS LIKED HAVING YOU TAG ALONG AFTER ME.
"HIBARI, I'LL COME TO YOUR PIANO LESSON WITH YOU."
"OKAY!"
You'll be good and quiet?
Yup!
YOU WERE THE CUTEST.
I WANT MY DAUGHTERS TO GROW UP CLOSE, LIKE WE DID.
WOULDN'T THAT BE LOVELY?
YOU'RE SPECIAL TO ME TOO.
THANKS FOR THESE GUYS!
HEE HEE!
YOU'RE ALWAYS FULL OF SURPRISES.

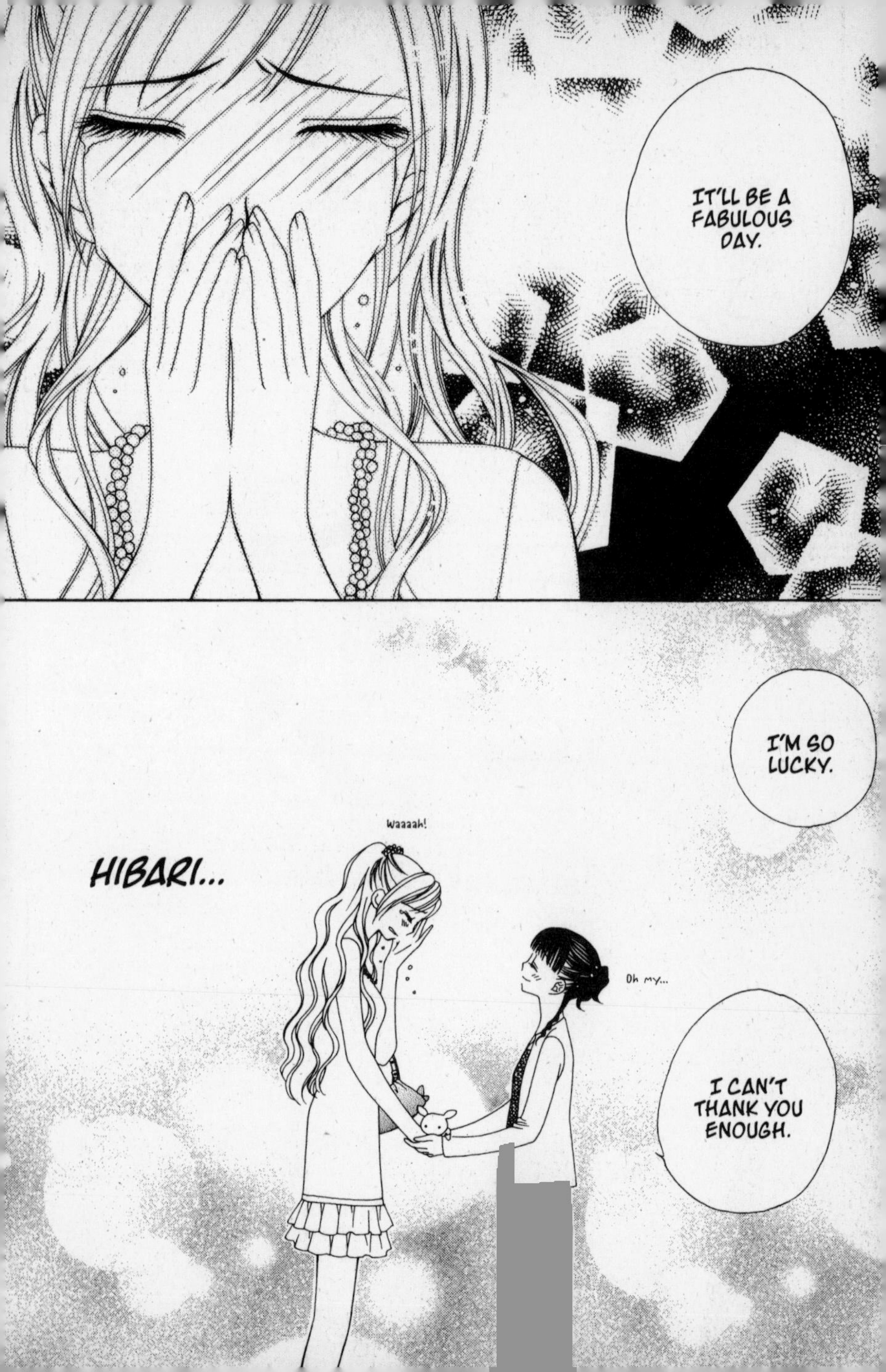
IT'LL BE A FABULOUS DAY.
I'M SO LUCKY.
I CAN'T THANK YOU ENOUGH.
Waaaah!
Oh my...
HIBARI...

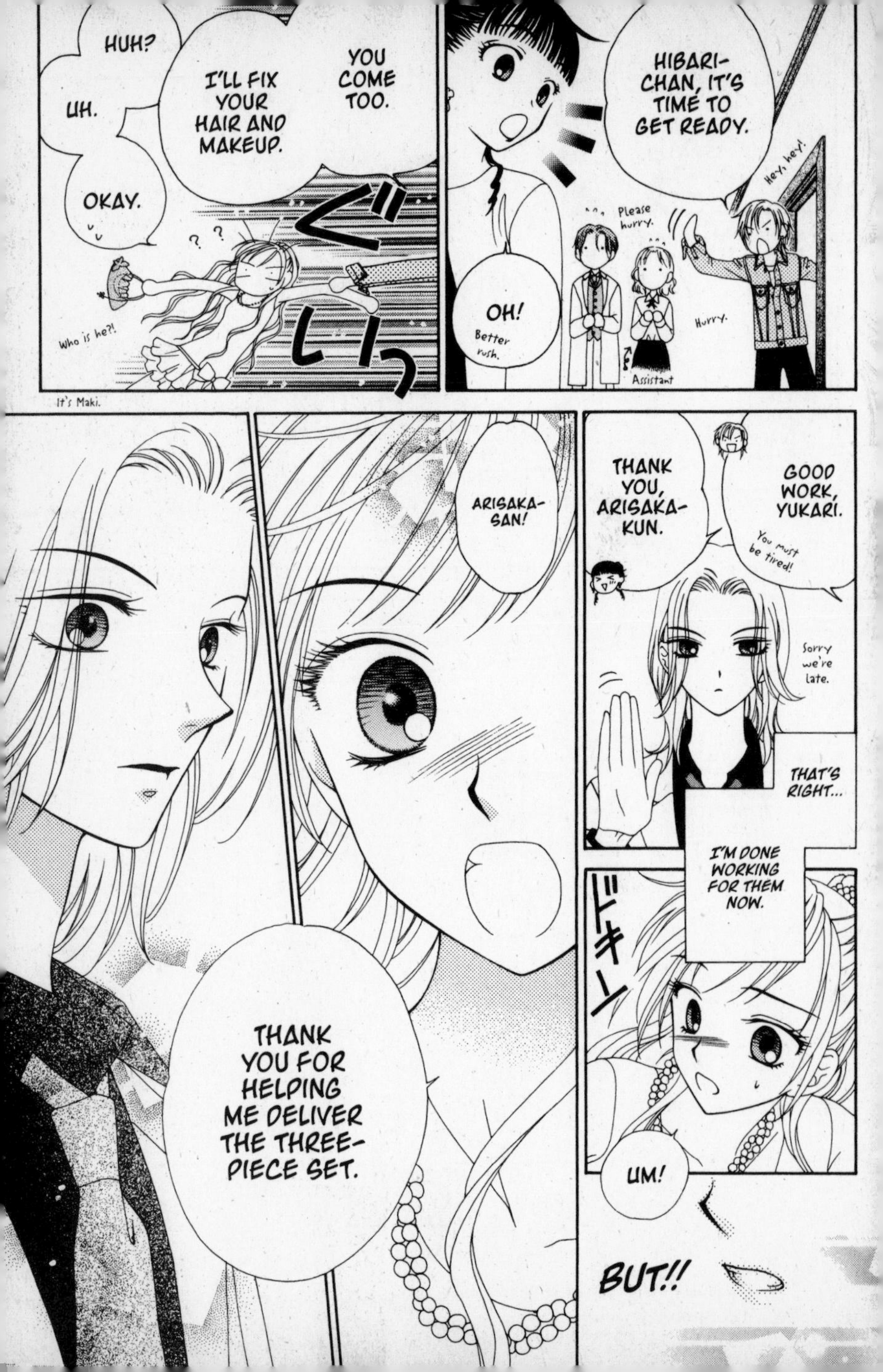
HIBARI-CHAN, IT'S TIME TO GET READY.
Hey, hey!
Please hurry.
Hurry.
Assistant
OH!
Better rush.
YOU COME TOO.
I'LL FIX YOUR HAIR AND MAKEUP.
HUH?
UH.
OKAY.
Who is he?!
It's Maki.
GOOD WORK, YUKARI.
You must be tired!
THANK YOU, ARISAKA-KUN.
Sorry we're late.
THAT'S RIGHT...
I'M DONE WORKING FOR THEM NOW.
ドキーン
UM!
BUT!!
ARISAKA-SAN!
THANK YOU FOR HELPING ME DELIVER THE THREE-PIECE SET.

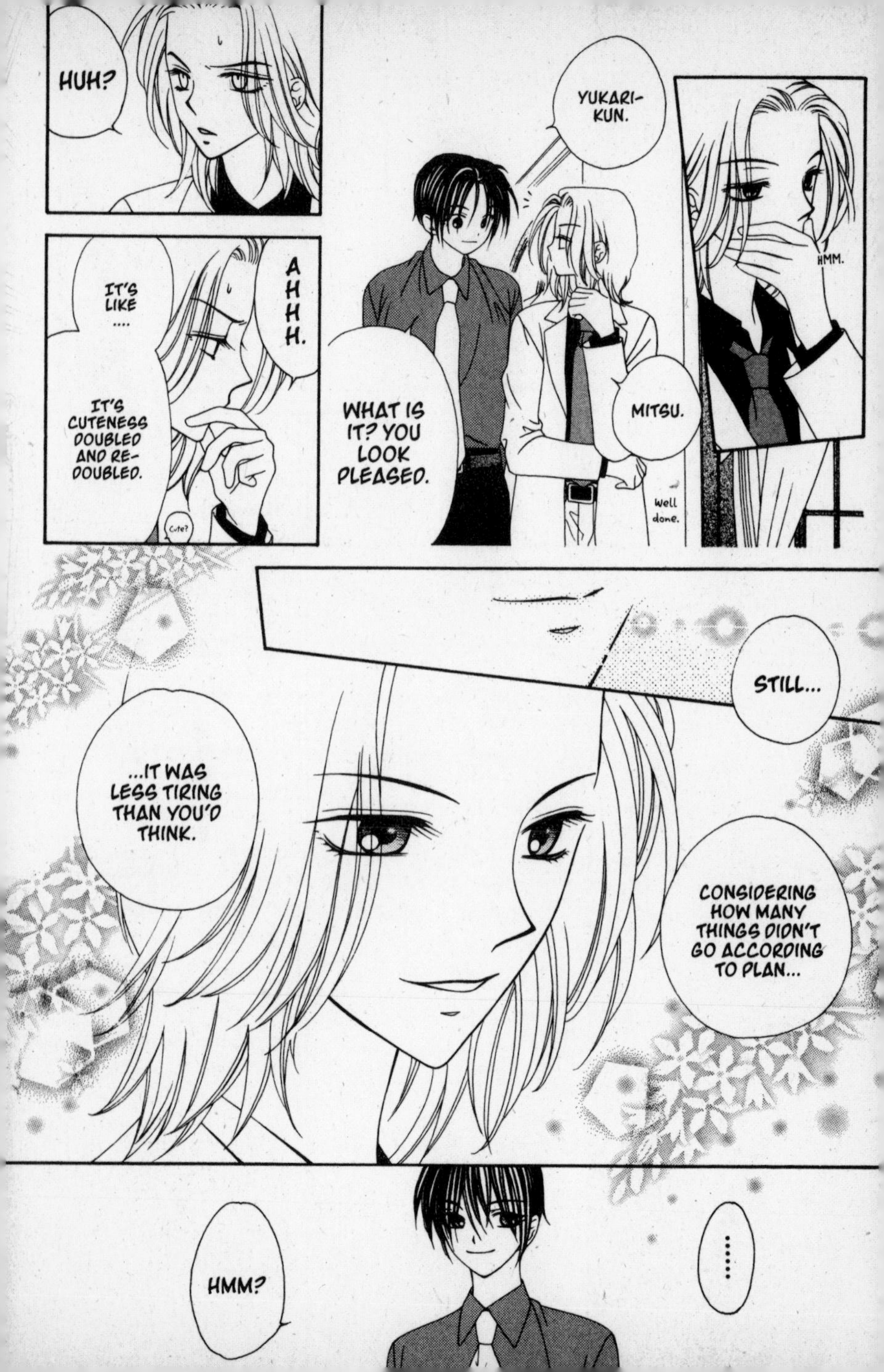
HMM.
YUKARI-KUN.
MITSU.
Well done.
WHAT IS IT? YOU LOOK PLEASED.
HUH?
AHHH.
IT'S LIKE ....
IT'S CUTENESS DOUBLED AND RE-DOUBLED.
Cute?
STILL...
CONSIDERING HOW MANY THINGS DIDN'T GO ACCORDING TO PLAN...
...IT WAS LESS TIRING THAN YOU'D THINK.
......
HMM?

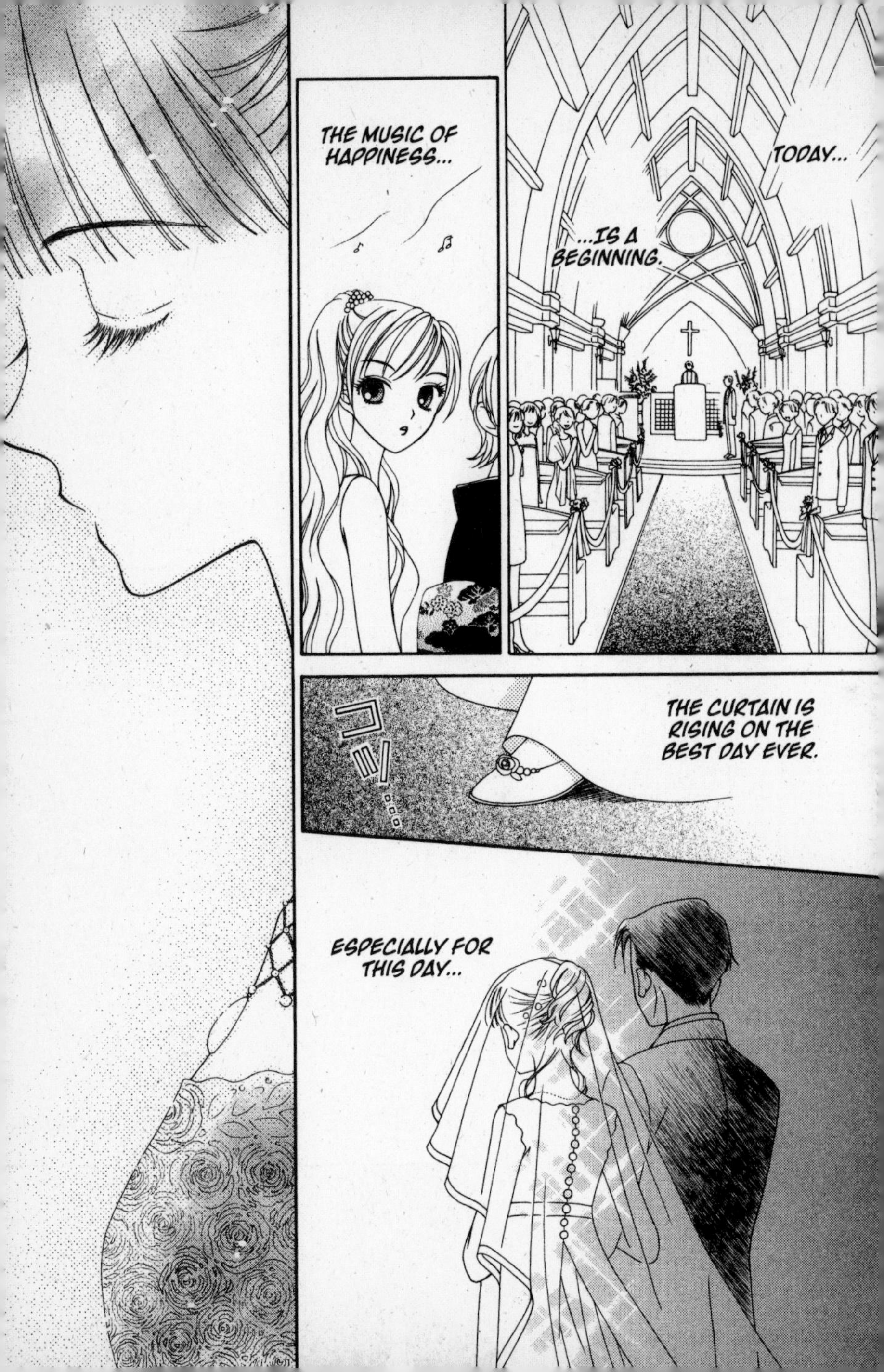
TODAY...
...IS A BEGINNING.
THE MUSIC OF HAPPINESS...
THE CURTAIN IS RISING ON THE BEST DAY EVER.
ESPECIALLY FOR THIS DAY...

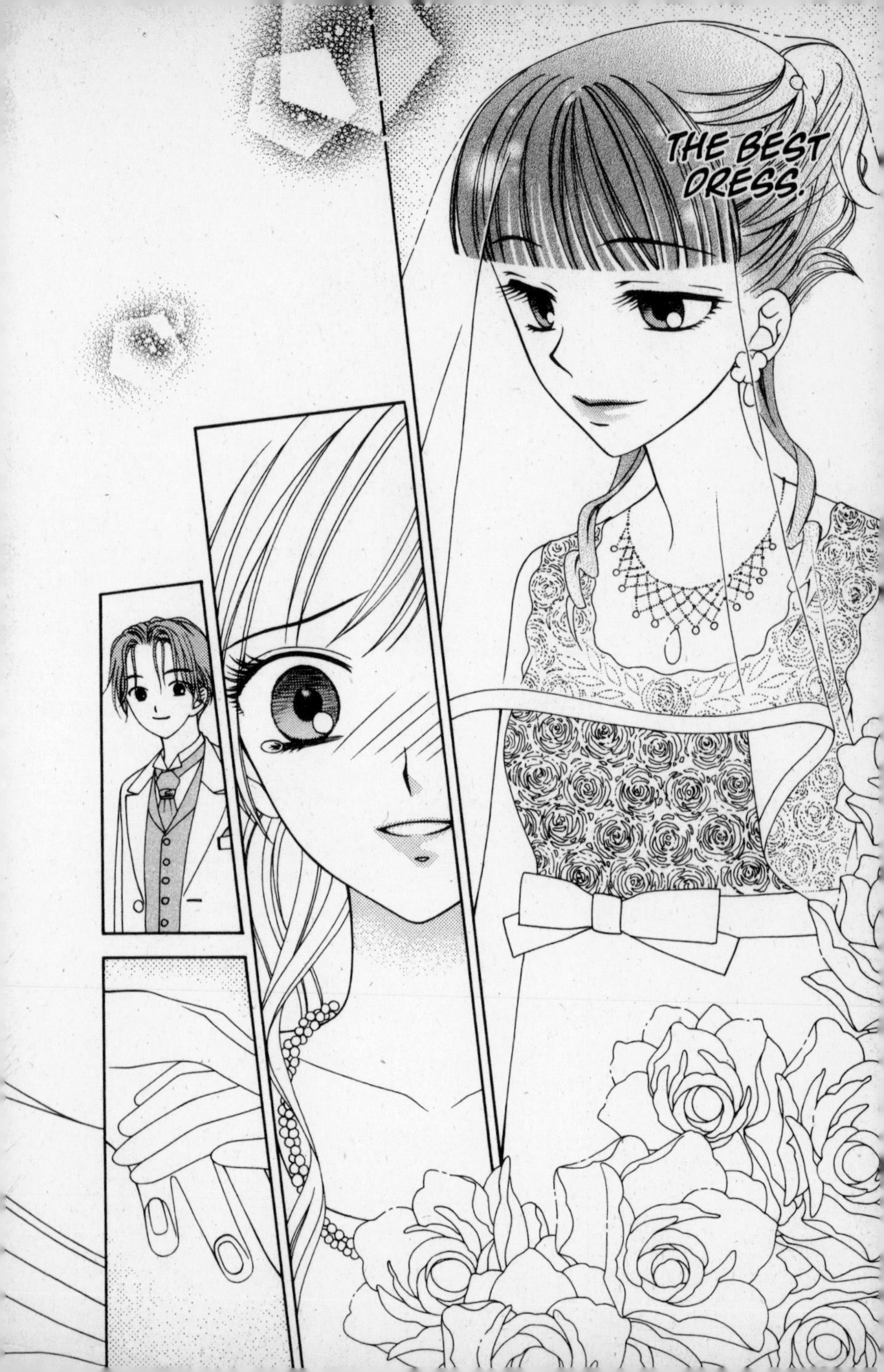
THE BEST DRESS.

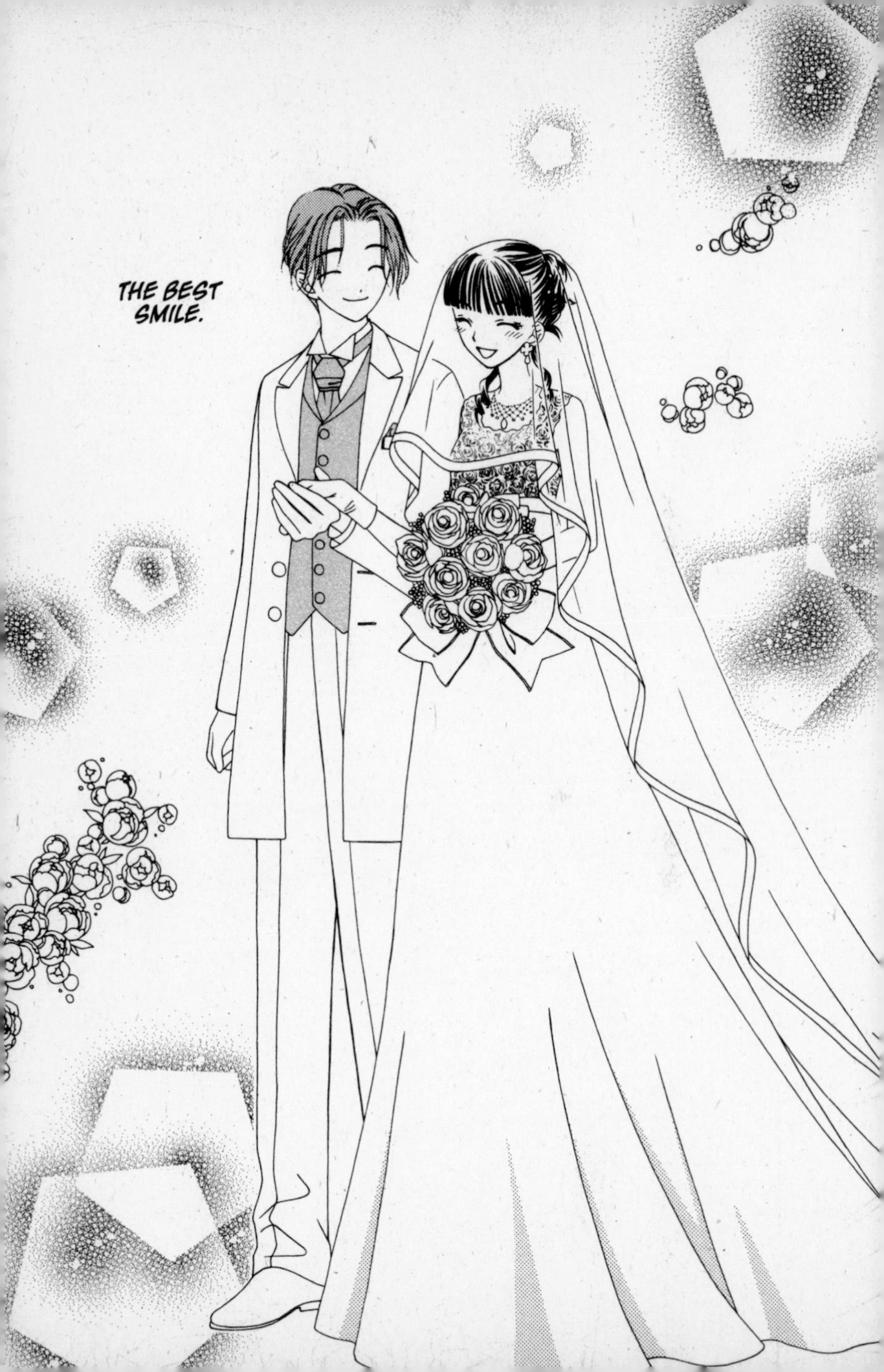
THE BEST SMILE.

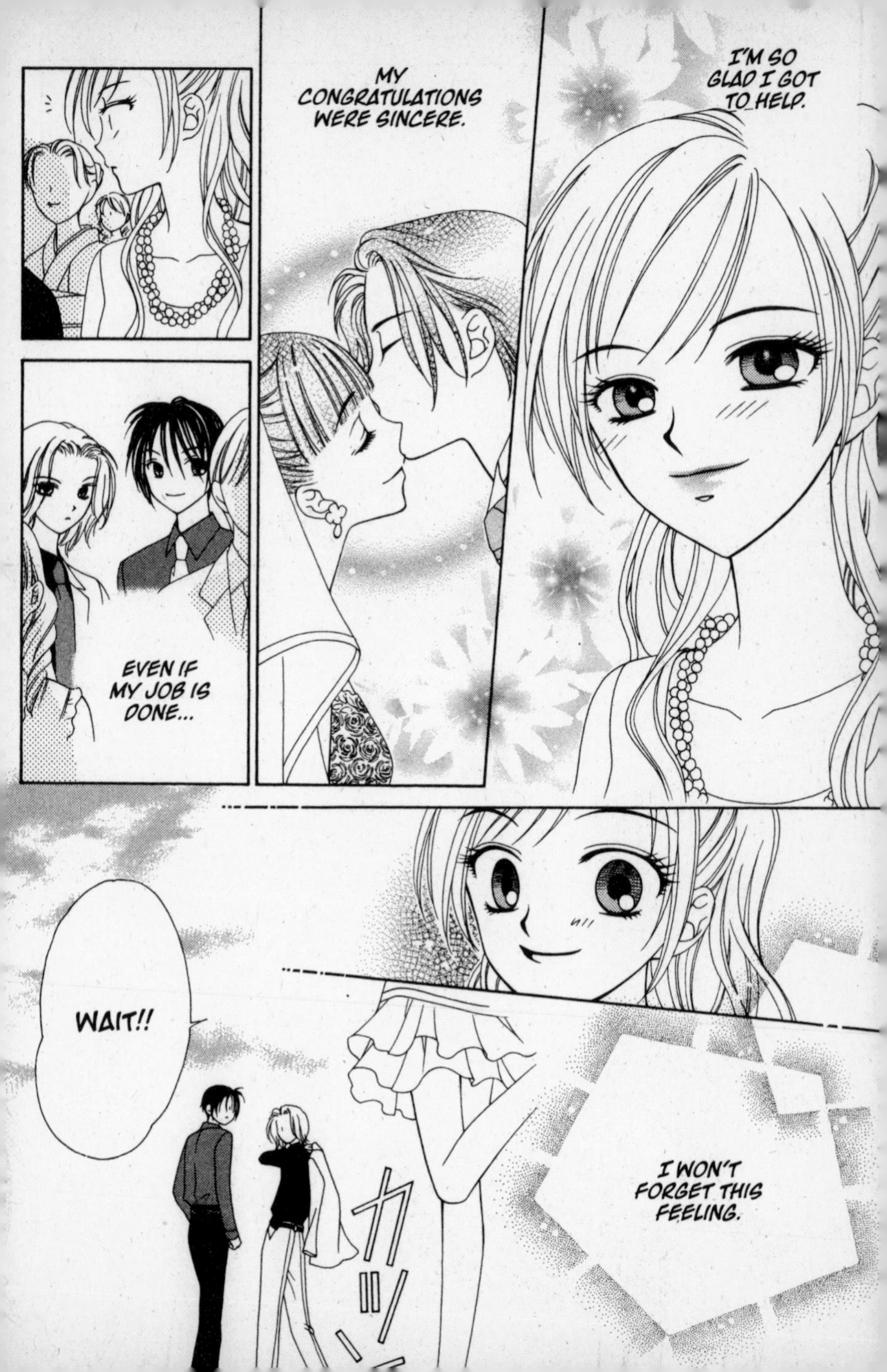
I'M SO GLAD I GOT TO HELP.
MY CONGRATULATIONS WERE SINCERE.
EVEN IF MY JOB IS DONE...
I WON'T FORGET THIS FEELING.
WAIT!!

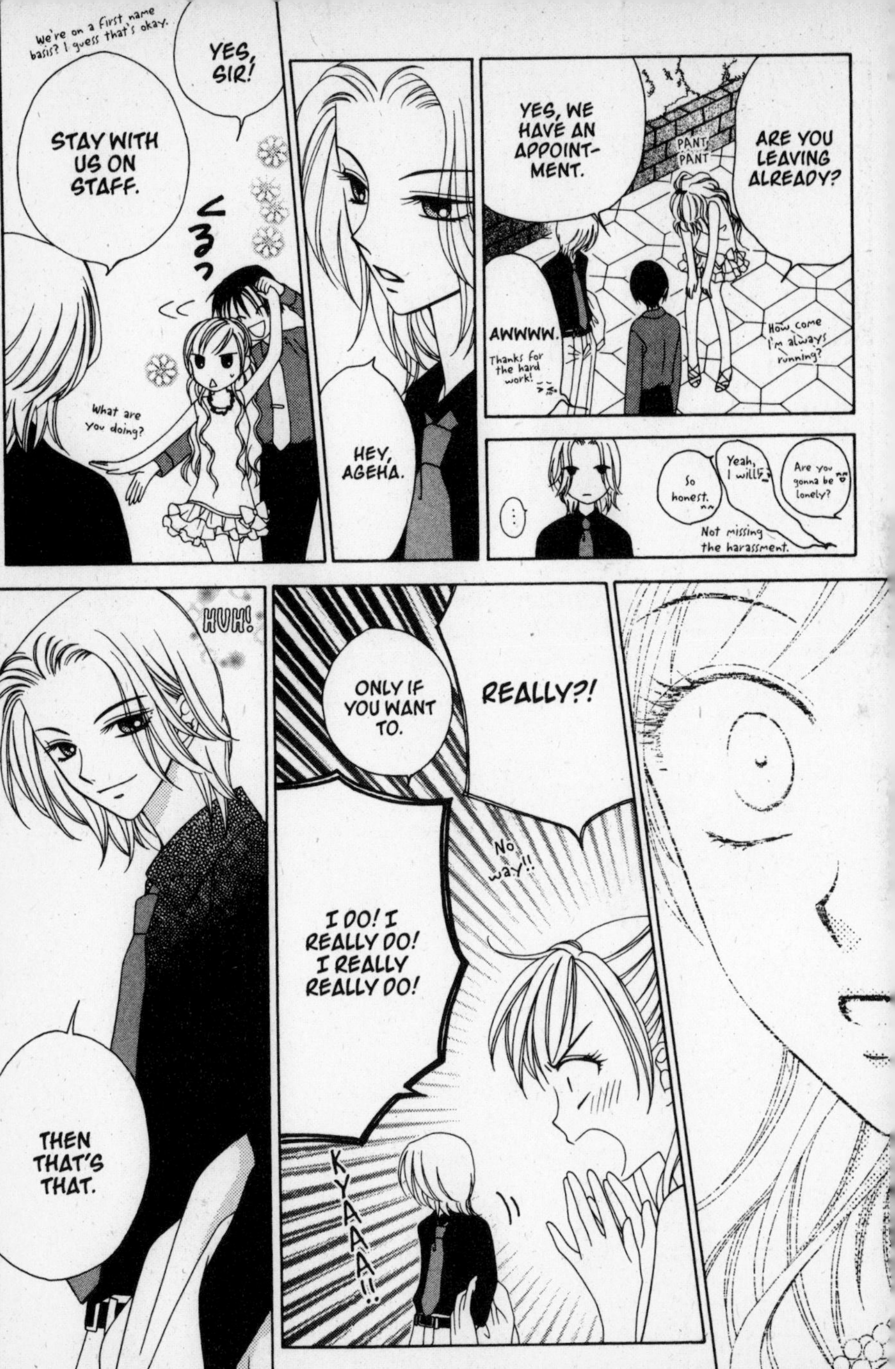
ARE YOU LEAVING ALREADY?
PANT PANT
YES, WE HAVE AN APPOINT-MENT.
How come I'm always running?
AWWWW.
Thanks for the hard work!
Are you gonna be lonely?
Yeah, I will!
So honest.
Not missing the harassment.
...
HEY, AGEHA.
YES, SIR!
We're on a first name basis? I guess that's okay.
STAY WITH US ON STAFF.
くるっ
What are you doing?
REALLY?!
ONLY IF YOU WANT TO.
No way!!
I DO! I REALLY DO! I REALLY REALLY DO!
KYAAA!!
HUH!
THEN THAT'S THAT.

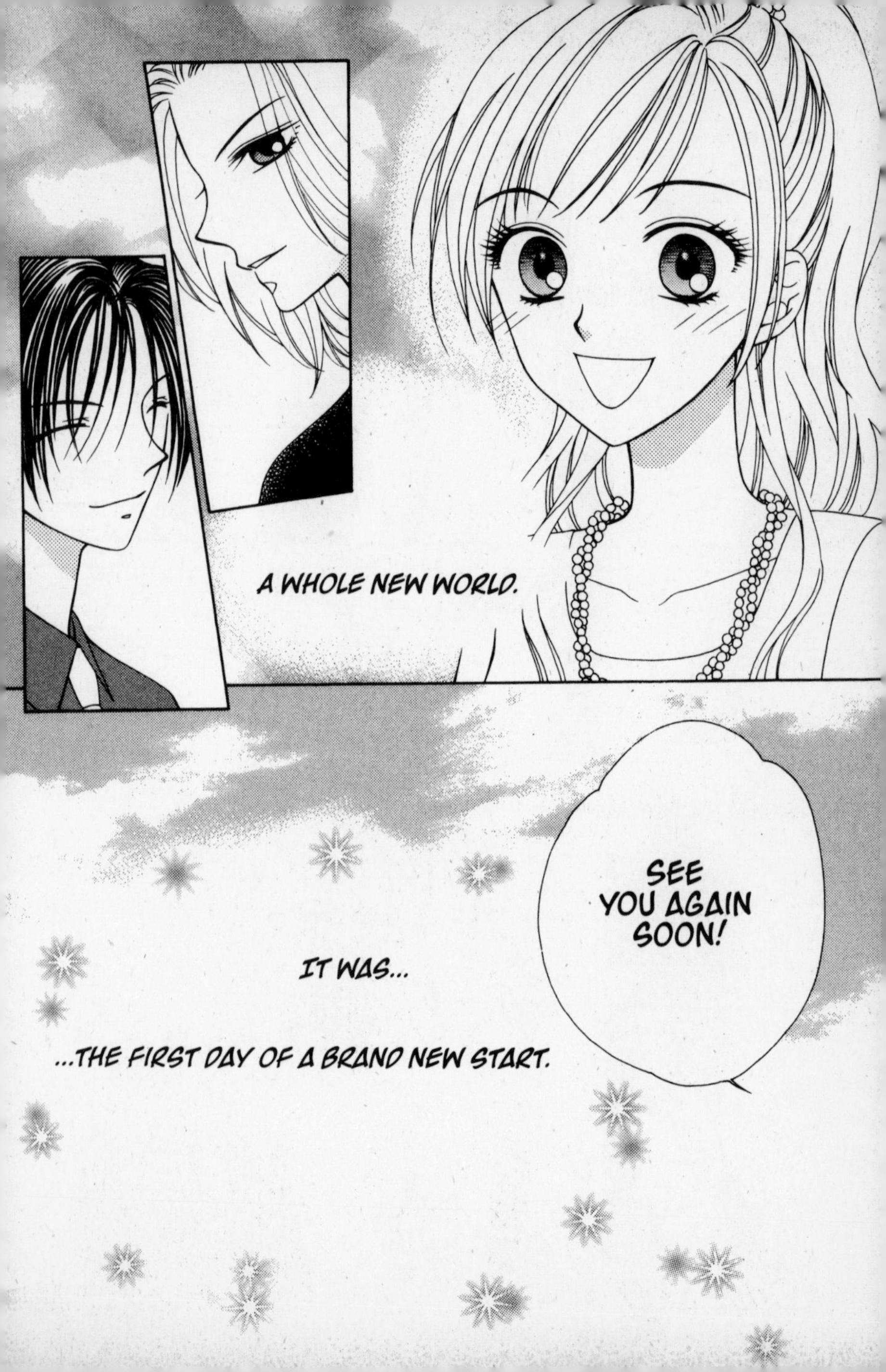
A WHOLE NEW WORLD.
SEE YOU AGAIN SOON!
IT WAS...
...THE FIRST DAY OF A BRAND NEW START.

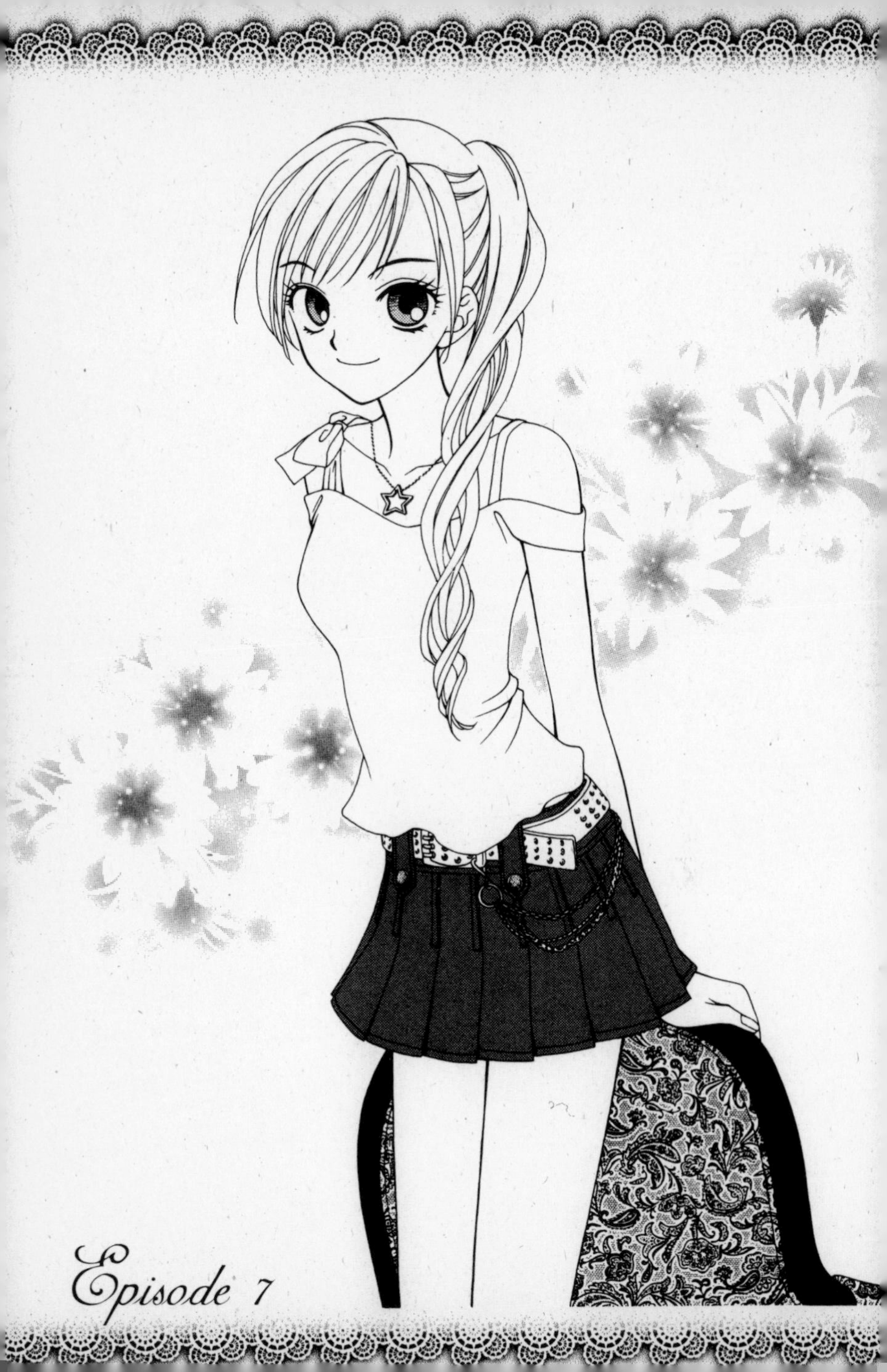
Episode 7

THE THINGS I LACK; THE THINGS I RESPECT...

SPARKLE SPARKLE...

THOSE ARE MY TREASURES.

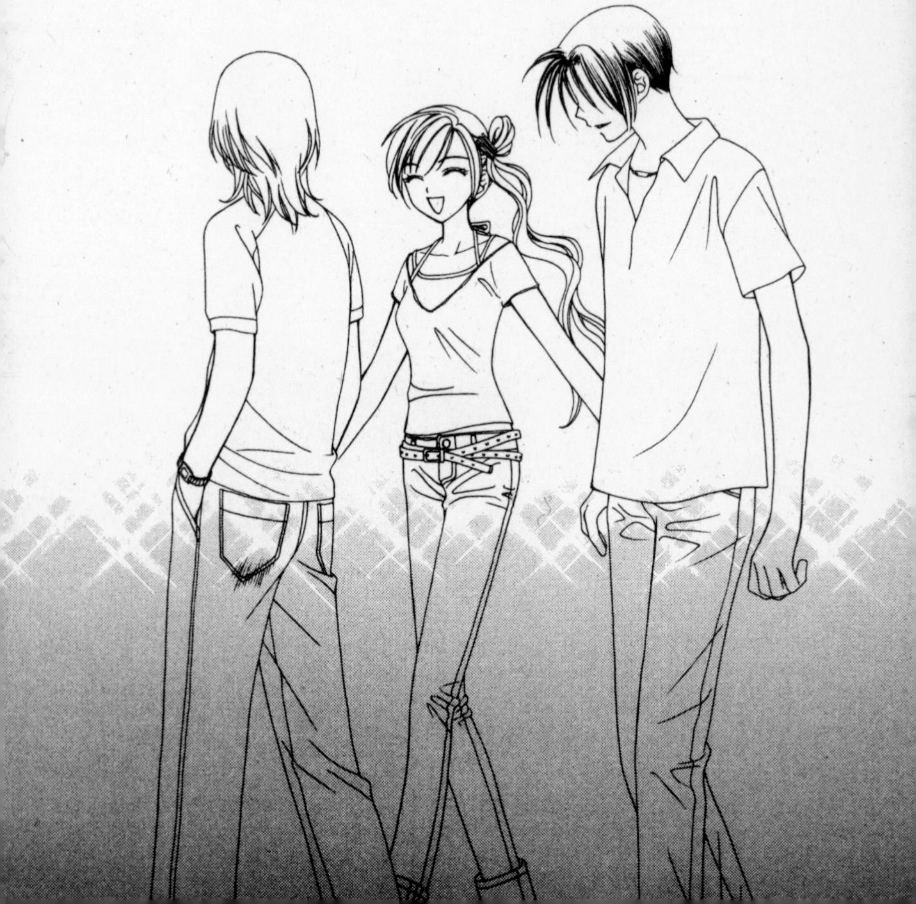

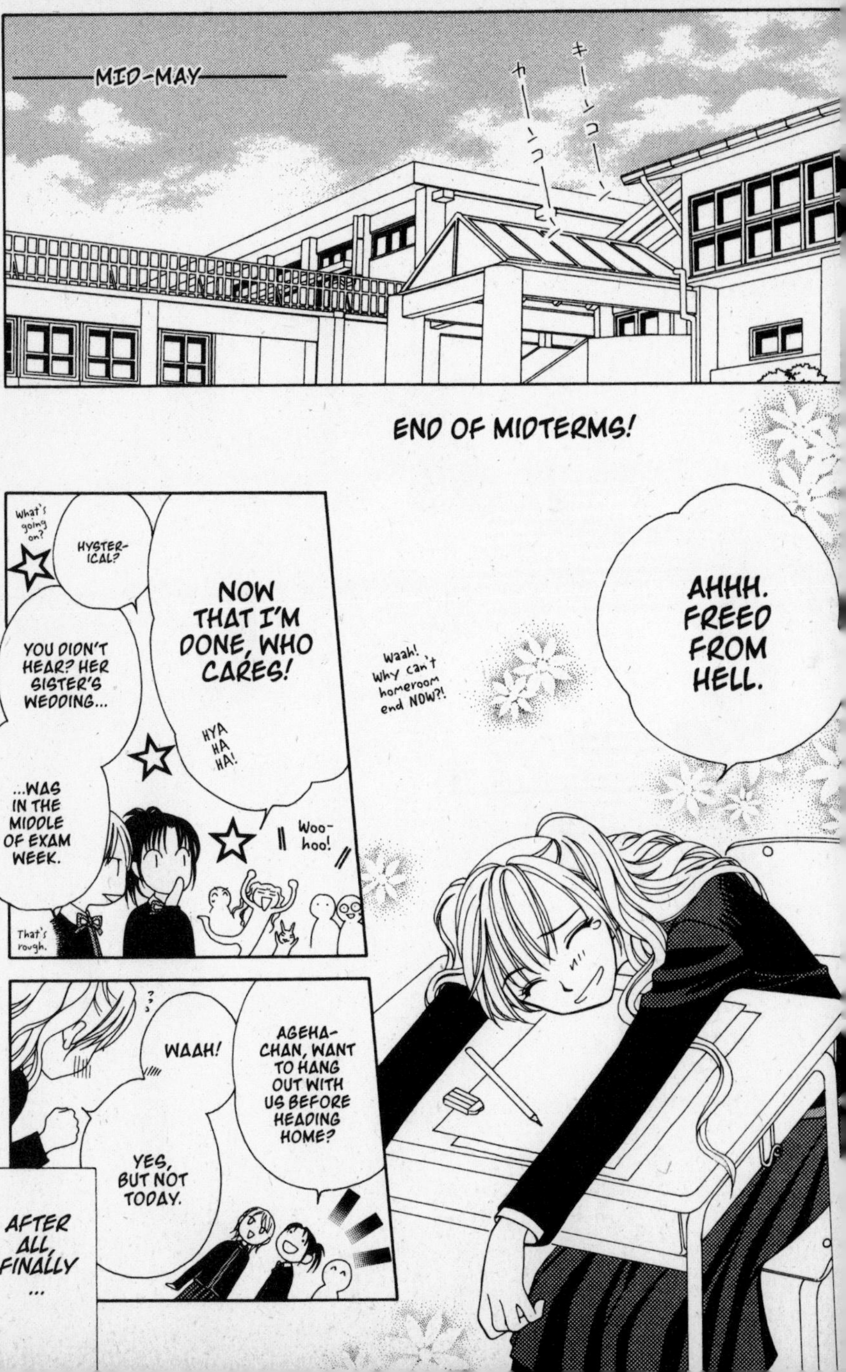
MID-MAY
キーンコーン
カーンコーン
END OF MIDTERMS!
AHHH. FREED FROM HELL.
Waah! Why can't homeroom end NOW?!
NOW THAT I'M DONE, WHO CARES!
HYA HA HA!
Woo-hoo!
HYSTER-ICAL?
What's going on?
YOU DIDN'T HEAR? HER SISTER'S WEDDING...
...WAS IN THE MIDDLE OF EXAM WEEK.
That's rough.
AGEHA-CHAN, WANT TO HANG OUT WITH US BEFORE HEADING HOME?
WAAH!
YES, BUT NOT TODAY.
AFTER ALL, FINALLY ...

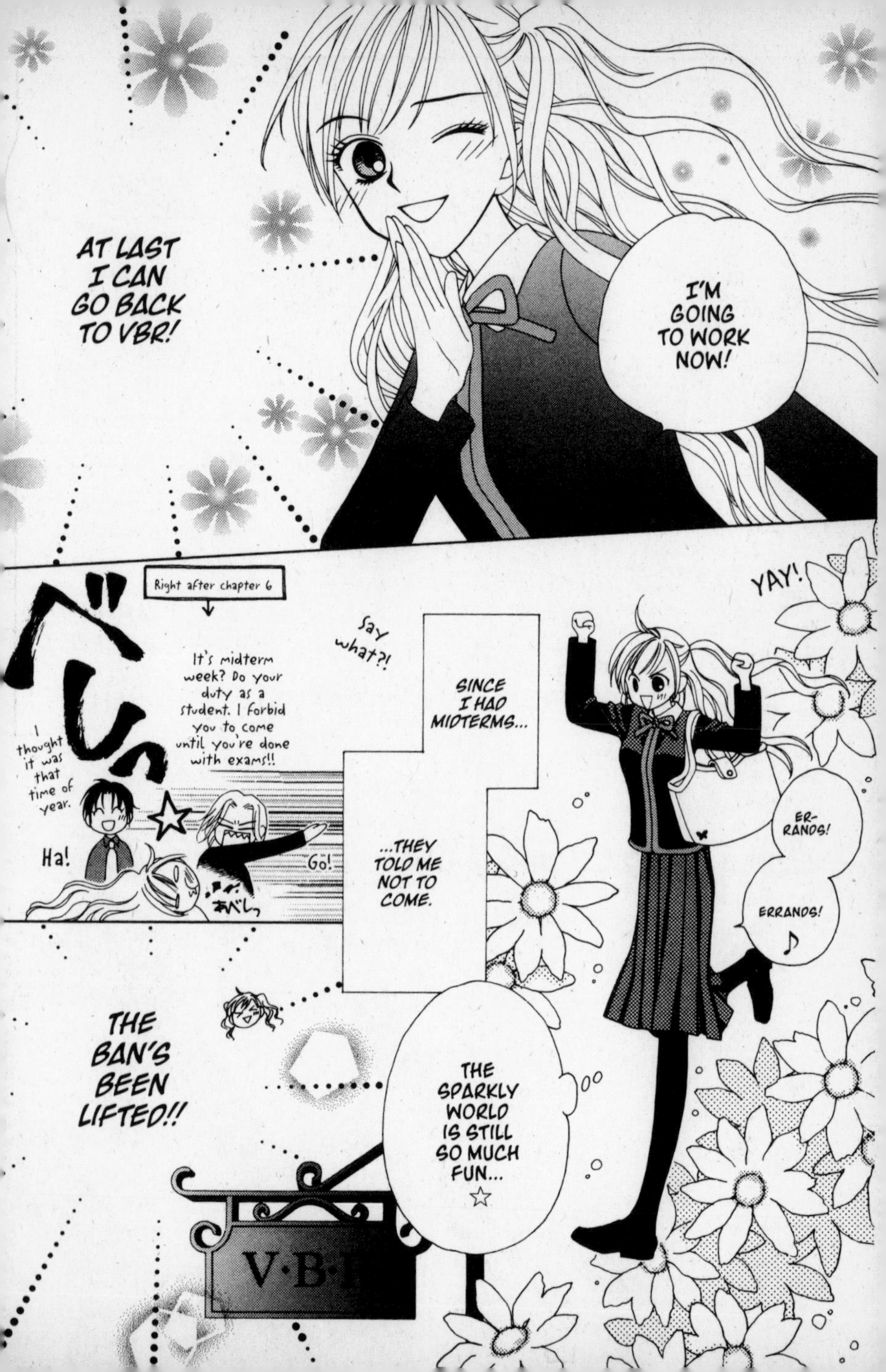
I'M GOING TO WORK NOW!
AT LAST I CAN GO BACK TO VBR!
YAY!
ER-RANDOS!
ERRANDOS! ♪
SINCE I HAD MIDTERMS...
...THEY TOLD ME NOT TO COME.
Right after chapter 6
Say what?!
It's midterm week? Do your duty as a student. I forbid you to come until you're done with exams!!
べしっ
I thought it was that time of year.
Ha!
Go!
あべしっ
THE SPARKLY WORLD IS STILL SO MUCH FUN... ☆
THE BAN'S BEEN LIFTED!!
V·B·I

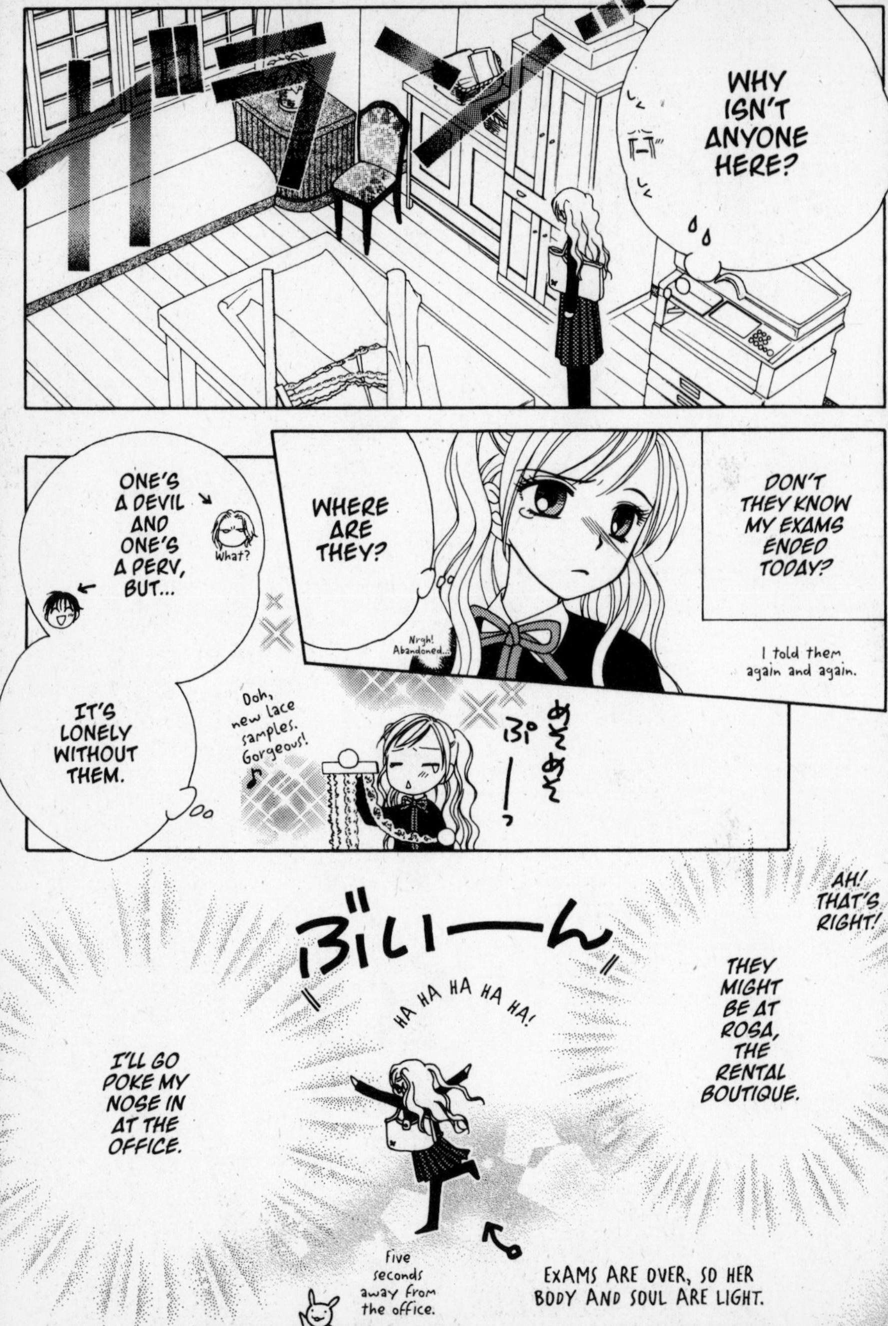
WHY ISN'T ANYONE HERE?
DON'T THEY KNOW MY EXAMS ENDED TODAY?
I told them again and again.
WHERE ARE THEY?
Nrgh! Abandoned...
ONE'S A DEVIL AND ONE'S A PERV, BUT...
What?
IT'S LONELY WITHOUT THEM.
めそめそ
ぷー
Ooh, new lace samples. Gorgeous!
AH! THAT'S RIGHT!
THEY MIGHT BE AT ROSA, THE RENTAL BOUTIQUE.
ぶいーん
HA HA HA HA HA!
I'LL GO POKE MY NOSE IN AT THE OFFICE.
EXAMS ARE OVER, SO HER BODY AND SOUL ARE LIGHT.
Five seconds away from the office.

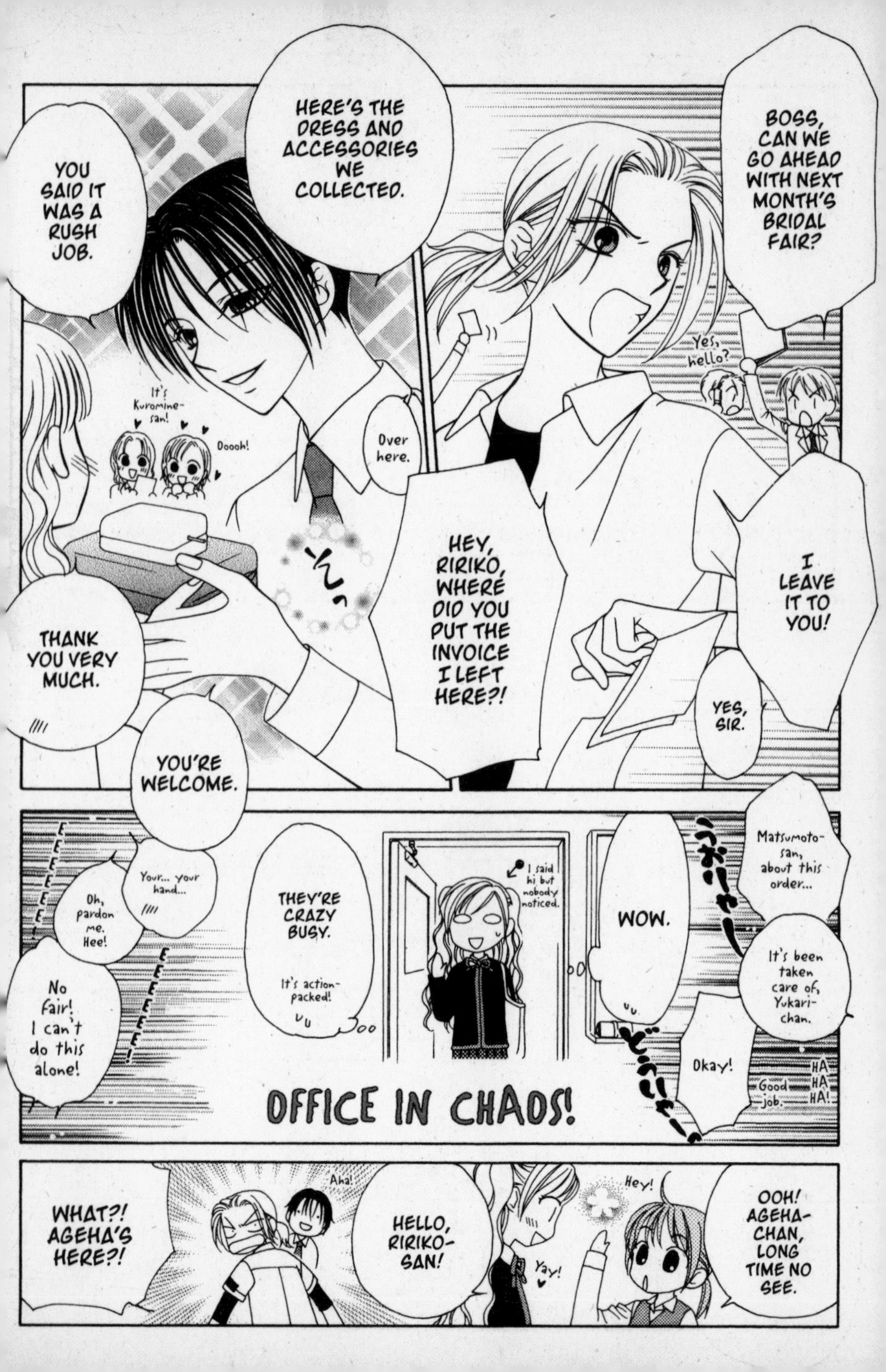
BOSS, CAN WE GO AHEAD WITH NEXT MONTH'S BRIDAL FAIR?
Yes, hello?
I LEAVE IT TO YOU!
YES, SIR.
HERE'S THE DRESS AND ACCESSORIES WE COLLECTED.
HEY, RIRIKO, WHERE DID YOU PUT THE INVOICE I LEFT HERE?!
Over here.
YOU SAID IT WAS A RUSH JOB.
It's Kuromine-san!
Doooh!
THANK YOU VERY MUCH.
YOU'RE WELCOME.
Matsumoto-san, about this order...
It's been taken care of, Yukari-chan.
Okay!
Good job.
HA HA HA!
WOW.
I said hi but nobody noticed.
THEY'RE CRAZY BUSY.
It's action-packed!
Your... your hand...
Oh, pardon me. Hee!
No fair! I can't do this alone!
OFFICE IN CHAOS!
OOH! AGEHA-CHAN, LONG TIME NO SEE.
Hey!
Yay!
HELLO, RIRIKO-SAN!
Aha!
WHAT?! AGEHA'S HERE?!

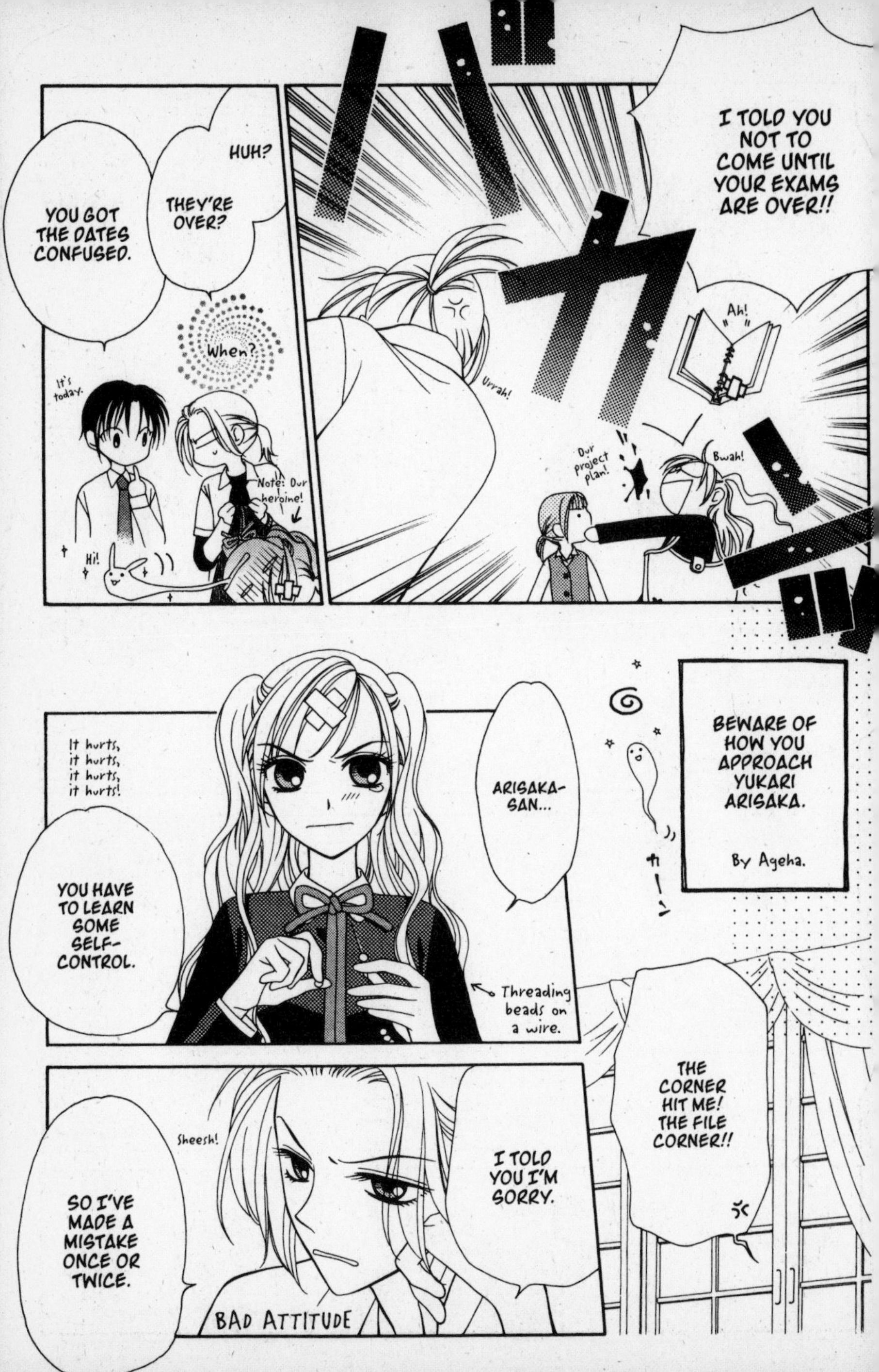
I TOLD YOU NOT TO COME UNTIL YOUR EXAMS ARE OVER!!
Urrah!
Ah!
Our project plan!
Bwah!
HUH? THEY'RE OVER?
When?
YOU GOT THE DATES CONFUSED.
It's today.
Note: Our heroine!
Hi!
BEWARE OF HOW YOU APPROACH YUKARI ARISAKA.
By Ageha.
ARISAKA-SAN...
It hurts, it hurts, it hurts, it hurts!
YOU HAVE TO LEARN SOME SELF-CONTROL.
Threading beads on a wire.
THE CORNER HIT ME! THE FILE CORNER!!
I TOLD YOU I'M SORRY.
Sheesh!
SO I'VE MADE A MISTAKE ONCE OR TWICE.
BAD ATTITUDE

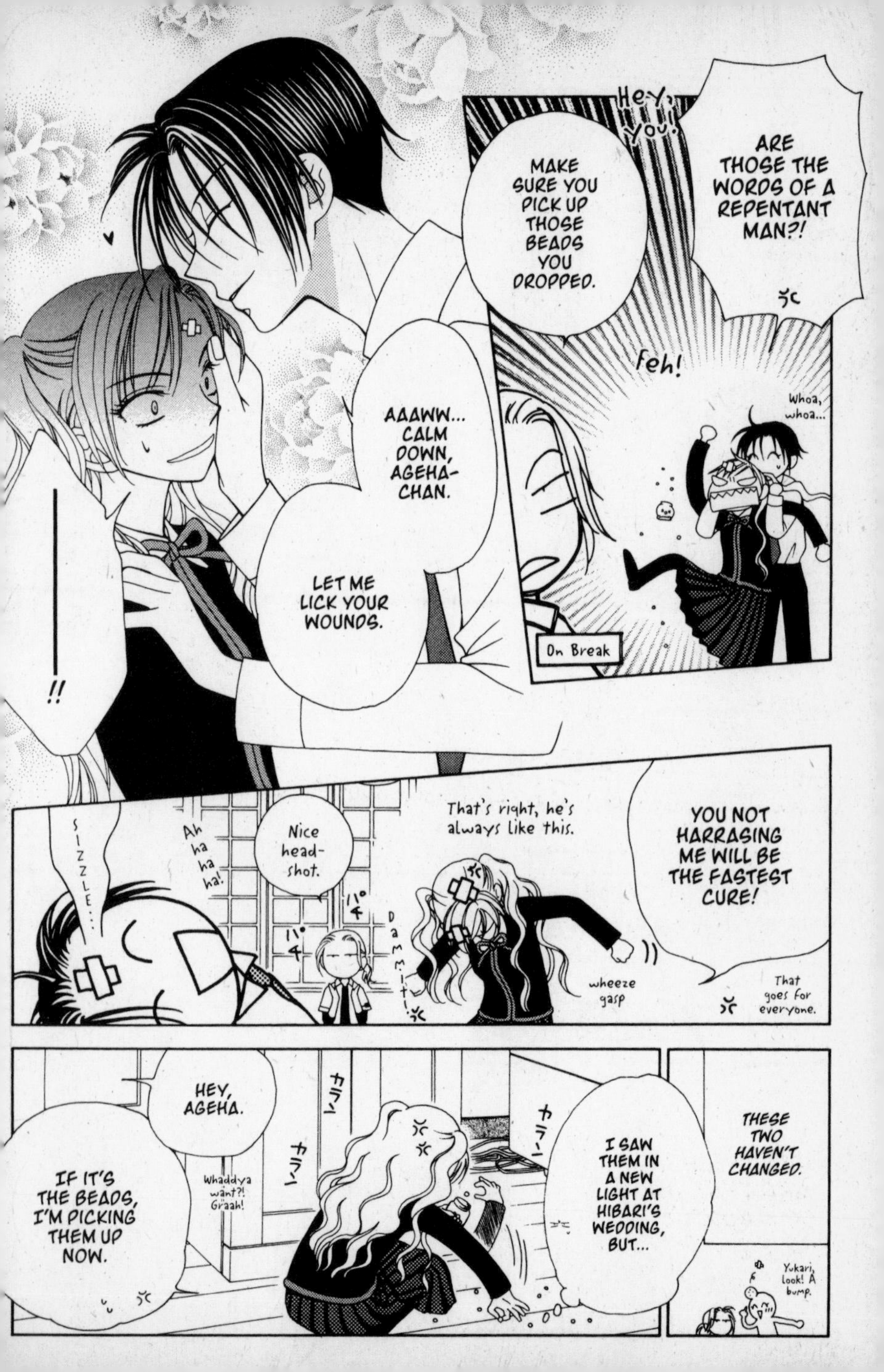
Hey, you!
ARE THOSE THE WORDS OF A REPENTANT MAN?!
MAKE SURE YOU PICK UP THOSE BEADS YOU DROPPED.
Feh!
Whoa, whoa...
On Break
AAAWW... CALM DOWN, AGEHA-CHAN.
LET ME LICK YOUR WOUNDS.
!!
YOU NOT HARRASING ME WILL BE THE FASTEST CURE!
That goes for everyone.
wheeze gasp
That's right, he's always like this.
DAMMIT...
パチ
パチ
Nice head-shot.
Ah ha ha ha!
SIZZLE...
THESE TWO HAVEN'T CHANGED.
Yukari, look! A bump.
I SAW THEM IN A NEW LIGHT AT HIBARI'S WEDDING, BUT...
カラン
カラン
カラン
HEY, AGEHA.
Whaddya want?! Graah!
IF IT'S THE BEADS, I'M PICKING THEM UP NOW.

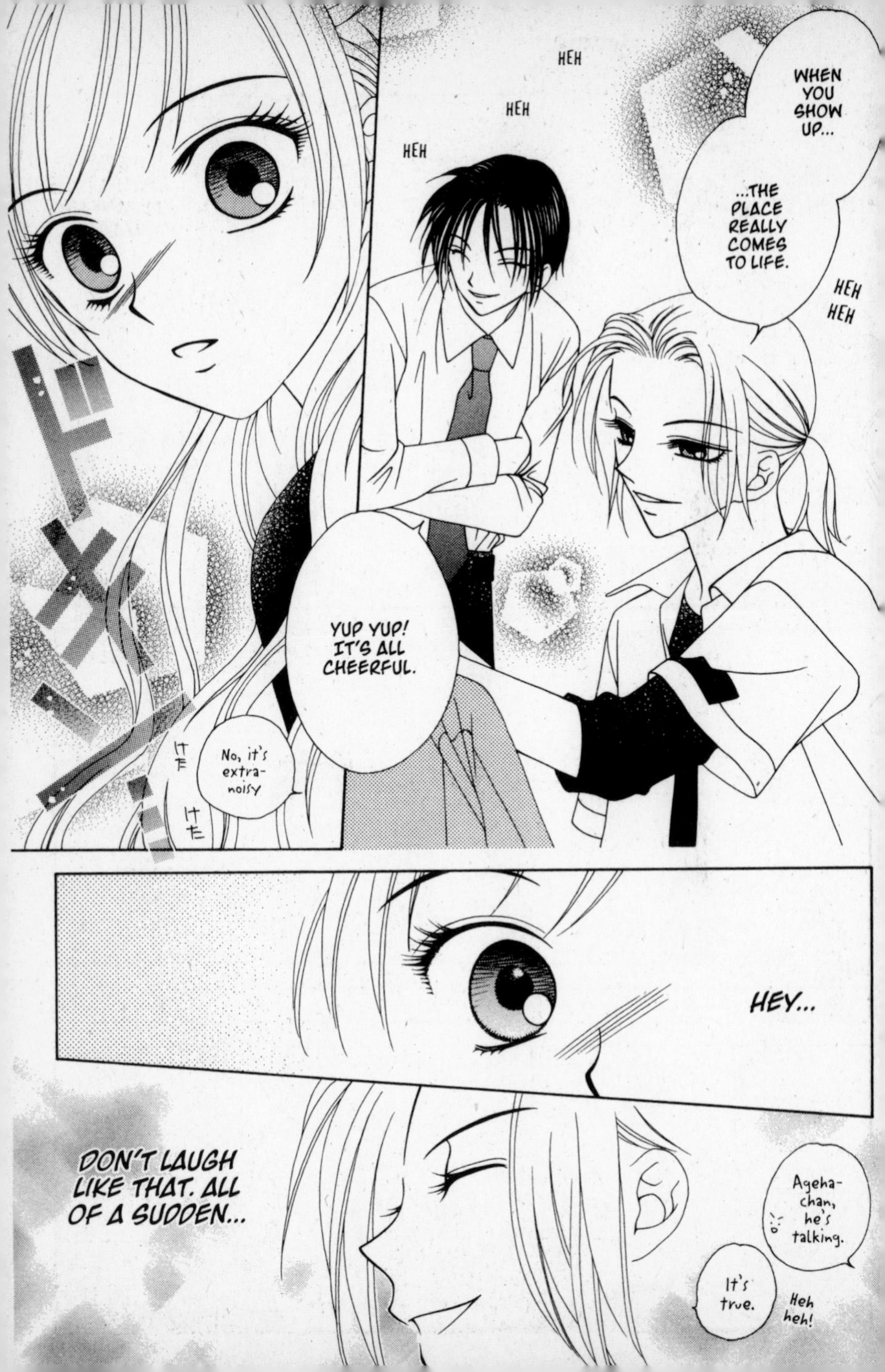
WHEN YOU SHOW UP...
...THE PLACE REALLY COMES TO LIFE.
HEH HEH
HEH
HEH
HEH
YUP YUP! IT'S ALL CHEERFUL.
けた
けた
No, it's extra-noisy
HEY...
Ageha-chan, he's talking.
Heh heh!
It's true.
DON'T LAUGH LIKE THAT. ALL OF A SUDDEN...

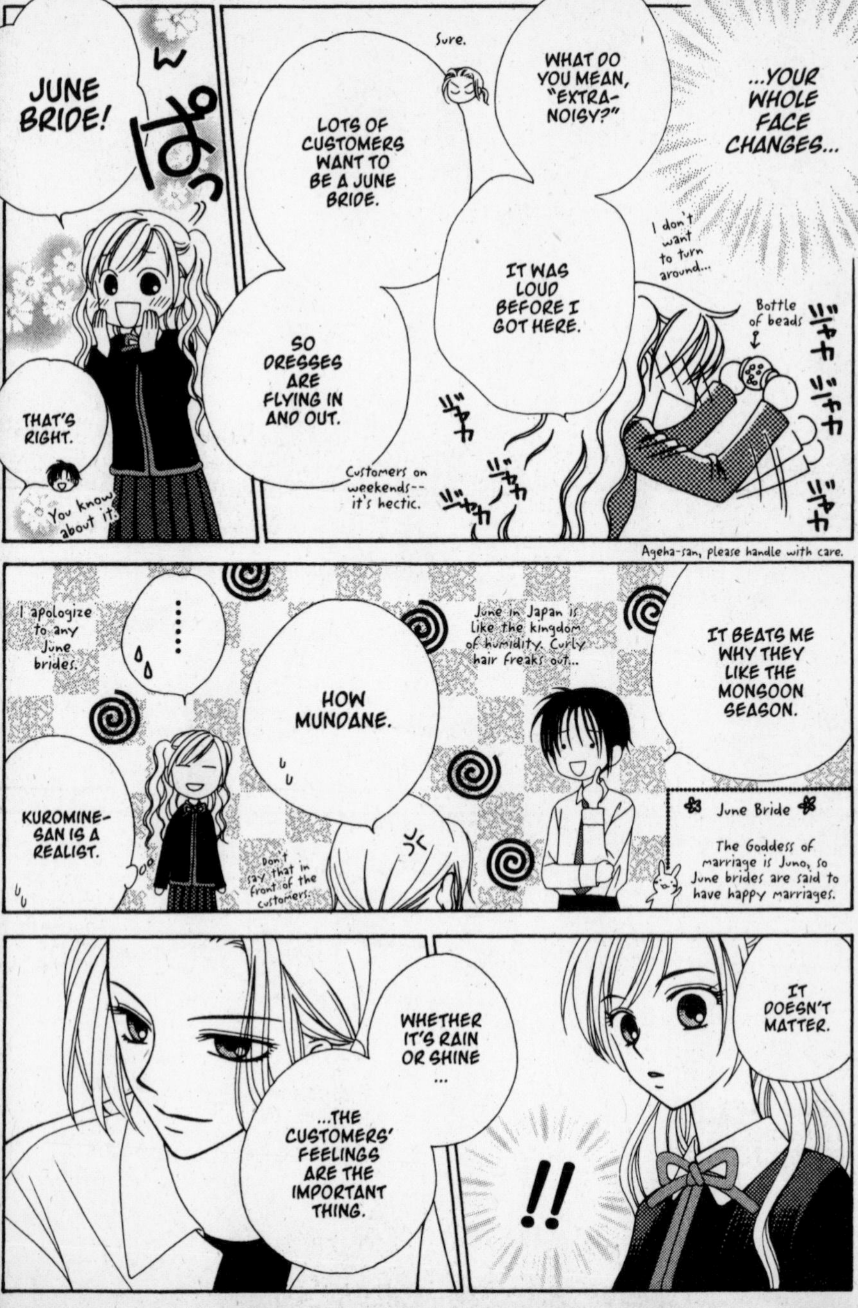
...YOUR WHOLE FACE CHANGES...
WHAT DO YOU MEAN, "EXTRA-NOISY?"
Sure.
LOTS OF CUSTOMERS WANT TO BE A JUNE BRIDE.
IT WAS LOUD BEFORE I GOT HERE.
I don't want to turn around...
Bottle of beads
ジャカ
ジャカ
SO DRESSES ARE FLYING IN AND OUT.
ジャカ
ジャカ
ジャカ
ジャカ
Customers on weekends-- it's hectic.
JUNE BRIDE!
ぱっ
THAT'S RIGHT.
You know about it.
Ageha-san, please handle with care.
IT BEATS ME WHY THEY LIKE THE MONSOON SEASON.
June Bride
The Goddess of marriage is Juno, so June brides are said to have happy marriages.
June in Japan is like the kingdom of humidity. Curly hair freaks out...
HOW MUNDANE.
Don't say that in front of the customers.
......
I apologize to any June brides.
KUROMINE-SAN IS A REALIST.
IT DOESN'T MATTER.
!!
WHETHER IT'S RAIN OR SHINE ...
...THE CUSTOMERS' FEELINGS ARE THE IMPORTANT THING.

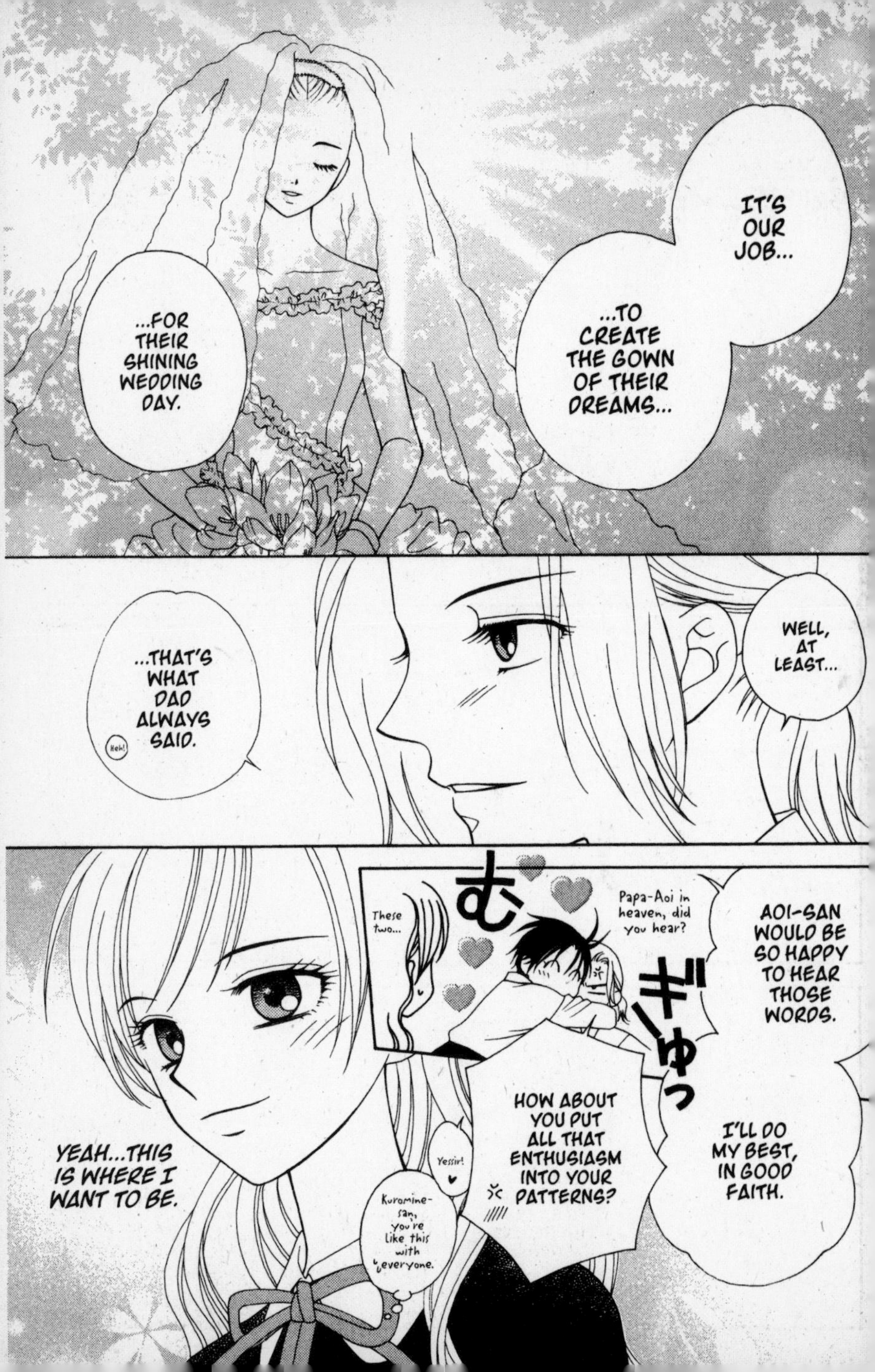
IT'S OUR JOB...
...TO CREATE THE GOWN OF THEIR DREAMS...
...FOR THEIR SHINING WEDDING DAY.
WELL, AT LEAST...
...THAT'S WHAT DAD ALWAYS SAID.
Heh!
AOI-SAN WOULD BE SO HAPPY TO HEAR THOSE WORDS.
I'LL DO MY BEST, IN GOOD FAITH.
ぎゅっ
Papa-Aoi in heaven, did you hear?
む
These two...
HOW ABOUT YOU PUT ALL THAT ENTHUSIASM INTO YOUR PATTERNS?
Yessir!
Kuromine-san, you're like this with everyone.
YEAH...THIS IS WHERE I WANT TO BE.

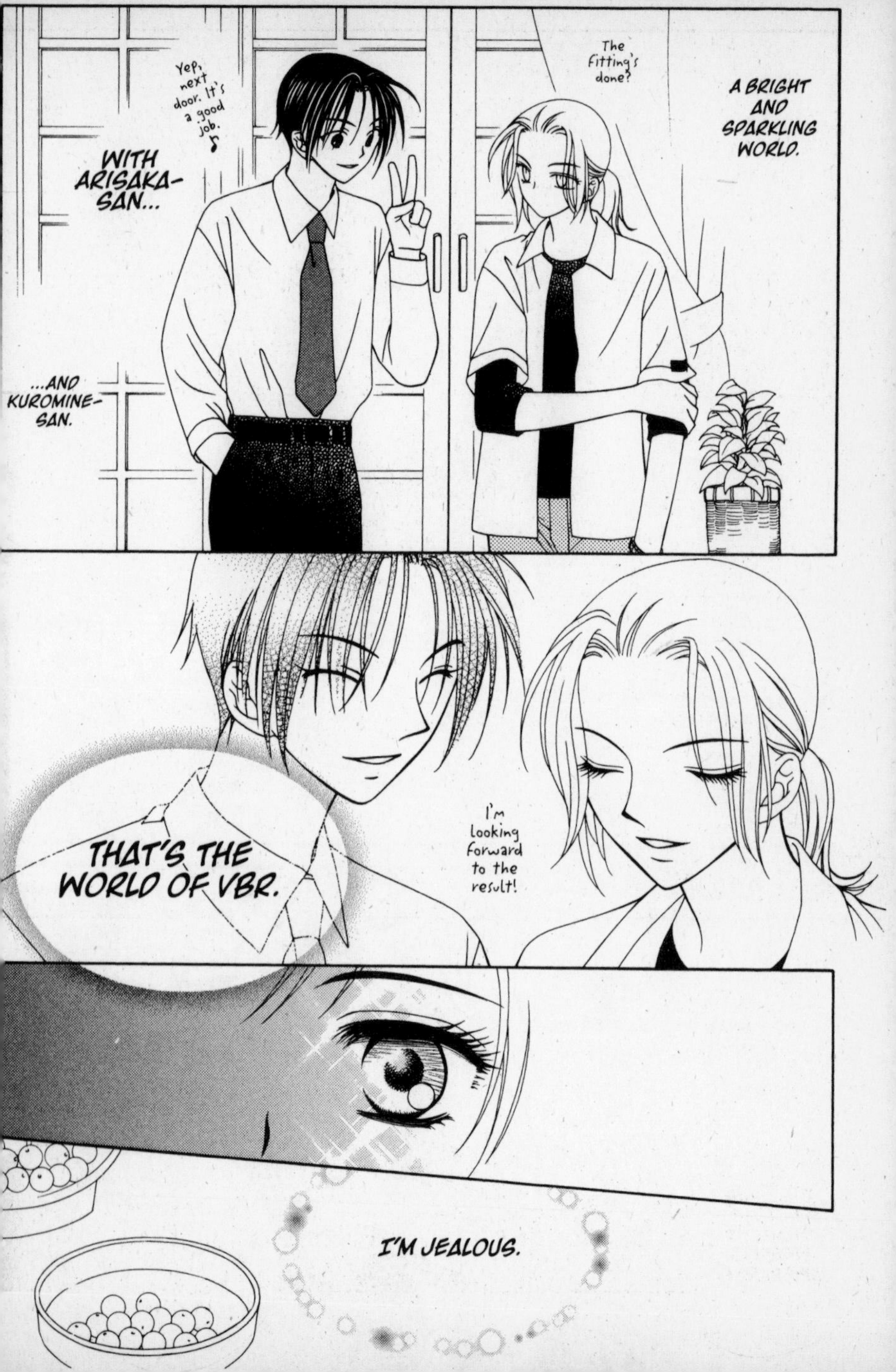
A BRIGHT AND SPARKLING WORLD.
The fitting's done?
Yep, next door. It's a good job. ♪
WITH ARISAKA-SAN...
...AND KUROMINE-SAN.
I'm looking forward to the result!
THAT'S THE WORLD OF VBR.
I'M JEALOUS.

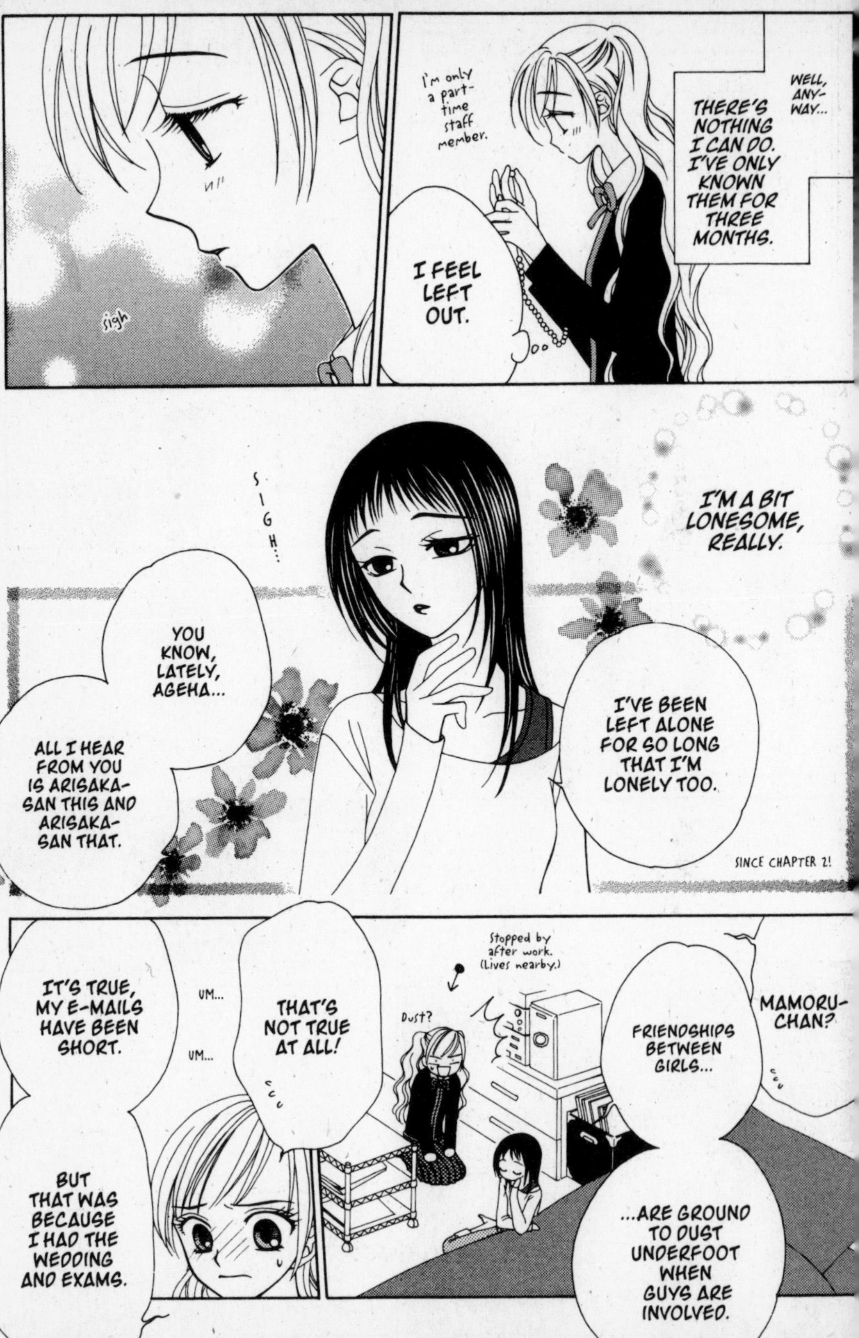
WELL, ANYWAY...
THERE'S NOTHING I CAN DO. I'VE ONLY KNOWN THEM FOR THREE MONTHS.
I'm only a part-time staff member.
I FEEL LEFT OUT.
sigh
I'M A BIT LONESOME, REALLY.
I'VE BEEN LEFT ALONE FOR SO LONG THAT I'M LONELY TOO.
SINCE CHAPTER 2!
SIGH...
YOU KNOW, LATELY, AGEHA...
ALL I HEAR FROM YOU IS ARISAKA-SAN THIS AND ARISAKA-SAN THAT.
MAMORU-CHAN?
FRIENDSHIPS BETWEEN GIRLS...
...ARE GROUND TO DUST UNDERFOOT WHEN GUYS ARE INVOLVED.
Stopped by after work. (Lives nearby.)
Dust?
THAT'S NOT TRUE AT ALL!
UM...
UM...
IT'S TRUE, MY E-MAILS HAVE BEEN SHORT.
BUT THAT WAS BECAUSE I HAD THE WEDDING AND EXAMS.

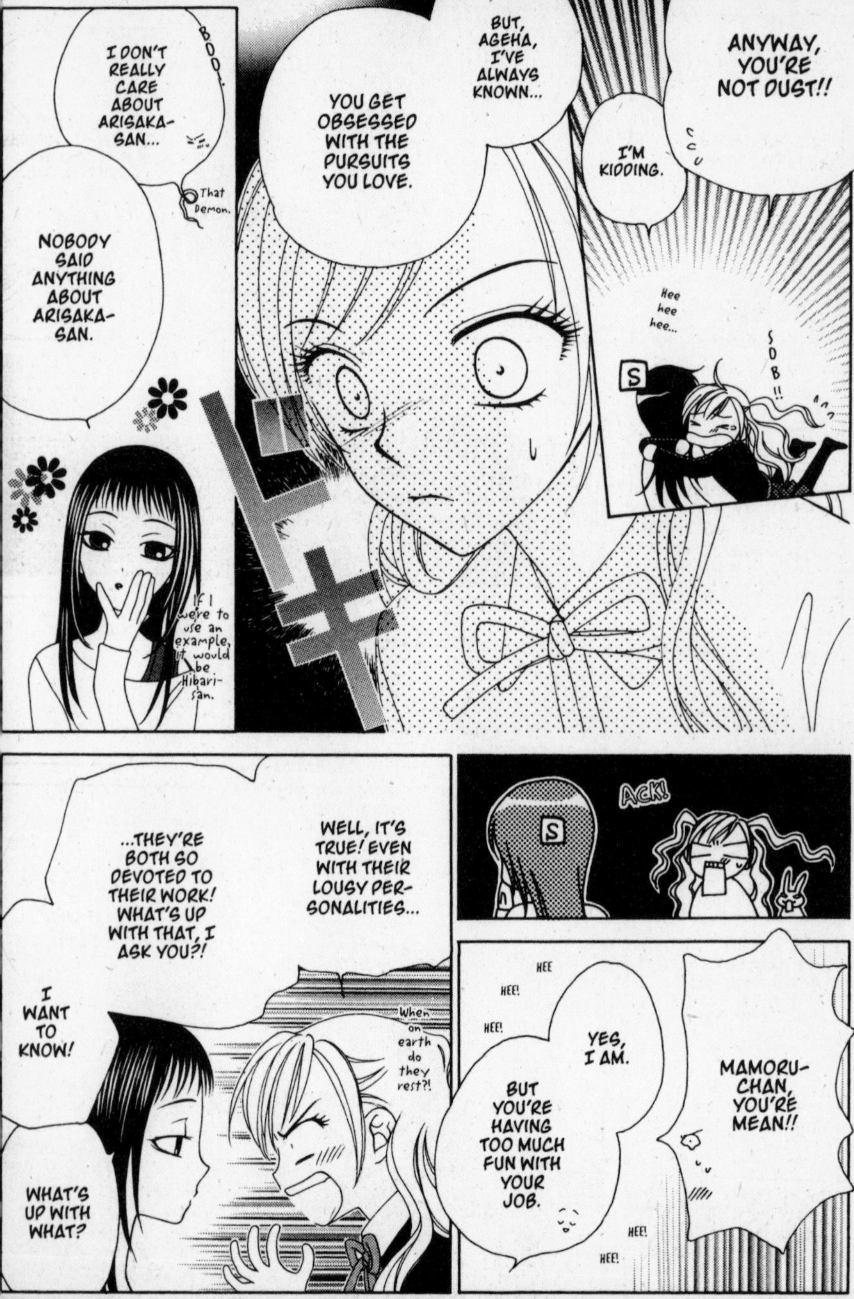
ANYWAY, YOU'RE NOT DUST!!
I'M KIDDING.
Hee hee hee...
SOB!!
S
BUT, AGEHA, I'VE ALWAYS KNOWN...
YOU GET OBSESSED WITH THE PURSUITS YOU LOVE.
BOO...
I DON'T REALLY CARE ABOUT ARISAKA-SAN...
That Demon.
NOBODY SAID ANYTHING ABOUT ARISAKA-SAN.
If I were to use an example, it would be Hibari-san.
ACK!
S
MAMORU-CHAN, YOU'RE MEAN!!
YES, I AM.
BUT YOU'RE HAVING TOO MUCH FUN WITH YOUR JOB.
HEE HEE! HEE!
HEE! HEE!
WELL, IT'S TRUE! EVEN WITH THEIR LOUSY PERSONALITIES...
...THEY'RE BOTH SO DEVOTED TO THEIR WORK! WHAT'S UP WITH THAT, I ASK YOU?!
When on earth do they rest?!
I WANT TO KNOW!
WHAT'S UP WITH WHAT?

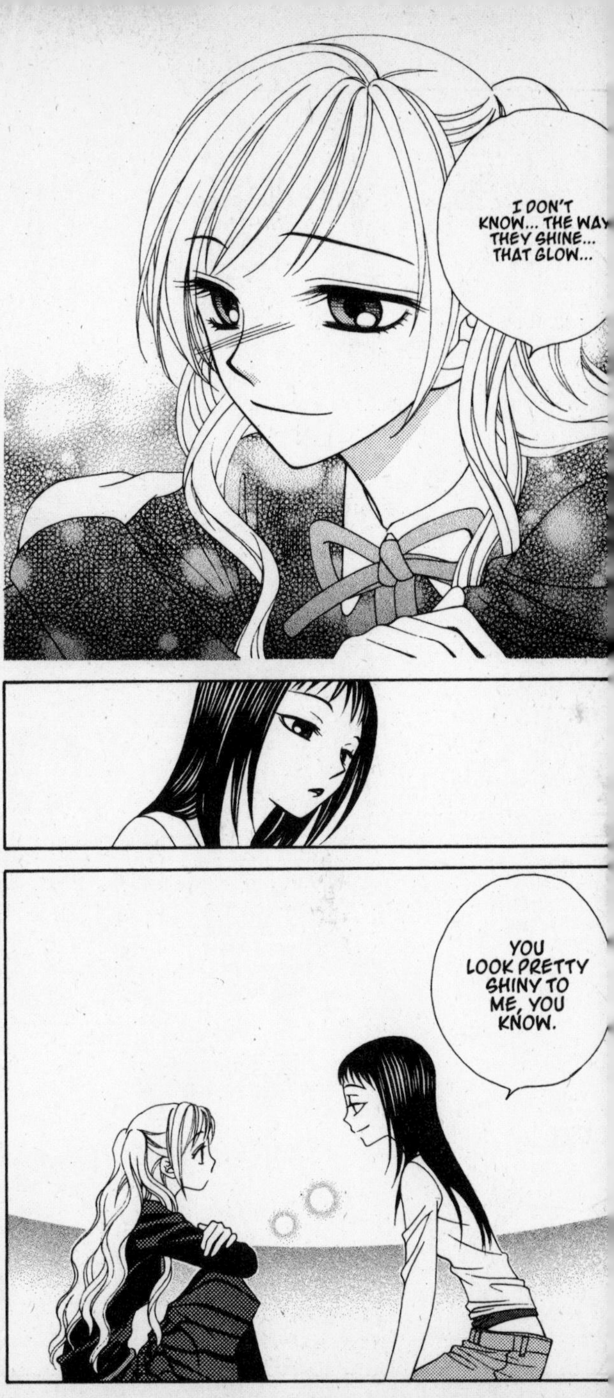
I DON'T KNOW... THE WAY THEY SHINE... THAT GLOW...
YOU LOOK PRETTY SHINY TO ME, YOU KNOW.

Hello, this is Banri Hidaka.

How have you been doing?

It's gotten really cold these days.

I don't do well with cold weather.

I wonder how cold it will be by the time this book is released? What will become of me in the ice of February?! Am I unusually vulnerable to cold, since I wear two layers of warm undershirts in October? But I love winter clothes!!

I got a flu shot this year, and I'm trying to keep up with daily life and away from cold viruses.

Strange, it's Hibari's wedding in Volume 2. I originally planned to have it in Episode 6 in Volume 1 but it somehow poured into volume 2, because the first two chapters had so many pages.

Please have fun with V.B. Rose Volume 2! It's my 28th comic book, with a whole cast of new characters!

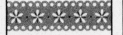

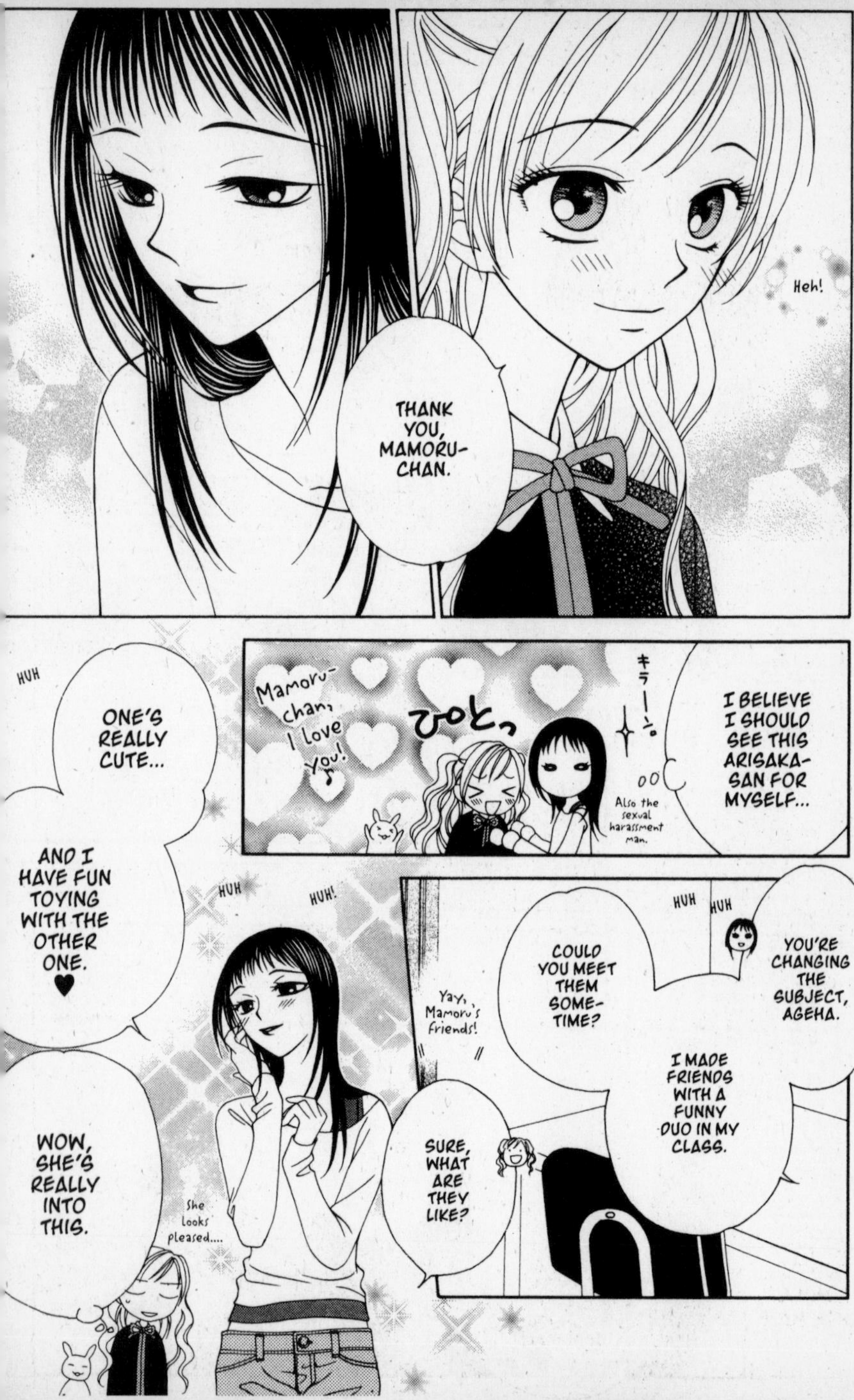
Heh!
THANK YOU, MAMORU-CHAN.
I BELIEVE I SHOULD SEE THIS ARISAKA-SAN FOR MYSELF...
キラー!
Also the sexual harassment man.
ぴとっ
Mamoru-chan, I love you! ♪
HUH
HUH
YOU'RE CHANGING THE SUBJECT, AGEHA.
COULD YOU MEET THEM SOME-TIME?
I MADE FRIENDS WITH A FUNNY DUO IN MY CLASS.
Yay, Mamoru's friends!
SURE, WHAT ARE THEY LIKE?
HUH
ONE'S REALLY CUTE...
HUH!
HUH
AND I HAVE FUN TOYING WITH THE OTHER ONE. ♥
WOW, SHE'S REALLY INTO THIS.
She looks pleased....

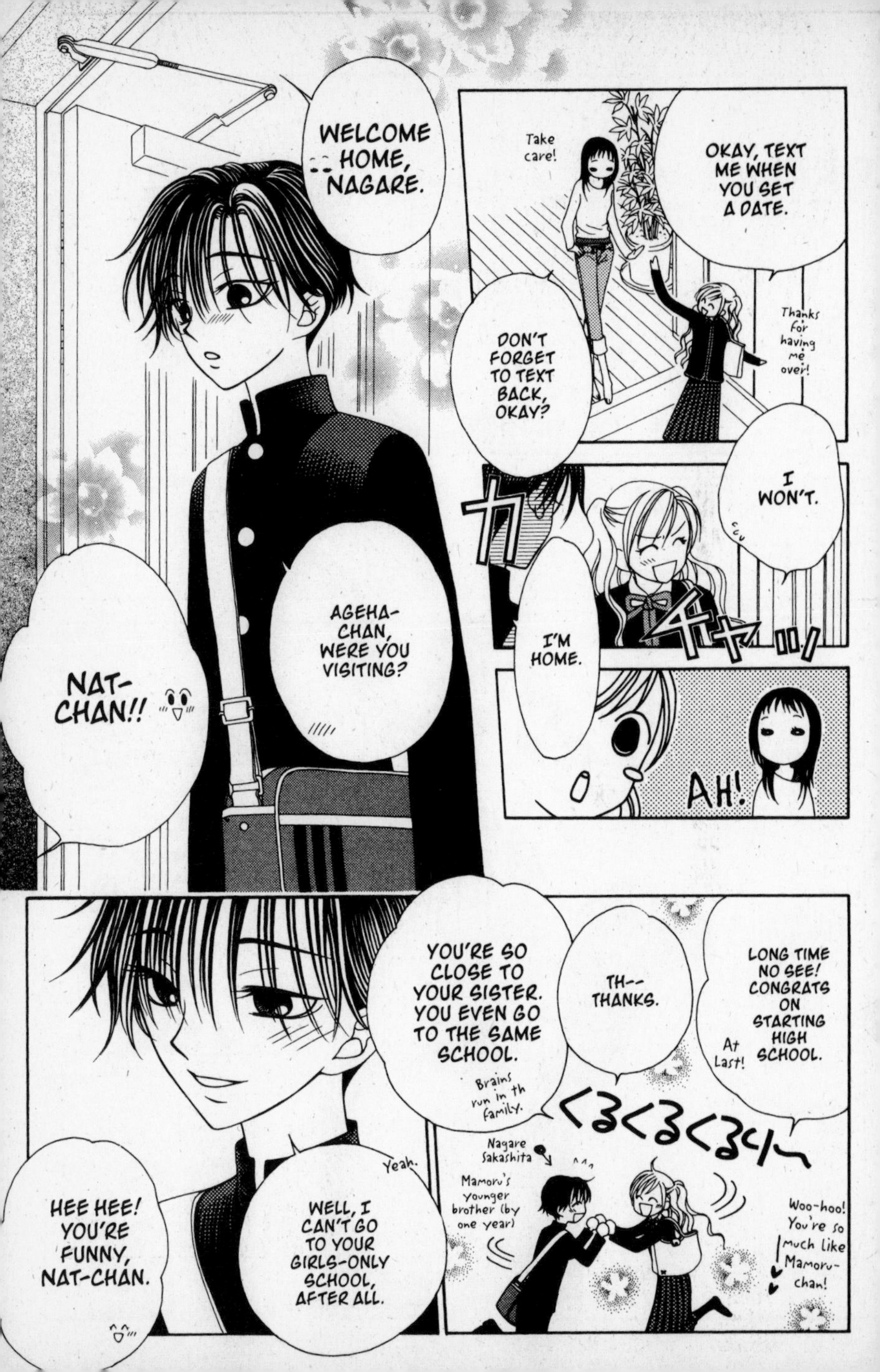
OKAY, TEXT ME WHEN YOU SET A DATE.
Thanks for having me over!
Take care!
DON'T FORGET TO TEXT BACK, OKAY?
I WON'T.
I'M HOME.
AH!
WELCOME HOME, NAGARE.
AGEHA-CHAN, WERE YOU VISITING?
NAT-CHAN!!
LONG TIME NO SEE! CONGRATS ON STARTING HIGH SCHOOL.
At Last!
TH--THANKS.
YOU'RE SO CLOSE TO YOUR SISTER. YOU EVEN GO TO THE SAME SCHOOL.
Brains run in th family.
くるくるくる〜
Woo-hoo! You're so much like Mamoru-chan!
Nagare Sakashita
Mamoru's younger brother (by one year)
Yeah.
WELL, I CAN'T GO TO YOUR GIRLS-ONLY SCHOOL, AFTER ALL.
HEE HEE! YOU'RE FUNNY, NAT-CHAN.

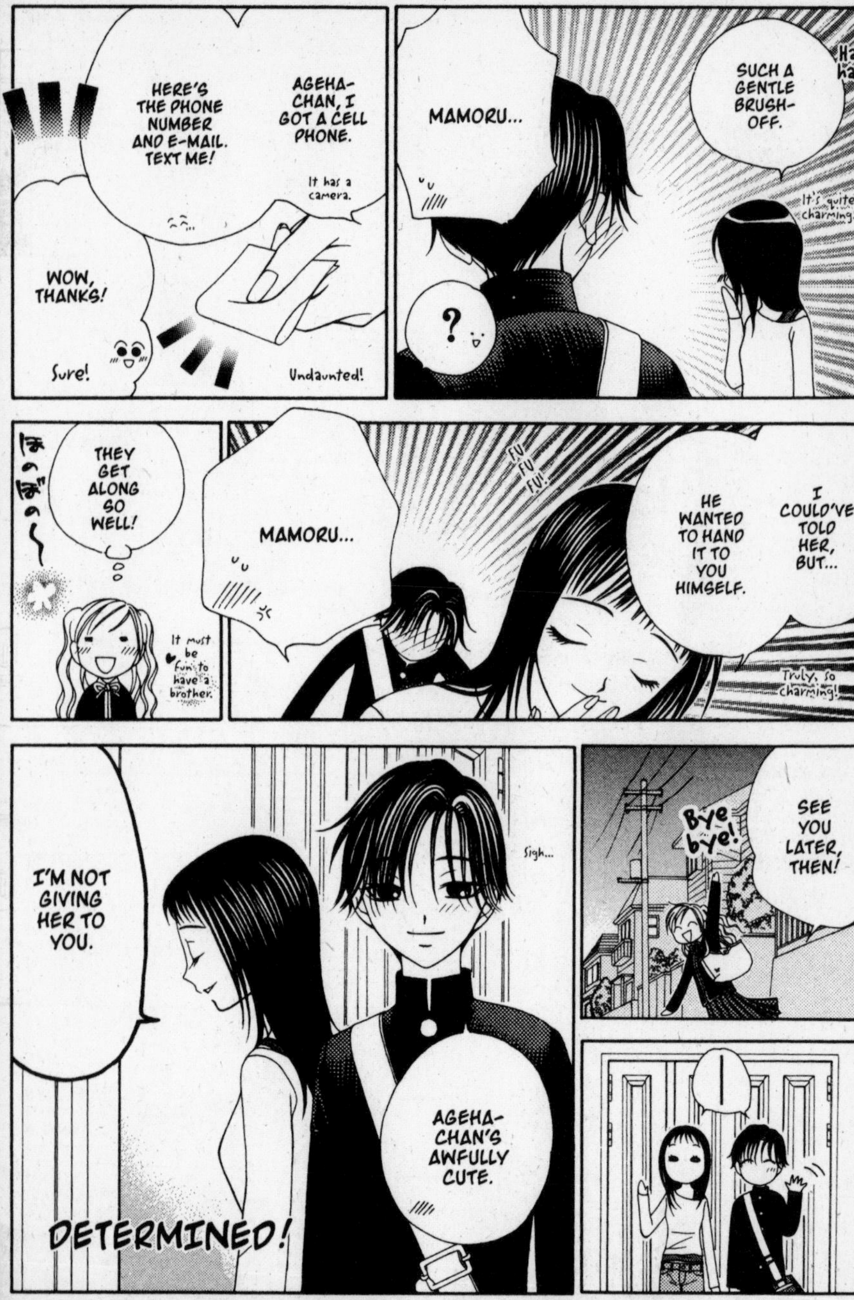
Ha ha.
SUCH A GENTLE BRUSH-OFF.
It's quite charming.
MAMORU...
?
AGEHA-CHAN, I GOT A CELL PHONE.
It has a camera.
HERE'S THE PHONE NUMBER AND E-MAIL. TEXT ME!
WOW, THANKS!
Sure!
Undaunted!
I COULD'VE TOLD HER, BUT...
HE WANTED TO HAND IT TO YOU HIMSELF.
FU FU FU!
Truly, so charming!
MAMORU...
THEY GET ALONG SO WELL!
ほのぼの~
It must be fun to have a brother.
SEE YOU LATER, THEN!
Bye bye!
!
AGEHA-CHAN'S AWFULLY CUTE.
Sigh...
I'M NOT GIVING HER TO YOU.
DETERMINED!

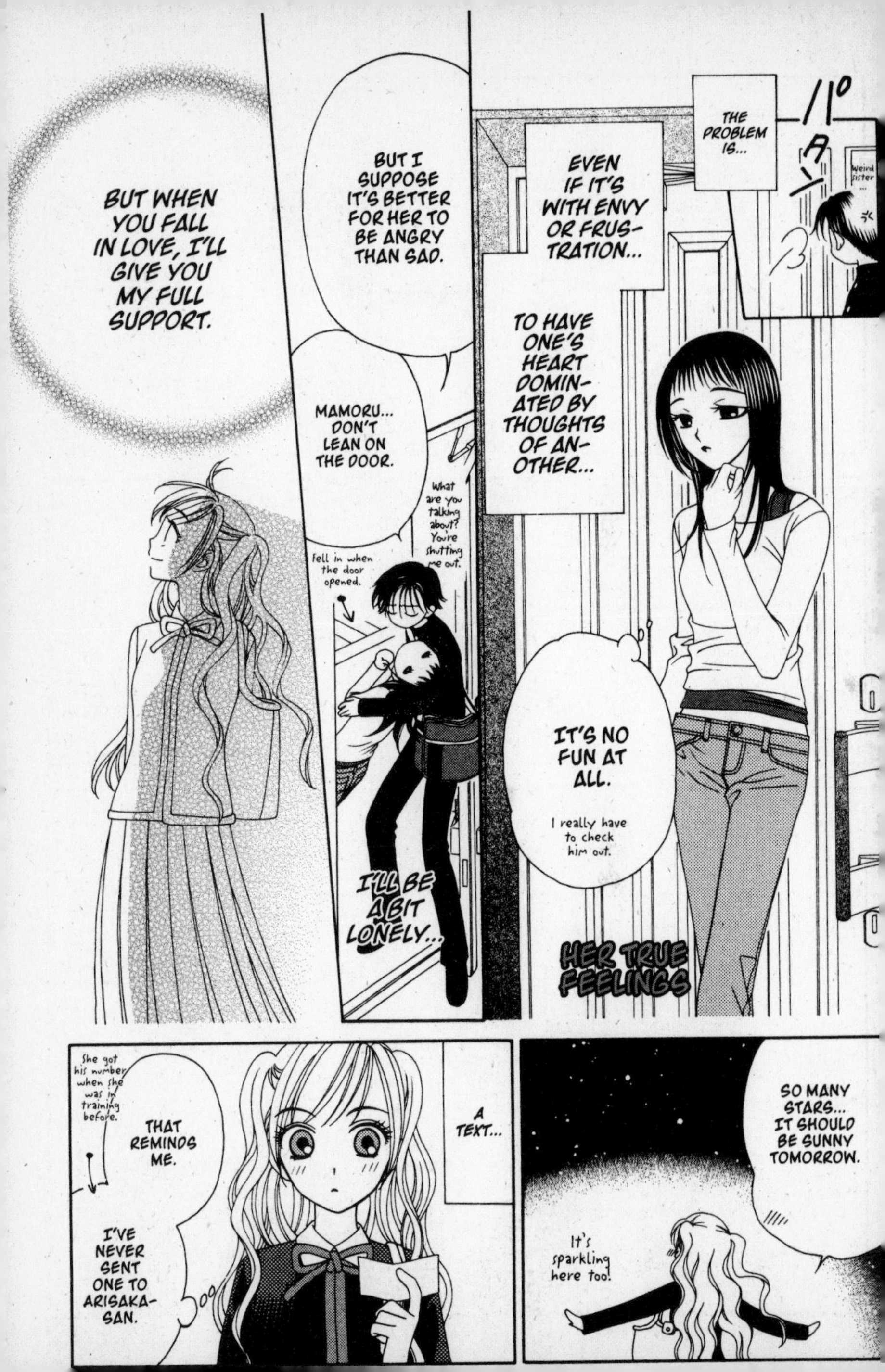
THE PROBLEM IS...
Weird sister ...
EVEN IF IT'S WITH ENVY OR FRUS-TRATION...
TO HAVE ONE'S HEART DOMIN-ATED BY THOUGHTS OF AN-OTHER...
IT'S NO FUN AT ALL.
I really have to check him out.
HER TRUE FEELINGS
BUT I SUPPOSE IT'S BETTER FOR HER TO BE ANGRY THAN SAD.
MAMORU... DON'T LEAN ON THE DOOR.
What are you talking about? You're shutting me out.
Fell in when the door opened.
I'LL BE A BIT LONELY...
BUT WHEN YOU FALL IN LOVE, I'LL GIVE YOU MY FULL SUPPORT.
SO MANY STARS... IT SHOULD BE SUNNY TOMORROW.
It's sparkling here too!
A TEXT...
THAT REMINDS ME.
She got his number when she was in training before.
I'VE NEVER SENT ONE TO ARISAKA-SAN.

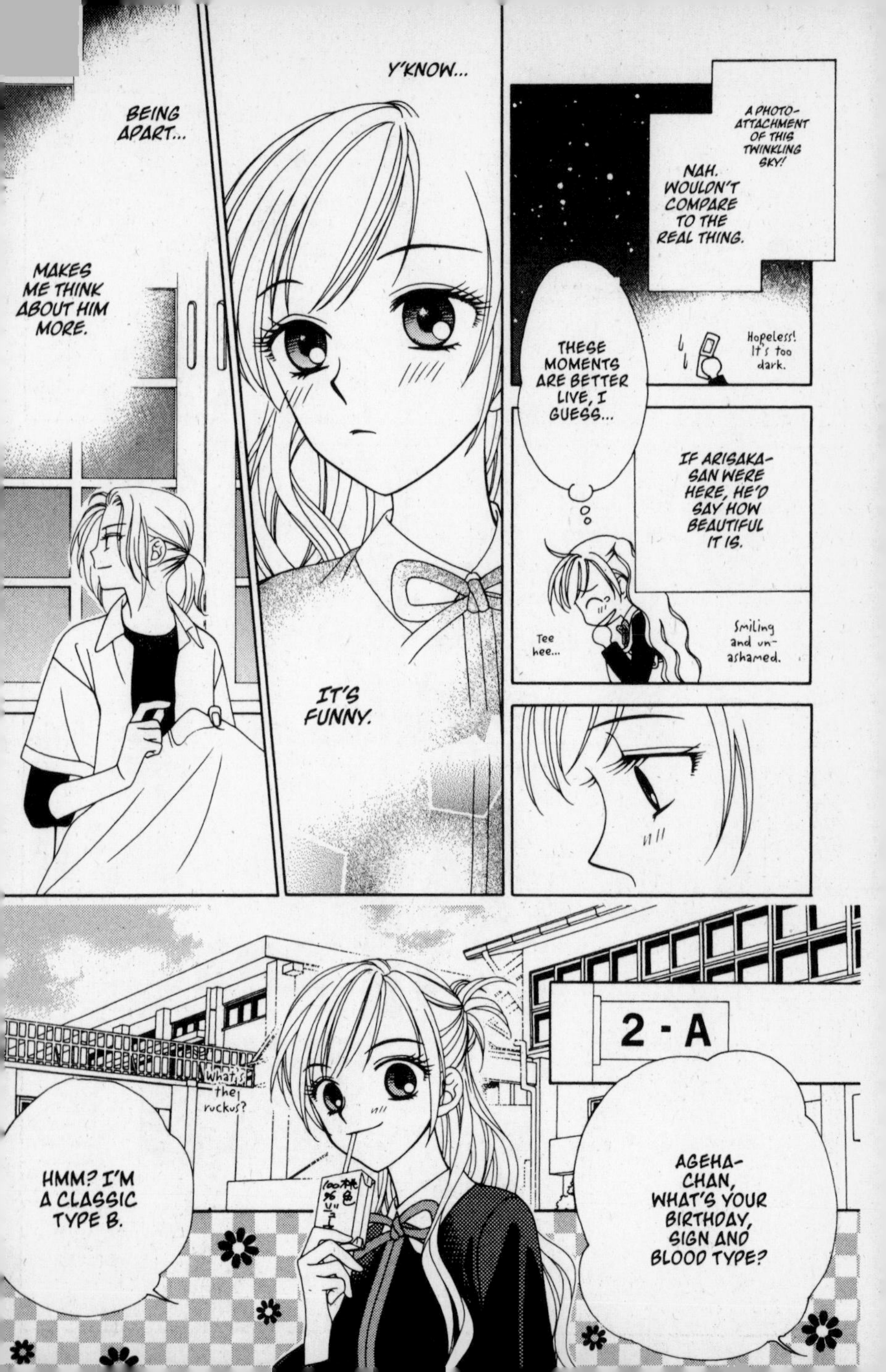
A PHOTO-ATTACHMENT OF THIS TWINKLING SKY!
NAH. WOULDN'T COMPARE TO THE REAL THING.
Hopeless! It's too dark.
THESE MOMENTS ARE BETTER LIVE, I GUESS...
IF ARISAKA-SAN WERE HERE, HE'D SAY HOW BEAUTIFUL IT IS.
Smiling and un-ashamed.
Tee hee...
Y'KNOW...
IT'S FUNNY.
BEING APART...
MAKES ME THINK ABOUT HIM MORE.
2 - A
AGEHA-CHAN, WHAT'S YOUR BIRTHDAY, SIGN AND BLOOD TYPE?
What's the ruckus?
HMM? I'M A CLASSIC TYPE B.

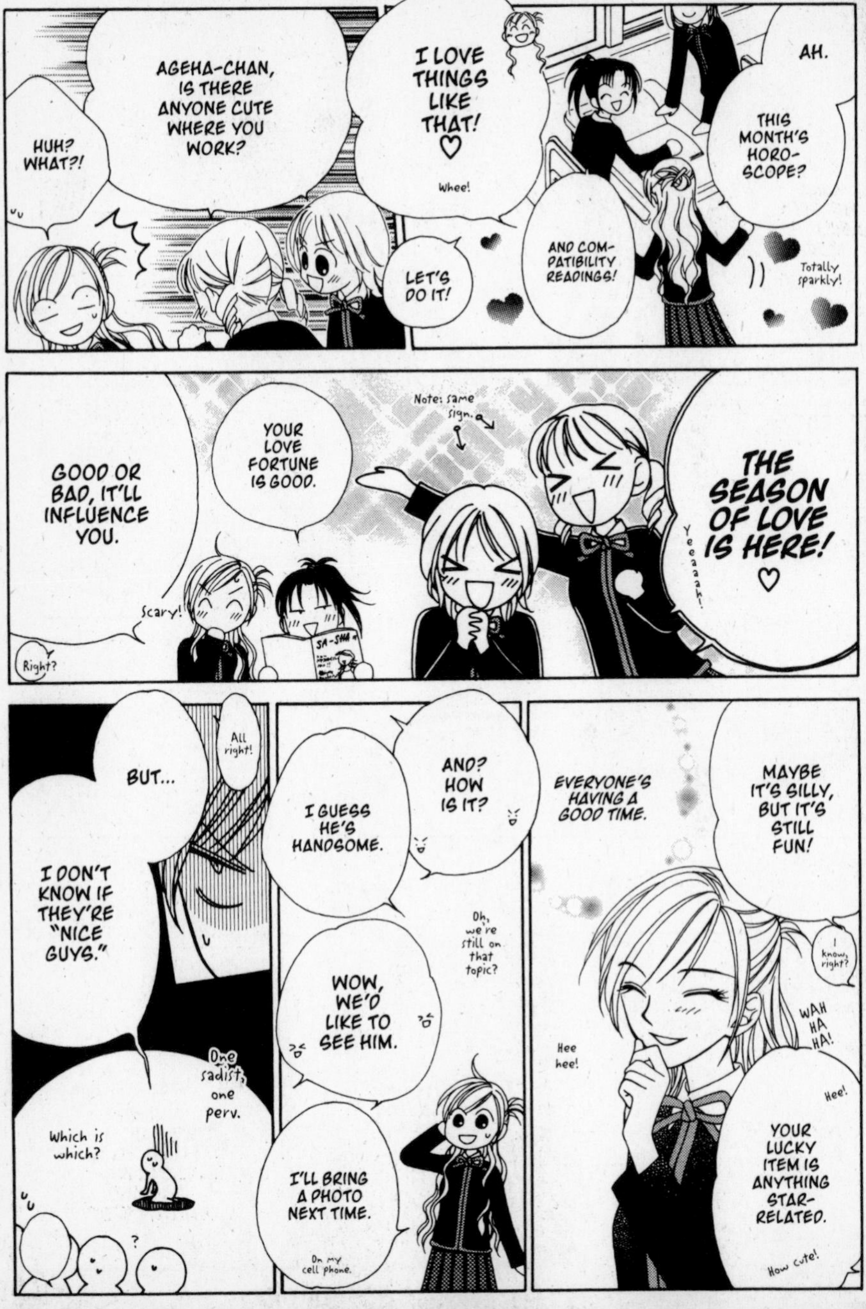
AH.
THIS MONTH'S HORO-SCOPE?
Totally sparkly!
AND COM-PATIBILITY READINGS!
I LOVE THINGS LIKE THAT! ♡
Whee!
LET'S DO IT!
AGEHA-CHAN, IS THERE ANYONE CUTE WHERE YOU WORK?
HUH? WHAT?!
THE SEASON OF LOVE IS HERE! ♡
Yeeaaaah!
Note: same sign.
YOUR LOVE FORTUNE IS GOOD.
GOOD OR BAD, IT'LL INFLUENCE YOU.
Scary!
Right?
MAYBE IT'S SILLY, BUT IT'S STILL FUN!
EVERYONE'S HAVING A GOOD TIME.
I know, right?
WAH HA HA!
Hee!
Hee hee!
YOUR LUCKY ITEM IS ANYTHING STAR-RELATED.
How cute!
AND? HOW IS IT?
I GUESS HE'S HANDSOME.
Oh, we're still on that topic?
WOW, WE'D LIKE TO SEE HIM.
I'LL BRING A PHOTO NEXT TIME.
On my cell phone.
All right!
BUT...
I DON'T KNOW IF THEY'RE "NICE GUYS."
One sadist, one perv.
Which is which?

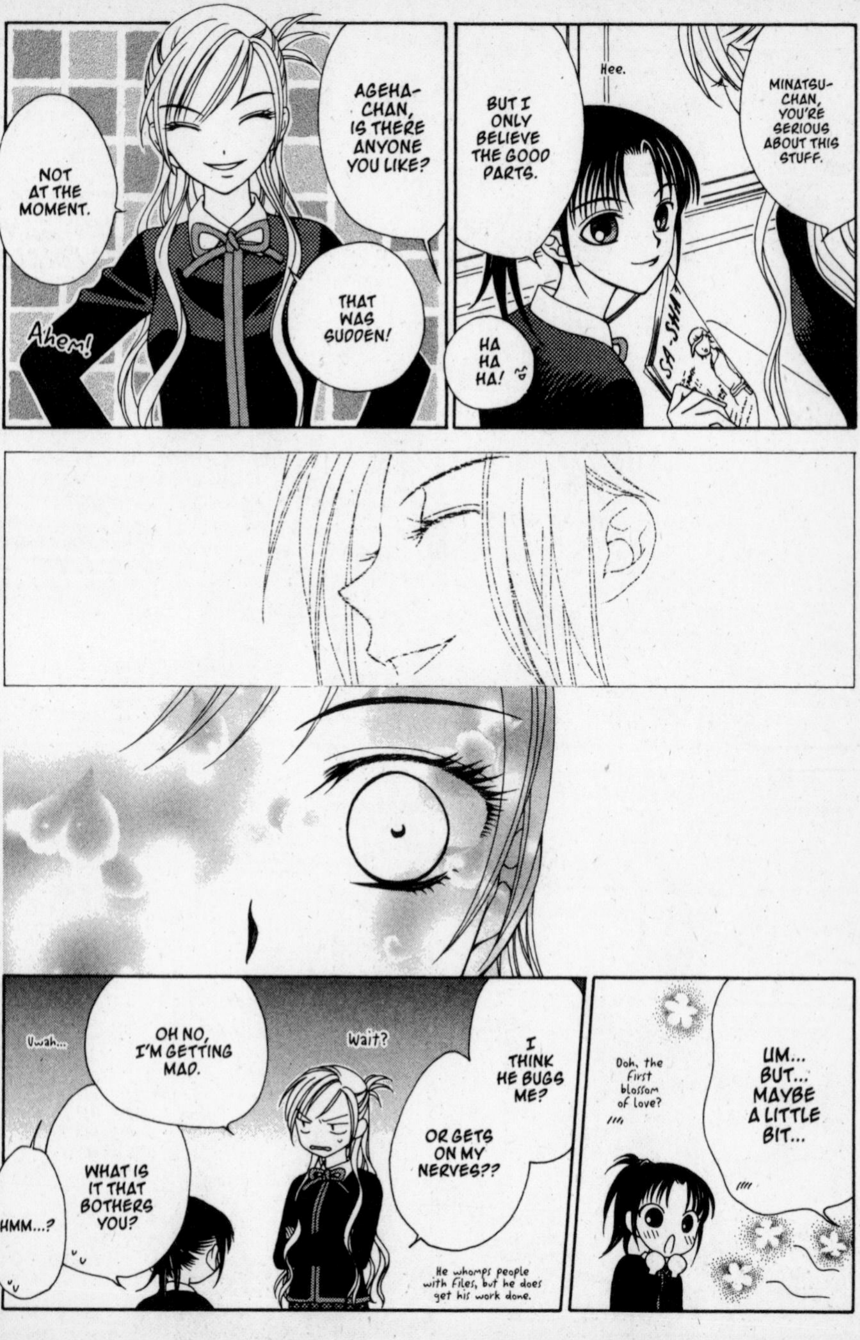

MINATSU-CHAN, YOU'RE SERIOUS ABOUT THIS STUFF.
Hee.
BUT I ONLY BELIEVE THE GOOD PARTS.
HA HA HA!
AGEHA-CHAN, IS THERE ANYONE YOU LIKE?
THAT WAS SUDDEN!
NOT AT THE MOMENT.
Ahem!
UM... BUT... MAYBE A LITTLE BIT...
Ooh, the first blossom of love?
I THINK HE BUGS ME?
Wait?
OR GETS ON MY NERVES??
OH NO, I'M GETTING MAD.
Uwah...
WHAT IS IT THAT BOTHERS YOU?
HMM...?
He whomps people with files, but he does get his work done.

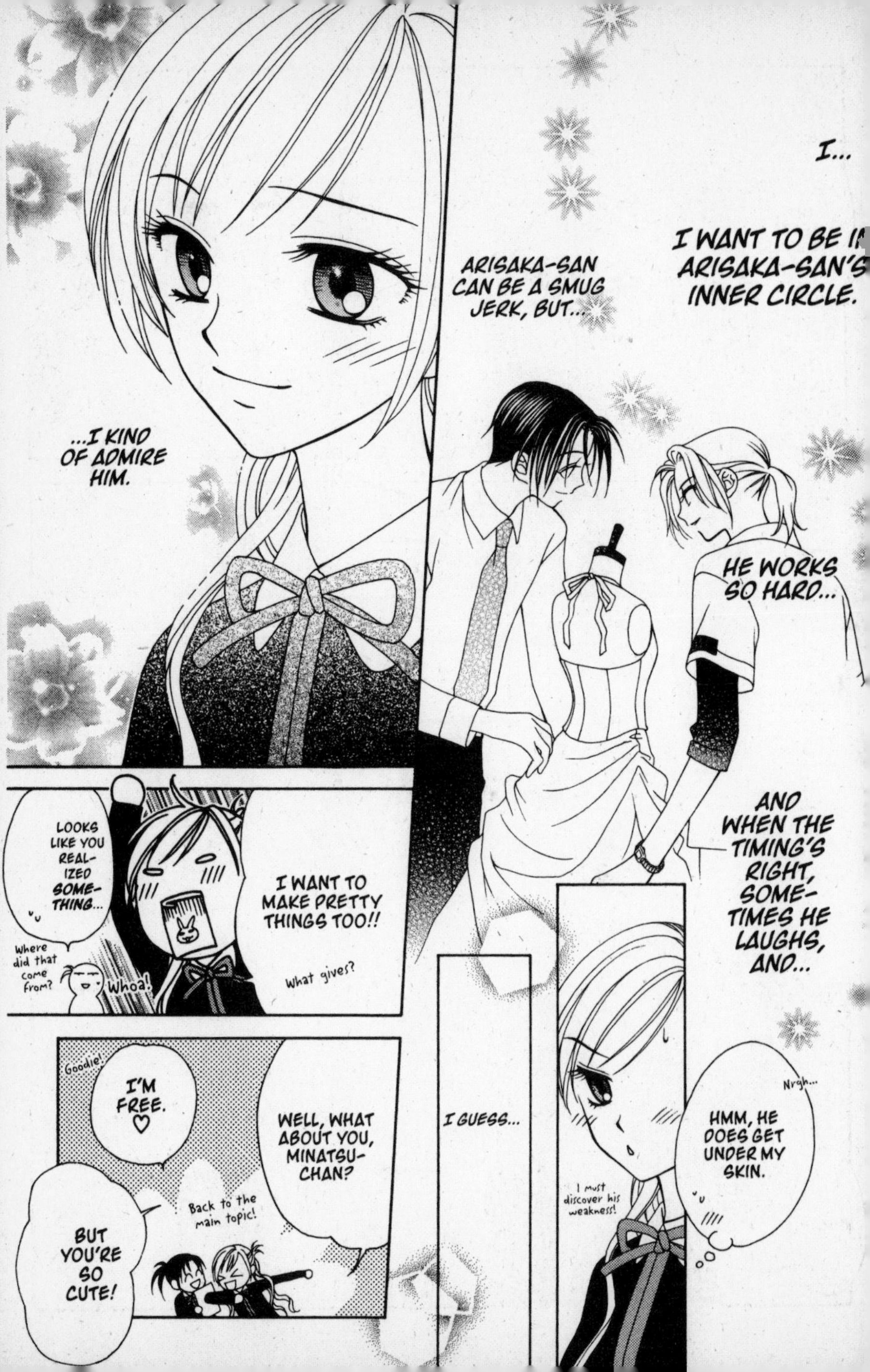
I...
I WANT TO BE I
ARISAKA-SAN'S INNER CIRCLE.
ARISAKA-SAN CAN BE A SMUG JERK, BUT...
HE WORKS SO HARD...
AND WHEN THE TIMING'S RIGHT, SOME-TIMES HE LAUGHS, AND...
...I KIND OF ADMIRE HIM.
I WANT TO MAKE PRETTY THINGS TOO!!
What gives?
LOOKS LIKE YOU REAL-IZED SOME-THING...
Where did that come from?
Whoa!
WELL, WHAT ABOUT YOU, MINATSU-CHAN?
I GUESS...
HMM, HE DOES GET UNDER MY SKIN.
Nrgh...
I must discover his weakness!
I'M FREE. ♡
Goodie!
BUT YOU'RE SO CUTE!
Back to the main topic!

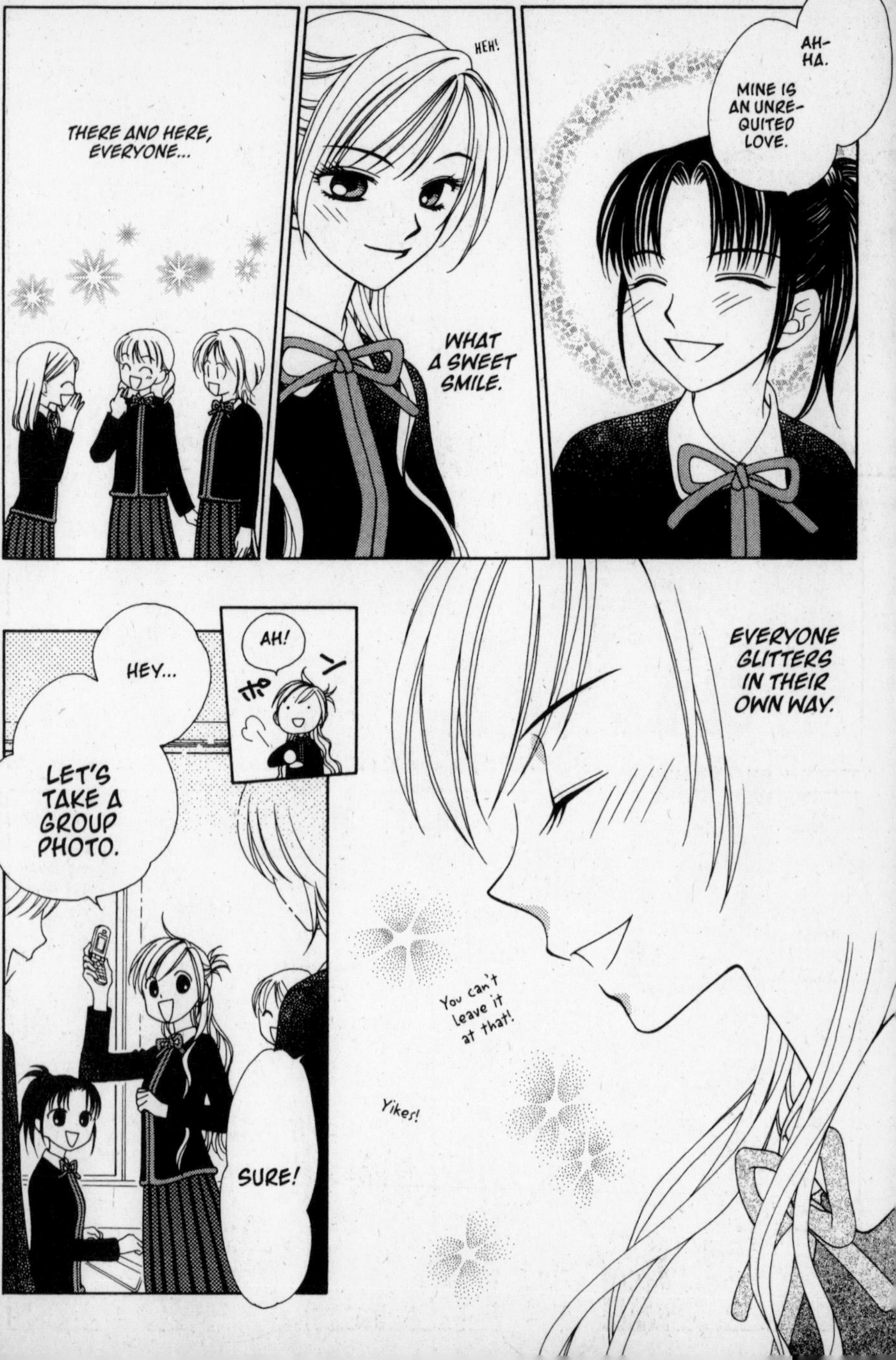
AH-HA.
MINE IS AN UNREQUITED LOVE.
HEH!
WHAT A SWEET SMILE.
THERE AND HERE, EVERYONE...
EVERYONE GLITTERS IN THEIR OWN WAY.
You can't leave it at that!
Yikes!
ン
AH!
ポ
HEY...
LET'S TAKE A GROUP PHOTO.
SURE!

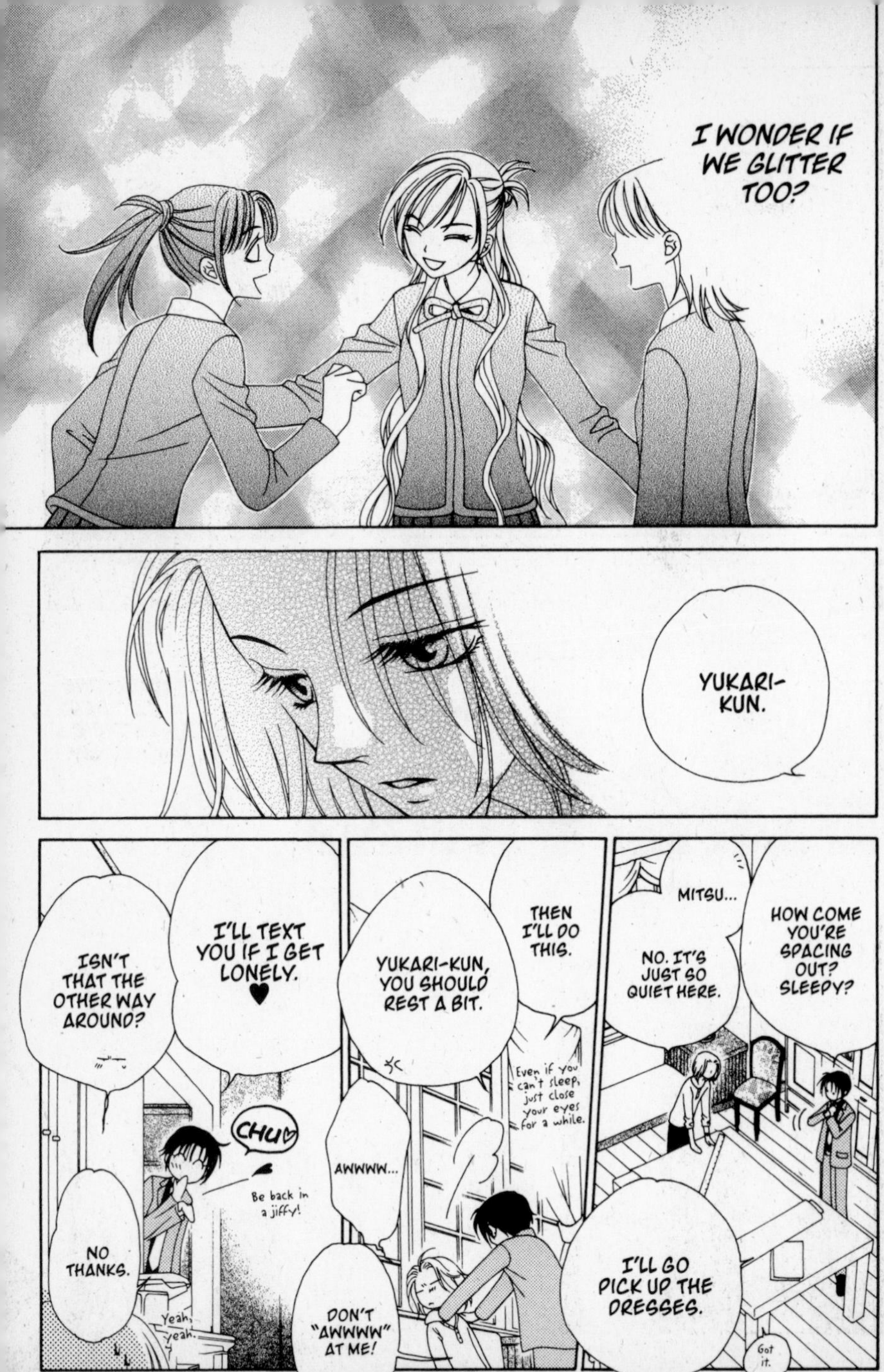
I WONDER IF WE GLITTER TOO?
YUKARI-KUN.
HOW COME YOU'RE SPACING OUT? SLEEPY?
MITSU...
NO. IT'S JUST SO QUIET HERE.
I'LL GO PICK UP THE DRESSES.
Got it.
THEN I'LL DO THIS.
YUKARI-KUN, YOU SHOULD REST A BIT.
Even if you can't sleep, just close your eyes for a while.
AWWWW...
DON'T "AWWWW" AT ME!
I'LL TEXT YOU IF I GET LONELY. ♥
ISN'T THAT THE OTHER WAY AROUND?
CHU♥
Be back in a jiffy!
NO THANKS.
Yeah, yeah.

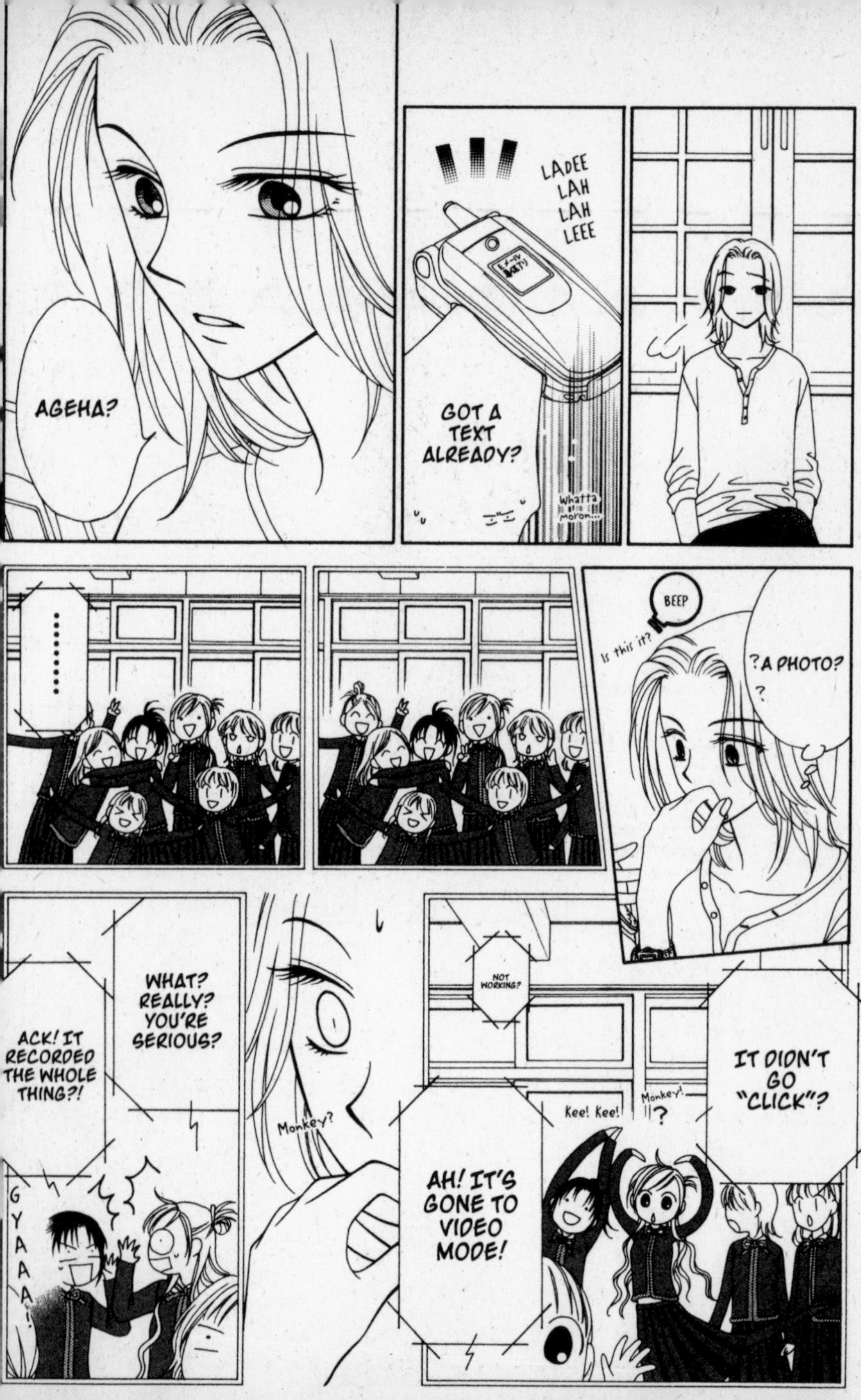
LADEE LAH LAH LEEE
GOT A TEXT ALREADY?
Whatta moron...
AGEHA?
BEEP
Is this it?
?A PHOTO?
......
NOT WORKING?
IT DIDN'T GO "CLICK"?
Monkey!!?
Kee! Kee!
AH! IT'S GONE TO VIDEO MODE!
Monkey?
WHAT? REALLY? YOU'RE SERIOUS?
ACK! IT RECORDED THE WHOLE THING?!
GYAAAA!

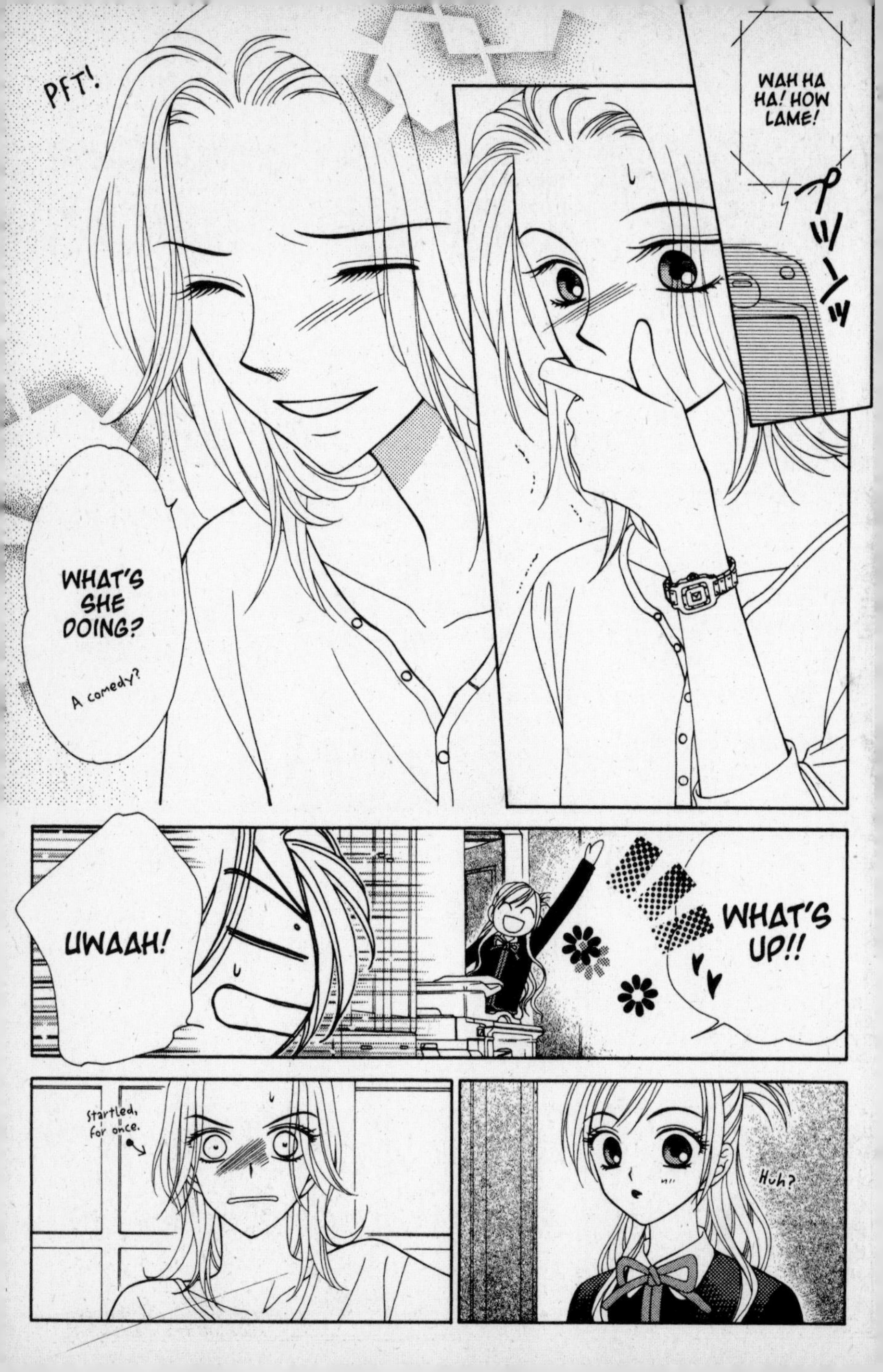
WAH HA HA! HOW LAME!
PFT!
WHAT'S SHE DOING?
A comedy?
WHAT'S UP!!
UWAAH!
Huh?
Startled, for once.

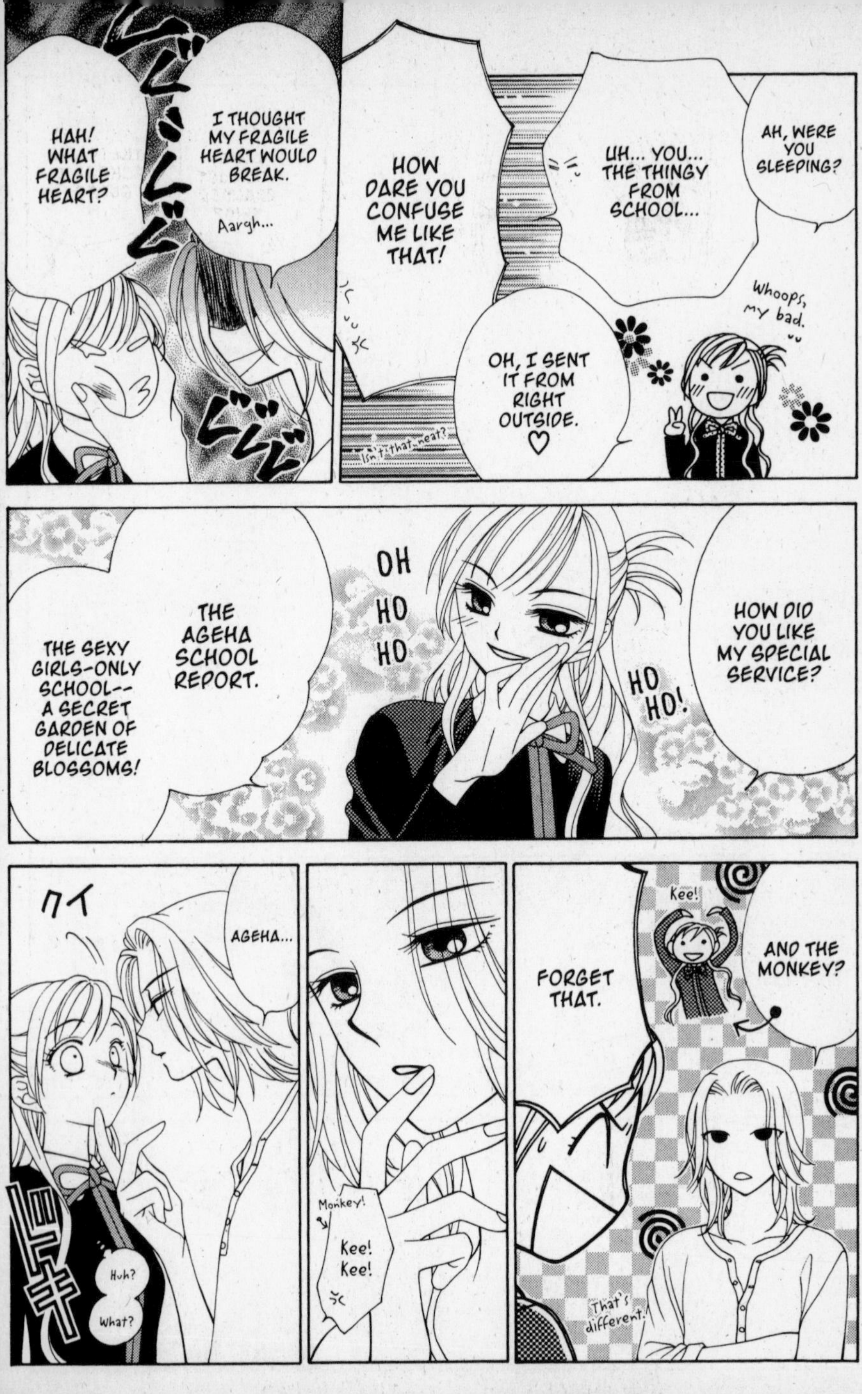

AH, WERE YOU SLEEPING?
UH... YOU... THE THINGY FROM SCHOOL...
Whoops, my bad.
OH, I SENT IT FROM RIGHT OUTSIDE. ♡
Isn't that neat?
HOW DARE YOU CONFUSE ME LIKE THAT!
I THOUGHT MY FRAGILE HEART WOULD BREAK.
Aargh...
HAH! WHAT FRAGILE HEART?
HOW DID YOU LIKE MY SPECIAL SERVICE?
HO HO!
OH HO HO
THE AGEHA SCHOOL REPORT.
THE SEXY GIRLS-ONLY SCHOOL-- A SECRET GARDEN OF DELICATE BLOSSOMS!
AND THE MONKEY?
Kee!
FORGET THAT.
That's different!
Monkey!
Kee! Kee!
AGEHA...
Huh?
What?

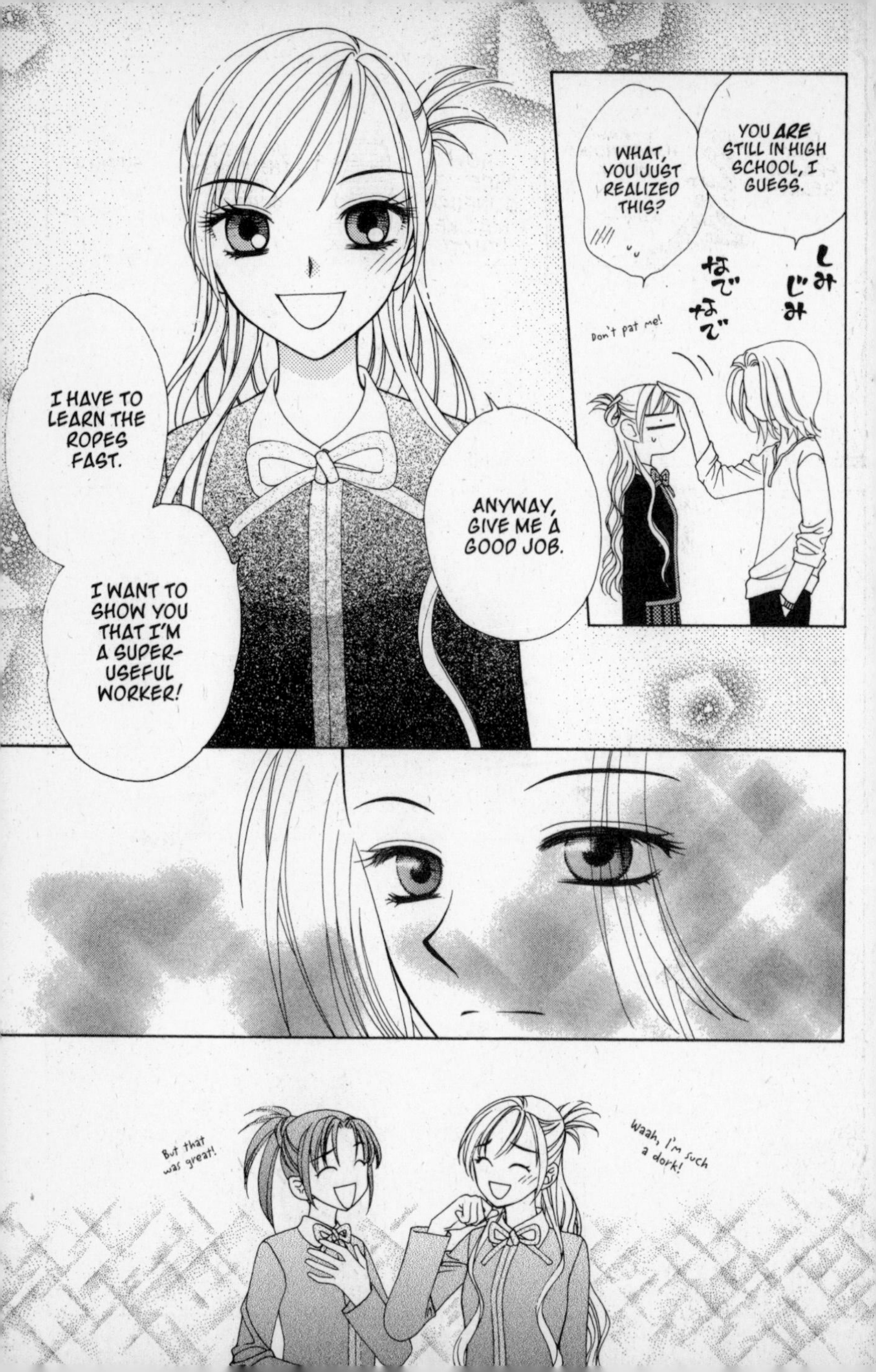
YOU ARE STILL IN HIGH SCHOOL, I GUESS.
WHAT, YOU JUST REALIZED THIS?
しみじみ
なでなで
Don't pat me!
ANYWAY, GIVE ME A GOOD JOB.
I HAVE TO LEARN THE ROPES FAST.
I WANT TO SHOW YOU THAT I'M A SUPER-USEFUL WORKER!
Waah, I'm such a dork!
But that was great!

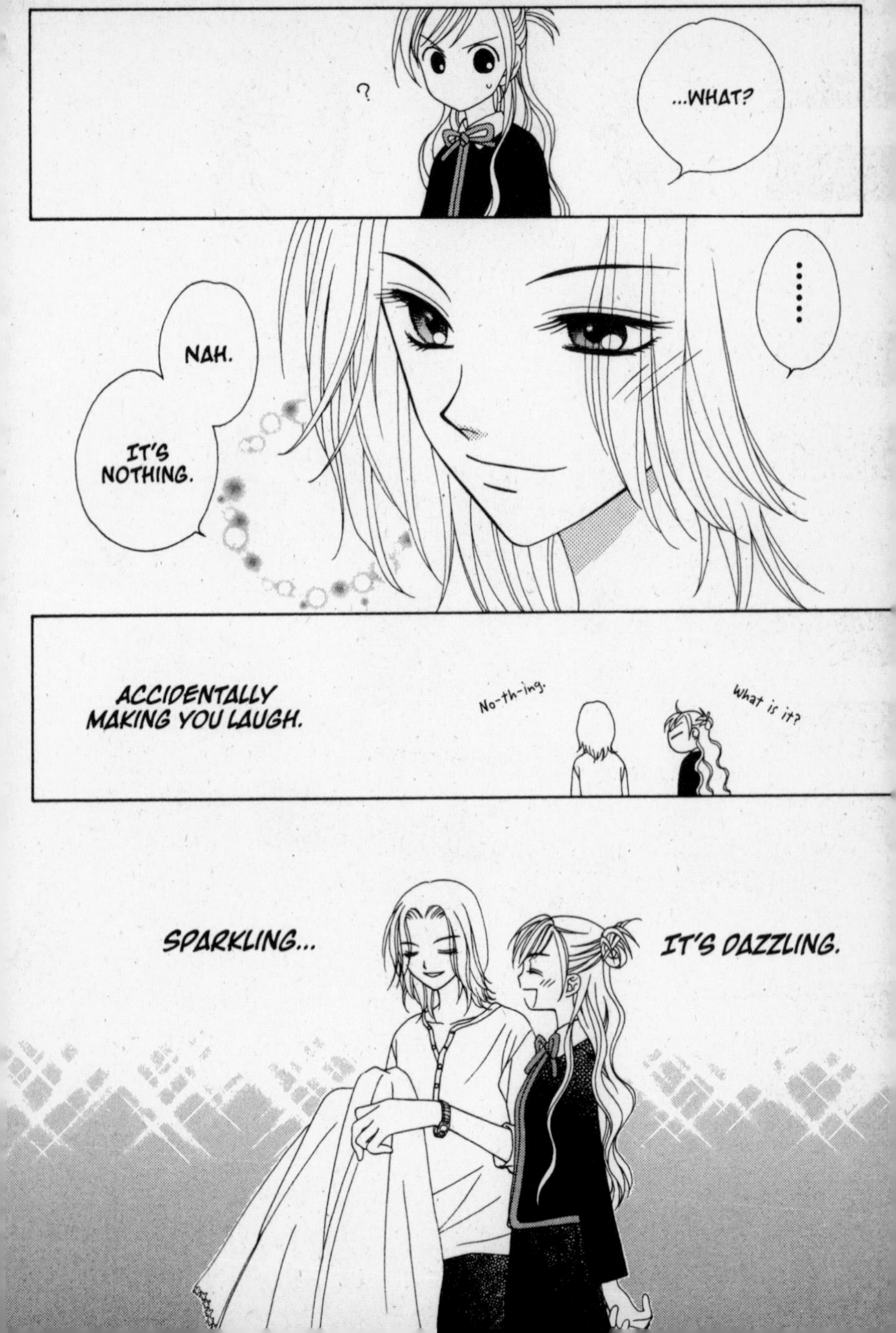
...WHAT?
?
......
NAH.
IT'S NOTHING.
What is it?
No-th-ing.
ACCIDENTALLY MAKING YOU LAUGH.
IT'S DAZZLING.
SPARKLING...

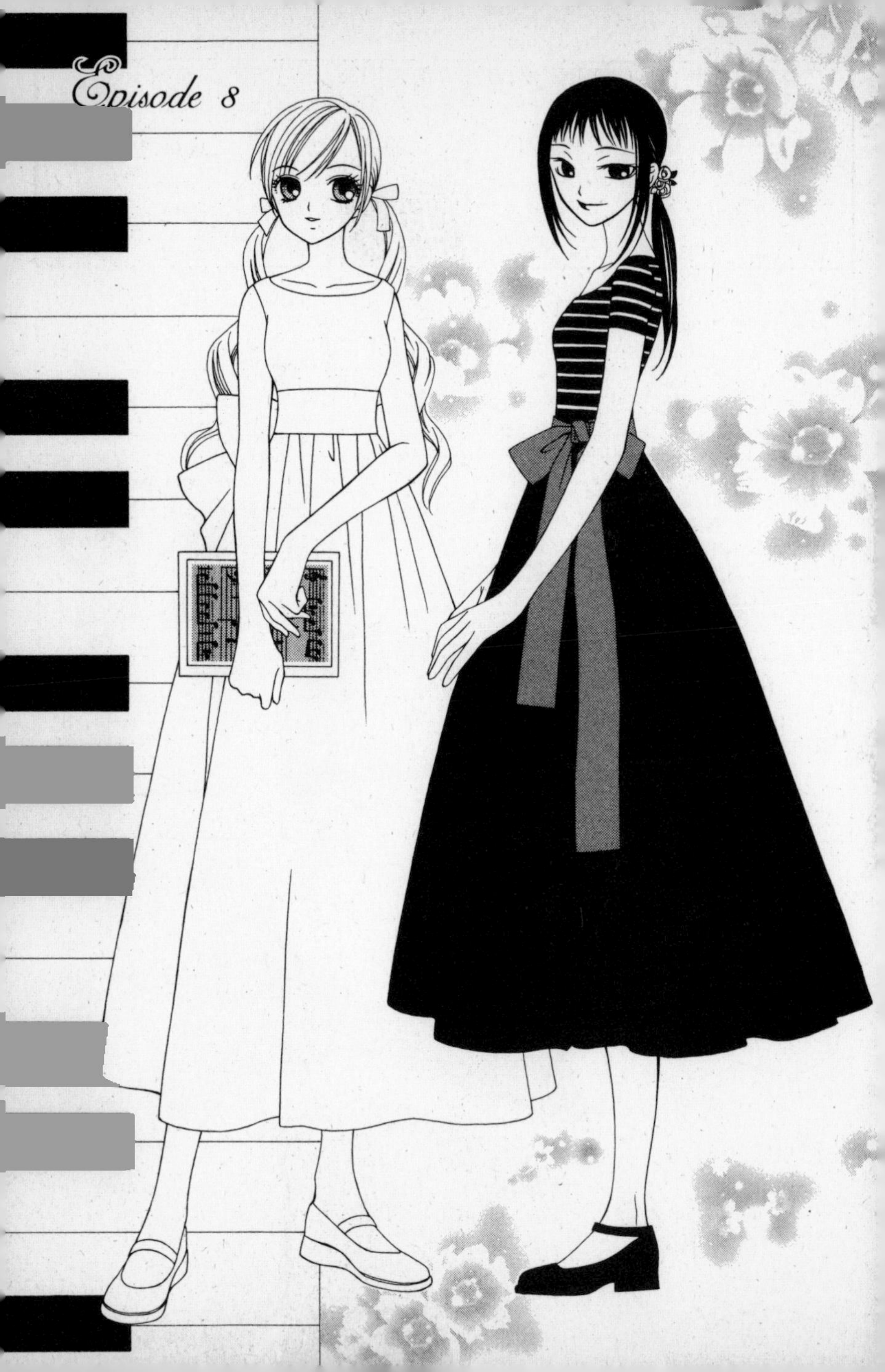
Episode 8

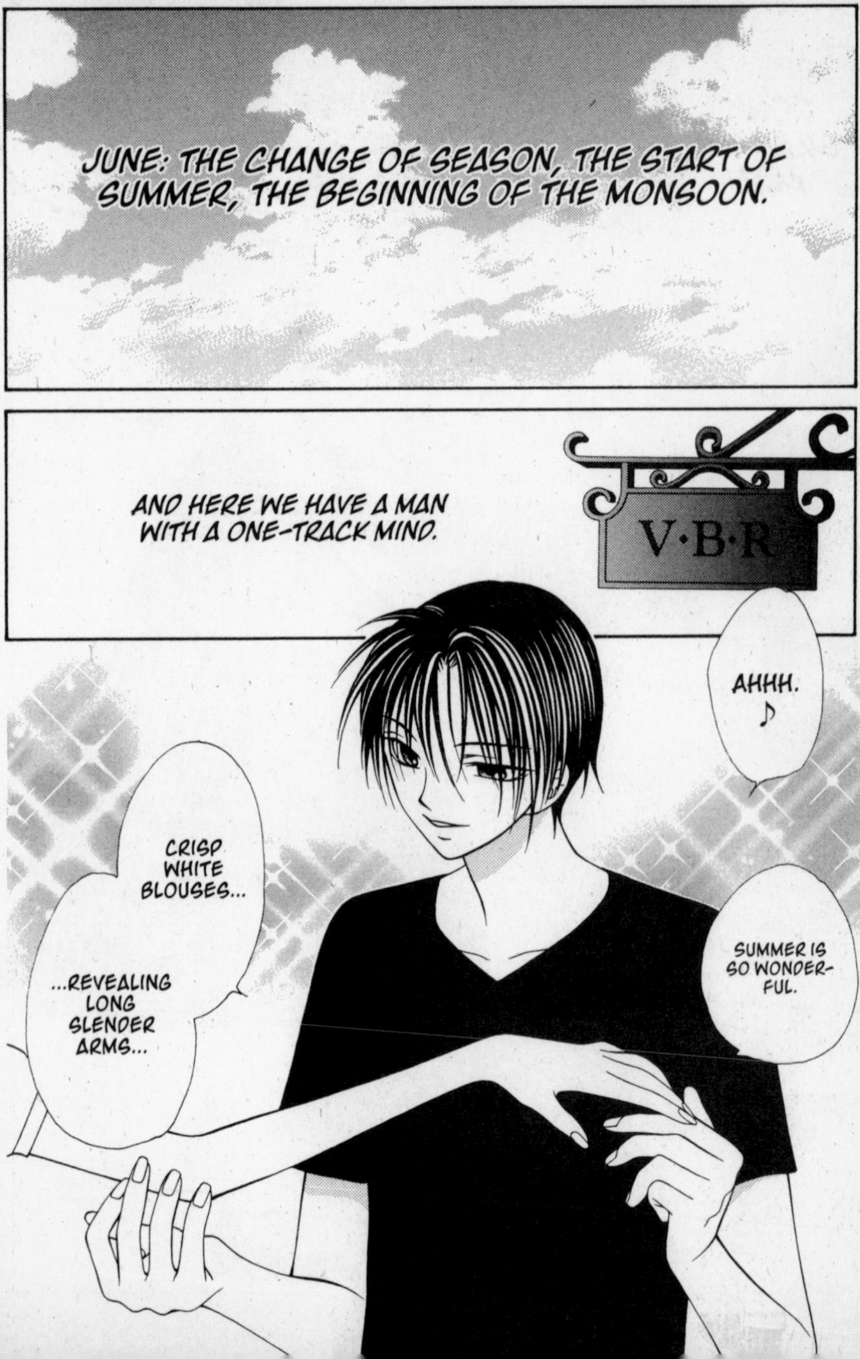
JUNE: THE CHANGE OF SEASON, THE START OF SUMMER, THE BEGINNING OF THE MONSOON.
V·B·R
AND HERE WE HAVE A MAN WITH A ONE-TRACK MIND.
AHHH. ♪
SUMMER IS SO WONDERFUL.
CRISP WHITE BLOUSES...
...REVEALING LONG SLENDER ARMS...

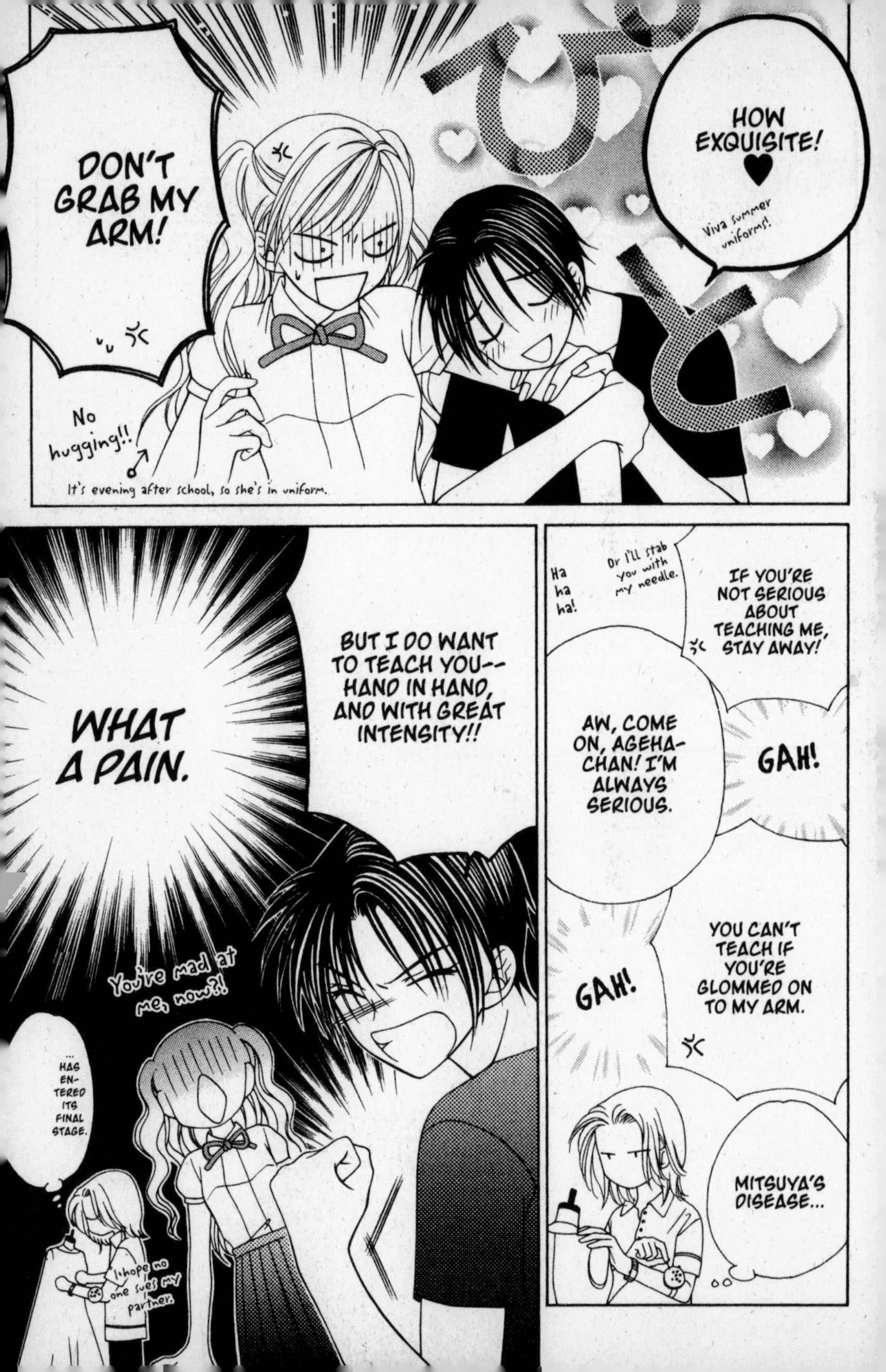
HOW EXQUISITE! ♥
Viva summer uniforms!
DON'T GRAB MY ARM!
No hugging!!
It's evening after school, so she's in uniform.
IF YOU'RE NOT SERIOUS ABOUT TEACHING ME, STAY AWAY!
Or I'll stab you with my needle.
Ha ha ha!
GAH!
AW, COME ON, AGEHA-CHAN! I'M ALWAYS SERIOUS.
YOU CAN'T TEACH IF YOU'RE GLOMMED ON TO MY ARM.
GAH!
MITSUYA'S DISEASE...
BUT I DO WANT TO TEACH YOU--HAND IN HAND, AND WITH GREAT INTENSITY!!
WHAT A PAIN.
You're mad at me, now?!
... HAS ENTERED ITS FINAL STAGE.
I hope no one sues my partner.

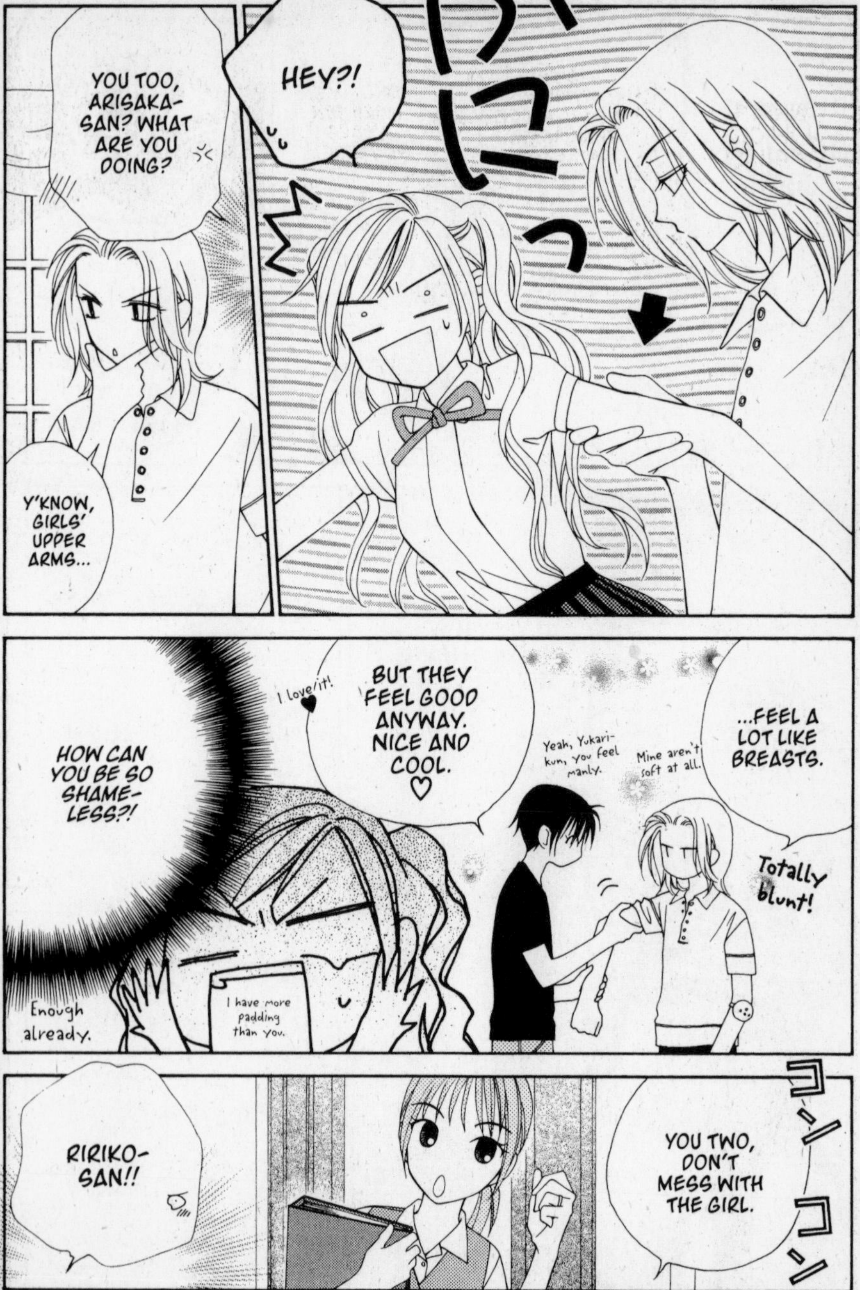
ふにっ
HEY?!
YOU TOO, ARISAKA-SAN? WHAT ARE YOU DOING?
Y'KNOW, GIRLS' UPPER ARMS...
...FEEL A LOT LIKE BREASTS.
Totally blunt!
Mine aren't soft at all.
Yeah, Yukari-kun, you feel manly.
BUT THEY FEEL GOOD ANYWAY. NICE AND COOL. ♡
I love it!
HOW CAN YOU BE SO SHAME-LESS?!
I have more padding than you.
Enough already.
コンコン
YOU TWO, DON'T MESS WITH THE GIRL.
RIRIKO-SAN!!

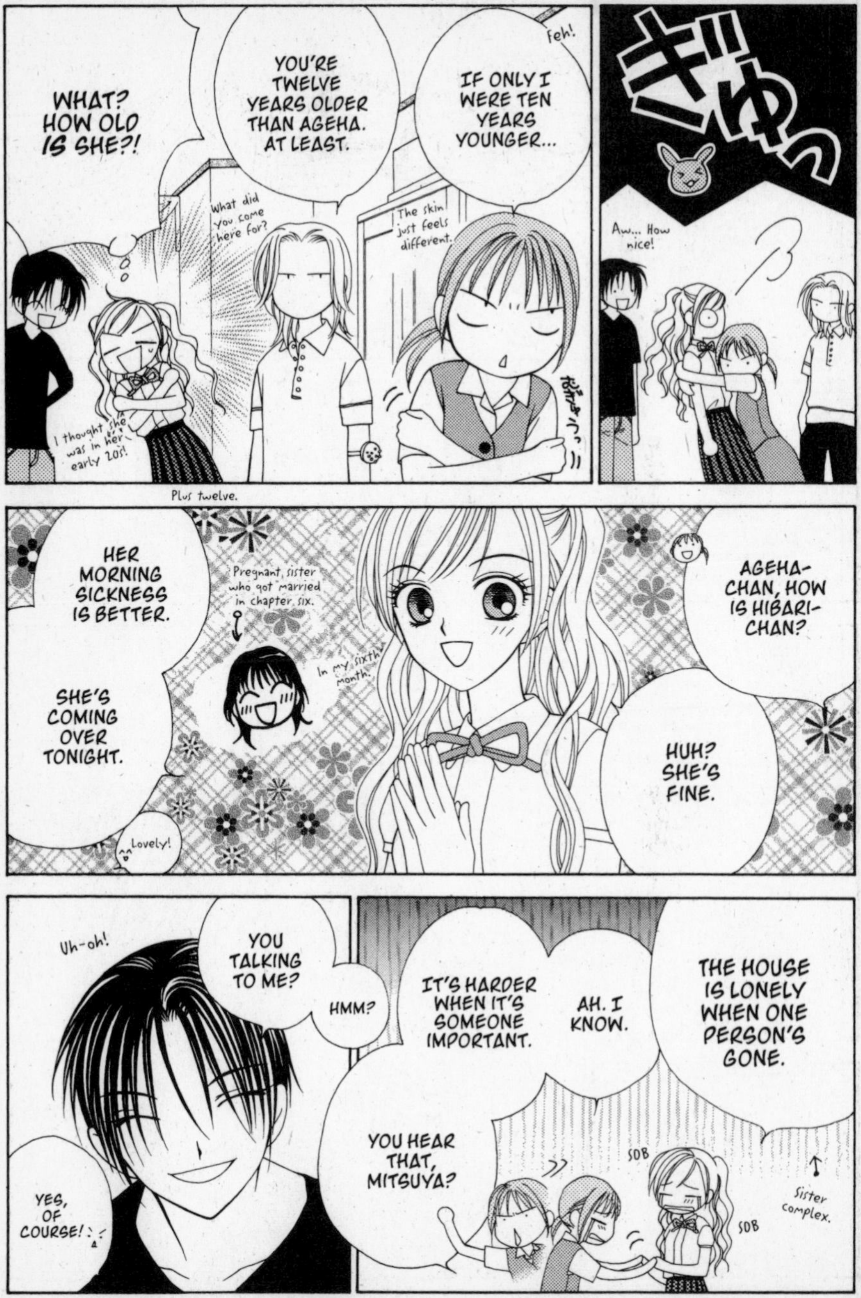
ぎゅっ
Aw... How nice!
Feh!
IF ONLY I WERE TEN YEARS YOUNGER...
The skin just feels different.
YOU'RE TWELVE YEARS OLDER THAN AGEHA. AT LEAST.
What did you come here for?
WHAT? HOW OLD IS SHE?!
I thought she was in her early 20s!
Plus twelve.
AGEHA-CHAN, HOW IS HIBARI-CHAN?
HUH? SHE'S FINE.
Pregnant, sister who got married in chapter six.
In my sixth month.
HER MORNING SICKNESS IS BETTER.
SHE'S COMING OVER TONIGHT.
Lovely!
THE HOUSE IS LONELY WHEN ONE PERSON'S GONE.
AH. I KNOW.
IT'S HARDER WHEN IT'S SOMEONE IMPORTANT.
Sister complex.
SOB
SOB
YOU HEAR THAT, MITSUYA?
HMM?
YOU TALKING TO ME?
Uh-oh!
YES, OF COURSE!

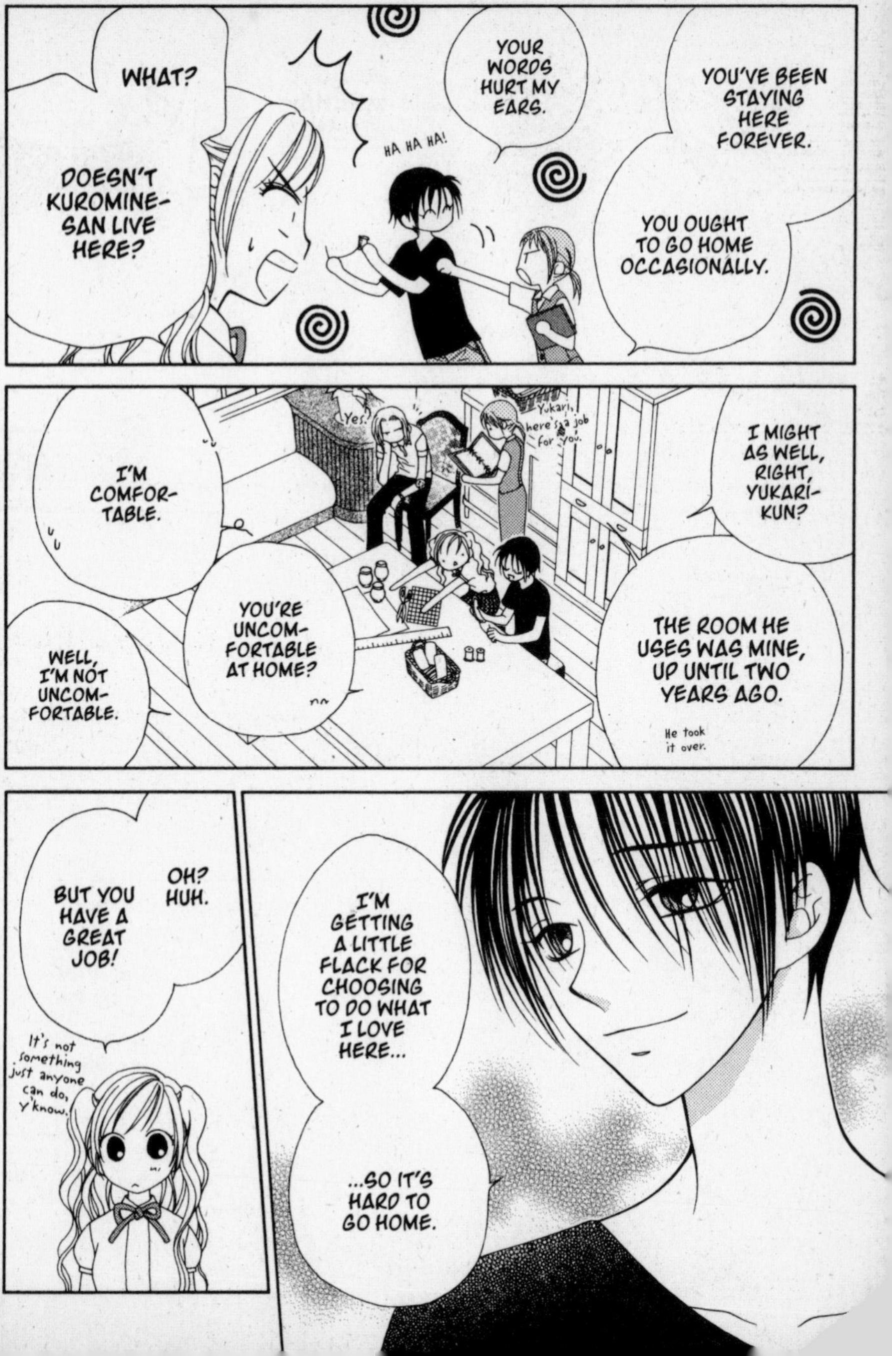
YOU'VE BEEN STAYING HERE FOREVER.
YOU OUGHT TO GO HOME OCCASIONALLY.
YOUR WORDS HURT MY EARS.
HA HA HA!
WHAT?
DOESN'T KUROMINE-SAN LIVE HERE?
I MIGHT AS WELL, RIGHT, YUKARI-KUN?
Yukari, here's a job for you.
Yes.
THE ROOM HE USES WAS MINE, UP UNTIL TWO YEARS AGO.
He took it over.
I'M COMFORTABLE.
YOU'RE UNCOMFORTABLE AT HOME?
WELL, I'M NOT UNCOMFORTABLE.
I'M GETTING A LITTLE FLACK FOR CHOOSING TO DO WHAT I LOVE HERE...
...SO IT'S HARD TO GO HOME.
OH? HUH.
BUT YOU HAVE A GREAT JOB!
It's not something just anyone can do, y'know.

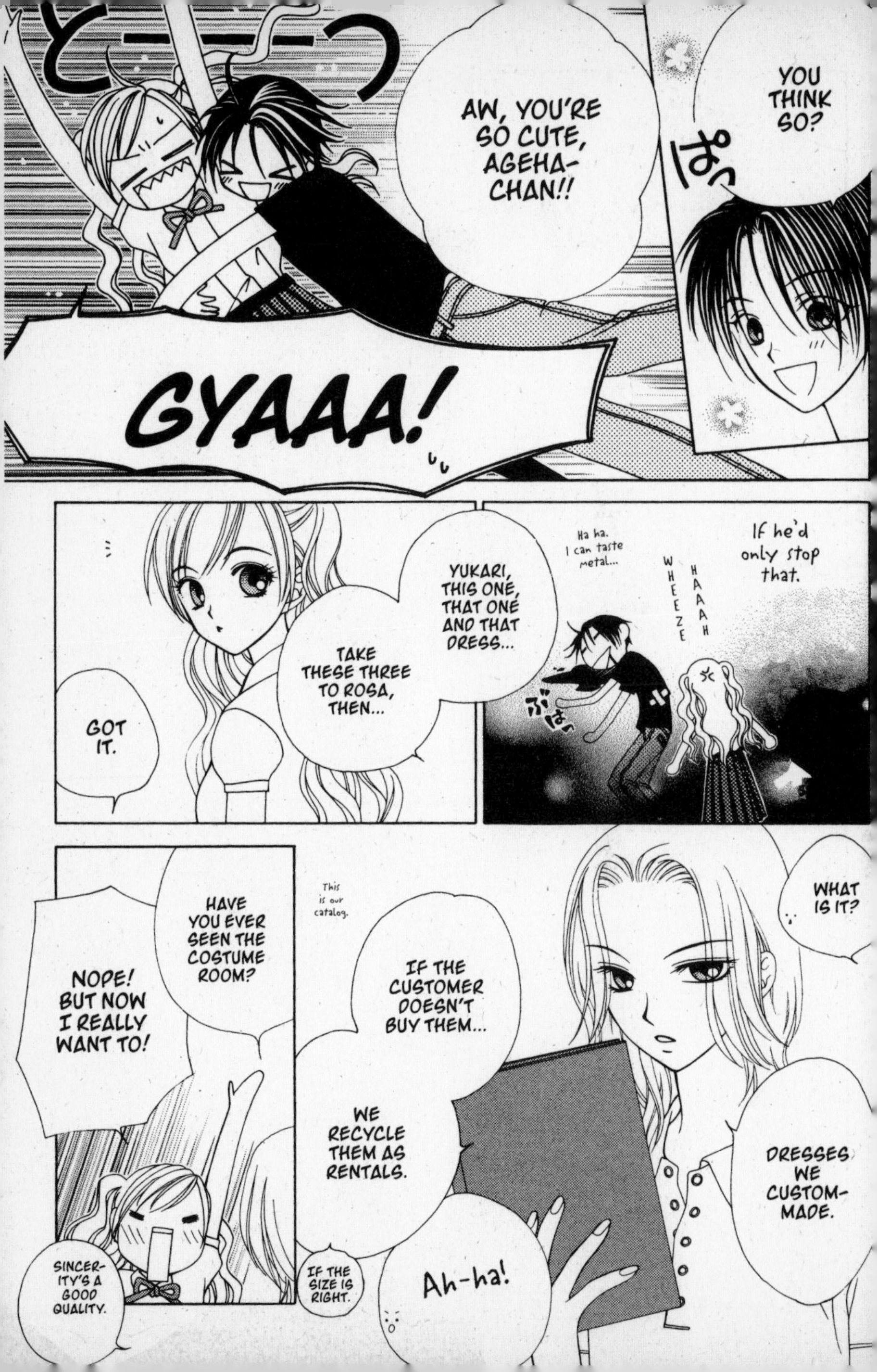
YOU THINK SO?
ぱっ
どーーっ
AW, YOU'RE SO CUTE, AGEHA-CHAN!!
GYAAA!
If he'd only stop that.
Ha ha. I can taste metal...
WHEEZE
HAAAH
ぶはっ
YUKARI, THIS ONE, THAT ONE AND THAT DRESS...
TAKE THESE THREE TO ROSA, THEN...
GOT IT.
WHAT IS IT?
This is our catalog.
DRESSES WE CUSTOM-MADE.
IF THE CUSTOMER DOESN'T BUY THEM...
WE RECYCLE THEM AS RENTALS.
Ah-ha!
IF THE SIZE IS RIGHT.
HAVE YOU EVER SEEN THE COSTUME ROOM?
NOPE! BUT NOW I REALLY WANT TO!
SINCERITY'S A GOOD QUALITY.

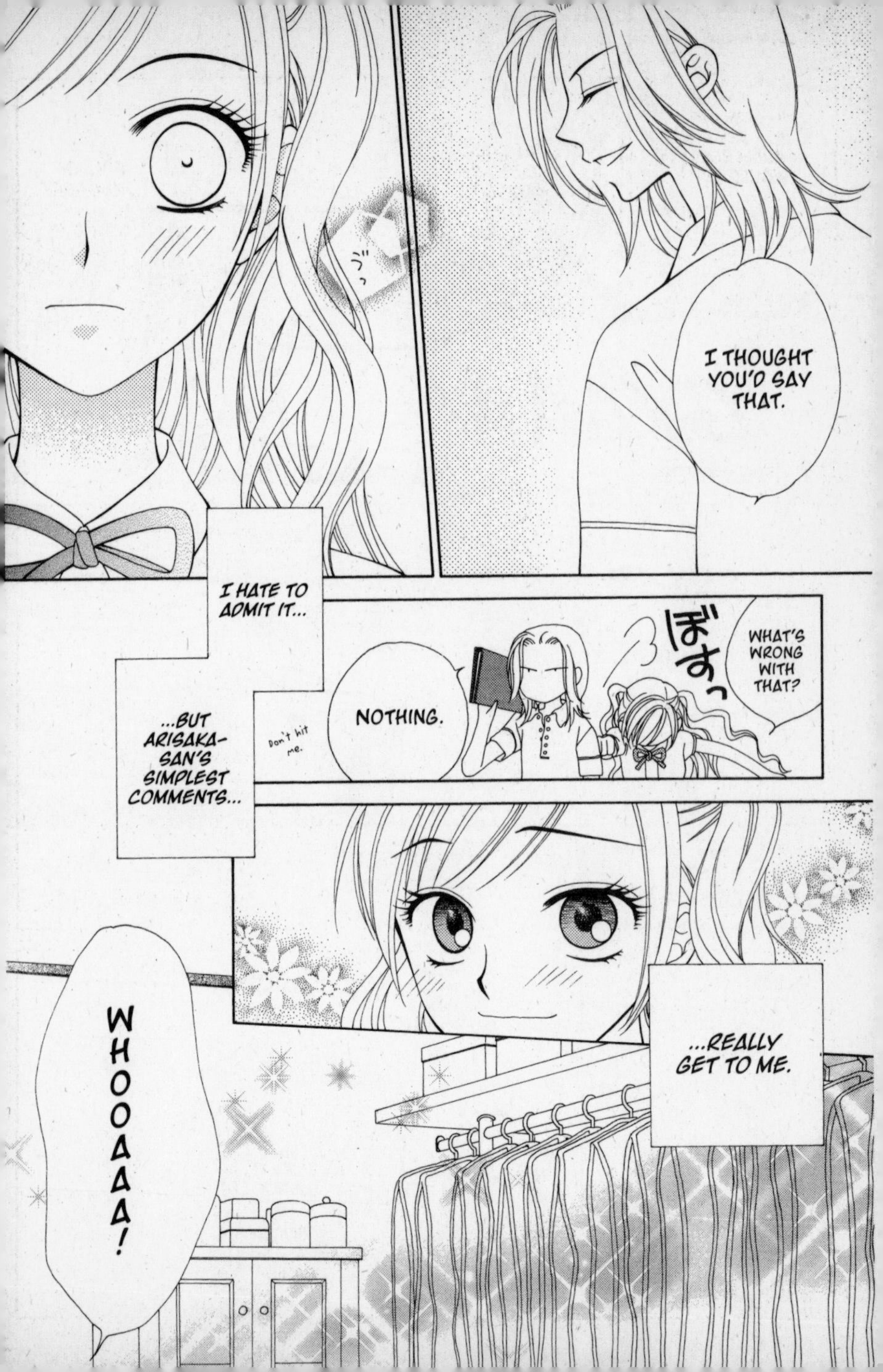
I THOUGHT YOU'D SAY THAT.
I HATE TO ADMIT IT...
WHAT'S WRONG WITH THAT?
ぼすっ
NOTHING.
Don't hit me.
...BUT ARISAKA-SAN'S SIMPLEST COMMENTS...
...REALLY GET TO ME.
WHOOAAAA!

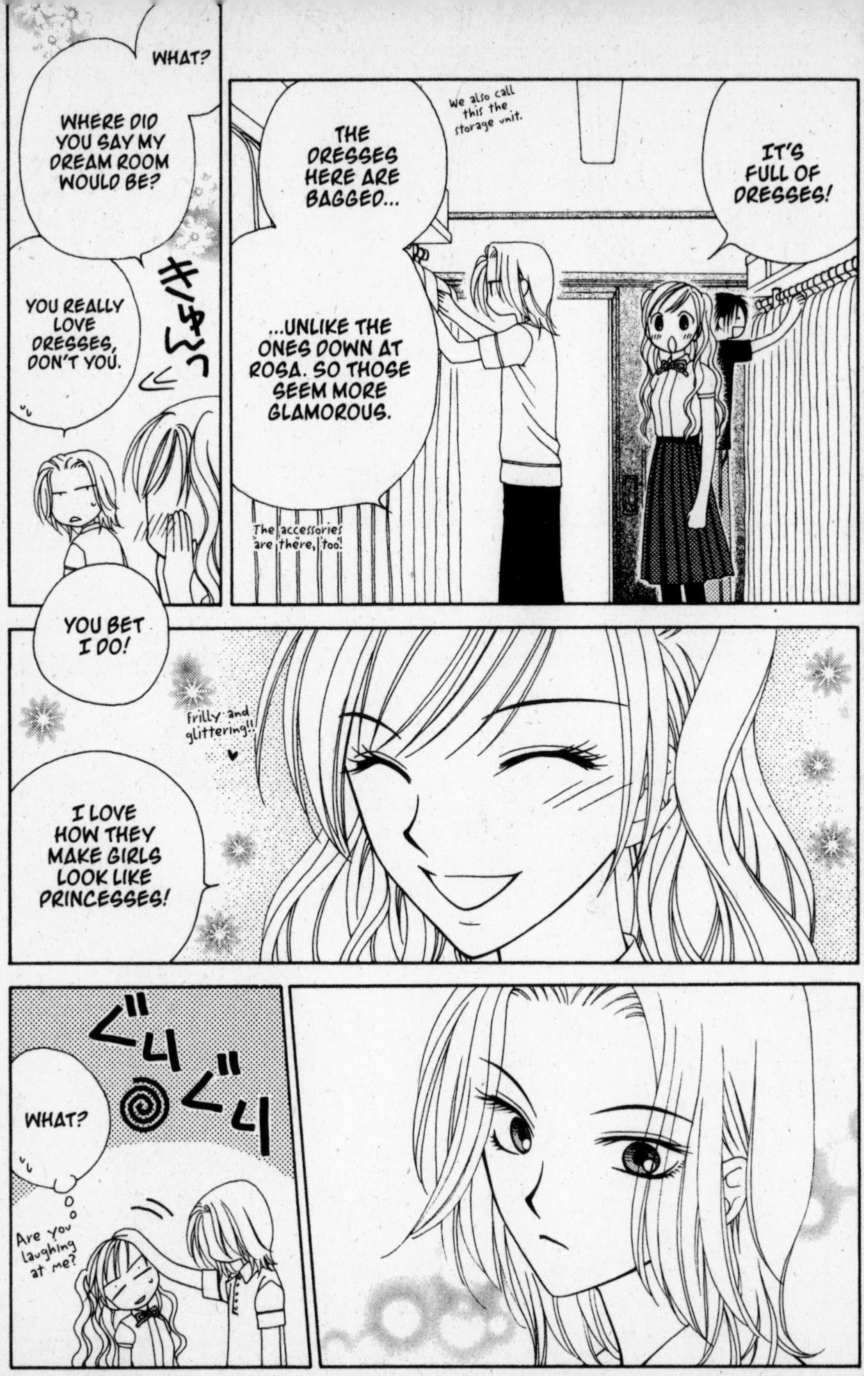
IT'S FULL OF DRESSES!
We also call this the storage unit.
THE DRESSES HERE ARE BAGGED...
...UNLIKE THE ONES DOWN AT ROSA. SO THOSE SEEM MORE GLAMOROUS.
The accessories are there, too!
WHAT?
WHERE DID YOU SAY MY DREAM ROOM WOULD BE?
きゅんっ
YOU REALLY LOVE DRESSES, DON'T YOU.
YOU BET I DO!
Frilly and glittering!!
I LOVE HOW THEY MAKE GIRLS LOOK LIKE PRINCESSES!
ぐりぐり
WHAT?
Are you laughing at me?

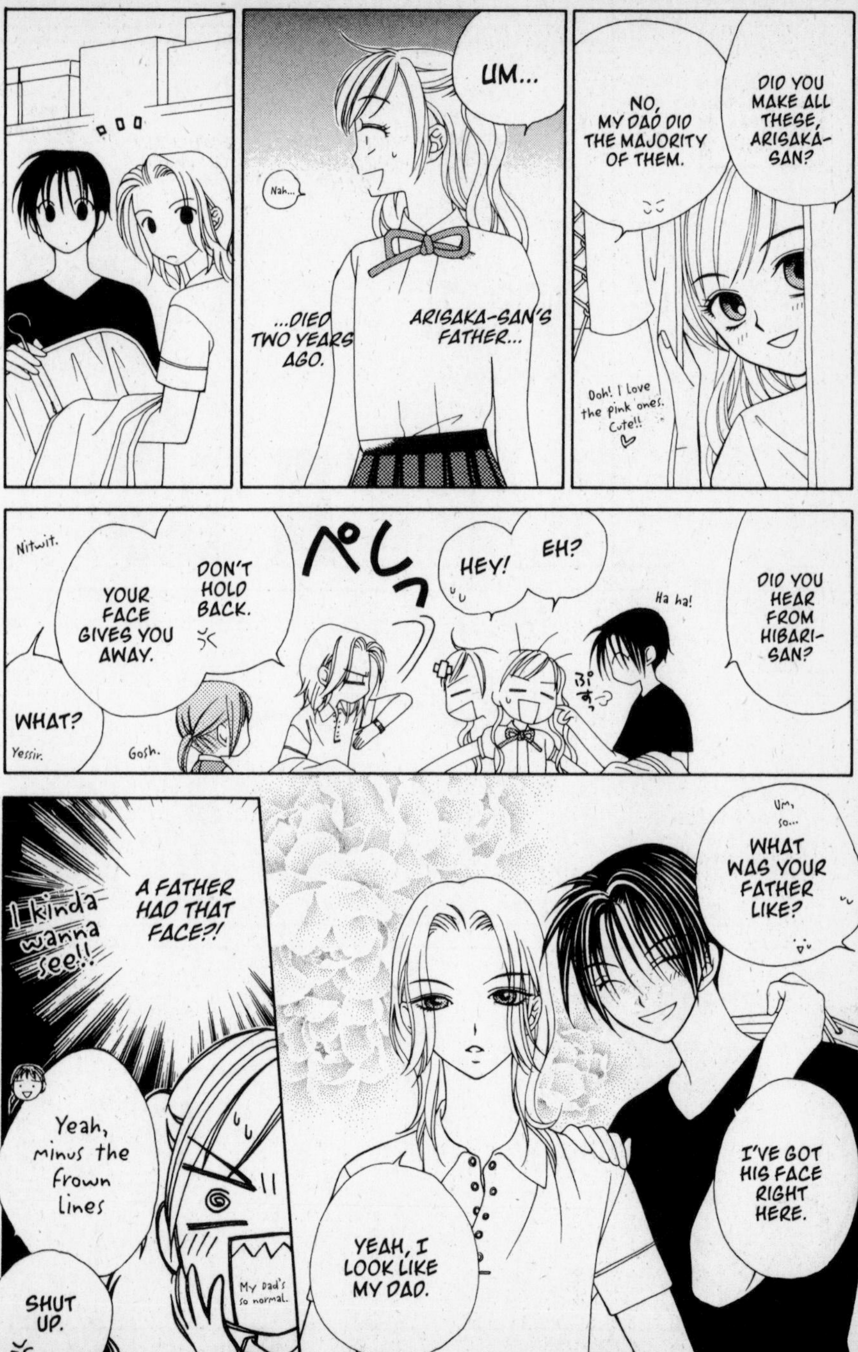
DID YOU MAKE ALL THESE, ARISAKA-SAN?
Ooh! I love the pink ones. Cute!!
NO, MY DAD DID THE MAJORITY OF THEM.
UM...
Nah...
ARISAKA-SAN'S FATHER...
...DIED TWO YEARS AGO.
DID YOU HEAR FROM HIBARI-SAN?
Ha ha!
ぷすっ
EH?
HEY!
ぺしっ
DON'T HOLD BACK.
YOUR FACE GIVES YOU AWAY.
Nitwit.
WHAT?
Gosh.
Yessir.
Um, so...
WHAT WAS YOUR FATHER LIKE?
I'VE GOT HIS FACE RIGHT HERE.
YEAH, I LOOK LIKE MY DAD.
A FATHER HAD THAT FACE?!
I kinda wanna see!!
My Dad's so normal.
Yeah, minus the frown lines
SHUT UP.

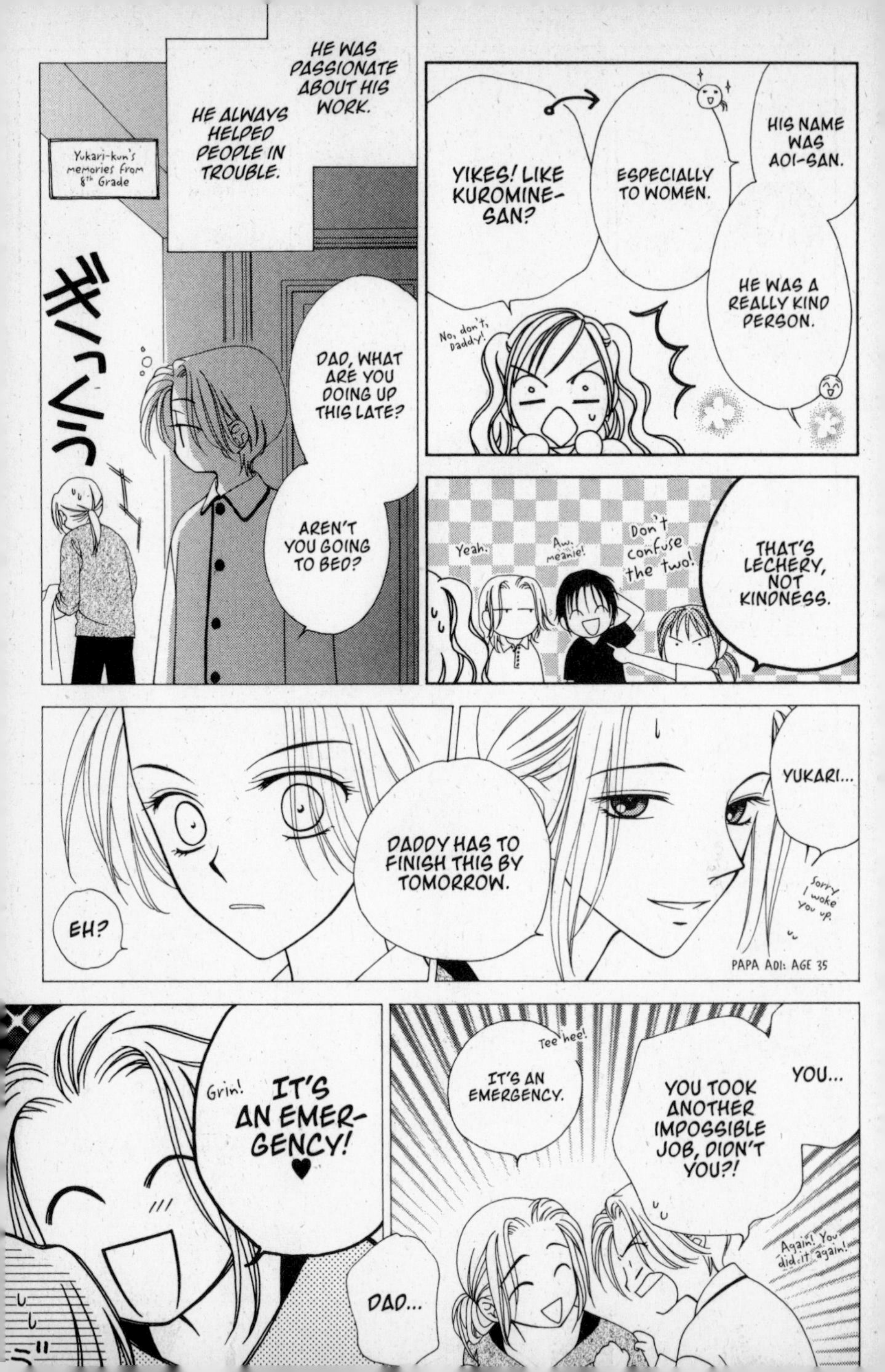
HIS NAME WAS AOI-SAN.
HE WAS A REALLY KIND PERSON.
ESPECIALLY TO WOMEN.
YIKES! LIKE KUROMINE-SAN?
No, don't, Daddy!
THAT'S LECHERY, NOT KINDNESS.
Don't confuse the two!
Aw, meanie!
Yeah.
HE WAS PASSIONATE ABOUT HIS WORK.
HE ALWAYS HELPED PEOPLE IN TROUBLE.
Yukari-kun's memories from 8th Grade
DAD, WHAT ARE YOU DOING UP THIS LATE?
AREN'T YOU GOING TO BED?
YUKARI...
Sorry I woke you up.
PAPA AOI: AGE 35
DADDY HAS TO FINISH THIS BY TOMORROW.
EH?
YOU...
YOU TOOK ANOTHER IMPOSSIBLE JOB, DIDN'T YOU?!
Again! You did it again!
IT'S AN EMERGENCY.
Tee hee!
DAD...
IT'S AN EMERGENCY! ♥
Grin!

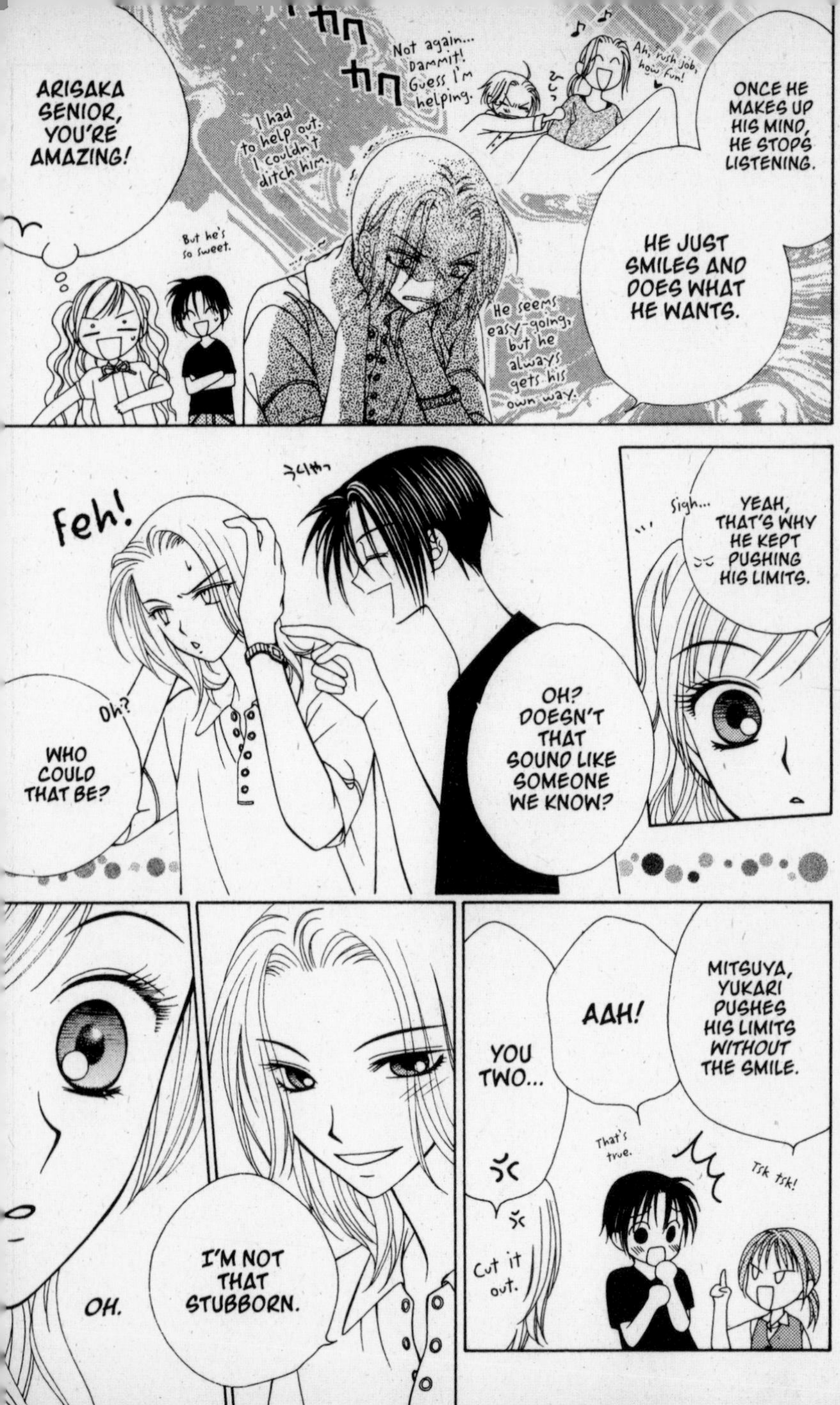

ONCE HE MAKES UP HIS MIND, HE STOPS LISTENING.
Ah, rush job, how fun!
Not again... Dammit! Guess I'm helping.
HE JUST SMILES AND DOES WHAT HE WANTS.
He seems easy-going, but he always gets his own way.
I had to help out. I couldn't ditch him.
ARISAKA SENIOR, YOU'RE AMAZING!
But he's so sweet.
Sigh...
YEAH, THAT'S WHY HE KEPT PUSHING HIS LIMITS.
OH? DOESN'T THAT SOUND LIKE SOMEONE WE KNOW?
Feh!
Oh?
WHO COULD THAT BE?
MITSUYA, YUKARI PUSHES HIS LIMITS WITHOUT THE SMILE.
AAH!
YOU TWO...
Tsk tsk!
That's true.
Cut it out.
I'M NOT THAT STUBBORN.
OH.

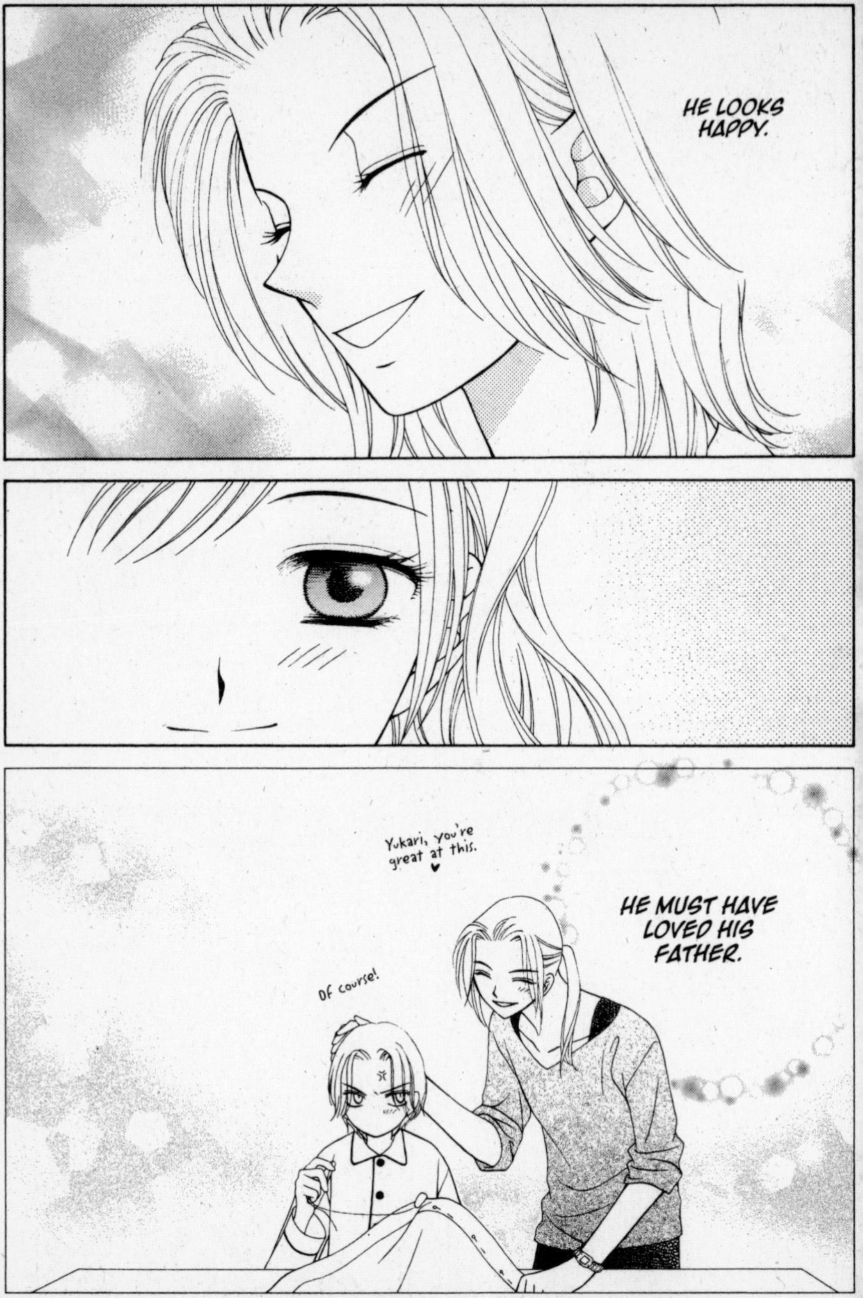
HE LOOKS HAPPY.
HE MUST HAVE LOVED HIS FATHER.
Yukari, you're great at this.
Of course!

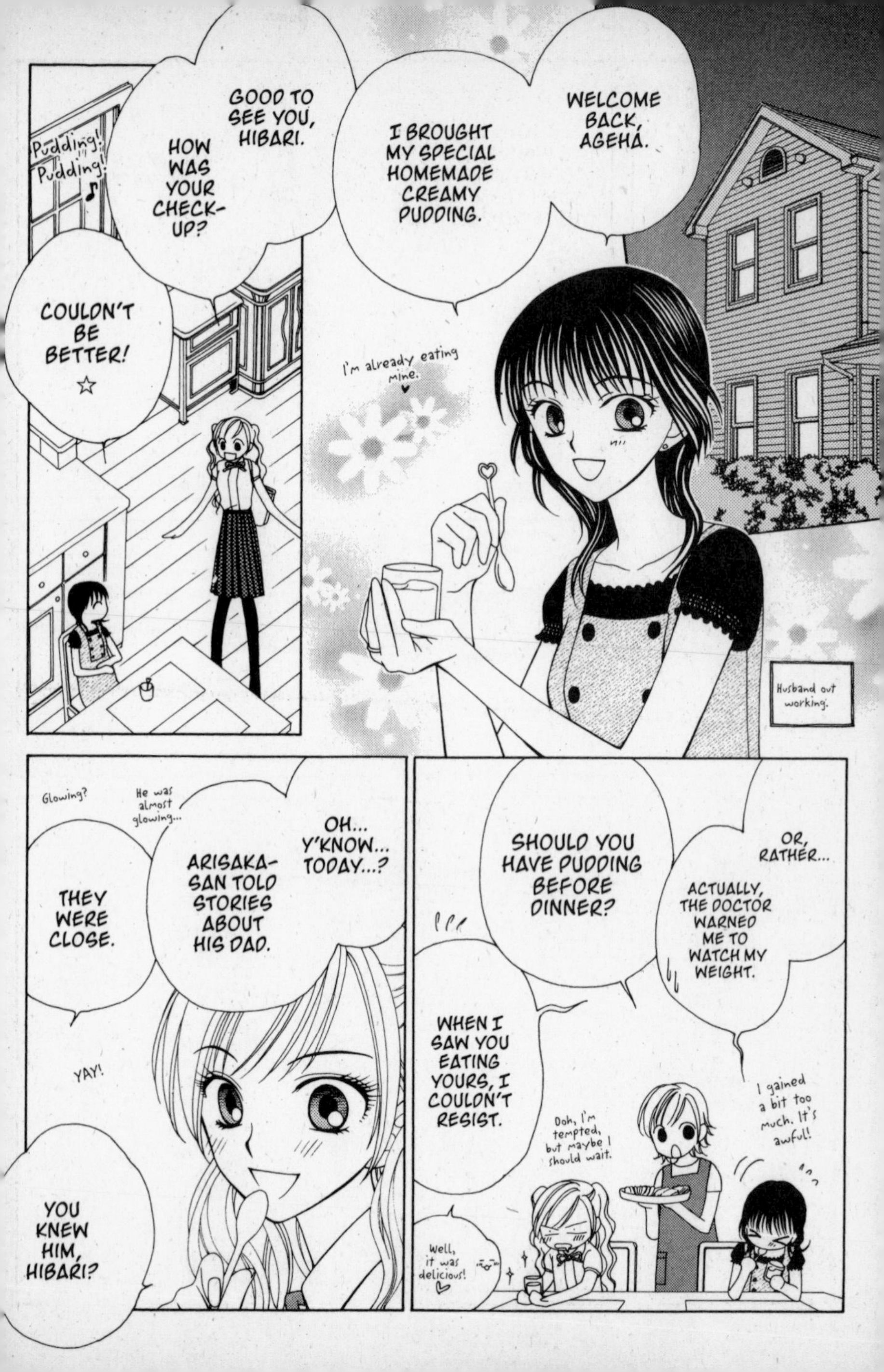
WELCOME BACK, AGEHA.
I BROUGHT MY SPECIAL HOMEMADE CREAMY PUDDING.
I'm already eating mine.
Husband out working.
GOOD TO SEE YOU, HIBARI.
HOW WAS YOUR CHECK-UP?
Pudding! Pudding!
COULDN'T BE BETTER! ☆
OR, RATHER...
ACTUALLY, THE DOCTOR WARNED ME TO WATCH MY WEIGHT.
SHOULD YOU HAVE PUDDING BEFORE DINNER?
I gained a bit too much. It's awful!
Ooh, I'm tempted, but maybe I should wait.
WHEN I SAW YOU EATING YOURS, I COULDN'T RESIST.
Well, it was delicious!
OH... Y'KNOW... TODAY...?
ARISAKA-SAN TOLD STORIES ABOUT HIS DAD.
He was almost glowing...
Glowing?
THEY WERE CLOSE.
YAY!
YOU KNEW HIM, HIBARI?

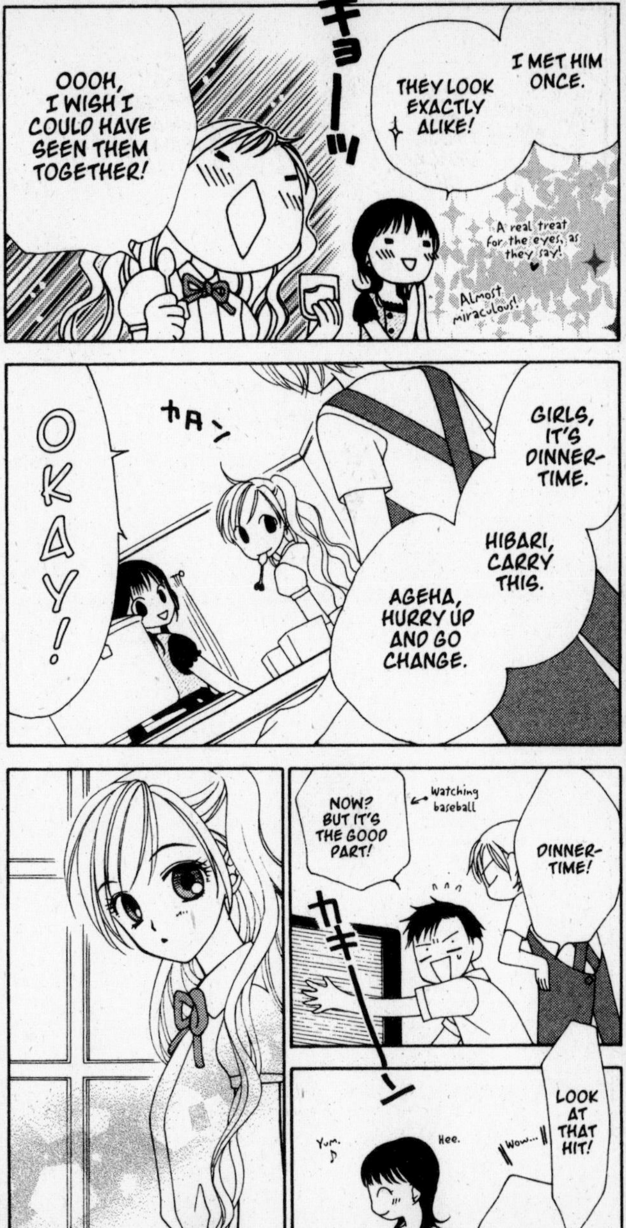
ケキョーッ
I MET HIM ONCE.
THEY LOOK EXACTLY ALIKE!
A real treat for the eyes, as they say!
Almost miraculous!
OOOH, I WISH I COULD HAVE SEEN THEM TOGETHER!
GIRLS, IT'S DINNER-TIME.
HIBARI, CARRY THIS.
AGEHA, HURRY UP AND GO CHANGE.
カタン
OKAY!
DINNER-TIME!
NOW? BUT IT'S THE GOOD PART!
Watching baseball
カキーン
LOOK AT THAT HIT!
IT'S A HOME RUN.
Wow...
Hee.
Yum.

I love shoes. ♥ I have all the sandals Ageha wears. The ones in chapter 13 are especially comfortable. I love them.

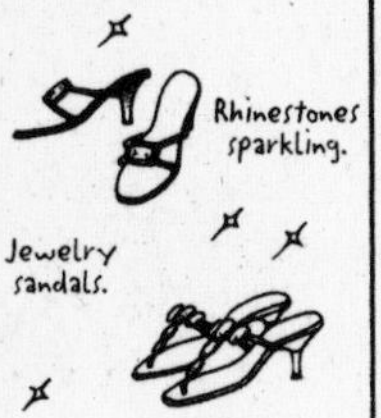
Rhinestones sparkling.
Jewelry sandals.

I bought boots in August this year. I can hear the voices now, saying there's no point buying boots when I never leave the house. ♪ But I like to have them just in case. If I ever need them, I'll be prepared.

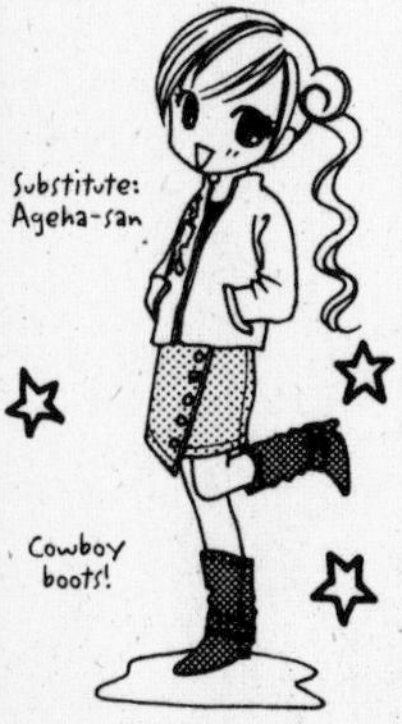
Substitute: Ageha-san
Cowboy boots!

Gosh, Ageha's hair is long.

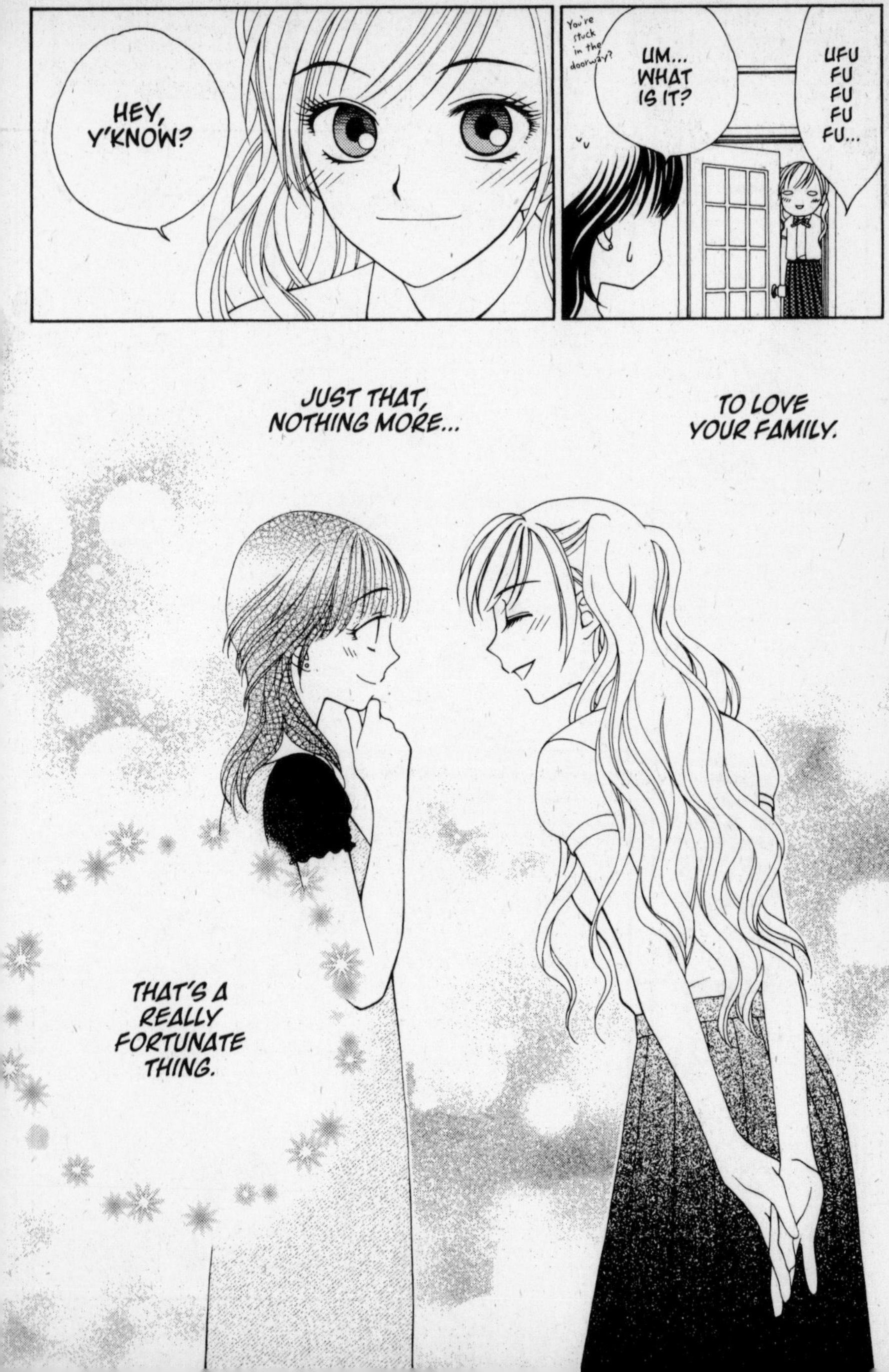
UFU FU FU FU FU...
UM... WHAT IS IT?
You're stuck in the doorway?
HEY, Y'KNOW?
TO LOVE YOUR FAMILY.
JUST THAT, NOTHING MORE...
THAT'S A REALLY FORTUNATE THING.

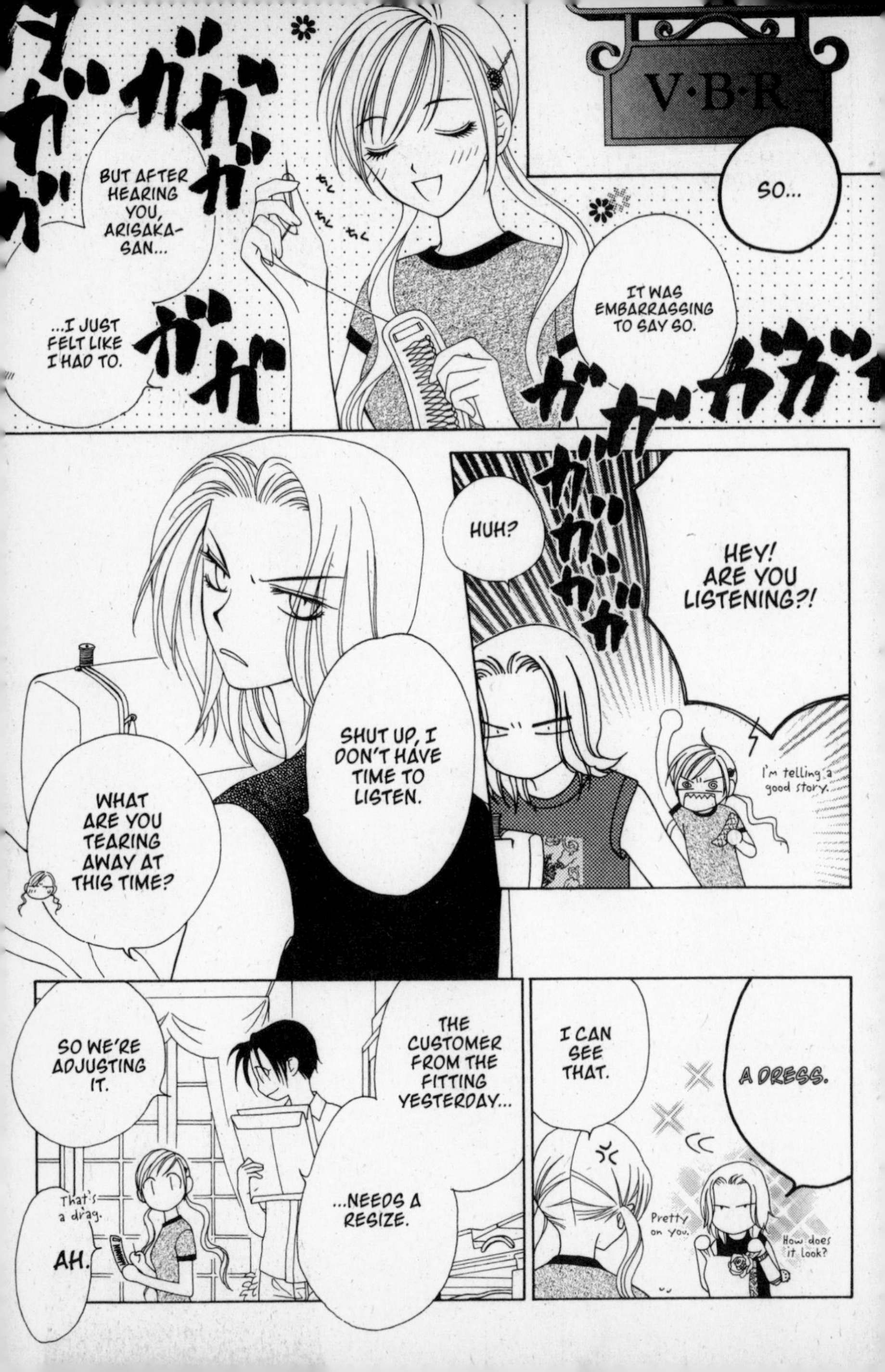
V·B·R
SO...
IT WAS EMBARRASSING TO SAY SO.
BUT AFTER HEARING YOU, ARISAKA-SAN...
...I JUST FELT LIKE I HAD TO.
HUH?
HEY! ARE YOU LISTENING?!
I'm telling a good story.
SHUT UP, I DON'T HAVE TIME TO LISTEN.
WHAT ARE YOU TEARING AWAY AT THIS TIME?
A DRESS.
I CAN SEE THAT.
How does it look?
Pretty on you.
THE CUSTOMER FROM THE FITTING YESTERDAY...
...NEEDS A RESIZE.
SO WE'RE ADJUSTING IT.
That's a drag.
AH.

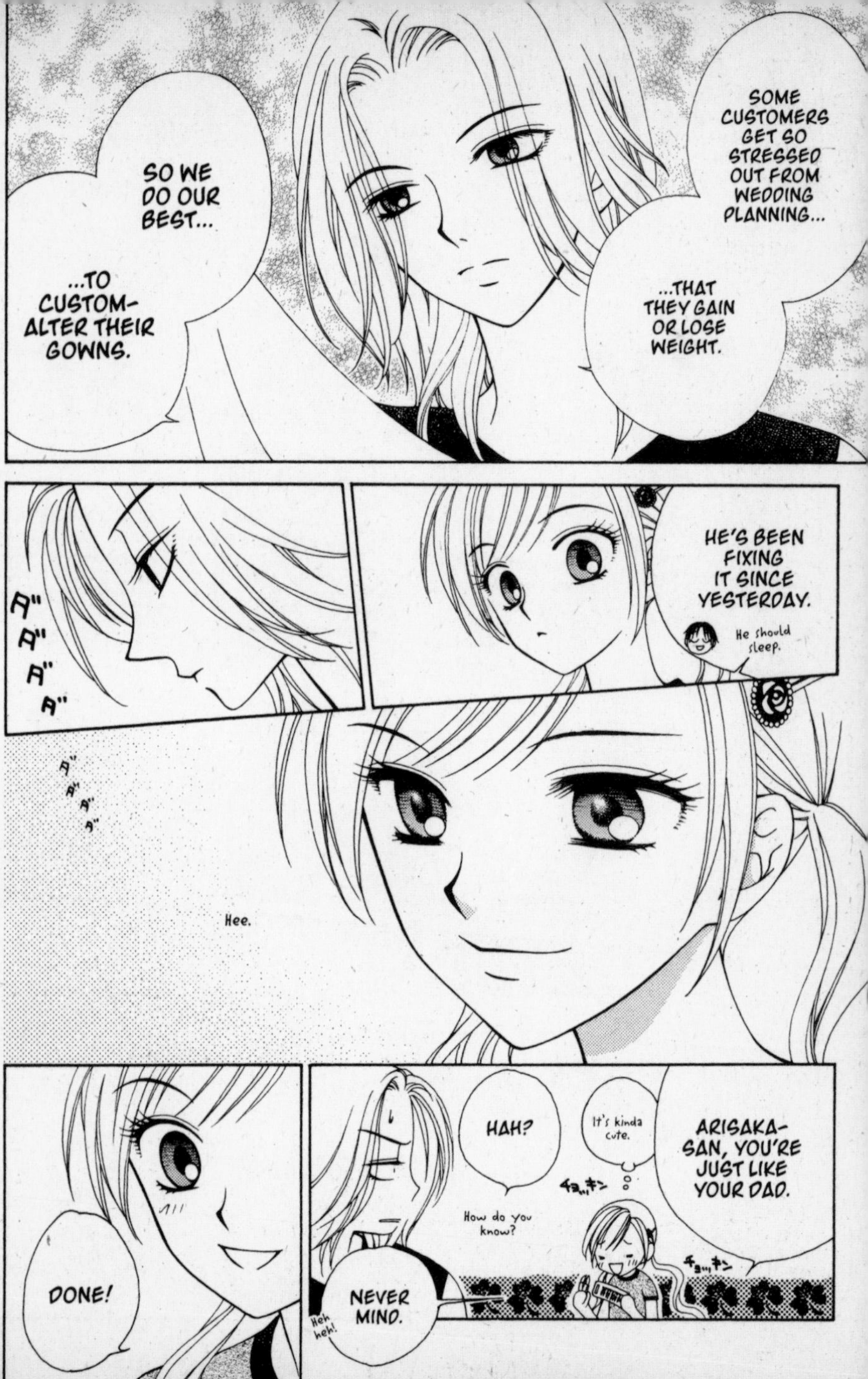
SOME CUSTOMERS GET SO STRESSED OUT FROM WEDDING PLANNING...
...THAT THEY GAIN OR LOSE WEIGHT.
SO WE DO OUR BEST...
...TO CUSTOM-ALTER THEIR GOWNS.
HE'S BEEN FIXING IT SINCE YESTERDAY.
He should sleep.
Hee.
ARISAKA-SAN, YOU'RE JUST LIKE YOUR DAD.
チョッキン
It's kinda cute.
チョッキン
HAH?
How do you know?
NEVER MIND.
Heh heh!
DONE!

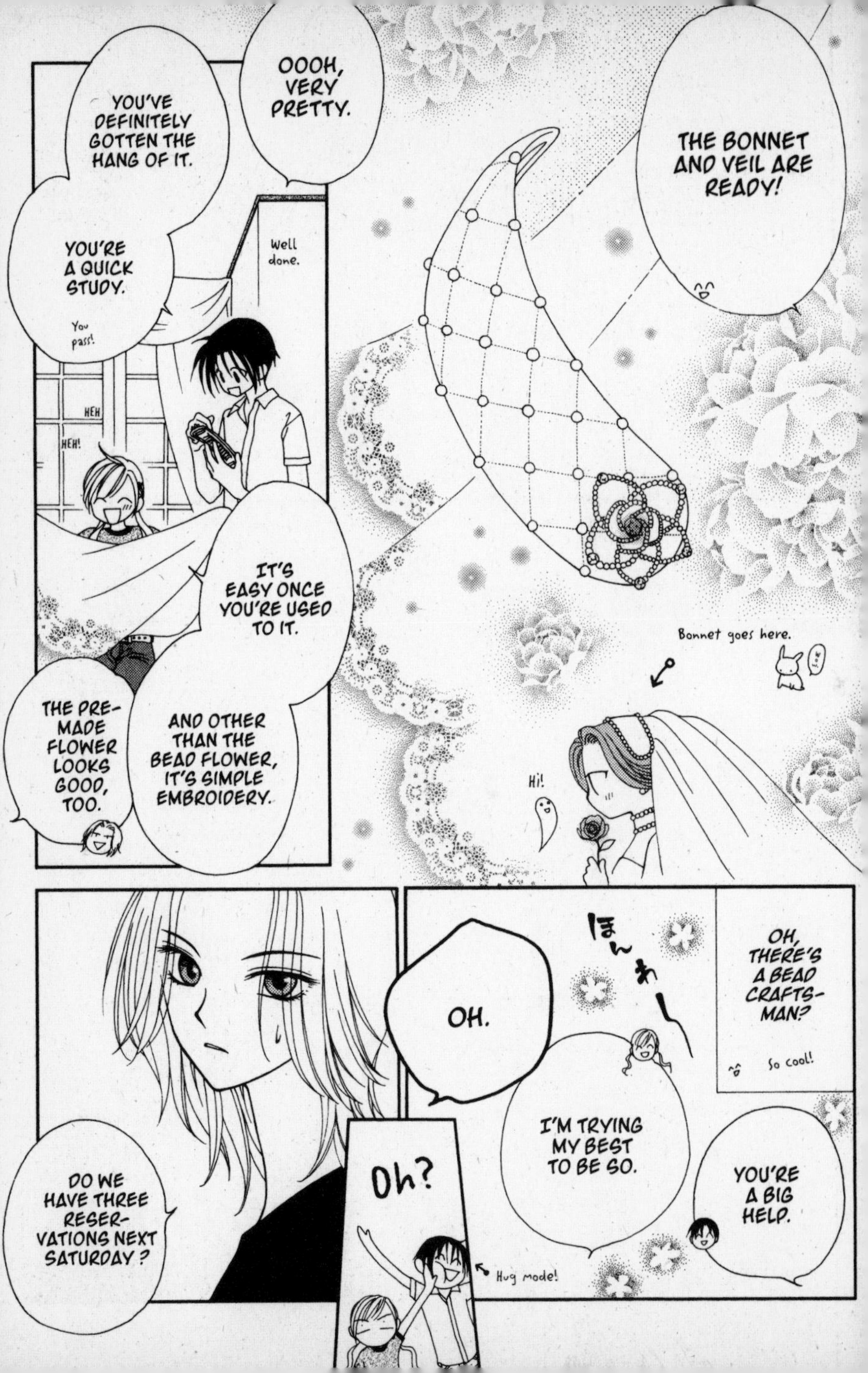
THE BONNET AND VEIL ARE READY!
Bonnet goes here.
Hi!
OOOH, VERY PRETTY.
YOU'VE DEFINITELY GOTTEN THE HANG OF IT.
Well done.
YOU'RE A QUICK STUDY.
You pass!
HEH
HEH!
IT'S EASY ONCE YOU'RE USED TO IT.
AND OTHER THAN THE BEAD FLOWER, IT'S SIMPLE EMBROIDERY.
THE PRE-MADE FLOWER LOOKS GOOD, TOO.
OH, THERE'S A BEAD CRAFTS-MAN?
So cool!
ほんわ〜
YOU'RE A BIG HELP.
I'M TRYING MY BEST TO BE SO.
OH.
Oh?
Hug mode!
DO WE HAVE THREE RESER-VATIONS NEXT SATURDAY ?

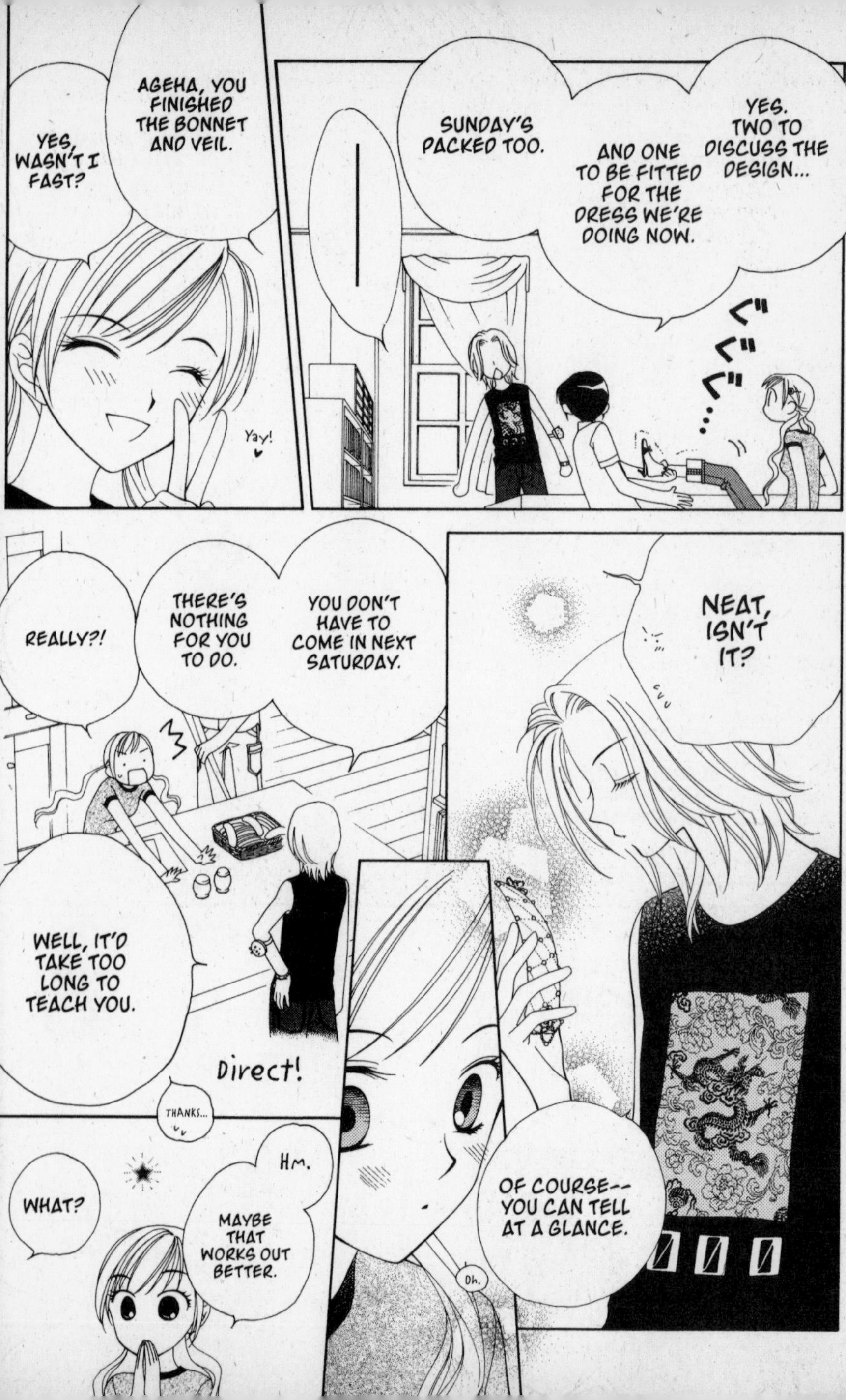
YES. TWO TO DISCUSS THE DESIGN...
AND ONE TO BE FITTED FOR THE DRESS WE'RE DOING NOW.
SUNDAY'S PACKED TOO.
じじじ...
AGEHA, YOU FINISHED THE BONNET AND VEIL.
YES, WASN'T I FAST?
Yay! ♥
NEAT, ISN'T IT?
OF COURSE-- YOU CAN TELL AT A GLANCE.
Oh.
YOU DON'T HAVE TO COME IN NEXT SATURDAY.
THERE'S NOTHING FOR YOU TO DO.
REALLY?!
WELL, IT'D TAKE TOO LONG TO TEACH YOU.
Direct!
THANKS...
Hm.
MAYBE THAT WORKS OUT BETTER.
WHAT?

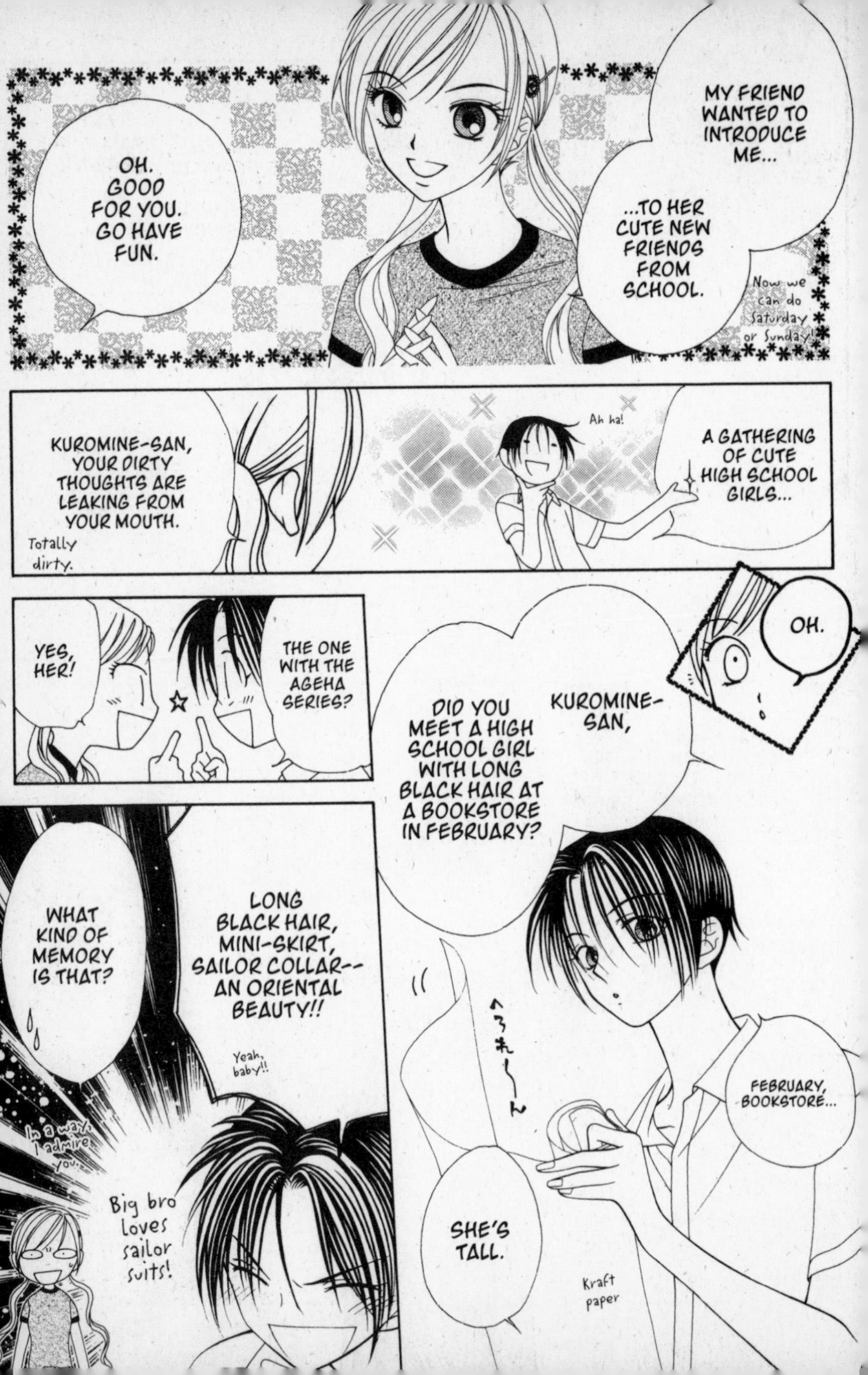
MY FRIEND WANTED TO INTRODUCE ME...
...TO HER CUTE NEW FRIENDS FROM SCHOOL.
Now we can do Saturday or Sunday!
OH. GOOD FOR YOU. GO HAVE FUN.
A GATHERING OF CUTE HIGH SCHOOL GIRLS...
Ah ha!
KUROMINE-SAN, YOUR DIRTY THOUGHTS ARE LEAKING FROM YOUR MOUTH.
Totally dirty.
OH.
KUROMINE-SAN,
DID YOU MEET A HIGH SCHOOL GIRL WITH LONG BLACK HAIR AT A BOOKSTORE IN FEBRUARY?
FEBRUARY, BOOKSTORE...
SHE'S TALL.
Kraft paper
THE ONE WITH THE AGEHA SERIES?
YES, HER!
LONG BLACK HAIR, MINI-SKIRT, SAILOR COLLAR--AN ORIENTAL BEAUTY!!
Yeah, baby!!
WHAT KIND OF MEMORY IS THAT?
In a way, I admire you.
Big bro loves sailor suits!

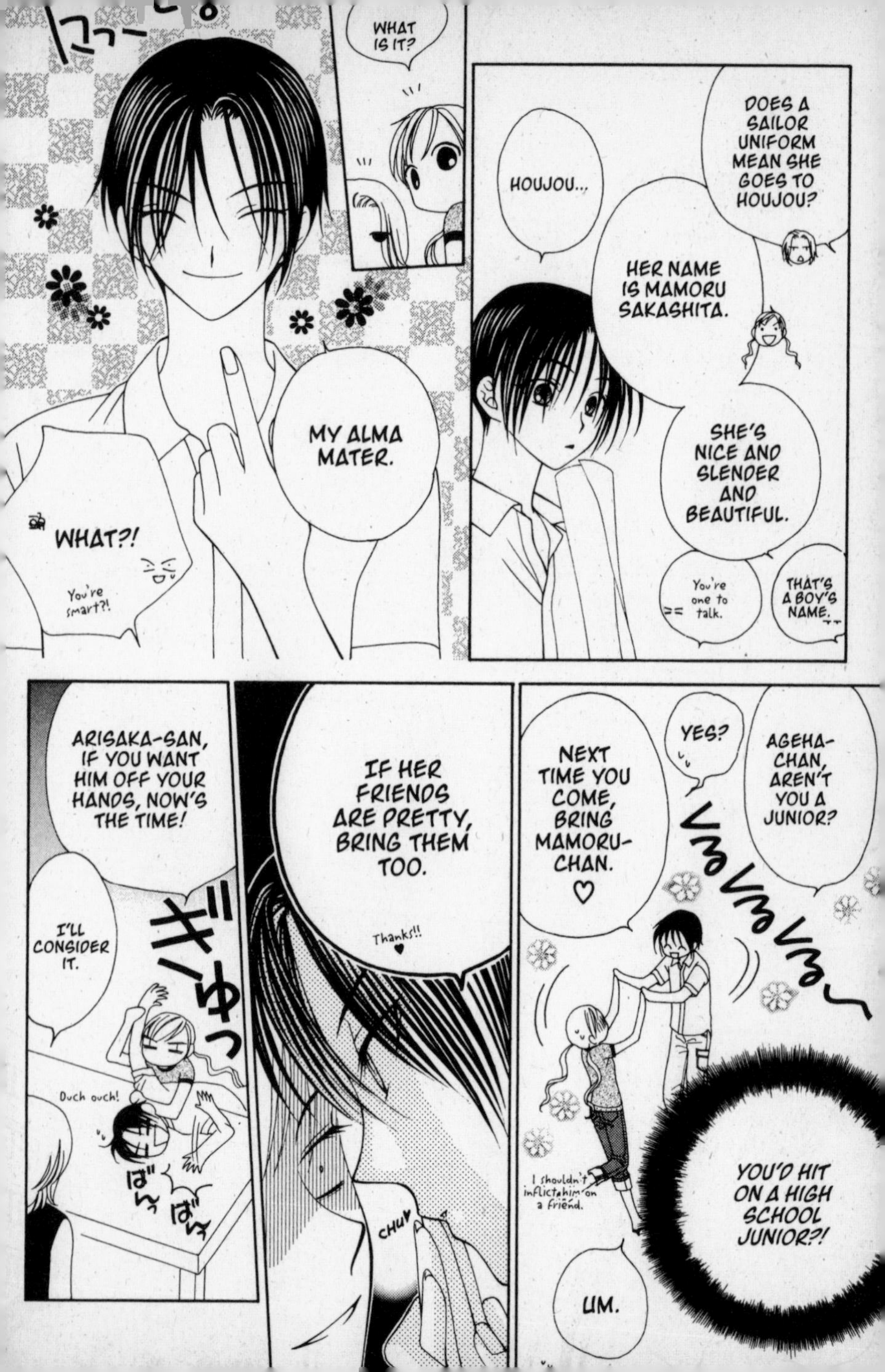
DOES A SAILOR UNIFORM MEAN SHE GOES TO HOUJOU?
HOUJOU...
HER NAME IS MAMORU SAKASHITA.
SHE'S NICE AND SLENDER AND BEAUTIFUL.
THAT'S A BOY'S NAME.
You're one to talk.
WHAT IS IT?
ニコー
MY ALMA MATER.
WHAT?!
You're smart?!
AGEHA-CHAN, AREN'T YOU A JUNIOR?
YES?
NEXT TIME YOU COME, BRING MAMORU-CHAN. ♡
くるくるくる～
YOU'D HIT ON A HIGH SCHOOL JUNIOR?!
I shouldn't inflict him on a friend.
UM.
IF HER FRIENDS ARE PRETTY, BRING THEM TOO.
Thanks!! ♥
CHU♥
ARISAKA-SAN, IF YOU WANT HIM OFF YOUR HANDS, NOW'S THE TIME!
I'LL CONSIDER IT.
ギューっ
Ouch ouch!
ばんっ ばんっ

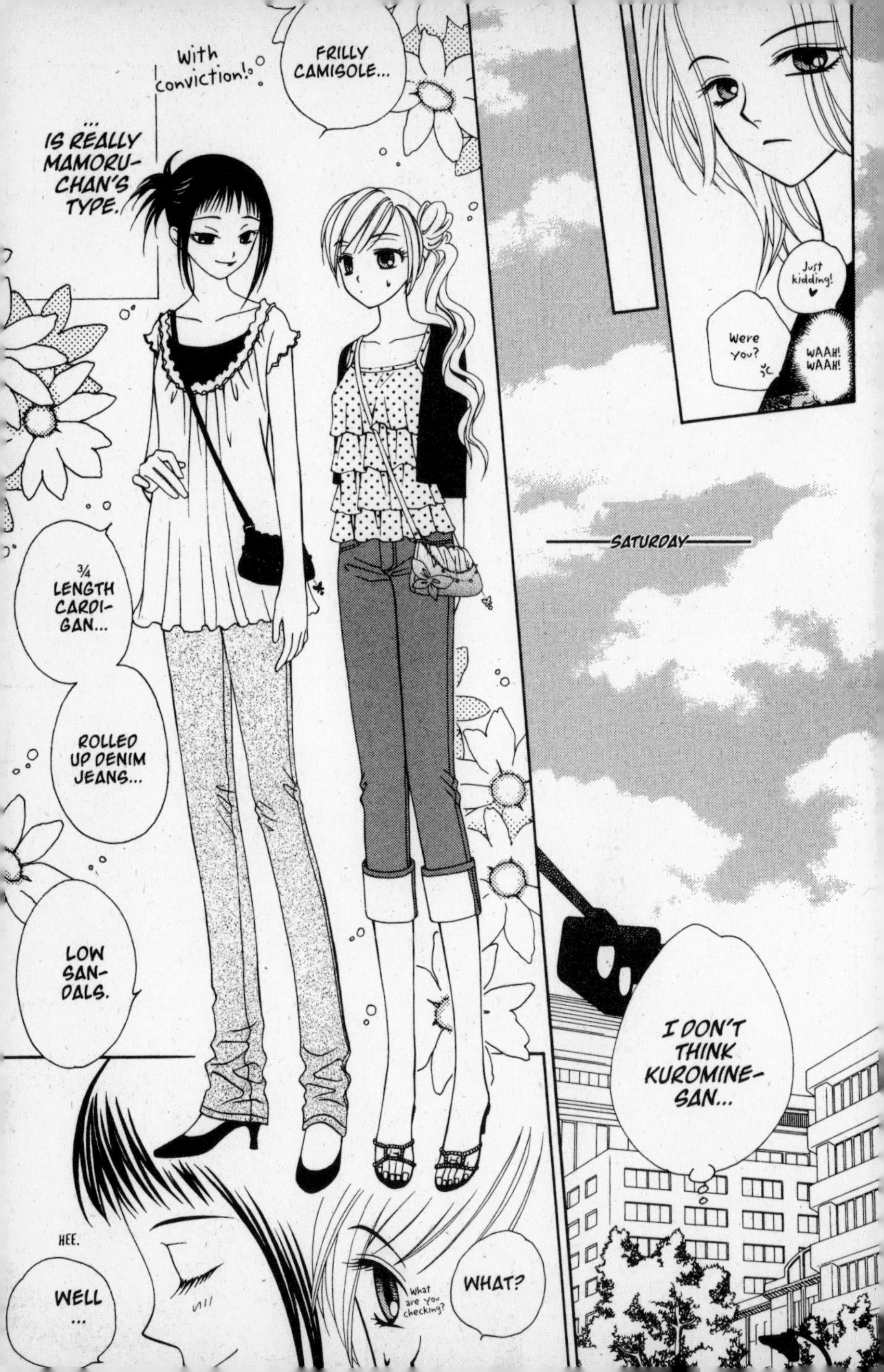
Just kidding! ♥
WAAH! WAAH!
Were you?
SATURDAY
I DON'T THINK KUROMINE-SAN...
FRILLY CAMISOLE...
With conviction!
... IS REALLY MAMORU-CHAN'S TYPE.
3/4 LENGTH CARDIGAN...
ROLLED UP DENIM JEANS...
LOW SANDALS.
WHAT?
What are you checking?
HEE.
WELL ...

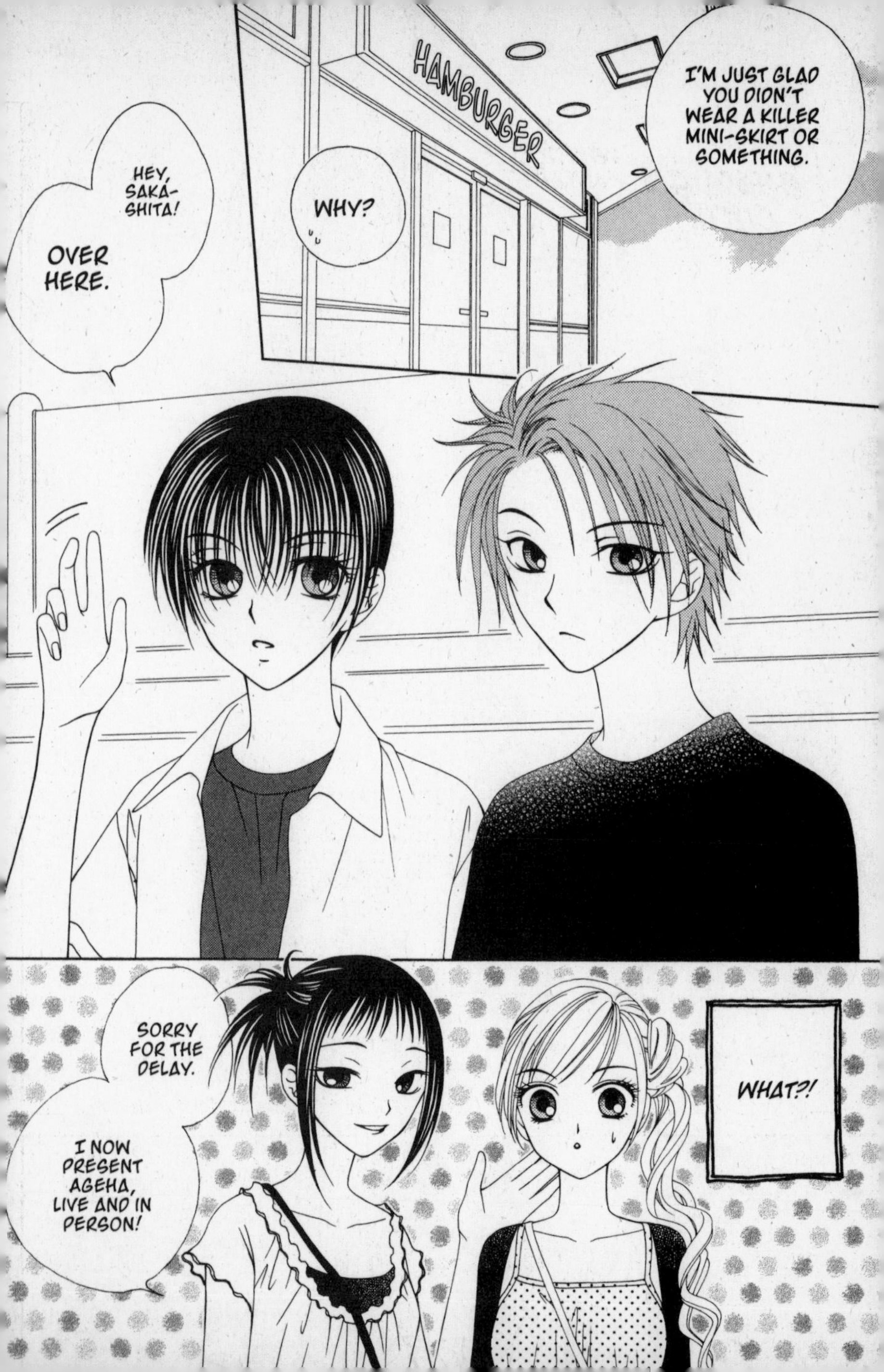
HAMBURGER
I'M JUST GLAD YOU DIDN'T WEAR A KILLER MINI-SKIRT OR SOMETHING.
WHY?
HEY, SAKA-SHITA!
OVER HERE.
WHAT?!
SORRY FOR THE DELAY.
I NOW PRESENT AGEHA, LIVE AND IN PERSON!

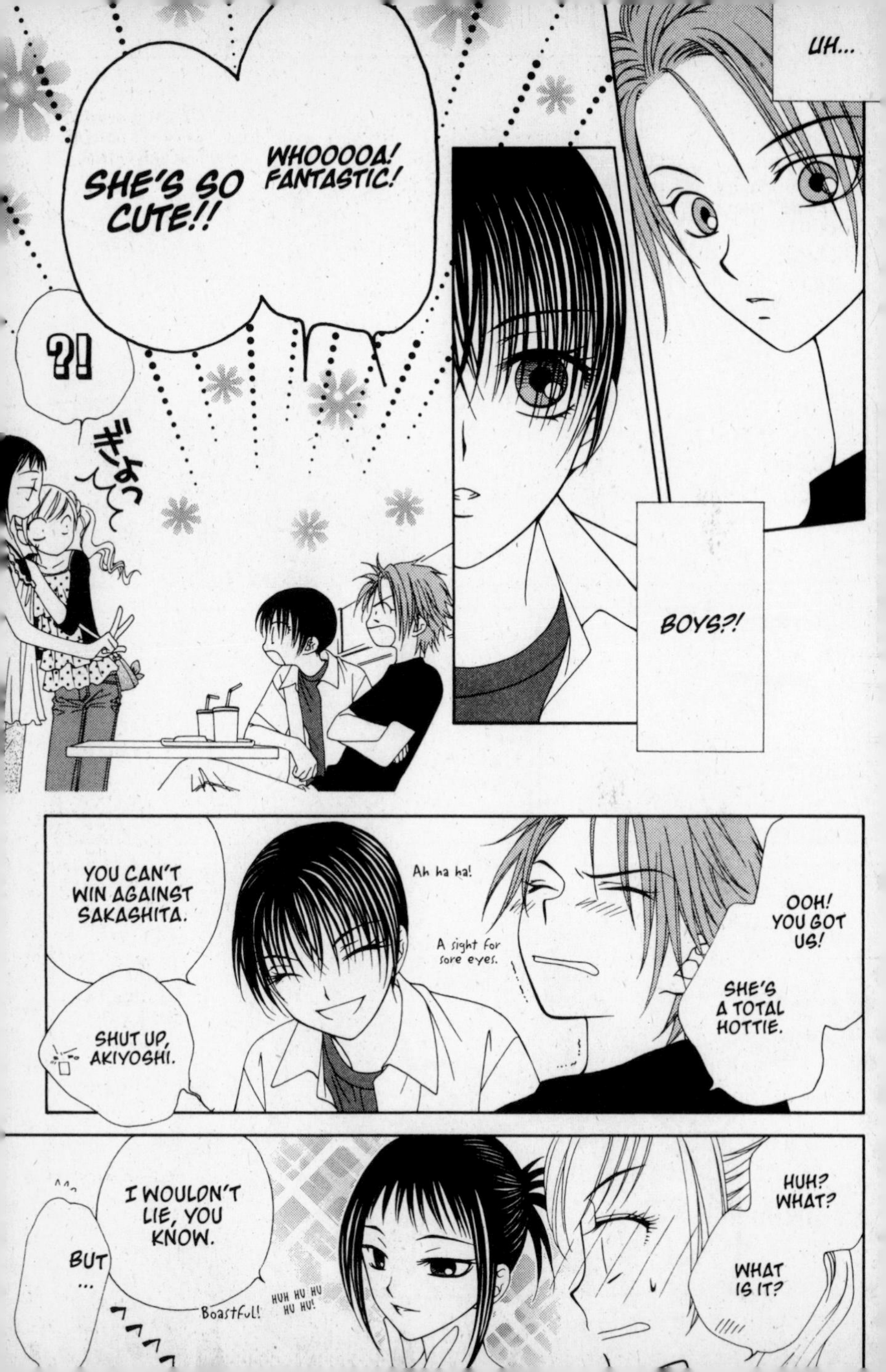
UH...
BOYS?!
WHOOOOA! FANTASTIC!
SHE'S SO CUTE!!
?!
ぎょっ
OOH! YOU GOT US!
SHE'S A TOTAL HOTTIE.
A sight for sore eyes.
Ah ha ha!
YOU CAN'T WIN AGAINST SAKASHITA.
SHUT UP, AKIYOSHI.
HUH? WHAT?
WHAT IS IT?
HUH HU HU HU HU!
I WOULDN'T LIE, YOU KNOW.
Boastful!
BUT ...

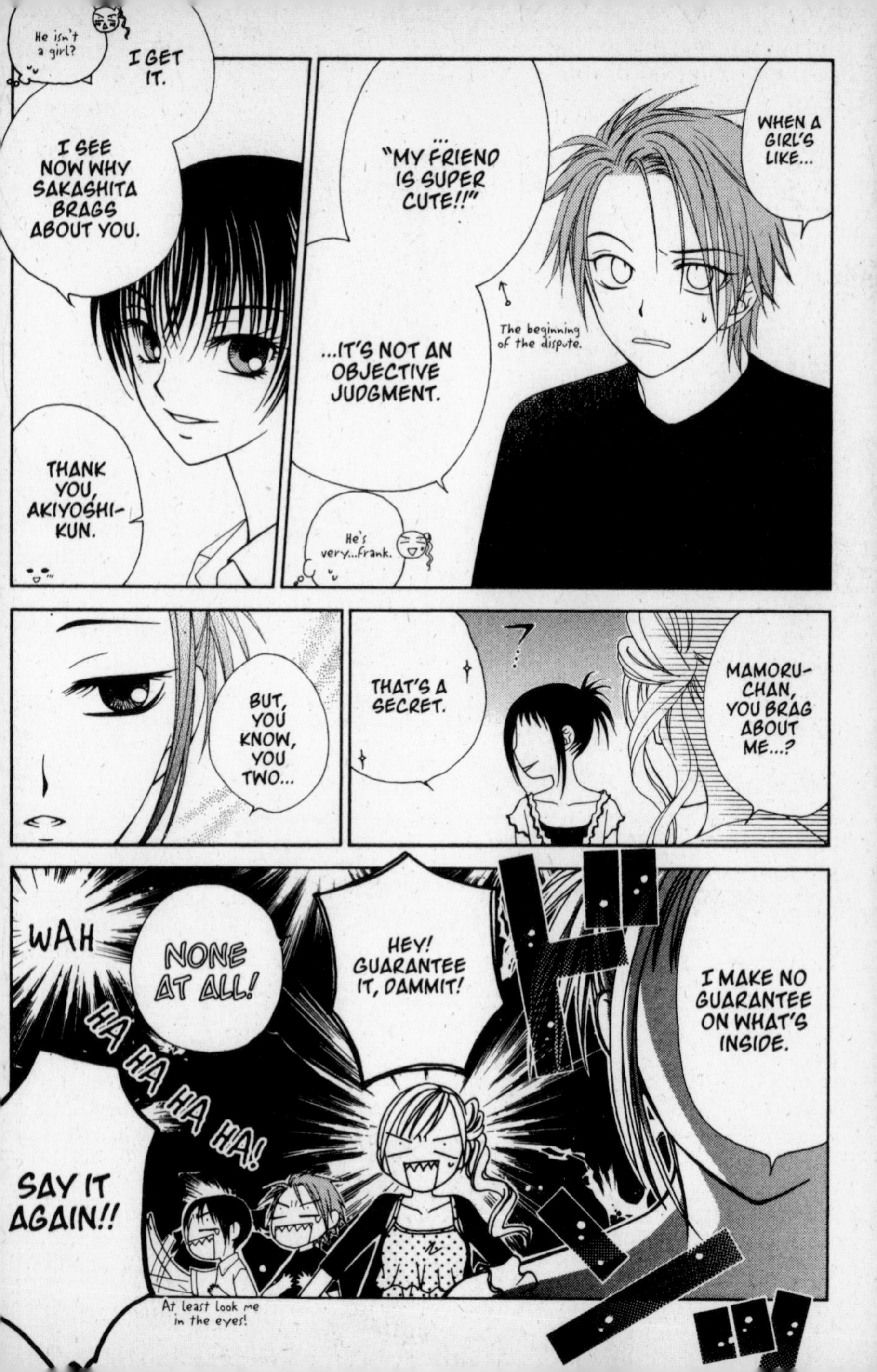
WHEN A GIRL'S LIKE...
... "MY FRIEND IS SUPER CUTE!!"
...IT'S NOT AN OBJECTIVE JUDGMENT.
The beginning of the dispute.
He's very...frank.
I GET IT.
He isn't a girl?
I SEE NOW WHY SAKASHITA BRAGS ABOUT YOU.
THANK YOU, AKIYOSHI-KUN.
MAMORU-CHAN, YOU BRAG ABOUT ME...?
THAT'S A SECRET.
BUT, YOU KNOW, YOU TWO...
I MAKE NO GUARANTEE ON WHAT'S INSIDE.
HEY! GUARANTEE IT, DAMMIT!
NONE AT ALL!
WAH
HA HA HA HA HA!
SAY IT AGAIN!!
At least look me in the eyes!

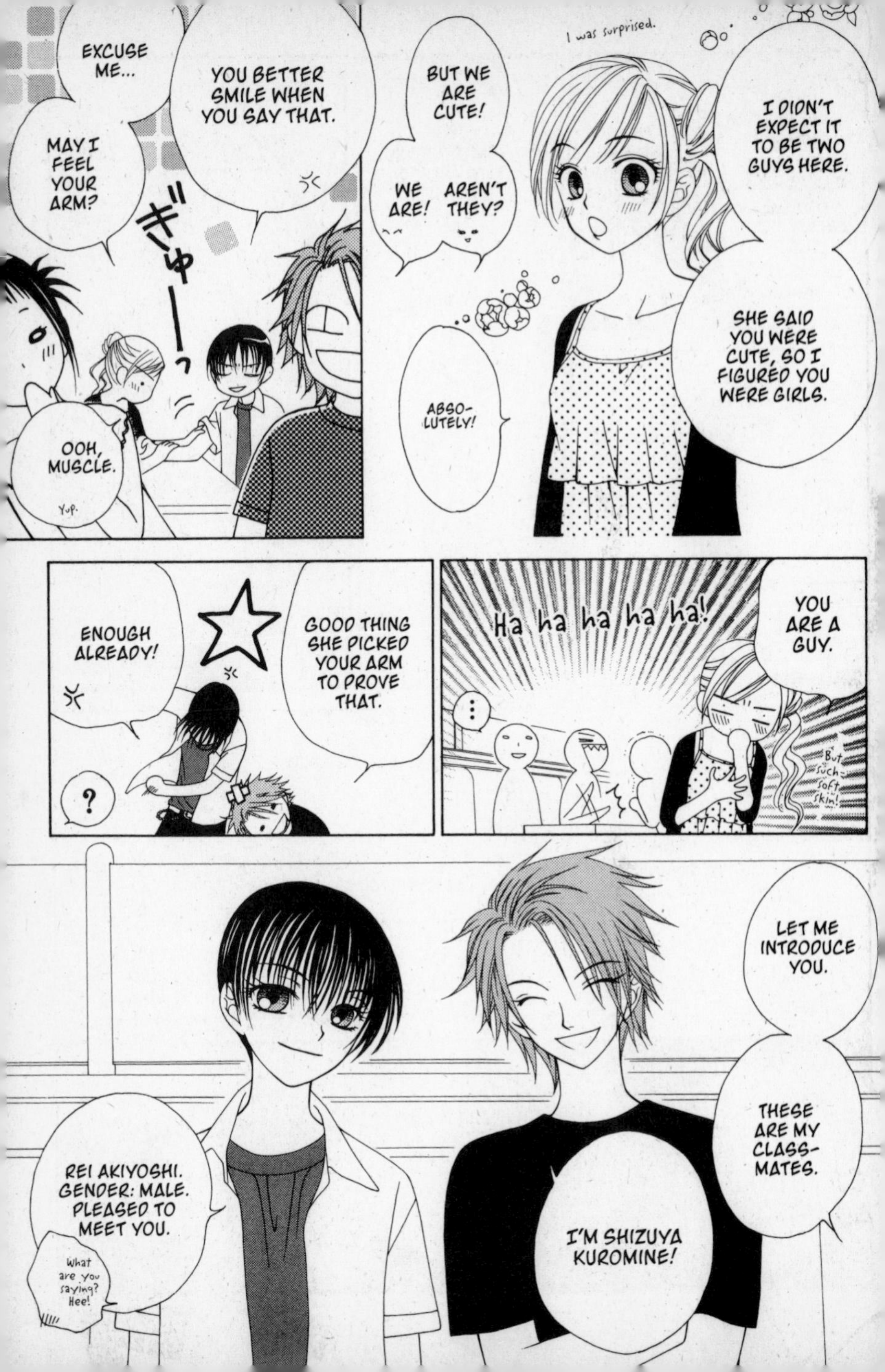
I was surprised.
I DIDN'T EXPECT IT TO BE TWO GUYS HERE.
BUT WE ARE CUTE!
SHE SAID YOU WERE CUTE, SO I FIGURED YOU WERE GIRLS.
AREN'T THEY?
WE ARE!
ABSOLUTELY!
YOU BETTER SMILE WHEN YOU SAY THAT.
EXCUSE ME...
MAY I FEEL YOUR ARM?
ギゅーっ
OOH, MUSCLE.
Yup.
YOU ARE A GUY.
Ha ha ha ha ha!
But such soft skin!
...
GOOD THING SHE PICKED YOUR ARM TO PROVE THAT.
ENOUGH ALREADY!
?
LET ME INTRODUCE YOU.
THESE ARE MY CLASSMATES.
I'M SHIZUYA KUROMINE!
REI AKIYOSHI. GENDER: MALE. PLEASED TO MEET YOU.
What are you saying? Hee!

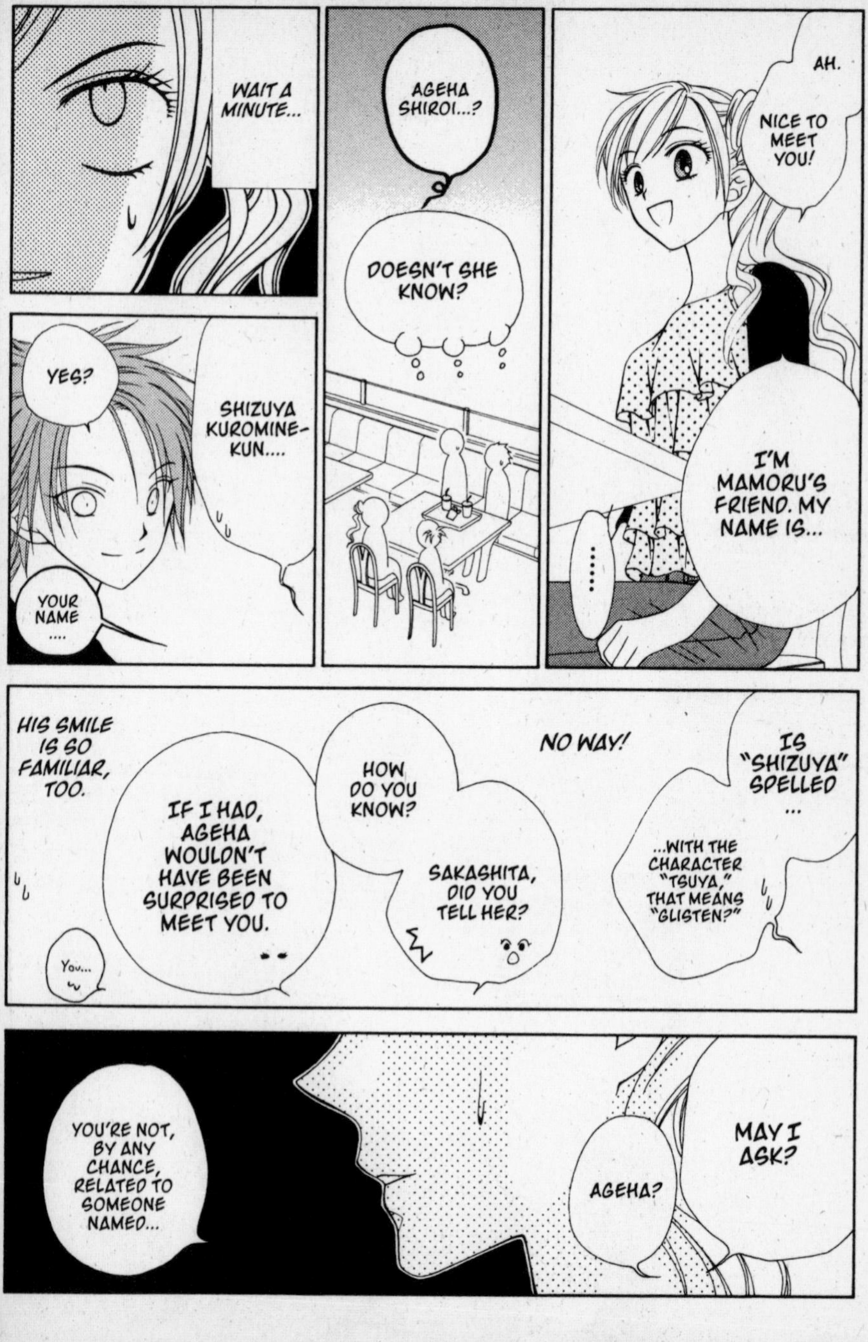
AH.
NICE TO MEET YOU!
I'M MAMORU'S FRIEND. MY NAME IS...
......
AGEHA SHIROI...?
DOESN'T SHE KNOW?
WAIT A MINUTE...
SHIZUYA KUROMINE-KUN....
YES?
YOUR NAME ....
IS "SHIZUYA" SPELLED ...
...WITH THE CHARACTER "TSUYA," THAT MEANS "GLISTEN?"
NO WAY!
HOW DO YOU KNOW?
SAKASHITA, DID YOU TELL HER?
IF I HAD, AGEHA WOULDN'T HAVE BEEN SURPRISED TO MEET YOU.
HIS SMILE IS SO FAMILIAR, TOO.
You...
MAY I ASK?
AGEHA?
YOU'RE NOT, BY ANY CHANCE, RELATED TO SOMEONE NAMED...

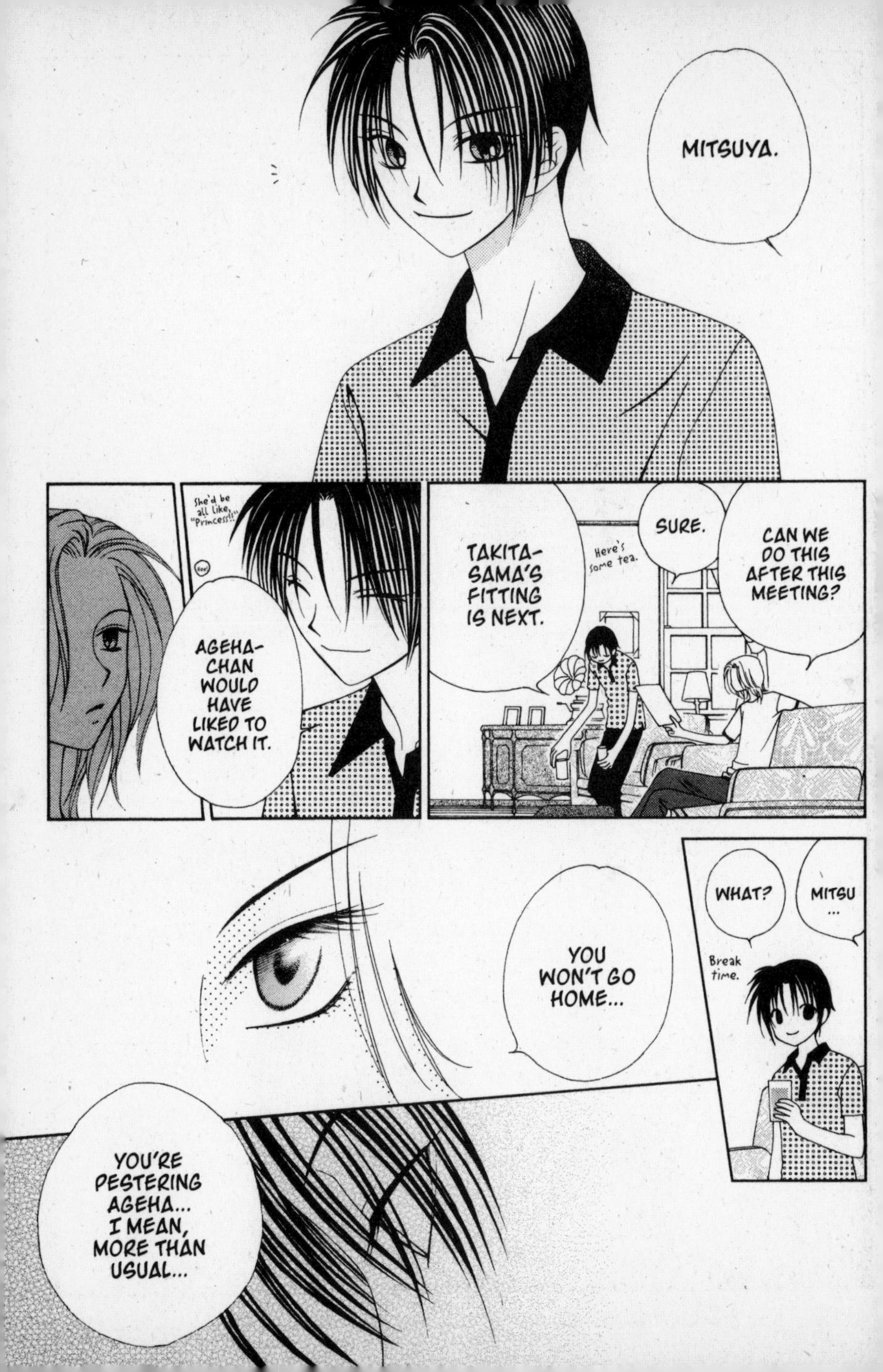
MITSUYA.
CAN WE DO THIS AFTER THIS MEETING?
SURE.
TAKITA-SAMA'S FITTING IS NEXT.
Here's some tea.
She'd be all like, "Princess!!"
Hee!
AGEHA-CHAN WOULD HAVE LIKED TO WATCH IT.
MITSU ...
WHAT?
Break time.
YOU WON'T GO HOME...
YOU'RE PESTERING AGEHA... I MEAN, MORE THAN USUAL...

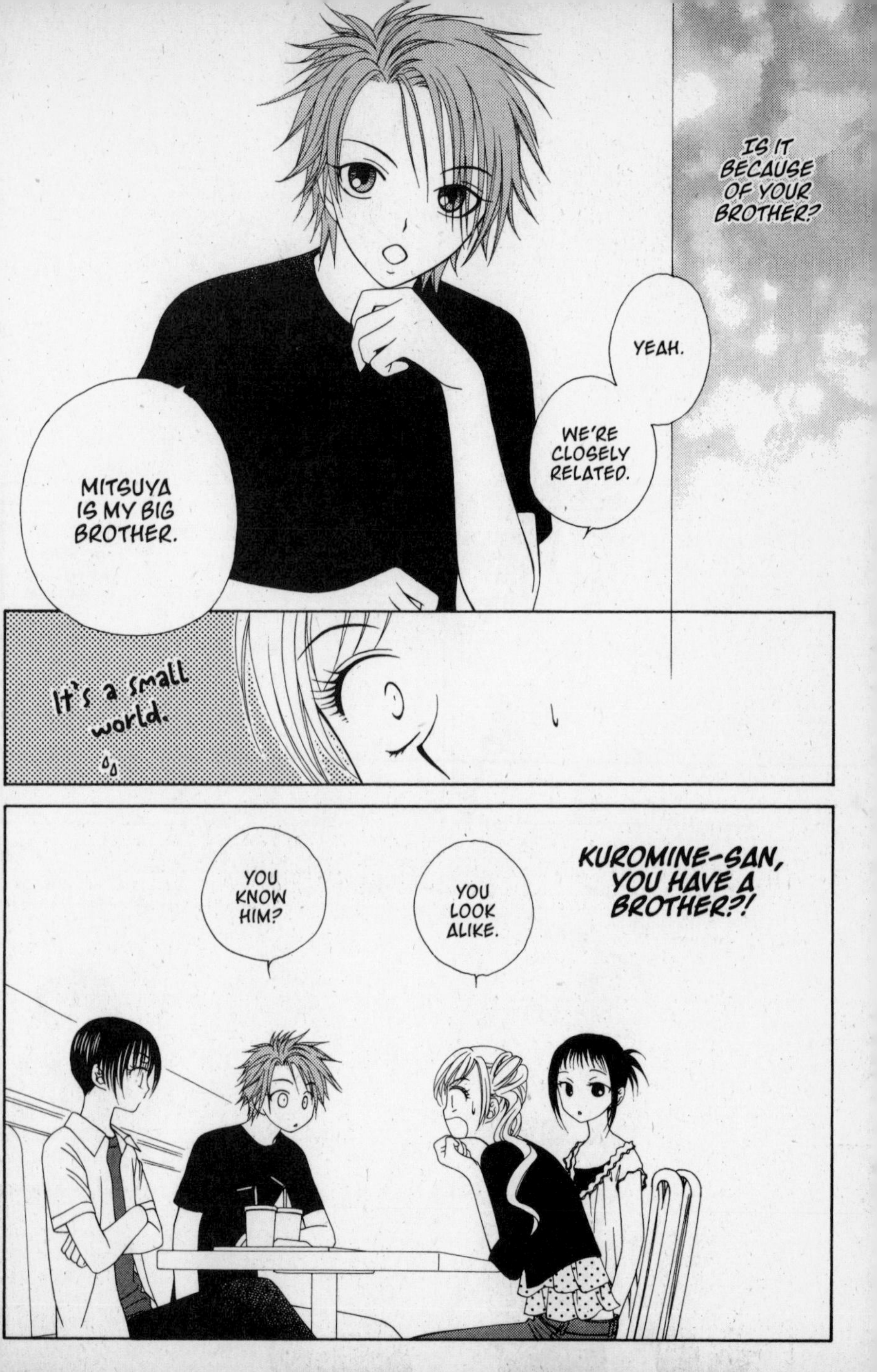
IS IT BECAUSE OF YOUR BROTHER?
YEAH.
WE'RE CLOSELY RELATED.
MITSUYA IS MY BIG BROTHER.
It's a small world.
KUROMINE-SAN, YOU HAVE A BROTHER?!
YOU LOOK ALIKE.
YOU KNOW HIM?

Episode 9

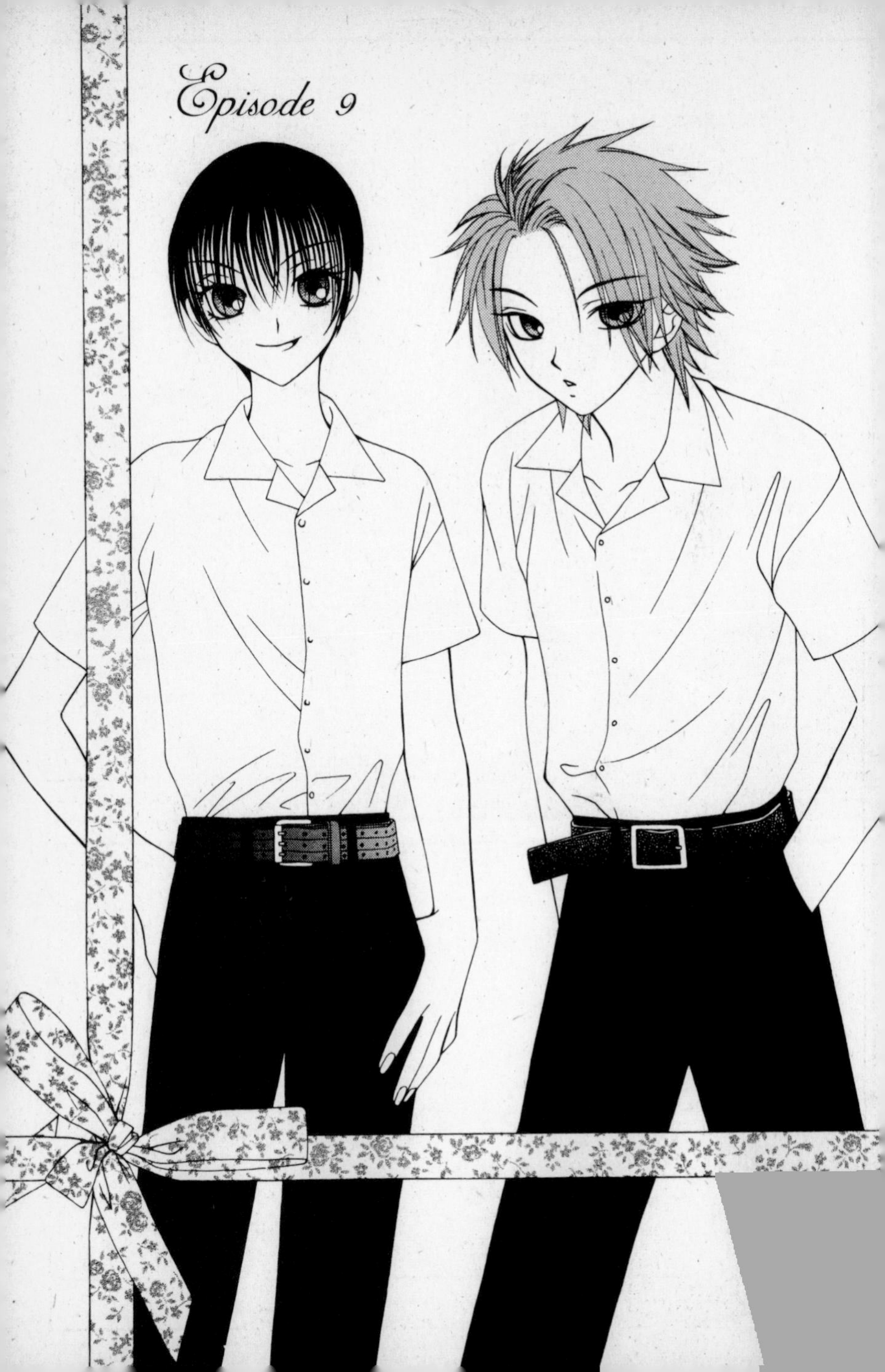

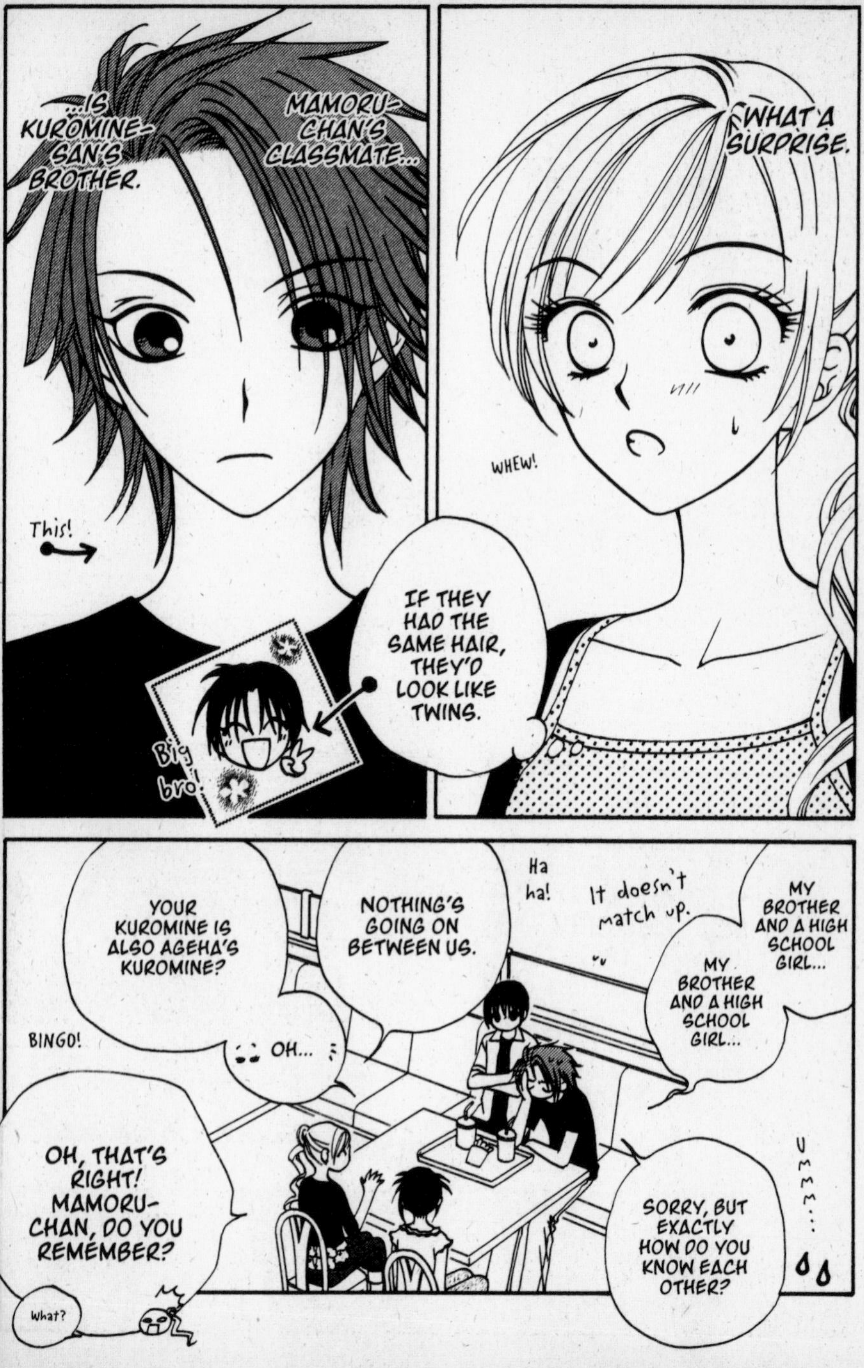
WHAT A SURPRISE.
WHEW!
IF THEY HAD THE SAME HAIR, THEY'D LOOK LIKE TWINS.
MAMORU-CHAN'S CLASSMATE...
...IS KUROMINE-SAN'S BROTHER.
This!
Big bro!
MY BROTHER AND A HIGH SCHOOL GIRL...
MY BROTHER AND A HIGH SCHOOL GIRL...
It doesn't match up.
Ha ha!
NOTHING'S GOING ON BETWEEN US.
YOUR KUROMINE IS ALSO AGEHA'S KUROMINE?
BINGO!
OH...
UMMM...
SORRY, BUT EXACTLY HOW DO YOU KNOW EACH OTHER?
OH, THAT'S RIGHT! MAMORU-CHAN, DO YOU REMEMBER?
What?

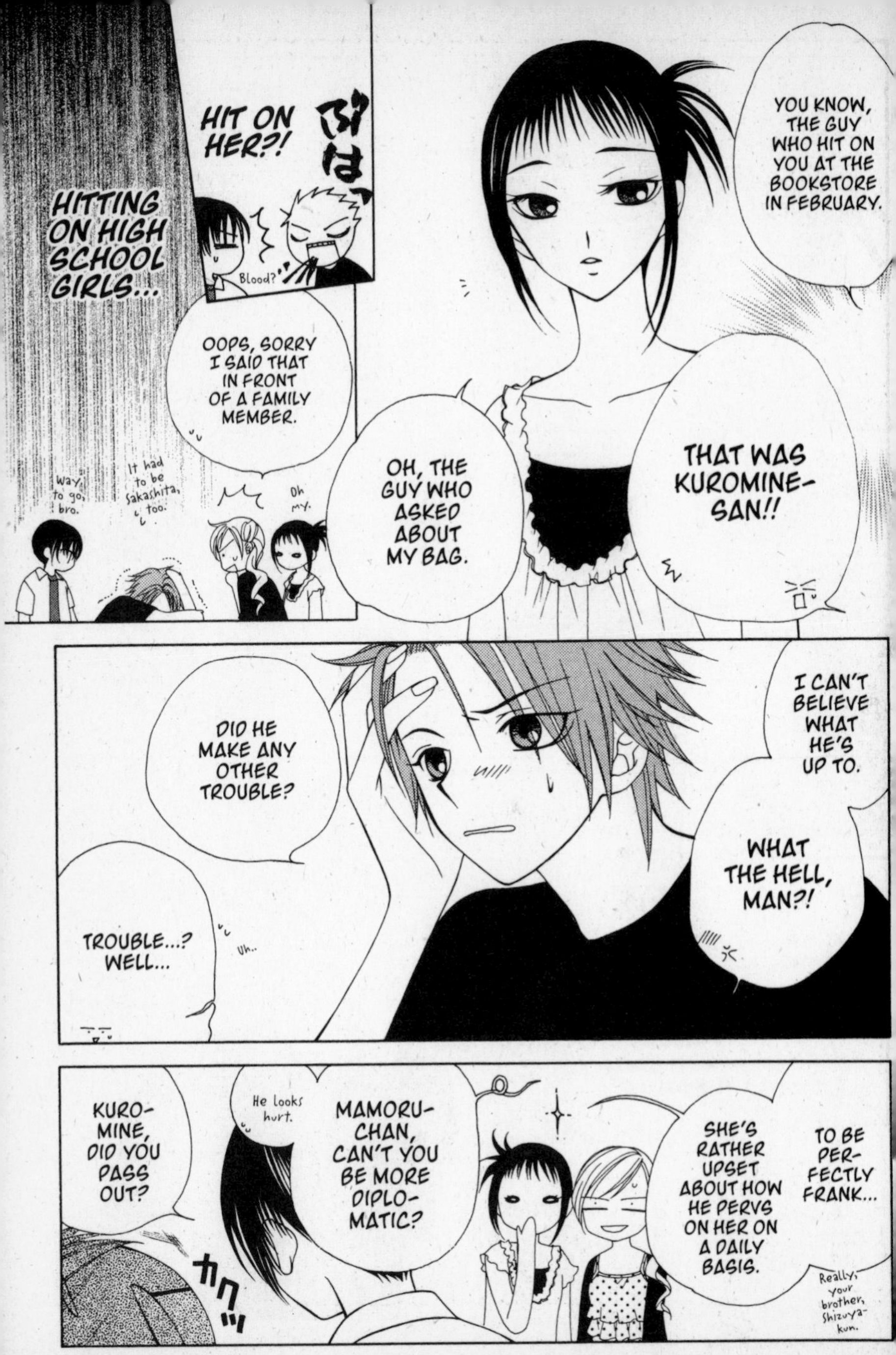
YOU KNOW, THE GUY WHO HIT ON YOU AT THE BOOKSTORE IN FEBRUARY.
OH, THE GUY WHO ASKED ABOUT MY BAG.
THAT WAS KUROMINE-SAN!!
HIT ON HER?!
ぶはっ
Blood?
HITTING ON HIGH SCHOOL GIRLS...
OOPS, SORRY I SAID THAT IN FRONT OF A FAMILY MEMBER.
Oh my.
It had to be Sakashita, too.
Way to go, bro.
I CAN'T BELIEVE WHAT HE'S UP TO.
WHAT THE HELL, MAN?!
DID HE MAKE ANY OTHER TROUBLE?
Uh..
TROUBLE...? WELL...
TO BE PERFECTLY FRANK...
SHE'S RATHER UPSET ABOUT HOW HE PERVS ON HER ON A DAILY BASIS.
Really, your brother, Shizuya-kun.
MAMORU-CHAN, CAN'T YOU BE MORE DIPLOMATIC?
He looks hurt.
KURO-MINE, DID YOU PASS OUT?
カクッ

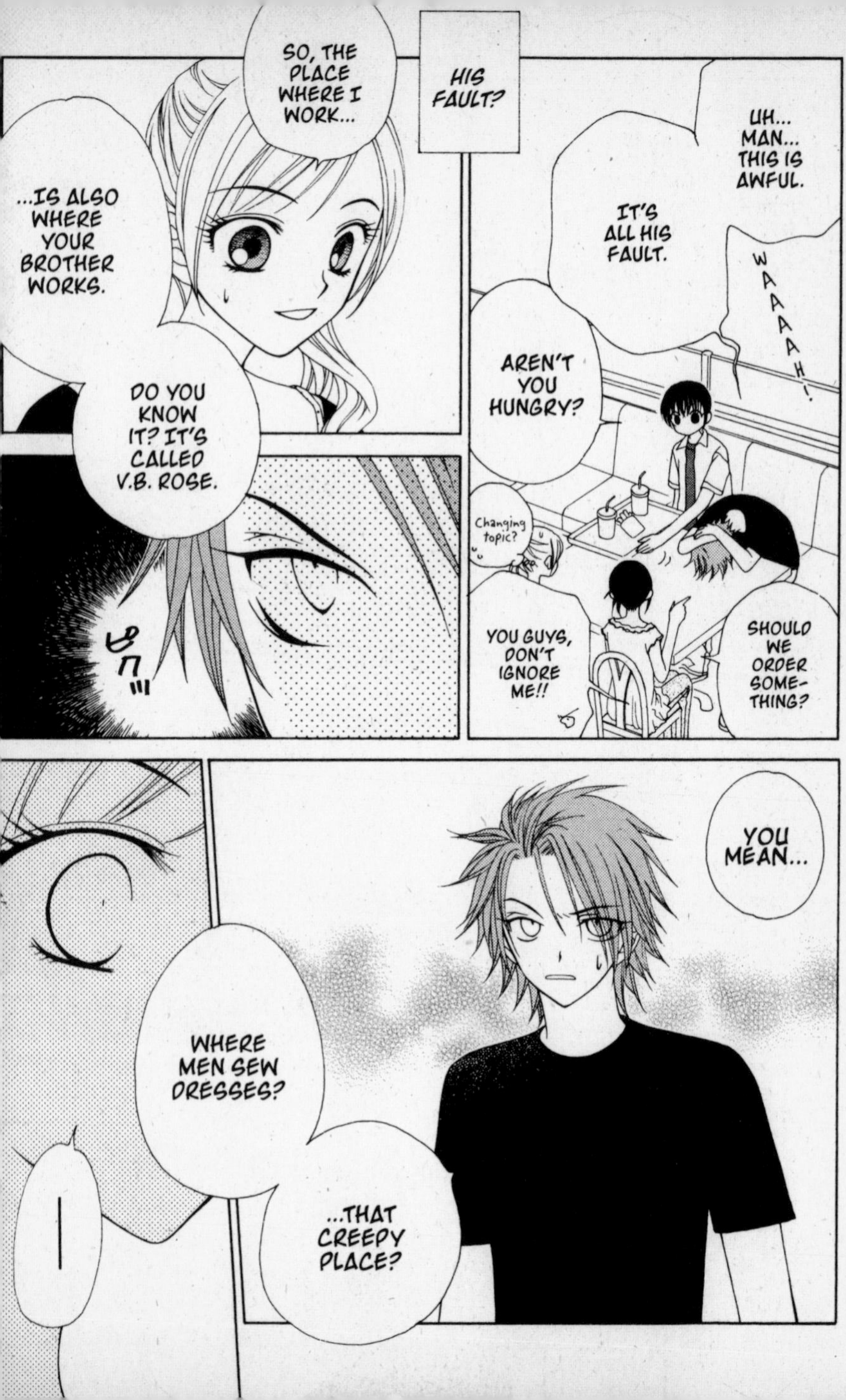
UH... MAN... THIS IS AWFUL.
WAAAAAH!
IT'S ALL HIS FAULT.
AREN'T YOU HUNGRY?
Changing topic?
SHOULD WE ORDER SOME-THING?
YOU GUYS, DON'T IGNORE ME!!
HIS FAULT?
SO, THE PLACE WHERE I WORK...
...IS ALSO WHERE YOUR BROTHER WORKS.
DO YOU KNOW IT? IT'S CALLED V.B. ROSE.
YOU MEAN...
WHERE MEN SEW DRESSES?
...THAT CREEPY PLACE?

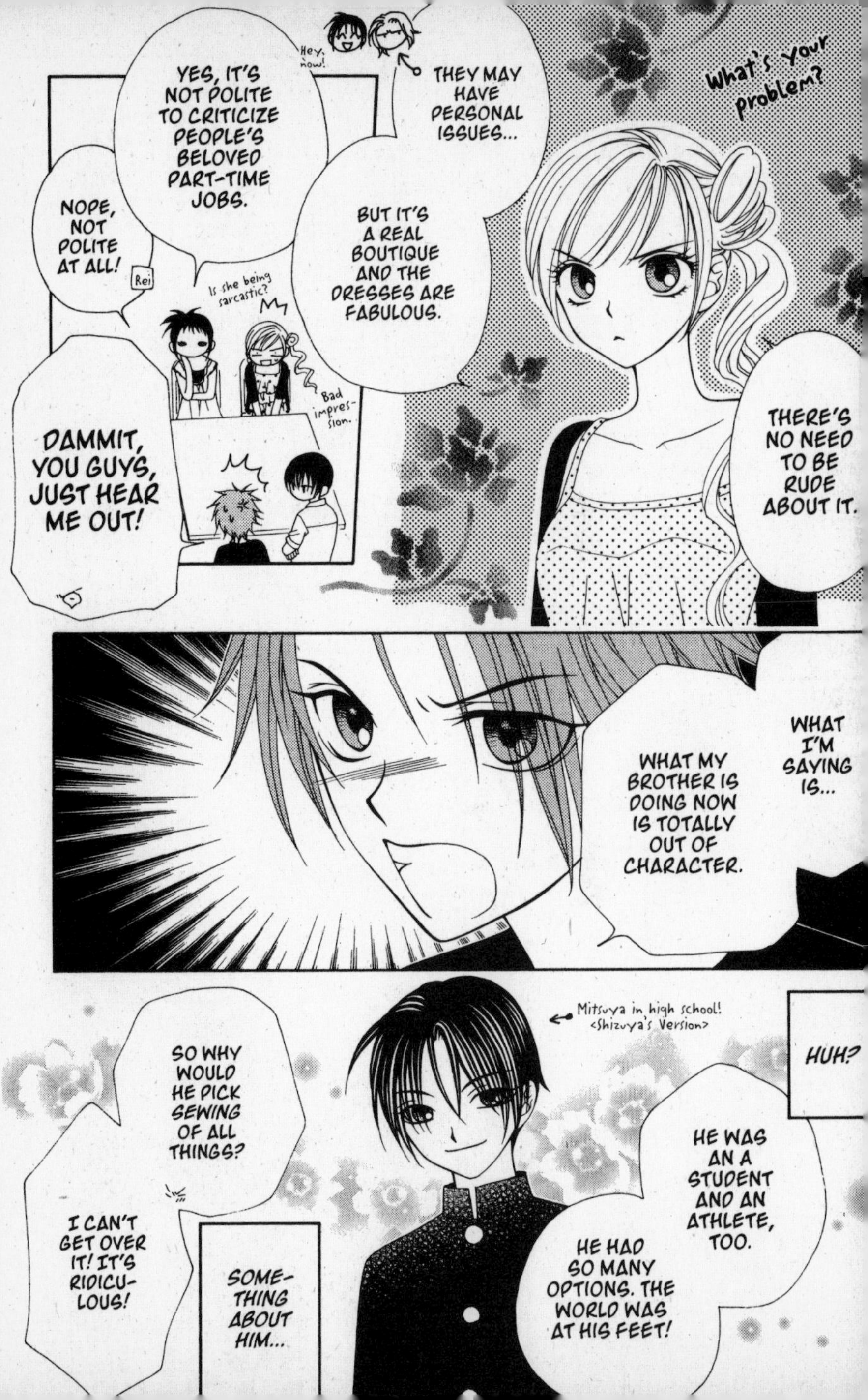
What's your problem?
THERE'S NO NEED TO BE RUDE ABOUT IT.
THEY MAY HAVE PERSONAL ISSUES...
Hey, now!
BUT IT'S A REAL BOUTIQUE AND THE DRESSES ARE FABULOUS.
YES, IT'S NOT POLITE TO CRITICIZE PEOPLE'S BELOVED PART-TIME JOBS.
NOPE, NOT POLITE AT ALL!
Rei
Is she being sarcastic?
Bad impression.
DAMMIT, YOU GUYS, JUST HEAR ME OUT!
WHAT I'M SAYING IS...
WHAT MY BROTHER IS DOING NOW IS TOTALLY OUT OF CHARACTER.
HUH?
Mitsuya in high school! <Shizuya's Version>
HE WAS AN A STUDENT AND AN ATHLETE, TOO.
HE HAD SO MANY OPTIONS. THE WORLD WAS AT HIS FEET!
SO WHY WOULD HE PICK SEWING OF ALL THINGS?
SOME-THING ABOUT HIM...
I CAN'T GET OVER IT! IT'S RIDICU-LOUS!

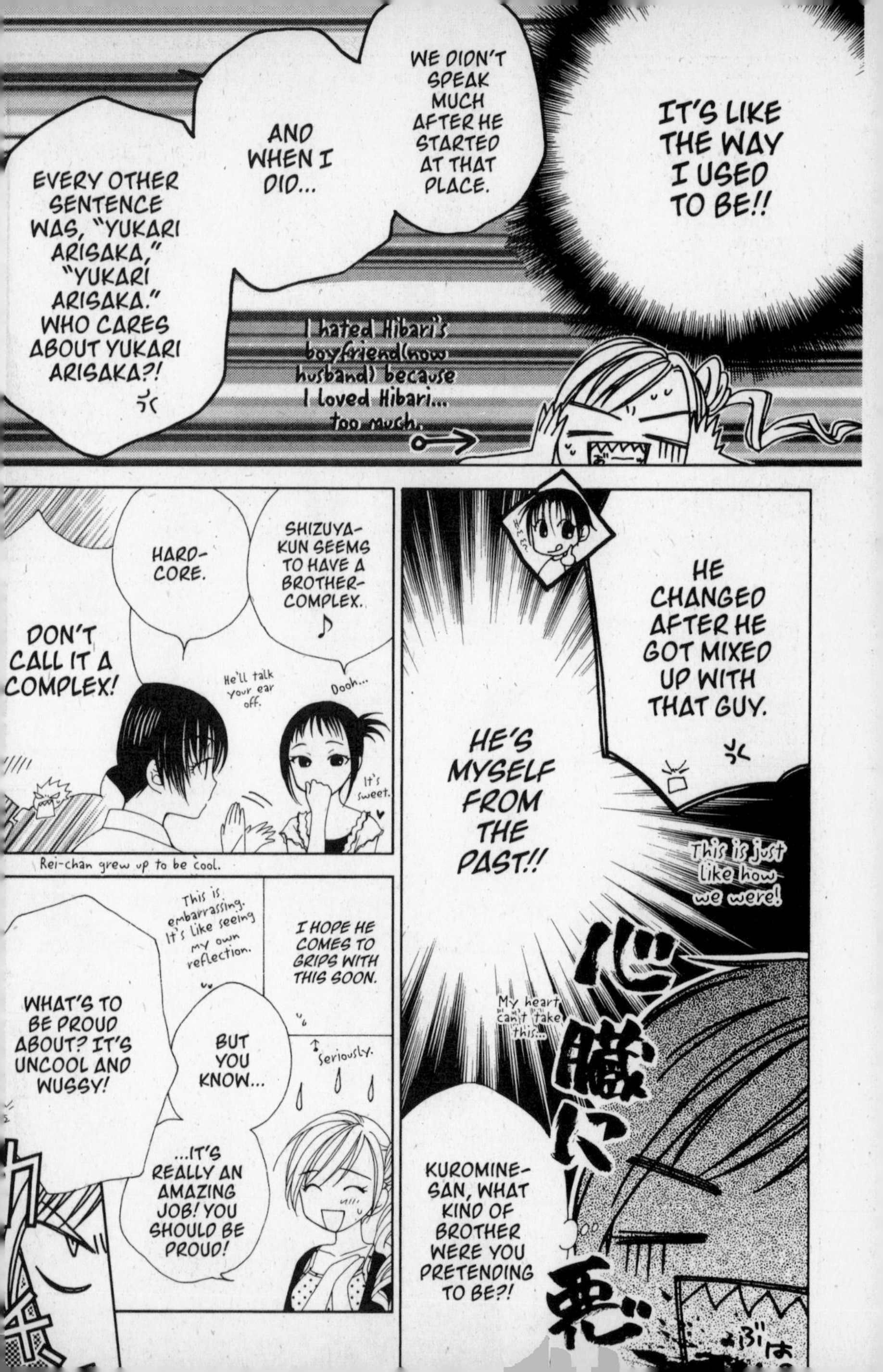
IT'S LIKE THE WAY I USED TO BE!!
WE DIDN'T SPEAK MUCH AFTER HE STARTED AT THAT PLACE.
AND WHEN I DID...
EVERY OTHER SENTENCE WAS, "YUKARI ARISAKA," "YUKARI ARISAKA." WHO CARES ABOUT YUKARI ARISAKA?!
I hated Hibari's boyfriend(now husband) because I loved Hibari... too much.
HE CHANGED AFTER HE GOT MIXED UP WITH THAT GUY.
HE'S MYSELF FROM THE PAST!!
This is just like how we were!
My heart can't take this...
KUROMINE-SAN, WHAT KIND OF BROTHER WERE YOU PRETENDING TO BE?!
SHIZUYA-KUN SEEMS TO HAVE A BROTHER-COMPLEX. ♪
HARD-CORE.
Oooh...
He'll talk your ear off.
It's sweet.
DON'T CALL IT A COMPLEX!
Rei-chan grew up to be cool.
I HOPE HE COMES TO GRIPS WITH THIS SOON.
This is embarrassing. It's like seeing my own reflection.
BUT YOU KNOW...
Seriously.
...IT'S REALLY AN AMAZING JOB! YOU SHOULD BE PROUD!
WHAT'S TO BE PROUD ABOUT? IT'S UNCOOL AND WUSSY!

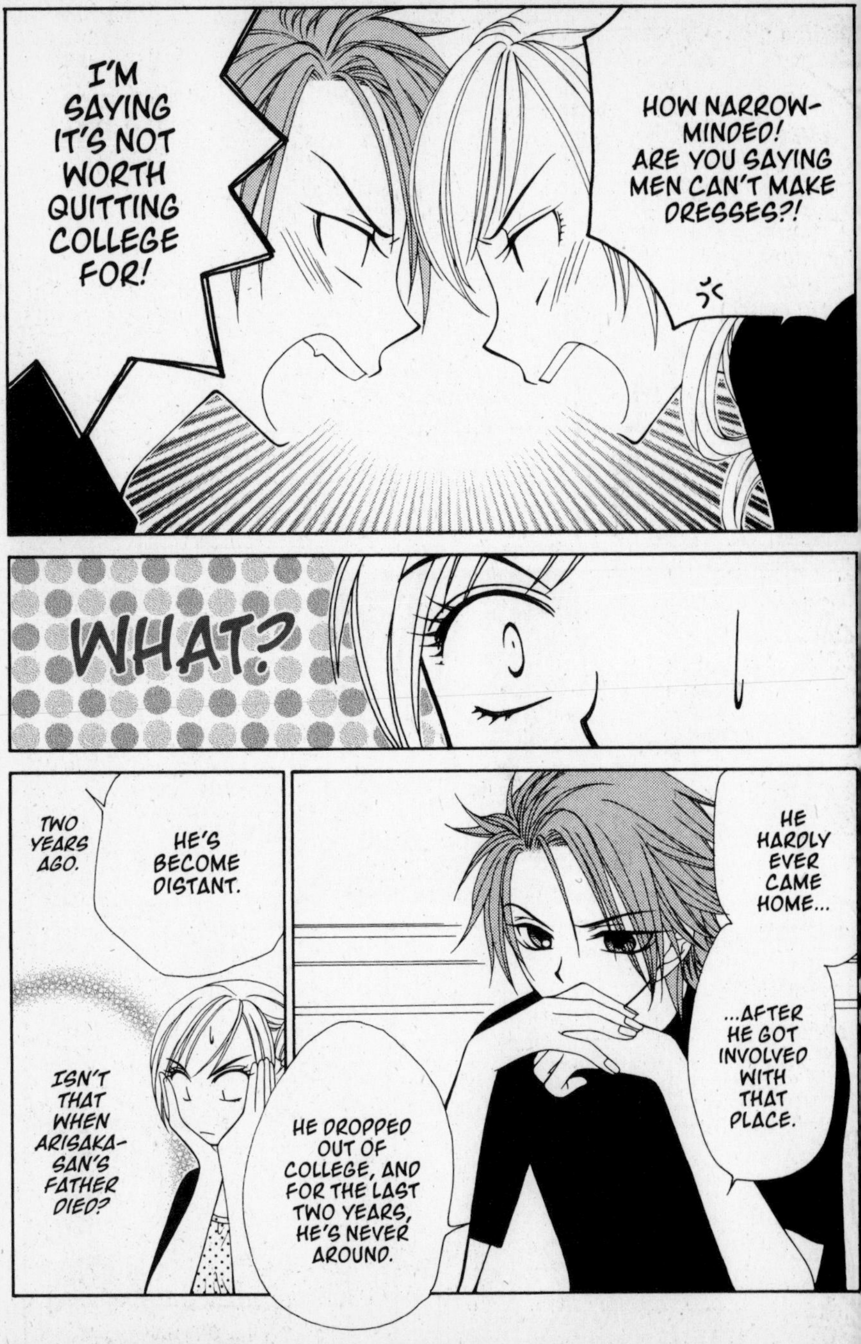
HOW NARROW-MINDED! ARE YOU SAYING MEN CAN'T MAKE DRESSES?!
I'M SAYING IT'S NOT WORTH QUITTING COLLEGE FOR!
WHAT?
HE HARDLY EVER CAME HOME...
...AFTER HE GOT INVOLVED WITH THAT PLACE.
HE DROPPED OUT OF COLLEGE, AND FOR THE LAST TWO YEARS, HE'S NEVER AROUND.
HE'S BECOME DISTANT.
TWO YEARS AGO.
ISN'T THAT WHEN ARISAKA-SAN'S FATHER DIED?

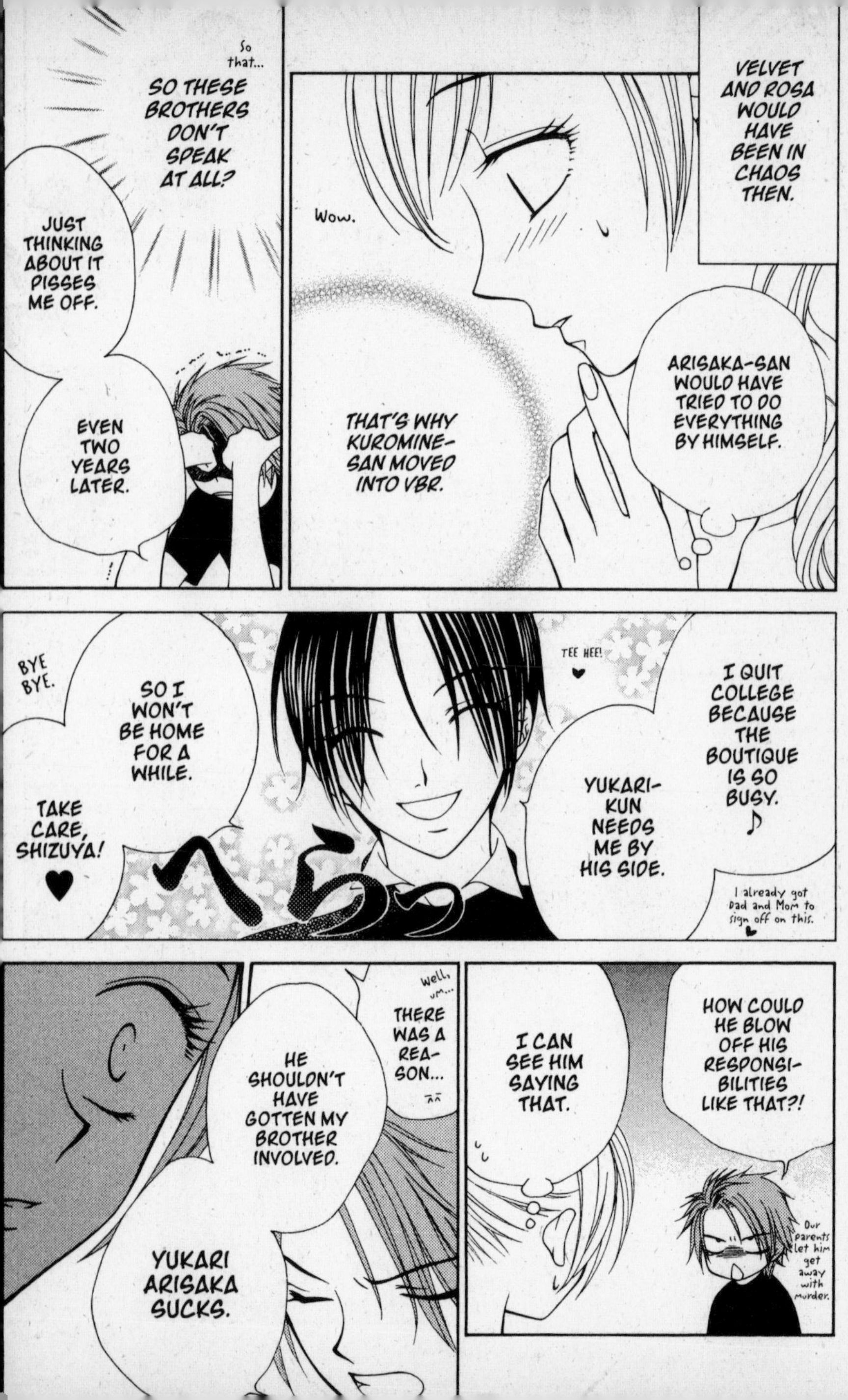
VELVET AND ROSA WOULD HAVE BEEN IN CHAOS THEN.
ARISAKA-SAN WOULD HAVE TRIED TO DO EVERYTHING BY HIMSELF.
THAT'S WHY KUROMINE-SAN MOVED INTO VBR.
Wow.
So that...
SO THESE BROTHERS DON'T SPEAK AT ALL?
JUST THINKING ABOUT IT PISSES ME OFF.
EVEN TWO YEARS LATER.
I QUIT COLLEGE BECAUSE THE BOUTIQUE IS SO BUSY. ♪
I already got Dad and Mom to sign off on this. ♥
TEE HEE! ♥
YUKARI-KUN NEEDS ME BY HIS SIDE.
SO I WON'T BE HOME FOR A WHILE.
BYE BYE.
TAKE CARE, SHIZUYA! ♥
HOW COULD HE BLOW OFF HIS RESPONSI-BILITIES LIKE THAT?!
Our parents let him get away with murder.
I CAN SEE HIM SAYING THAT.
Well, um...
THERE WAS A REA-SON...
HE SHOULDN'T HAVE GOTTEN MY BROTHER INVOLVED.
YUKARI ARISAKA SUCKS.

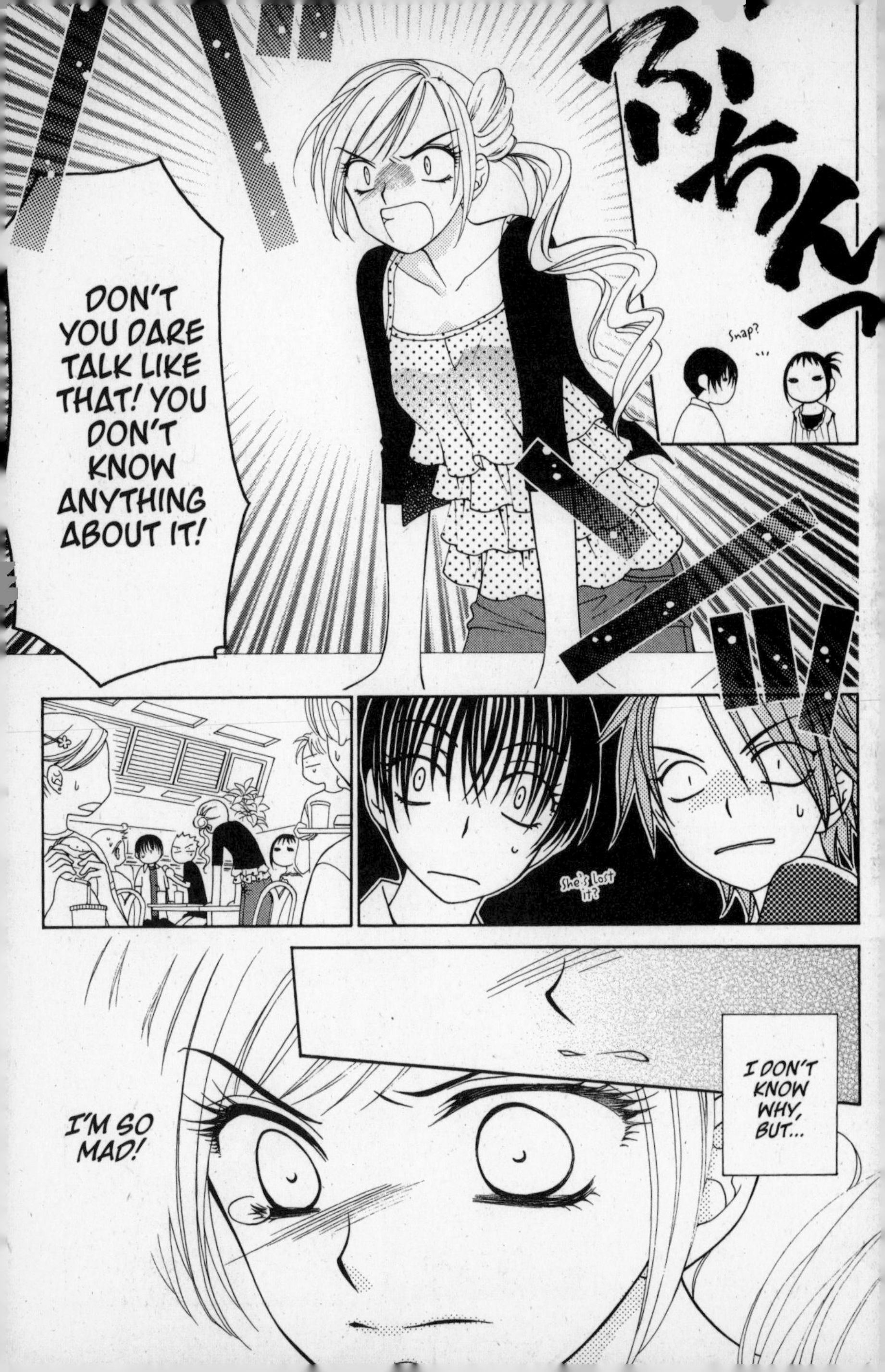
ふわん
Snap?
...
DON'T YOU DARE TALK LIKE THAT! YOU DON'T KNOW ANYTHING ABOUT IT!
She's lost it
I DON'T KNOW WHY, BUT...
I'M SO MAD!

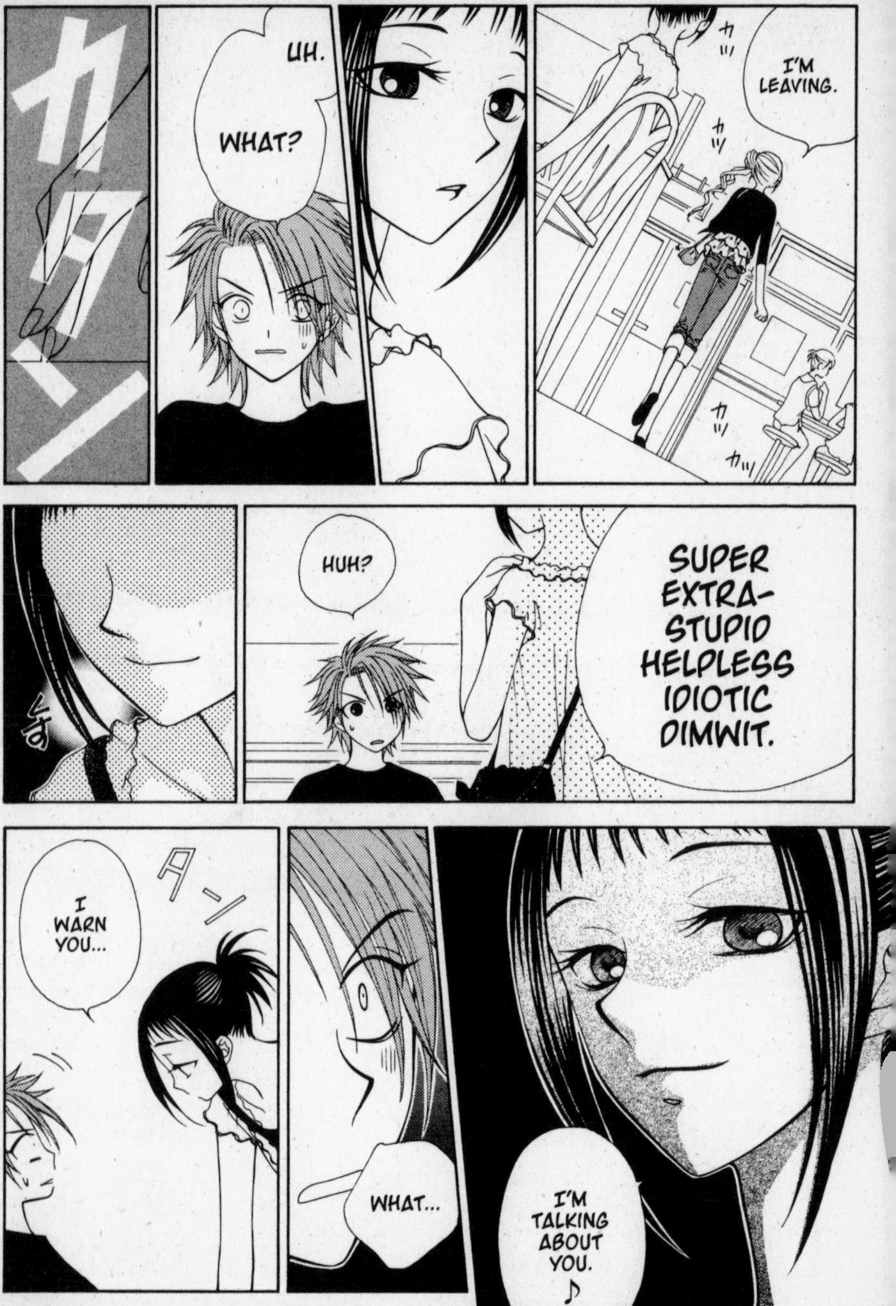
I'M LEAVING.
カツ
カツ
カツ
カツ
UH.
WHAT?
カタン
SUPER EXTRA-STUPID HELPLESS IDIOTIC DIMWIT.
HUH?
I'M TALKING ABOUT YOU. ♪
WHAT...
I WARN YOU...
ターン

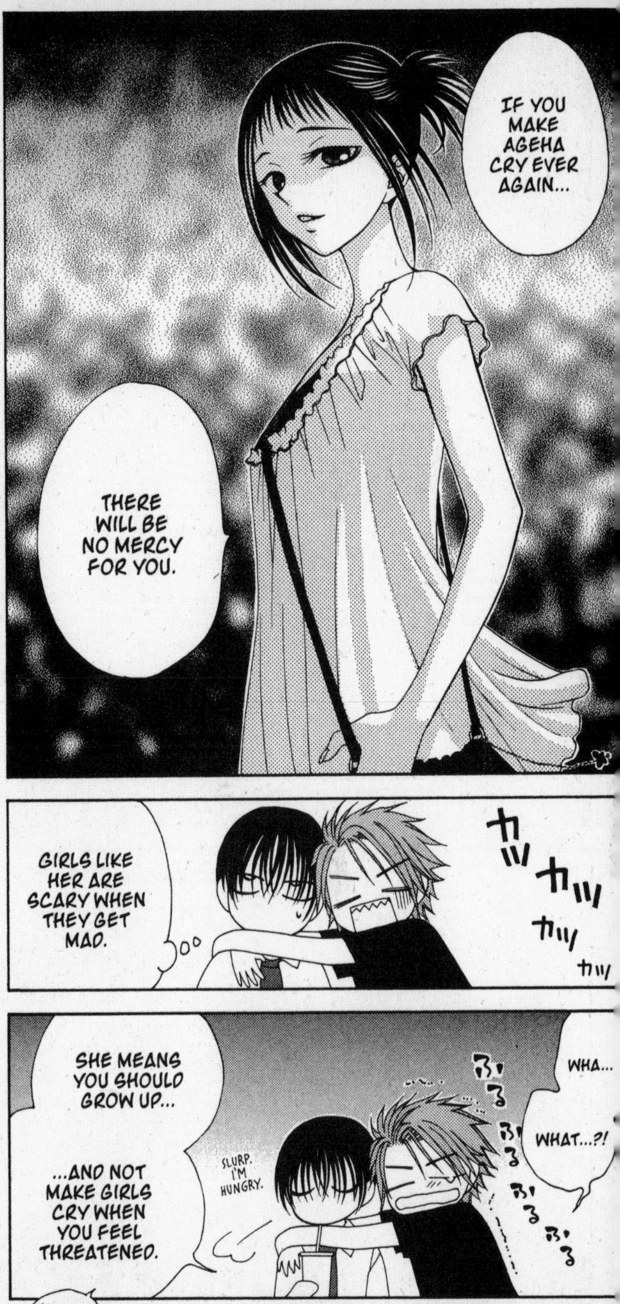
IF YOU MAKE AGEHA CRY EVER AGAIN...
THERE WILL BE NO MERCY FOR YOU.
カッ
カッ
カッ
カッ
GIRLS LIKE HER ARE SCARY WHEN THEY GET MAD.
WHA...
WHAT...?!
ふる
ふる
ふる
ふる
SLURP. I'M HUNGRY.
SHE MEANS YOU SHOULD GROW UP...
...AND NOT MAKE GIRLS CRY WHEN YOU FEEL THREATENED.

Rei grew up to become super dry.

Although that was pretty scary.

Many of you readers who know my *Akiyoshi Family* series or *Next It's You* may be surprised. How can Rei be all grown up now? For those who do not know him from earlier, that's fine (LOL) No problem story-wise. (But for those who are interested, please take a look!) Promoting in a small voice. ♪

I love it when characters cross over from one series to another.

But it's funny how Rei grew up influenced by his two older sisters. He still resembles Kazuha.

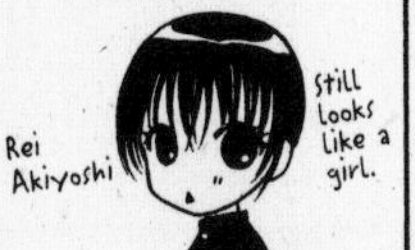
Rei Akiyoshi
Still looks like a girl.
High school 1st Year

I hope to write stories about the other characters, but I want this story to focus on Ageha. I really need to stop Ageha from getting involved with all these other people! Good luck to me! Good luck to Ageha!! Somehow it will all come together.

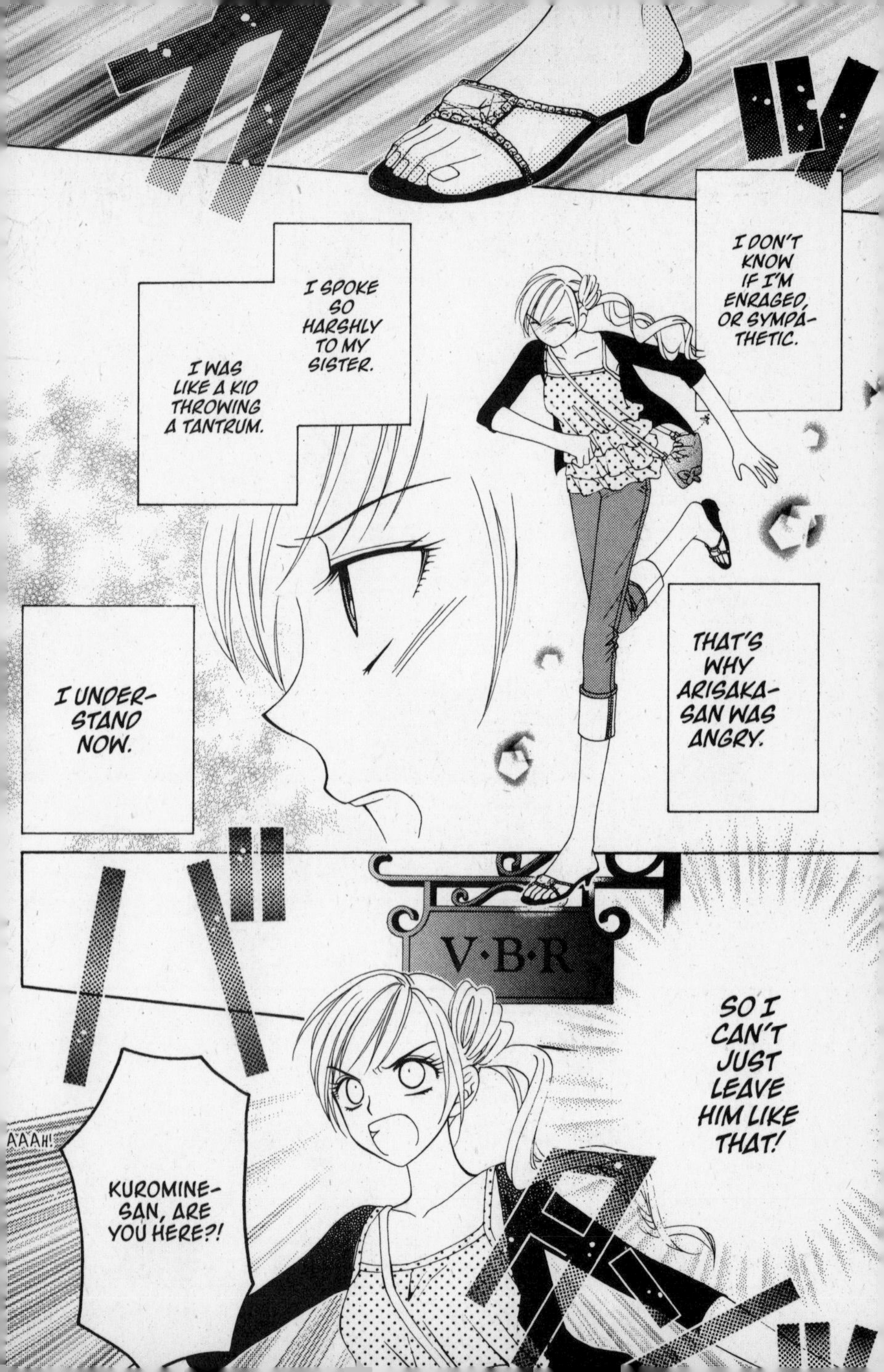

I DON'T KNOW IF I'M ENRAGED, OR SYMPATHETIC.
I SPOKE SO HARSHLY TO MY SISTER.
I WAS LIKE A KID THROWING A TANTRUM.
THAT'S WHY ARISAKA-SAN WAS ANGRY.
I UNDER-STAND NOW.
V·B·R
SO I CAN'T JUST LEAVE HIM LIKE THAT!
KUROMINE-SAN, ARE YOU HERE?!
AAAH!

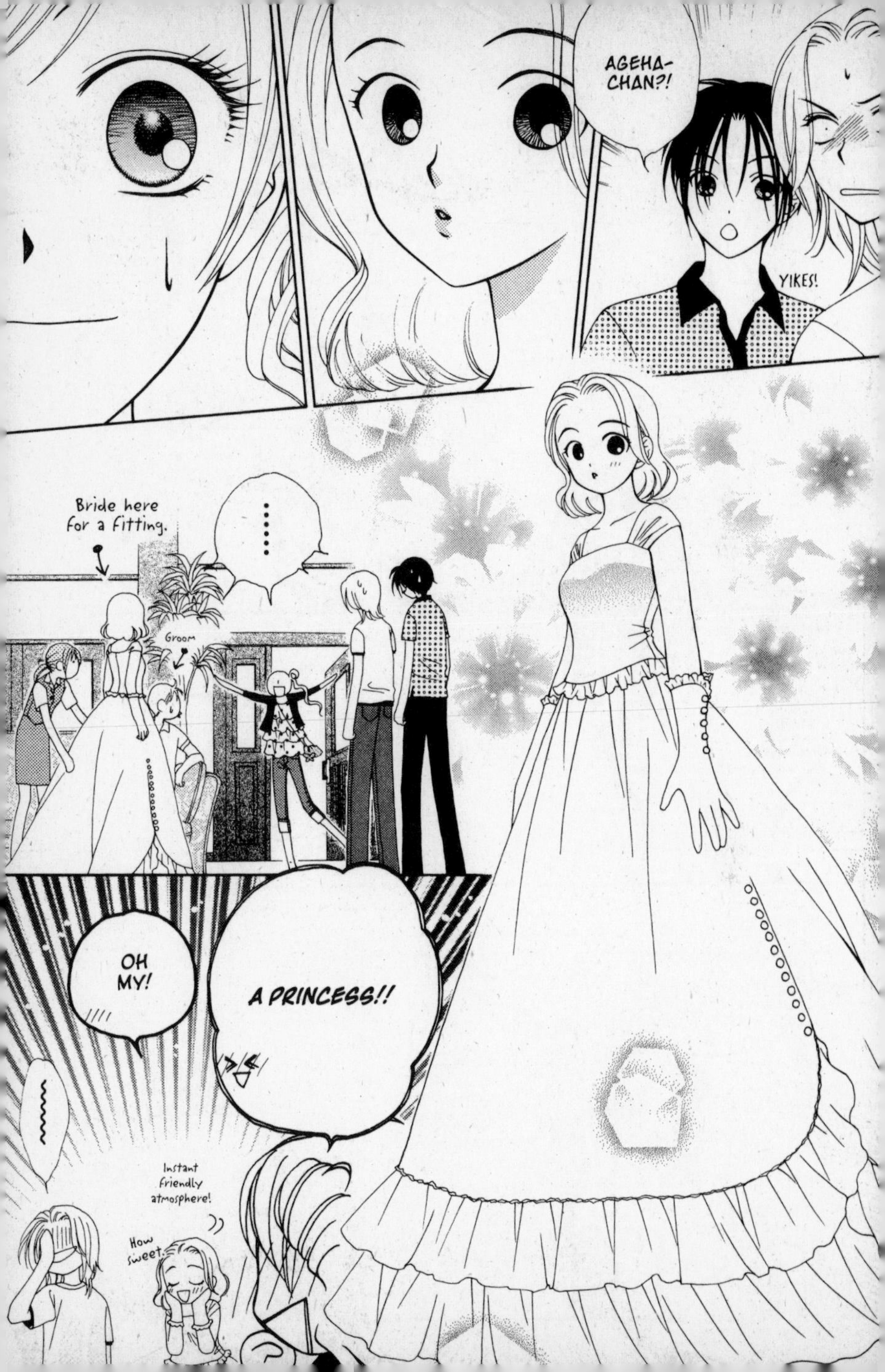
AGEHA-CHAN?!
YIKES!
Bride here for a fitting.
......
Groom
A PRINCESS!!
OH MY!
Instant friendly atmosphere!
How sweet.

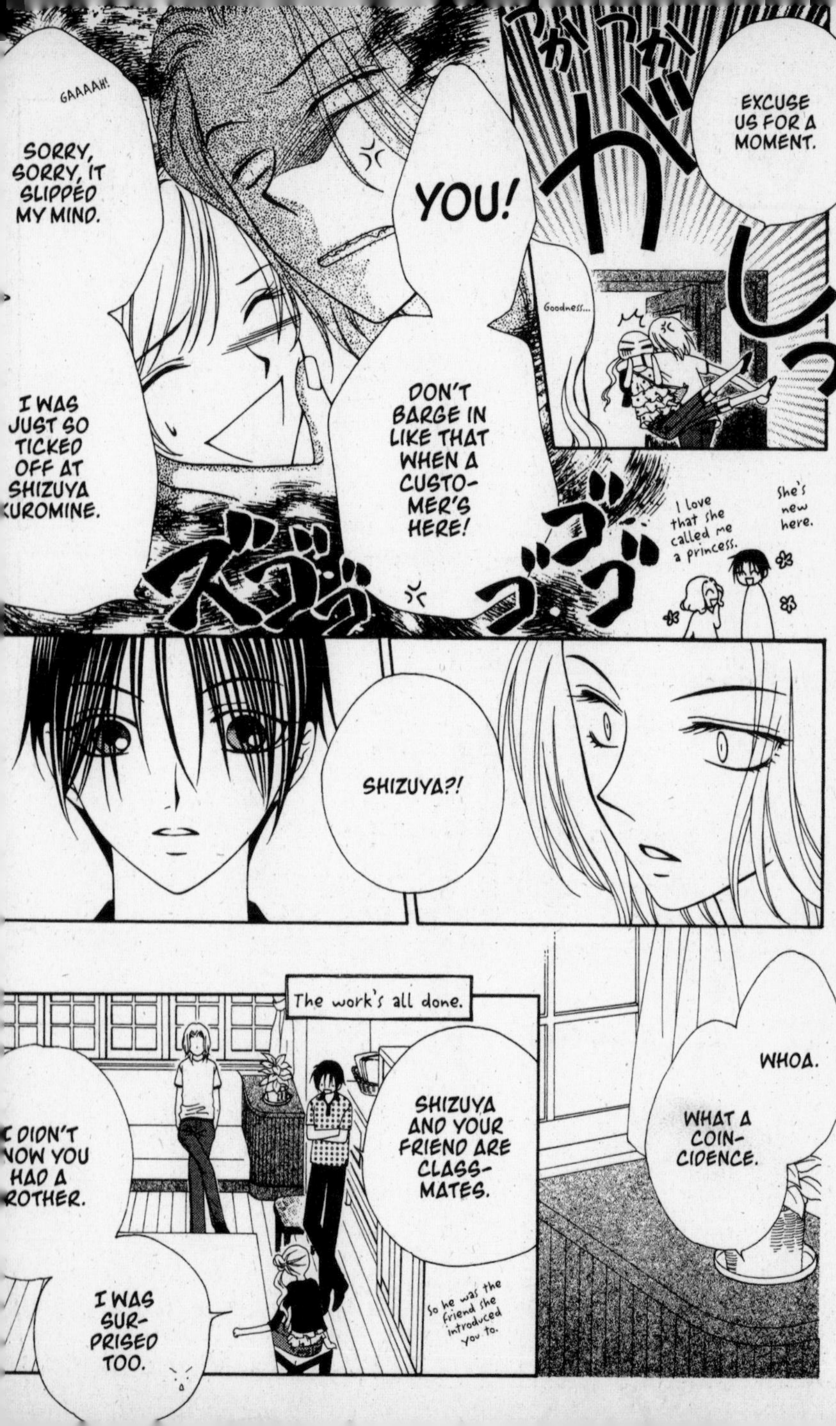
EXCUSE US FOR A MOMENT.
Goodness...
YOU!
DON'T BARGE IN LIKE THAT WHEN A CUSTOMER'S HERE!
GAAAAH!
SORRY, SORRY, IT SLIPPED MY MIND.
I WAS JUST SO TICKED OFF AT SHIZUYA KUROMINE.
She's new here.
I love that she called me a princess.
SHIZUYA?!
WHOA.
WHAT A COINCIDENCE.
The work's all done.
SHIZUYA AND YOUR FRIEND ARE CLASSMATES.
So he was the friend she introduced you to.
C DIDN'T NOW YOU HAD A ROTHER.
I WAS SURPRISED TOO.

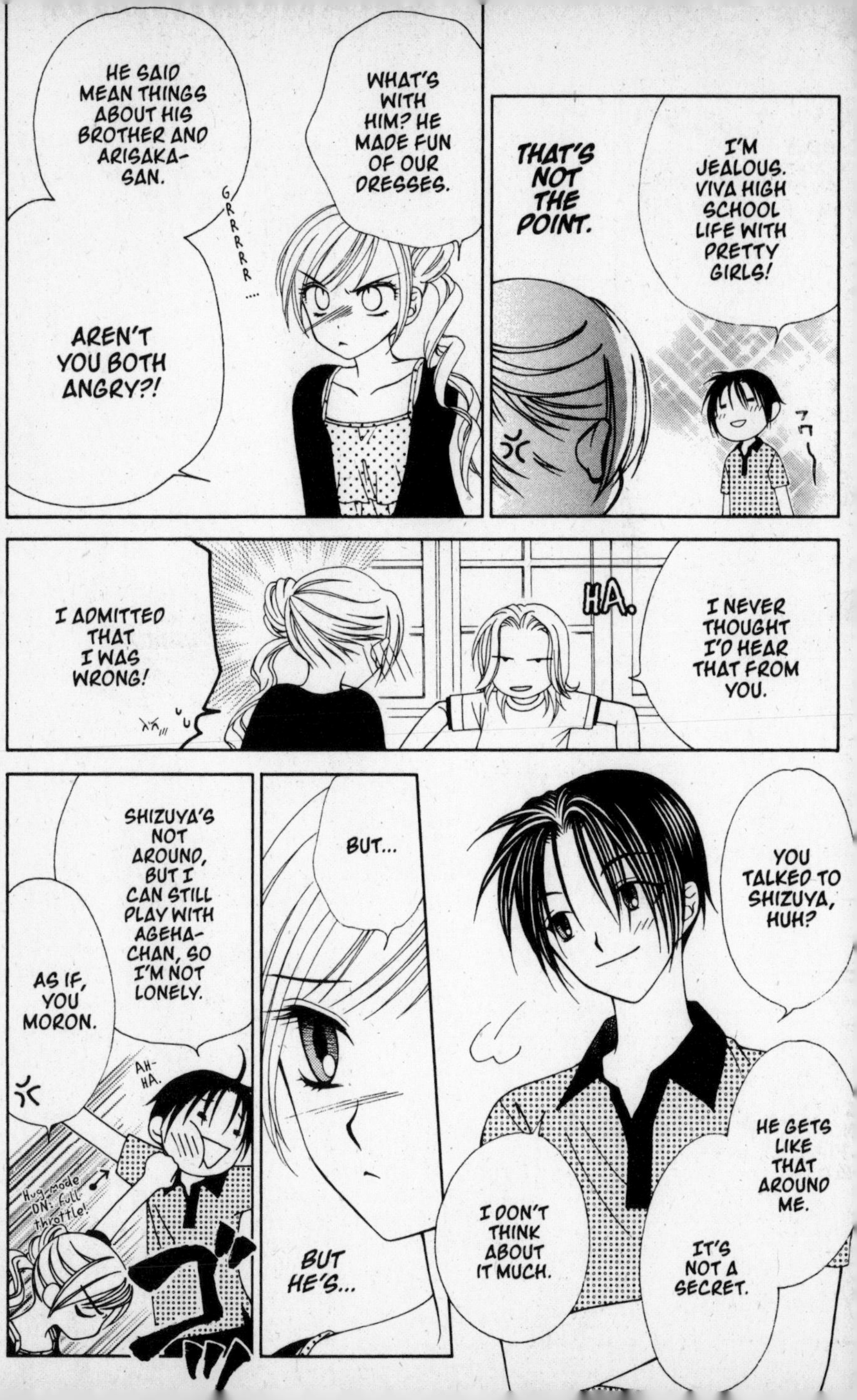
I'M JEALOUS. VIVA HIGH SCHOOL LIFE WITH PRETTY GIRLS!
THAT'S NOT THE POINT.
WHAT'S WITH HIM? HE MADE FUN OF OUR DRESSES.
HE SAID MEAN THINGS ABOUT HIS BROTHER AND ARISAKA-SAN.
GRRRRRR....
AREN'T YOU BOTH ANGRY?!
HA.
I NEVER THOUGHT I'D HEAR THAT FROM YOU.
I ADMITTED THAT I WAS WRONG!
YOU TALKED TO SHIZUYA, HUH?
BUT...
HE GETS LIKE THAT AROUND ME.
IT'S NOT A SECRET.
I DON'T THINK ABOUT IT MUCH.
BUT HE'S...
SHIZUYA'S NOT AROUND, BUT I CAN STILL PLAY WITH AGEHA-CHAN, SO I'M NOT LONELY.
AS IF, YOU MORON.
AH-HA.
Hug-mode ON: full-throttle!

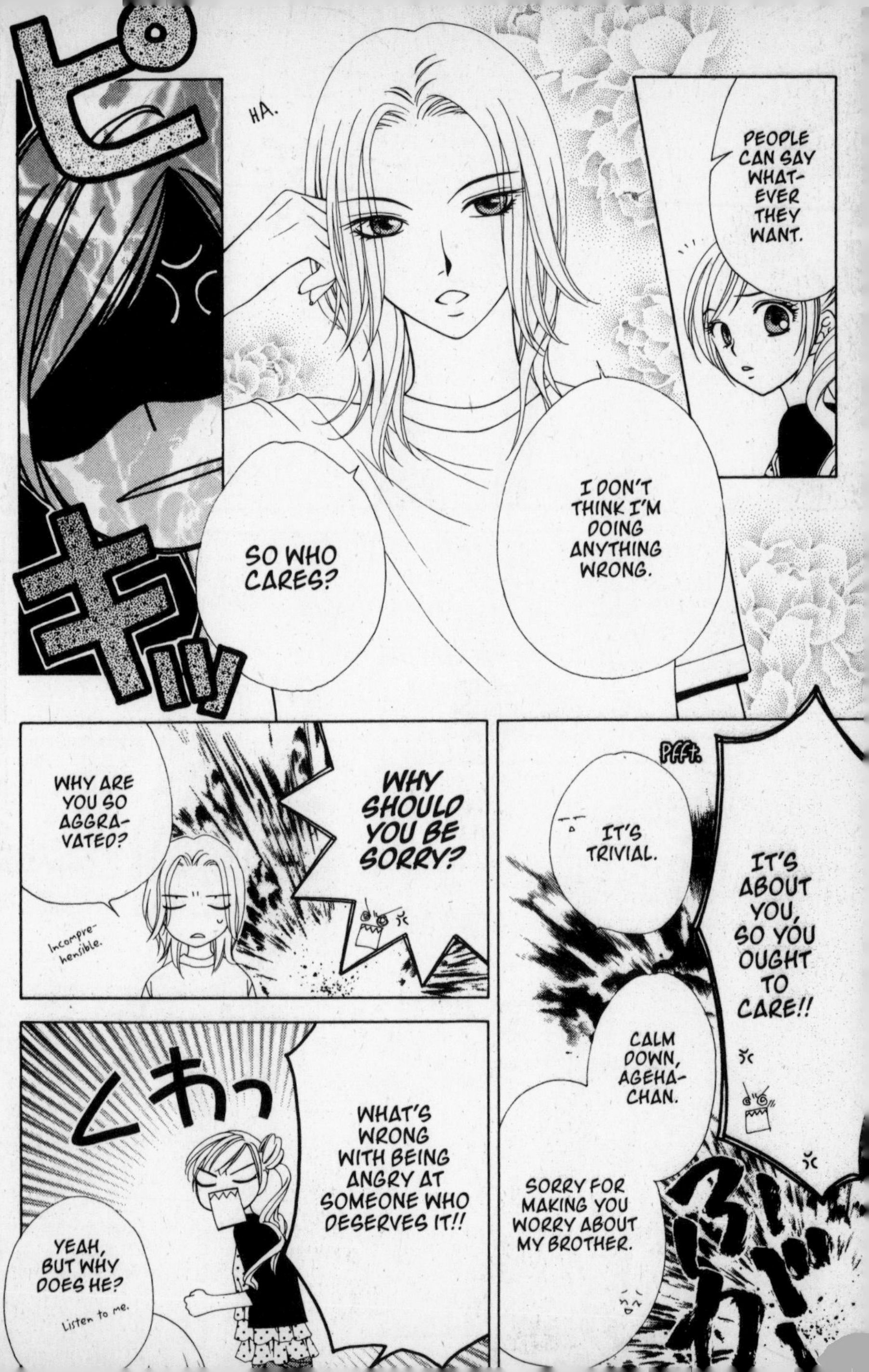
PEOPLE CAN SAY WHAT-EVER THEY WANT.
HA.
I DON'T THINK I'M DOING ANYTHING WRONG.
SO WHO CARES?
ピキッ
PFFT.
IT'S TRIVIAL.
IT'S ABOUT YOU, SO YOU OUGHT TO CARE!!
CALM DOWN, AGEHA-CHAN.
SORRY FOR MAKING YOU WORRY ABOUT MY BROTHER.
WHY SHOULD YOU BE SORRY?
WHY ARE YOU SO AGGRA-VATED?
Incompre-hensible.
くわっ
WHAT'S WRONG WITH BEING ANGRY AT SOMEONE WHO DESERVES IT!!
YEAH, BUT WHY DOES HE?
Listen to me.

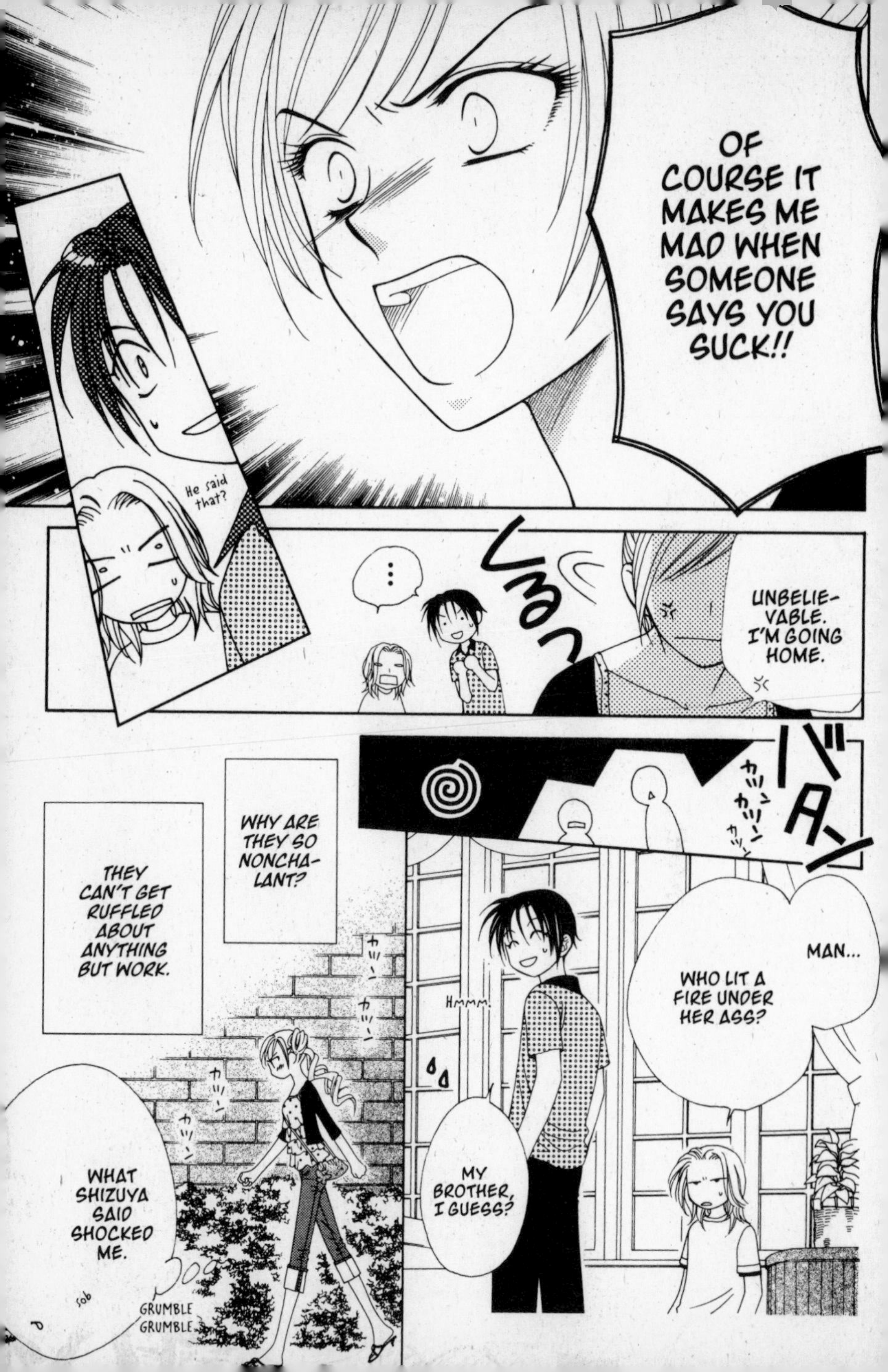
OF COURSE IT MAKES ME MAD WHEN SOMEONE SAYS YOU SUCK!!
He said that?
くるっ
UNBELIE-VABLE. I'M GOING HOME.
...
バタン
カツン カツン カツン
MAN...
WHO LIT A FIRE UNDER HER ASS?
MY BROTHER, I GUESS?
Hmmm.
WHY ARE THEY SO NONCHA-LANT?
THEY CAN'T GET RUFFLED ABOUT ANYTHING BUT WORK.
カツン カツン
カツン カツン
WHAT SHIZUYA SAID SHOCKED ME.
sob
GRUMBLE GRUMBLE

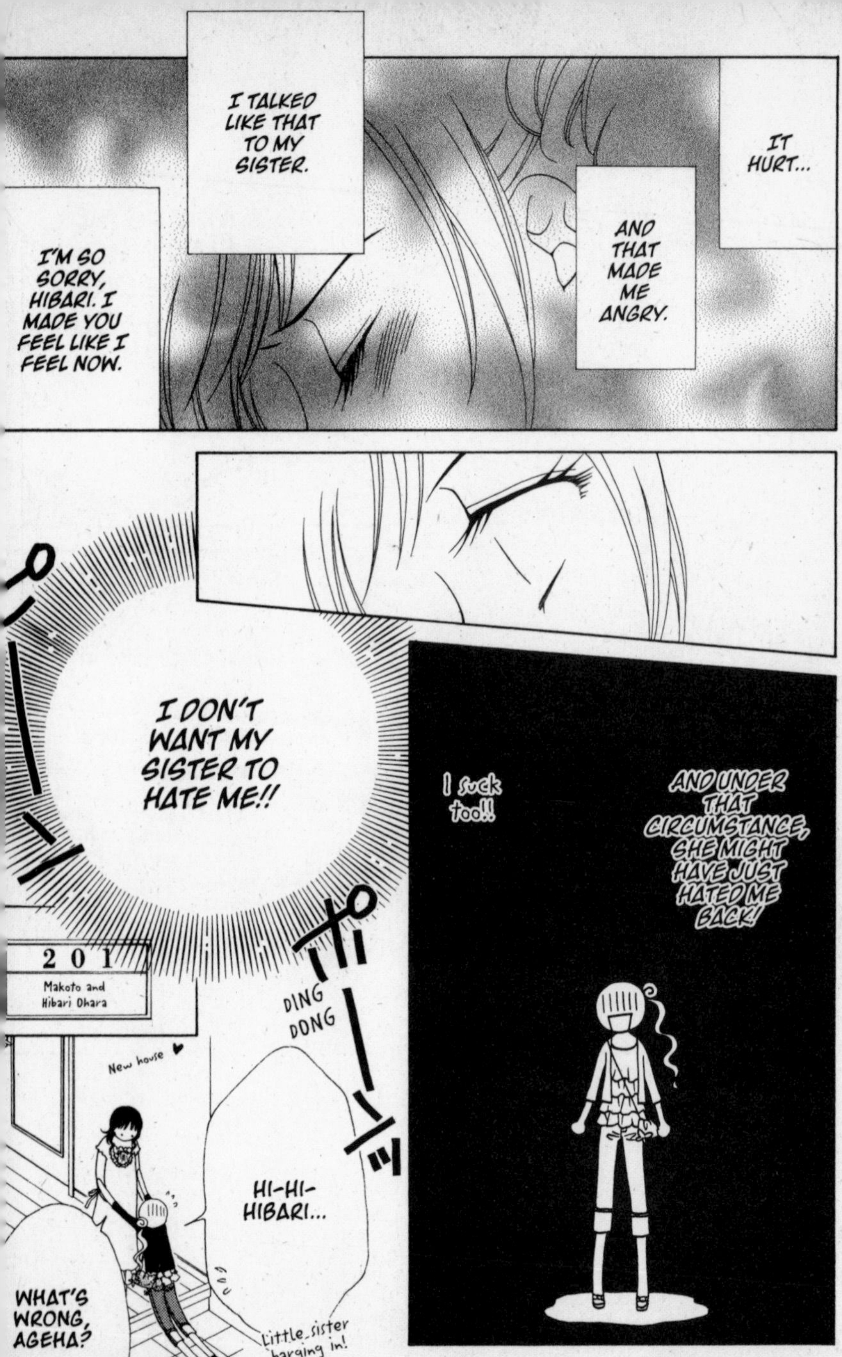
IT HURT...
AND THAT MADE ME ANGRY.
I TALKED LIKE THAT TO MY SISTER.
I'M SO SORRY, HIBARI. I MADE YOU FEEL LIKE I FEEL NOW.
I DON'T WANT MY SISTER TO HATE ME!!
AND UNDER THAT CIRCUMSTANCE, SHE MIGHT HAVE JUST HATED ME BACK!
I suck too!!
201
Makoto and Hibari Ohara
DING DONG
New house ♥
HI-HI-HIBARI...
WHAT'S WRONG, AGEHA?
Little sister barging in!

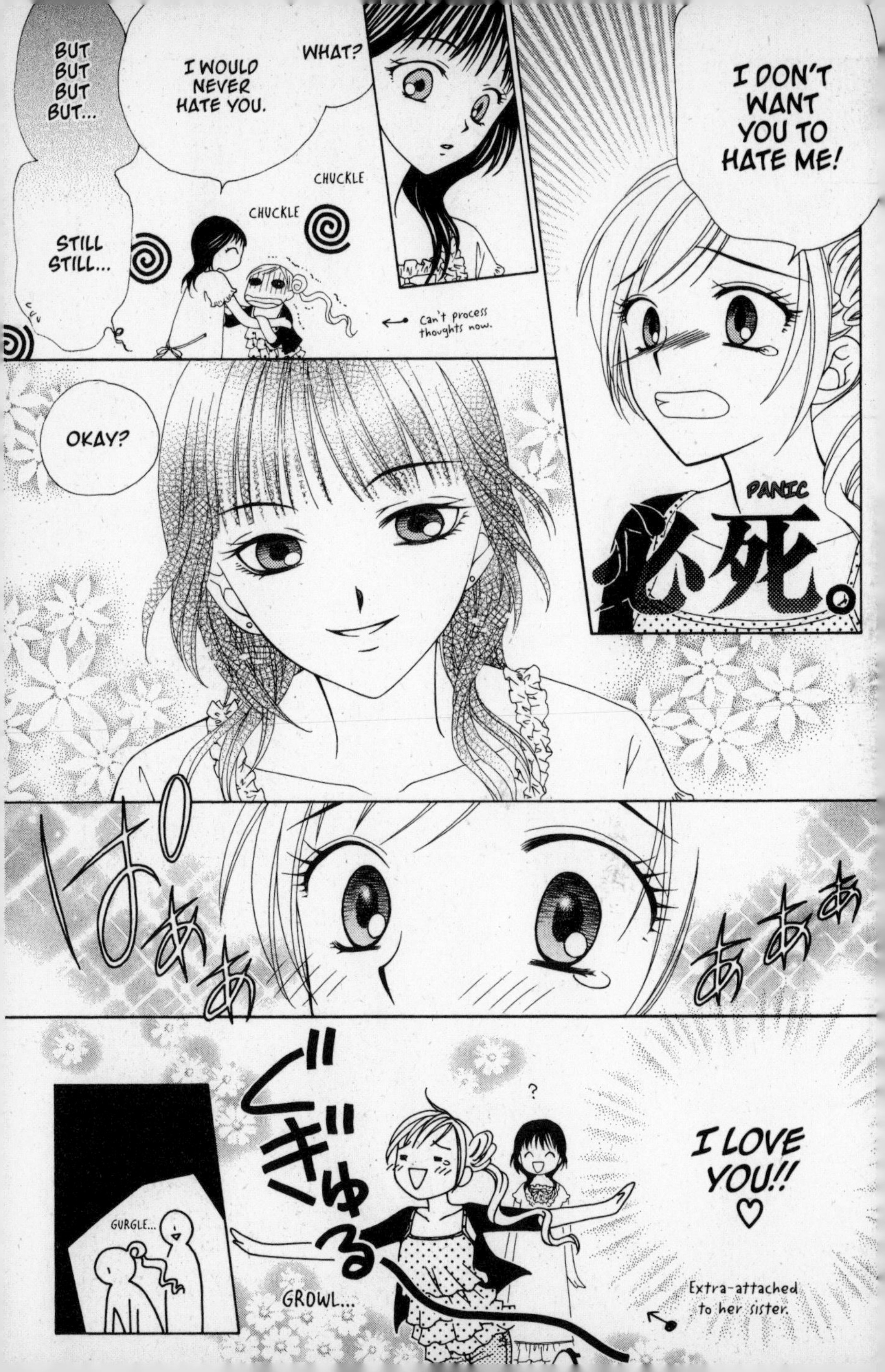
I DON'T WANT YOU TO HATE ME!
PANIC
必死。
WHAT?
I WOULD NEVER HATE YOU.
BUT BUT BUT BUT...
STILL STILL...
CHUCKLE
CHUCKLE
Can't process thoughts now.
OKAY?
I LOVE YOU!! ♡
Extra-attached to her sister.
ぎゅる
?
GROWL...
GURGLE...

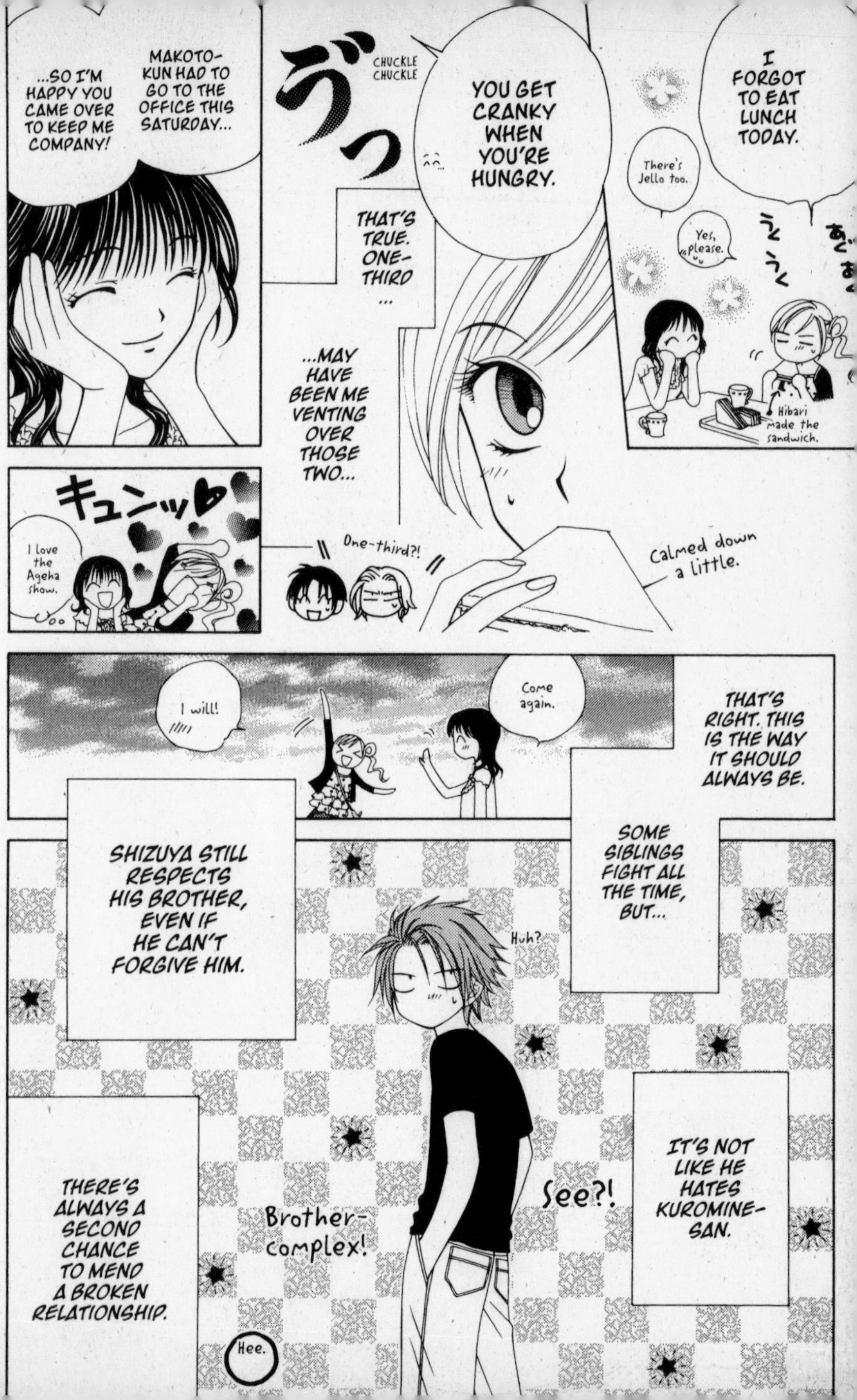
I FORGOT TO EAT LUNCH TODAY.
There's Jello too.
Yes, please.
Hibari made the sandwich.
YOU GET CRANKY WHEN YOU'RE HUNGRY.
うっ
CHUCKLE CHUCKLE
THAT'S TRUE. ONE-THIRD...
...MAY HAVE BEEN ME VENTING OVER THOSE TWO...
One-third?!
Calmed down a little.
MAKOTO-KUN HAD TO GO TO THE OFFICE THIS SATURDAY...
...SO I'M HAPPY YOU CAME OVER TO KEEP ME COMPANY!
キュンッ
I love the Ageha show.
Come again.
I will!
THAT'S RIGHT. THIS IS THE WAY IT SHOULD ALWAYS BE.
SOME SIBLINGS FIGHT ALL THE TIME, BUT...
SHIZUYA STILL RESPECTS HIS BROTHER, EVEN IF HE CAN'T FORGIVE HIM.
Huh?
IT'S NOT LIKE HE HATES KUROMINE-SAN.
See?!
Brother-complex!
THERE'S ALWAYS A SECOND CHANCE TO MEND A BROKEN RELATIONSHIP.
Hee.

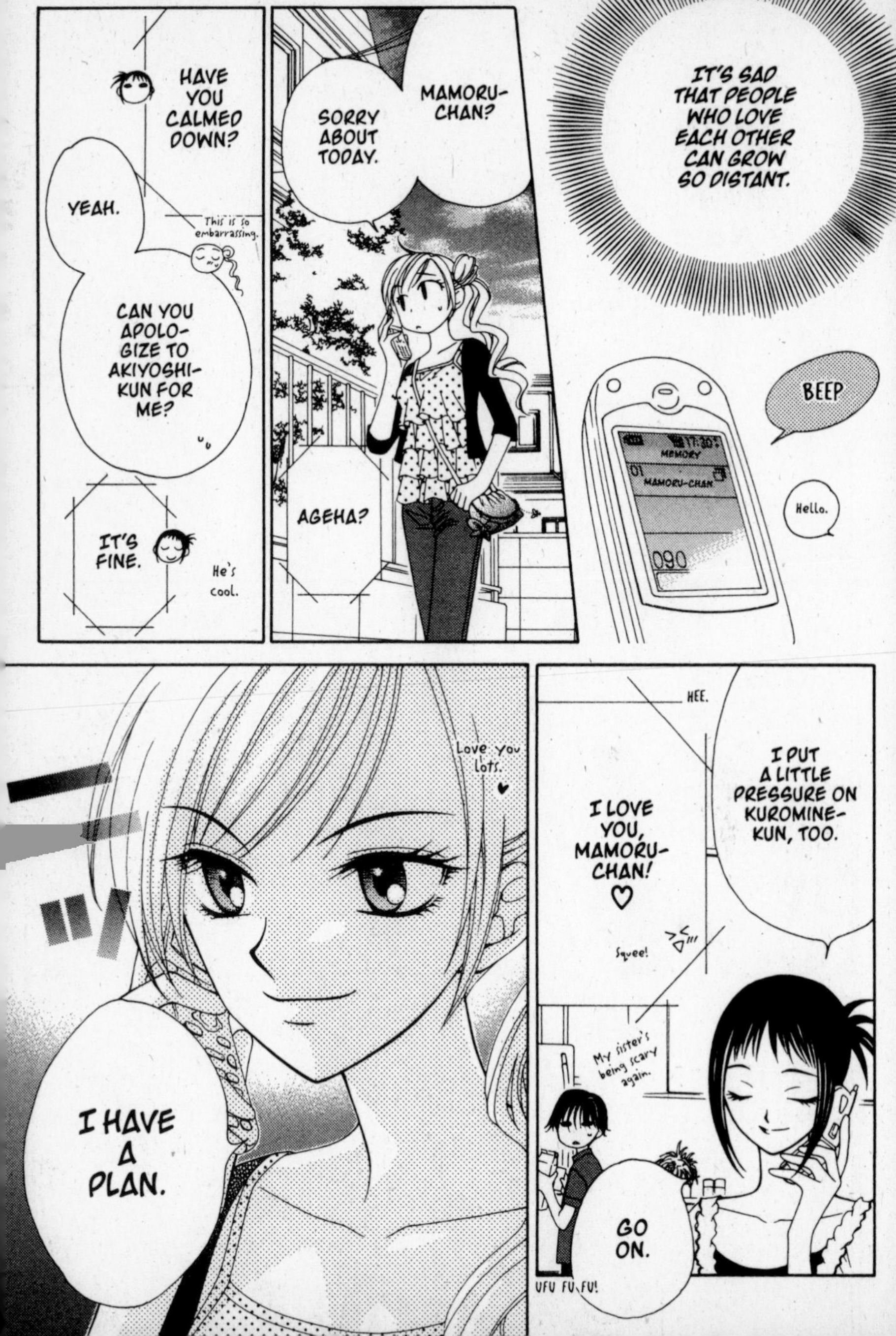
IT'S SAD THAT PEOPLE WHO LOVE EACH OTHER CAN GROW SO DISTANT.
BEEP
17:30
MEMORY
01
MAMORU-CHAN
090
Hello.
MAMORU-CHAN?
SORRY ABOUT TODAY.
AGEHA?
HAVE YOU CALMED DOWN?
YEAH.
This is so embarrassing.
CAN YOU APOLOGIZE TO AKIYOSHI-KUN FOR ME?
IT'S FINE.
He's cool.
HEE.
I PUT A LITTLE PRESSURE ON KUROMINE-KUN, TOO.
I LOVE YOU, MAMORU-CHAN! ♡
Squee!
My sister's being scary again.
GO ON.
UFU FU FU!
Love you lots. ♥
I HAVE A PLAN.

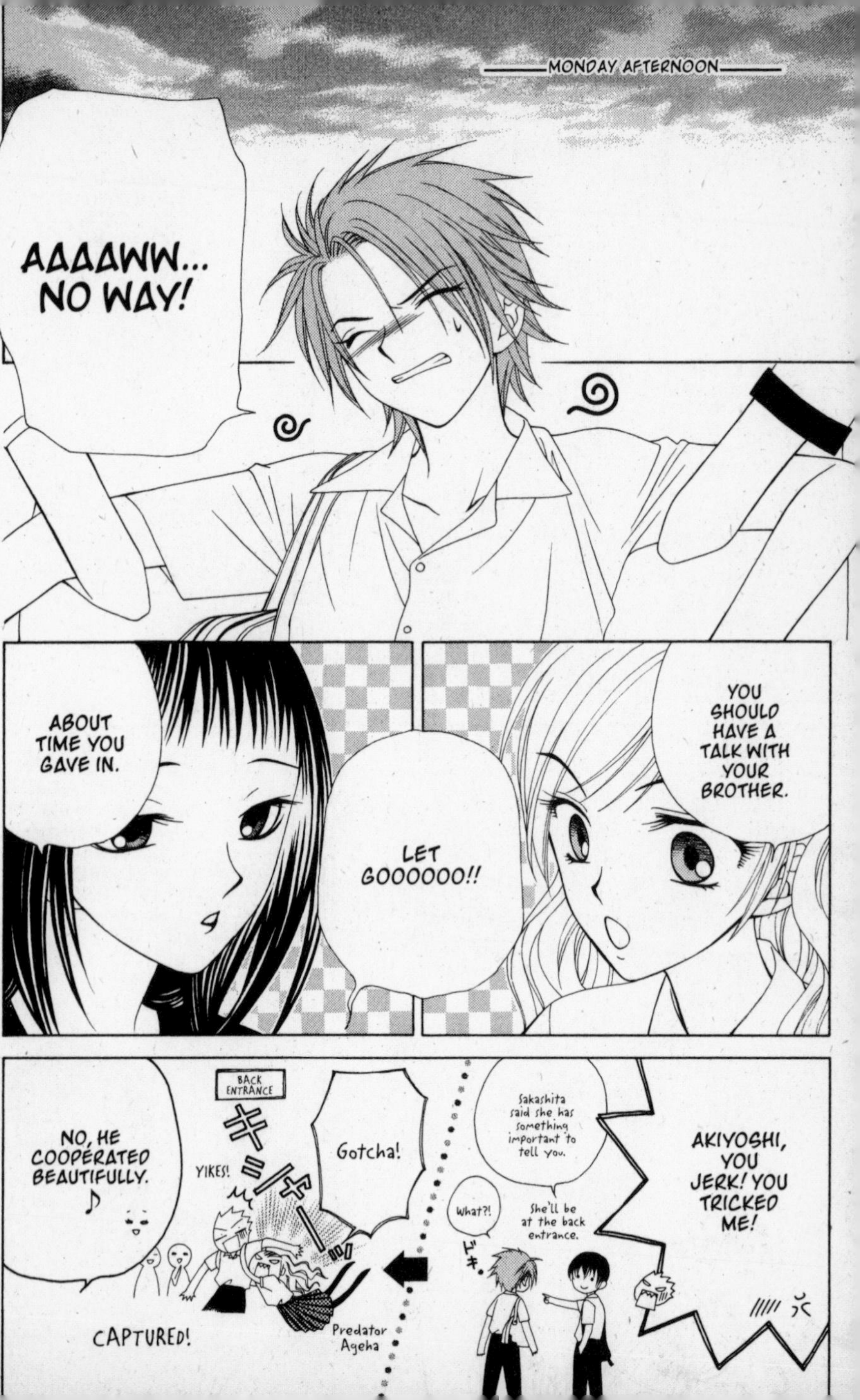

MONDAY AFTERNOON
AAAAWW... NO WAY!
YOU SHOULD HAVE A TALK WITH YOUR BROTHER.
LET GOOOOOO!!
ABOUT TIME YOU GAVE IN.
AKIYOSHI, YOU JERK! YOU TRICKED ME!
Sakashita said she has something important to tell you.
What?!
She'll be at the back entrance.
BACK ENTRANCE
Gotcha!
YIKES!
Predator Ageha
NO, HE COOPERATED BEAUTIFULLY. ♪
CAPTURED!

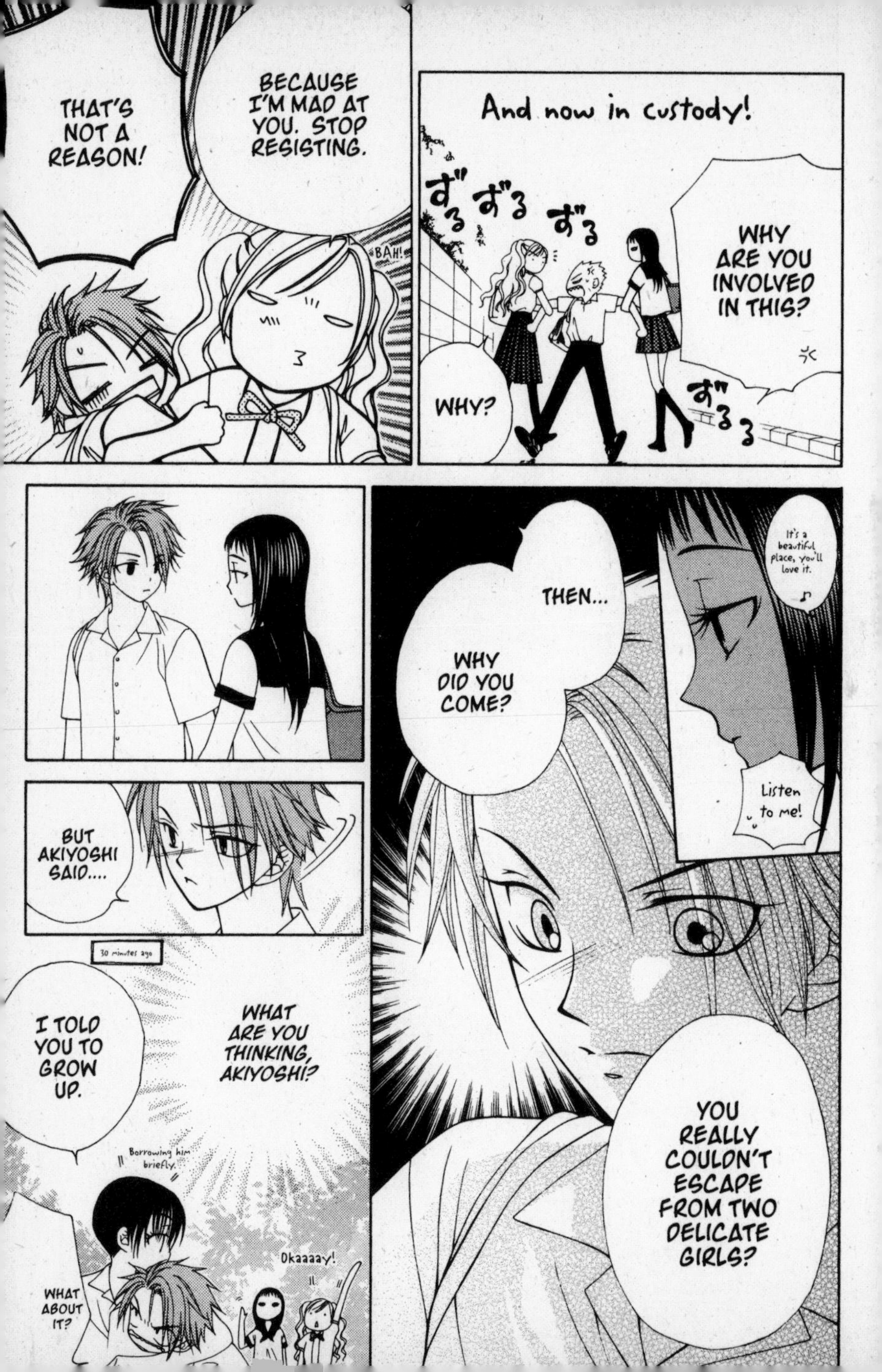
And now in custody!
WHY ARE YOU INVOLVED IN THIS?
ずるずる
ずる
ずるる
WHY?
BECAUSE I'M MAD AT YOU. STOP RESISTING.
BAH!
THAT'S NOT A REASON!
It's a beautiful place, you'll love it.
THEN...
WHY DID YOU COME?
Listen to me!
YOU REALLY COULDN'T ESCAPE FROM TWO DELICATE GIRLS?
BUT AKIYOSHI SAID....
30 minutes ago
WHAT ARE YOU THINKING, AKIYOSHI?
I TOLD YOU TO GROW UP.
Borrowing him briefly.
Okaaaay!
WHAT ABOUT IT?

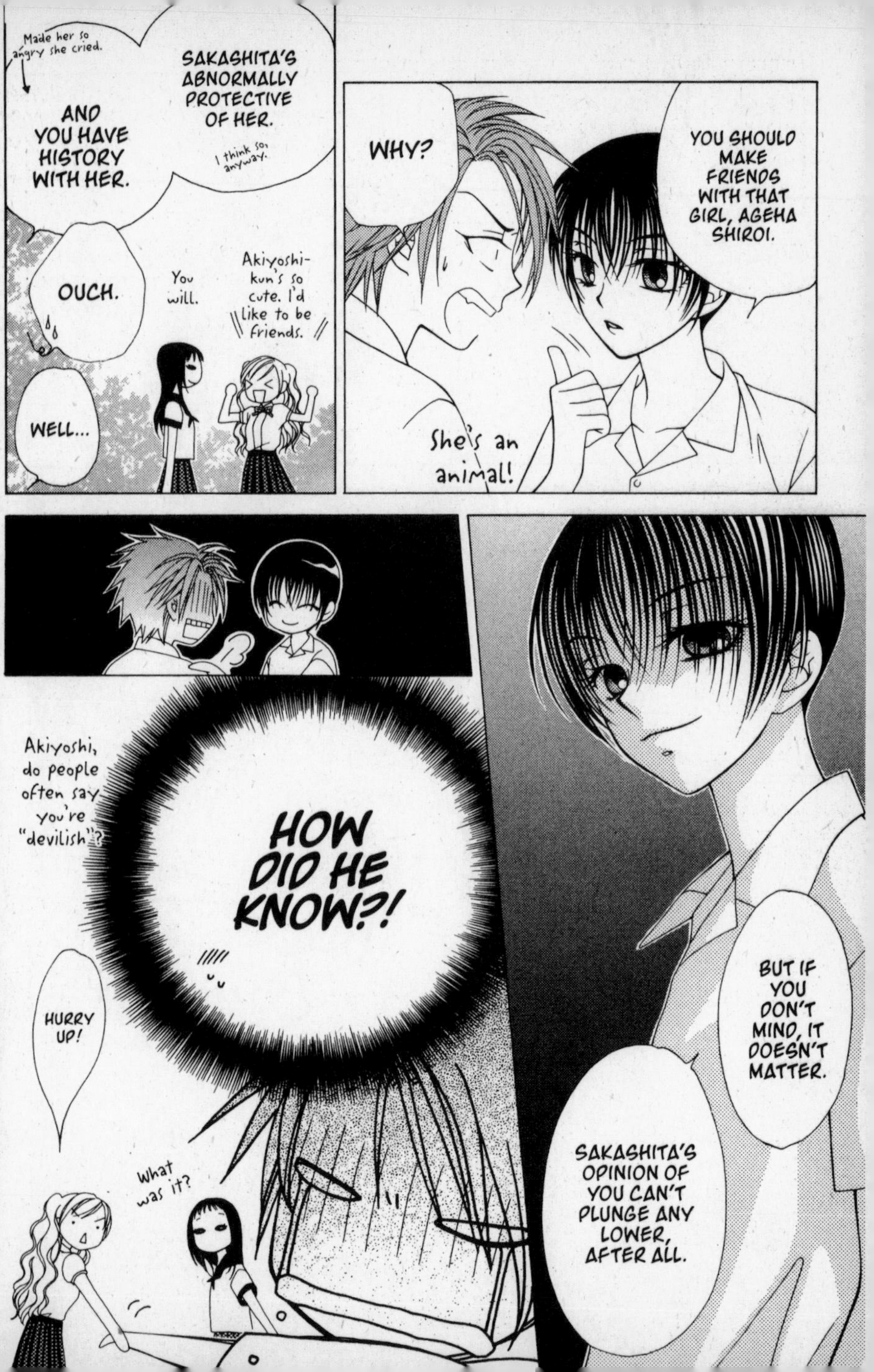

YOU SHOULD MAKE FRIENDS WITH THAT GIRL, AGEHA SHIROI.
WHY?
She's an animal!
SAKASHITA'S ABNORMALLY PROTECTIVE OF HER.
I think so, anyway.
AND YOU HAVE HISTORY WITH HER.
Made her so angry she cried.
OUCH.
WELL...
Akiyoshi-kun's so cute. I'd like to be friends.
You will.
BUT IF YOU DON'T MIND, IT DOESN'T MATTER.
SAKASHITA'S OPINION OF YOU CAN'T PLUNGE ANY LOWER, AFTER ALL.
HOW DID HE KNOW?!
Akiyoshi, do people often say you're "devilish"?
HURRY UP!
What was it?

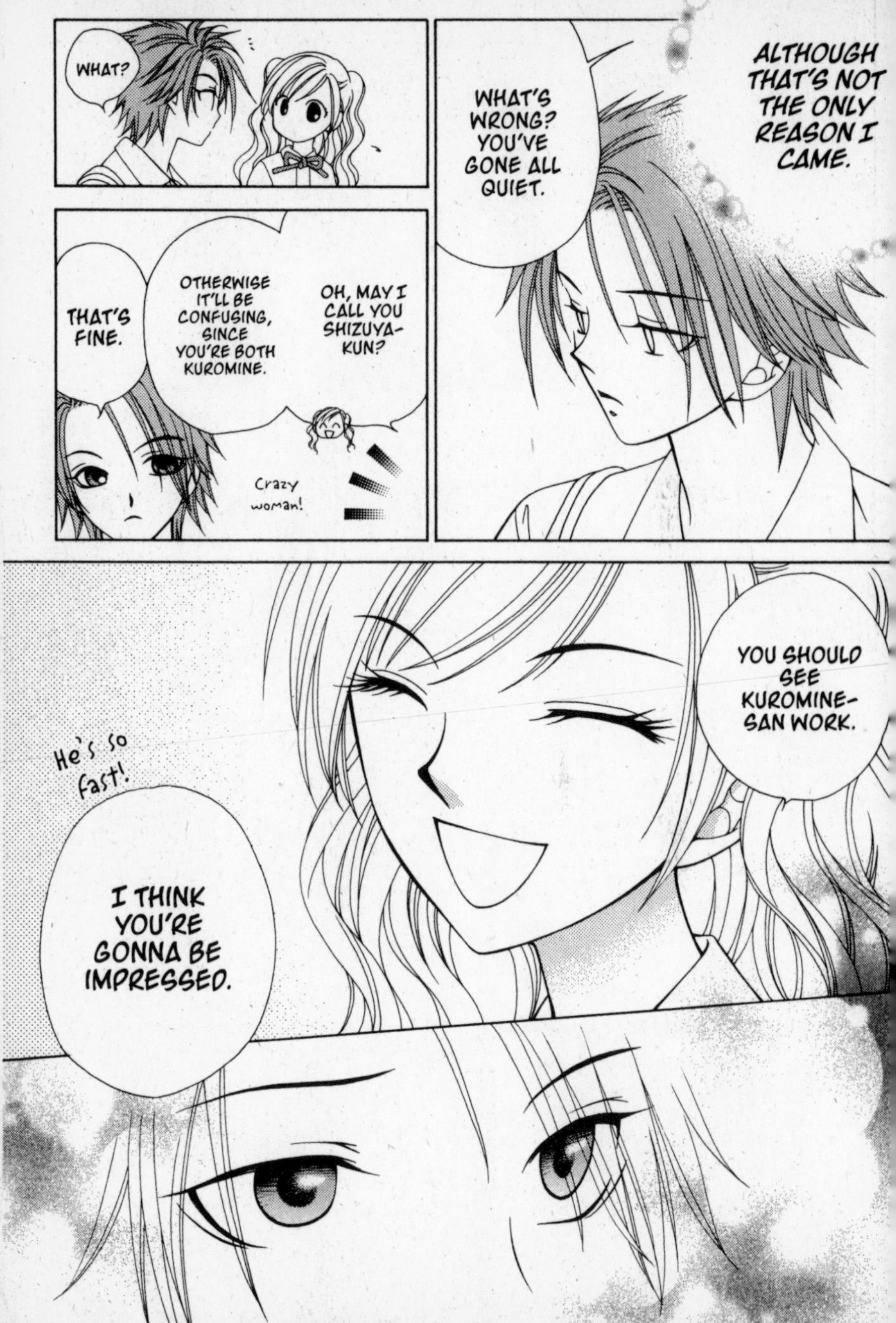
ALTHOUGH THAT'S NOT THE ONLY REASON I CAME.
WHAT'S WRONG? YOU'VE GONE ALL QUIET.
WHAT?
OH, MAY I CALL YOU SHIZUYA-KUN?
OTHERWISE IT'LL BE CONFUSING, SINCE YOU'RE BOTH KUROMINE.
THAT'S FINE.
Crazy woman!
YOU SHOULD SEE KUROMINE-SAN WORK.
He's so fast!
I THINK YOU'RE GONNA BE IMPRESSED.

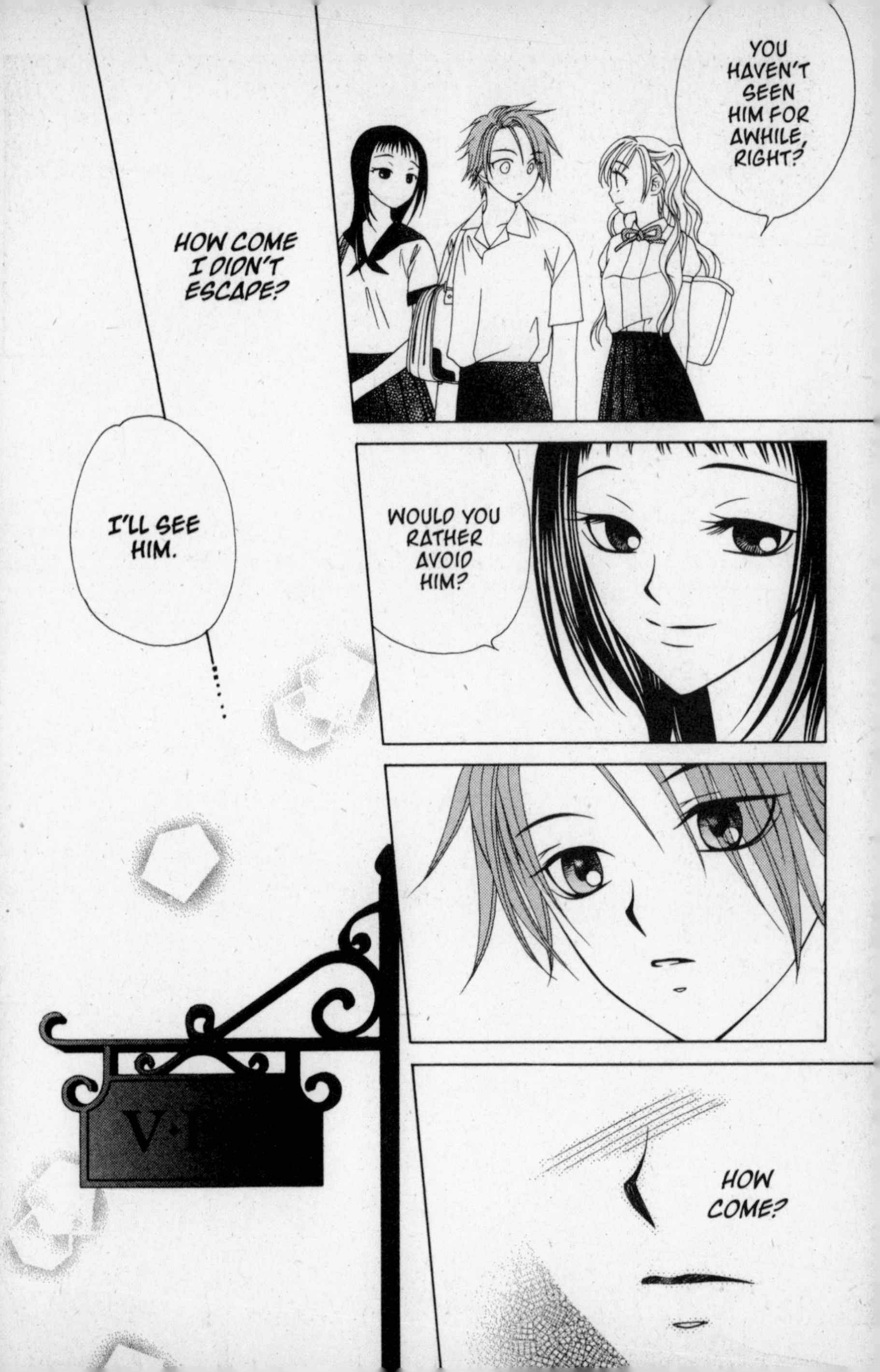
YOU HAVEN'T SEEN HIM FOR AWHILE, RIGHT?
HOW COME I DIDN'T ESCAPE?
WOULD YOU RATHER AVOID HIM?
I'LL SEE HIM.
.....
HOW COME?

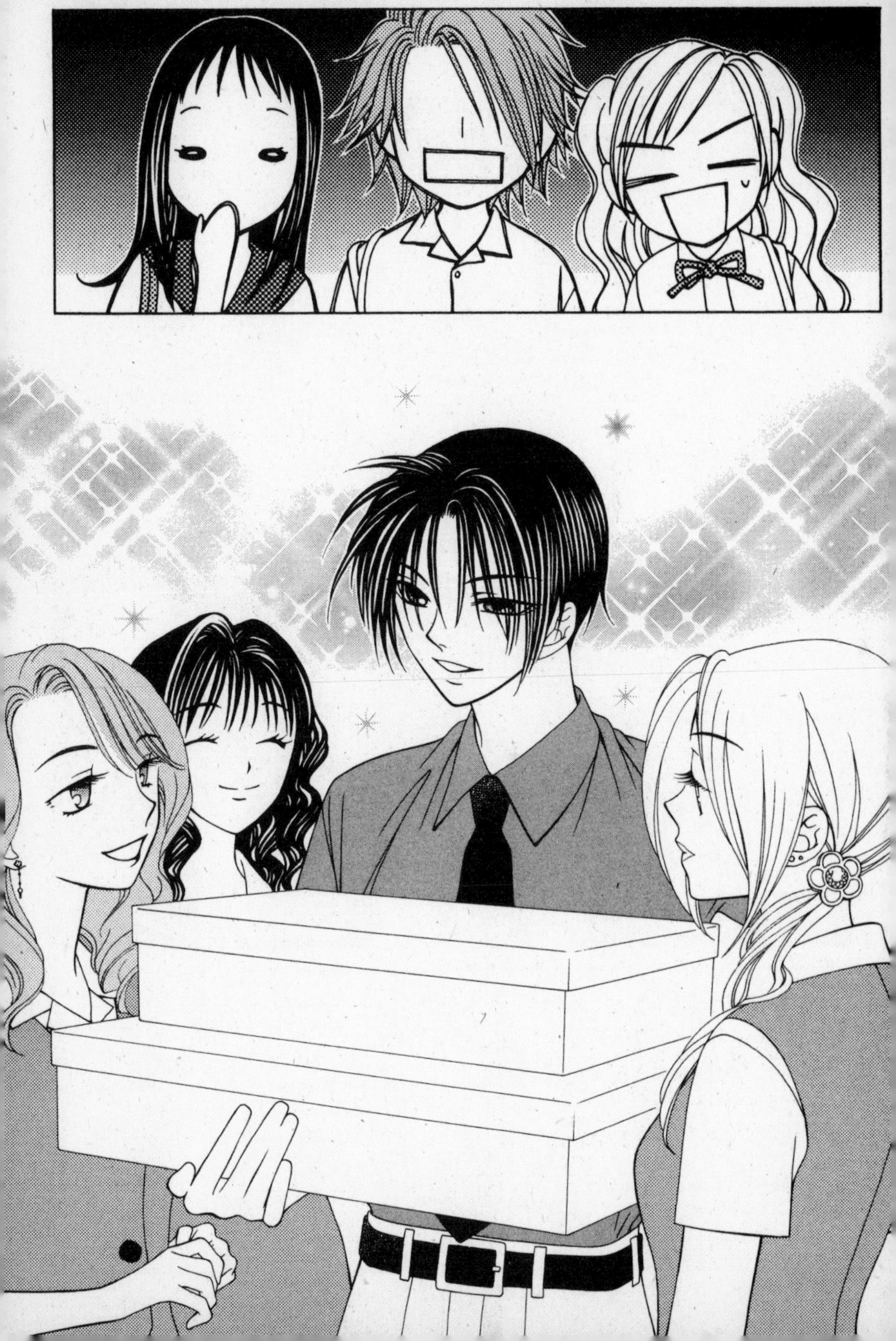

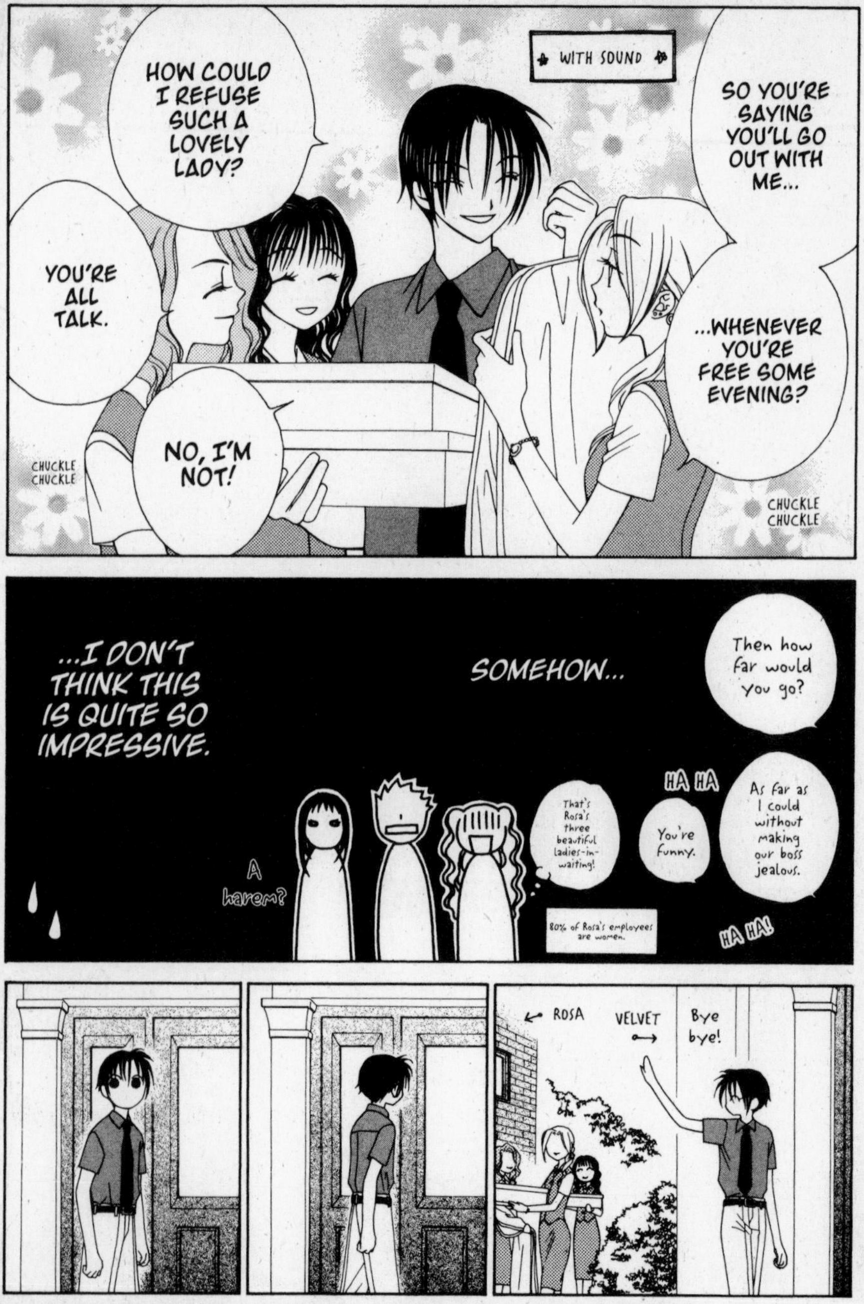
WITH SOUND
SO YOU'RE SAYING YOU'LL GO OUT WITH ME...
...WHENEVER YOU'RE FREE SOME EVENING?
CHUCKLE CHUCKLE
HOW COULD I REFUSE SUCH A LOVELY LADY?
YOU'RE ALL TALK.
NO, I'M NOT!
CHUCKLE CHUCKLE
Then how far would you go?
As far as I could without making our boss jealous.
HA HA
You're funny.
HA HA!
That's Rosa's three beautiful ladies-in-waiting!
80% of Rosa's employees are women.
SOMEHOW...
A harem?
...I DON'T THINK THIS IS QUITE SO IMPRESSIVE.
Bye bye!
VELVET
ROSA

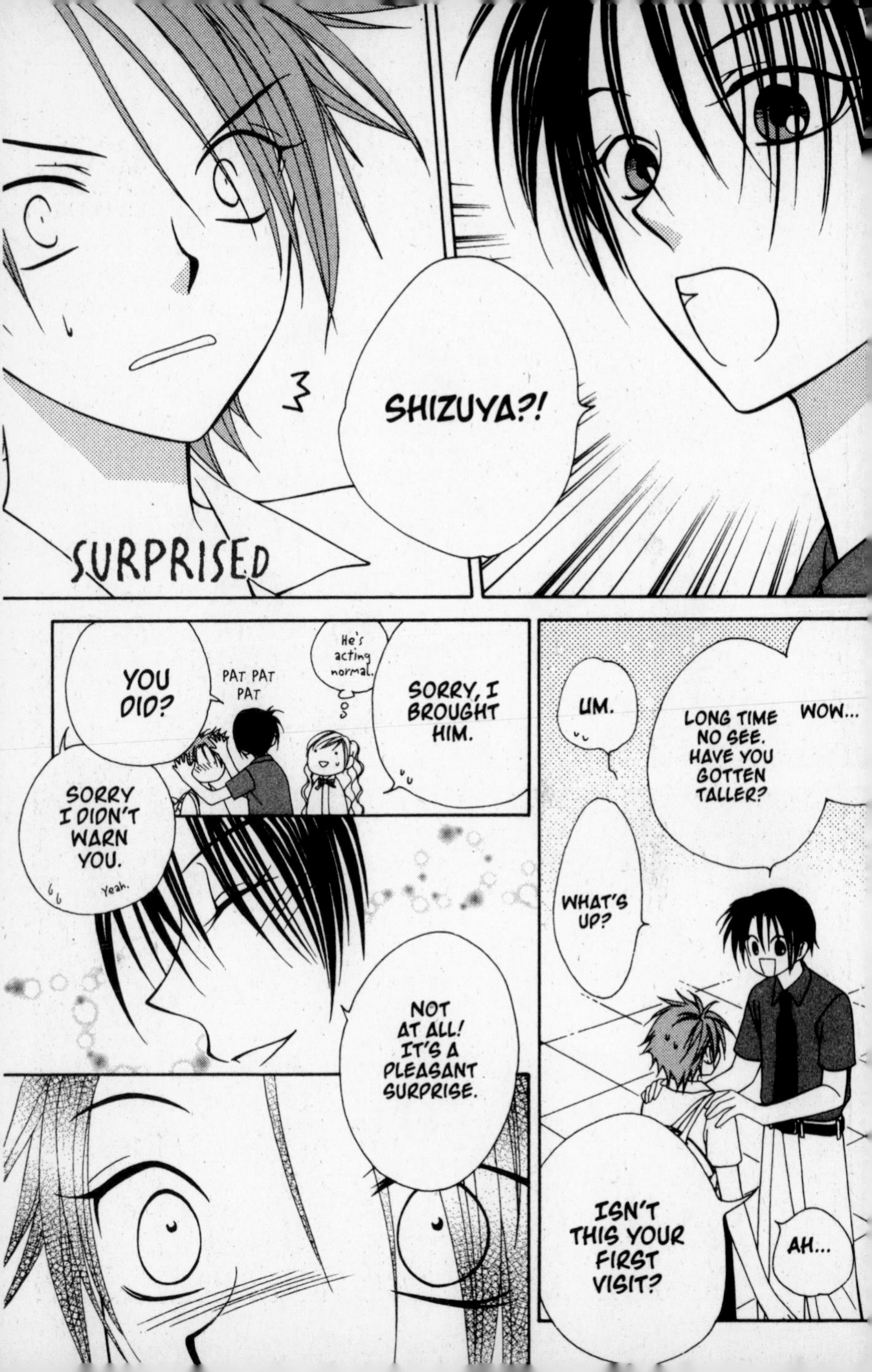
SHIZUYA?!
SURPRISED
WOW...
LONG TIME NO SEE. HAVE YOU GOTTEN TALLER?
UM.
WHAT'S UP?
AH...
ISN'T THIS YOUR FIRST VISIT?
SORRY, I BROUGHT HIM.
He's acting normal.
PAT PAT PAT
YOU DID?
SORRY I DIDN'T WARN YOU.
Yeah.
NOT AT ALL! IT'S A PLEASANT SURPRISE.

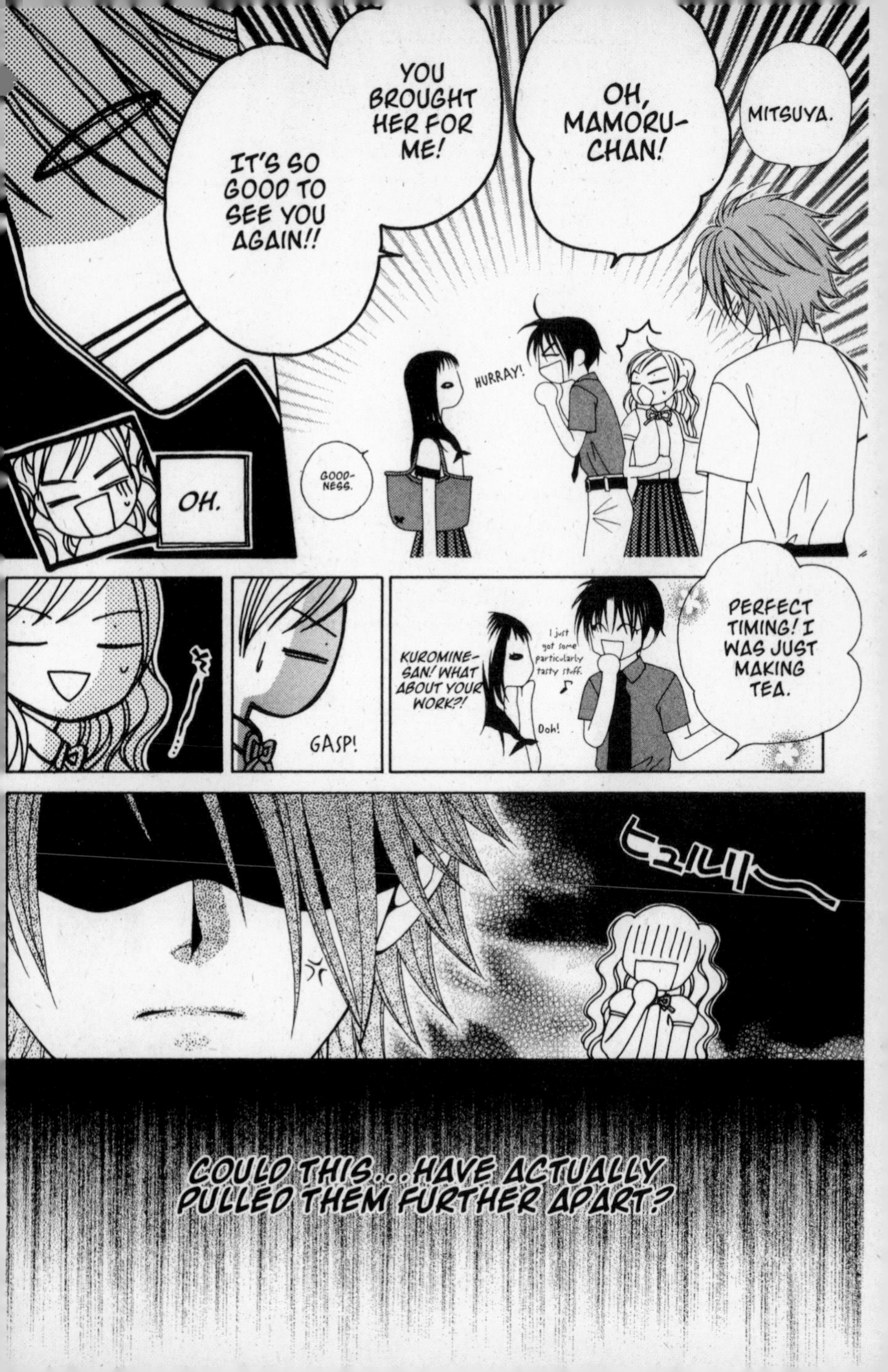
MITSUYA.
OH, MAMORU-CHAN!
YOU BROUGHT HER FOR ME!
IT'S SO GOOD TO SEE YOU AGAIN!!
HURRAY!
GOOD-NESS.
OH.
PERFECT TIMING! I WAS JUST MAKING TEA.
I just got some particularly tasty stuff.
Ooh!
KUROMINE-SAN! WHAT ABOUT YOUR WORK?!
GASP!
COULD THIS...HAVE ACTUALLY PULLED THEM FURTHER APART?

Instructions to Velvet V·6

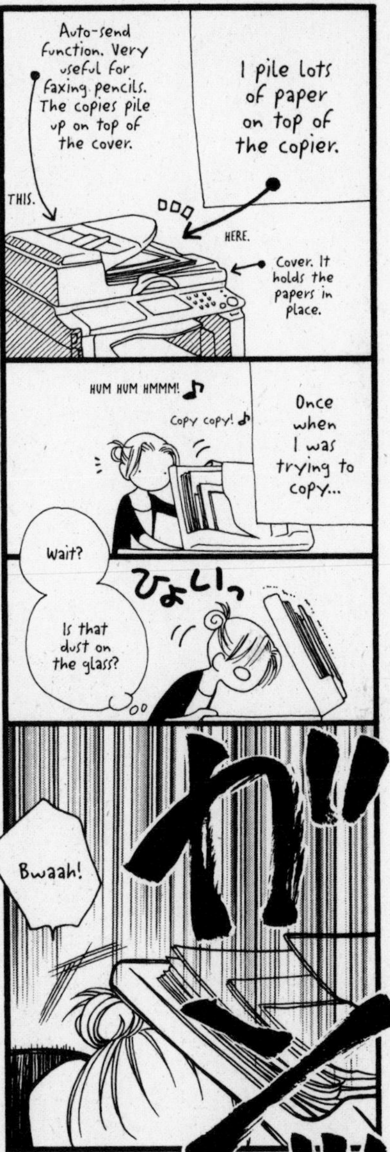
I pile lots of paper on top of the copier.
Auto-send function. Very useful for faxing pencils. The copies pile up on top of the cover.
THIS.
HERE.
Cover. It holds the papers in place.
Once when I was trying to copy...
HUM HUM HMMM!
Copy copy!
Wait?
ひょいっ
Is that dust on the glass?
Bwaah!

It really hurt.

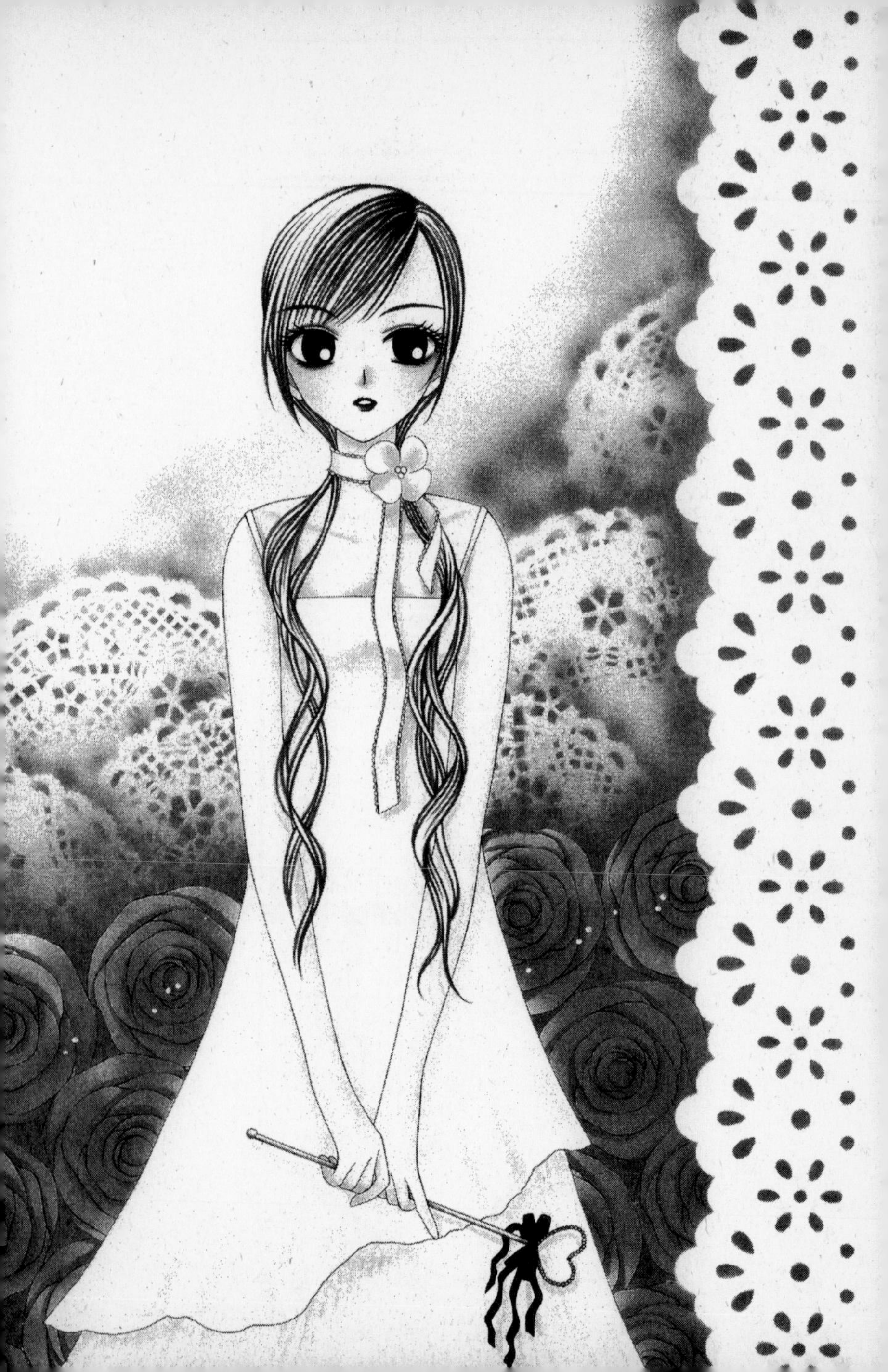

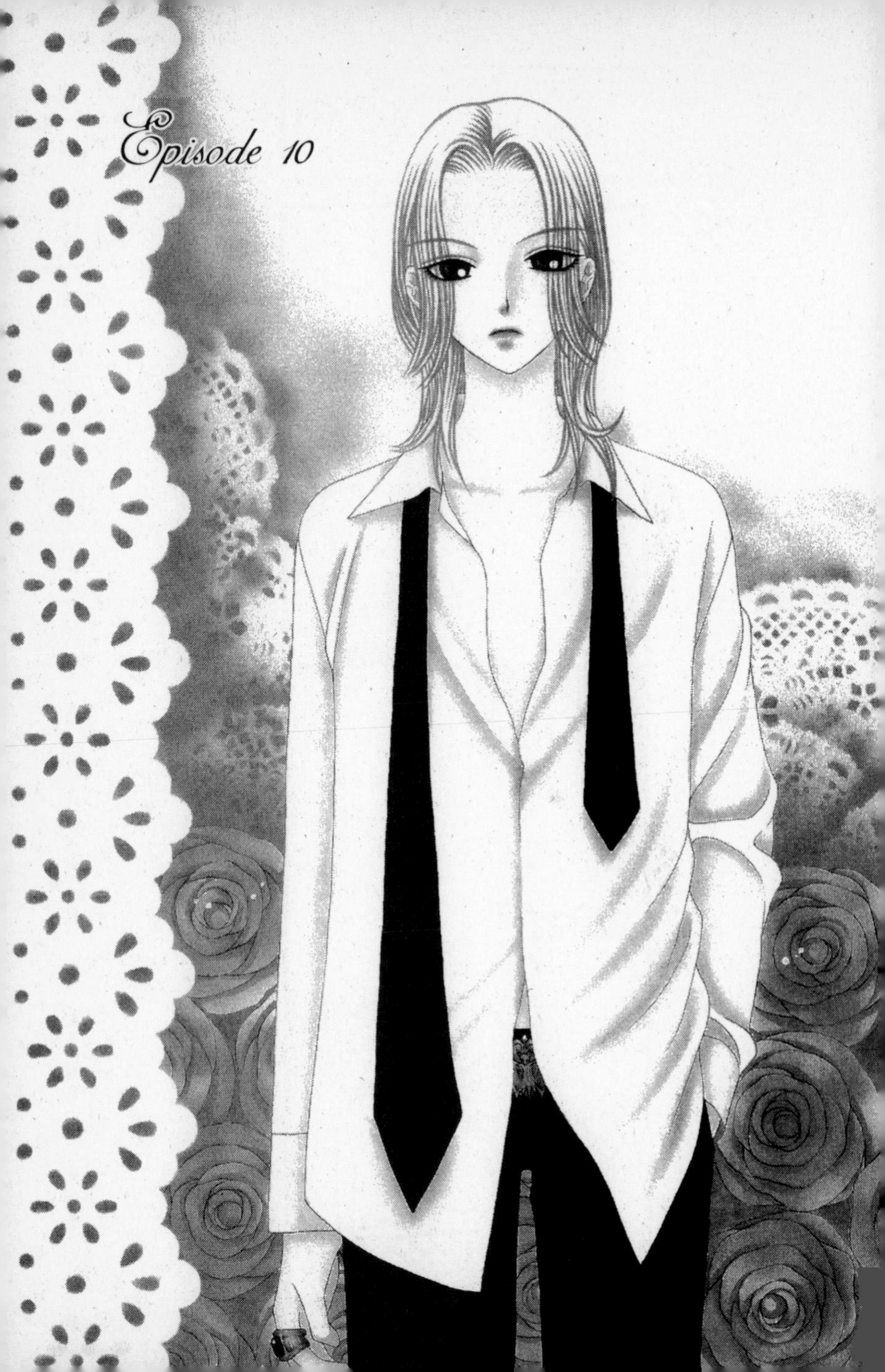
Episode 10

Instructions to Velvet V•7

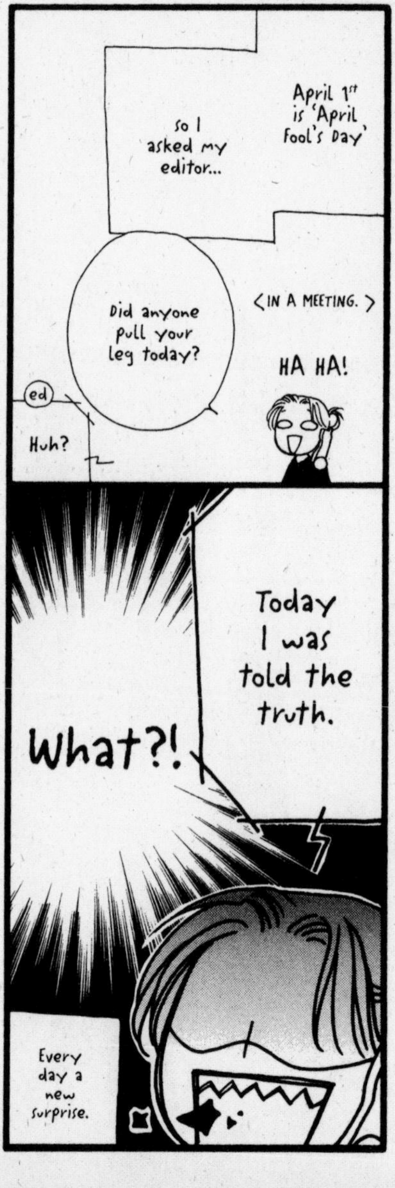
April 1st is 'April Fool's Day'
so I asked my editor...
<IN A MEETING.>
HA HA!
Did anyone pull your leg today?
ed
Huh?
Today I was told the truth.
What?!
Every day a new surprise.

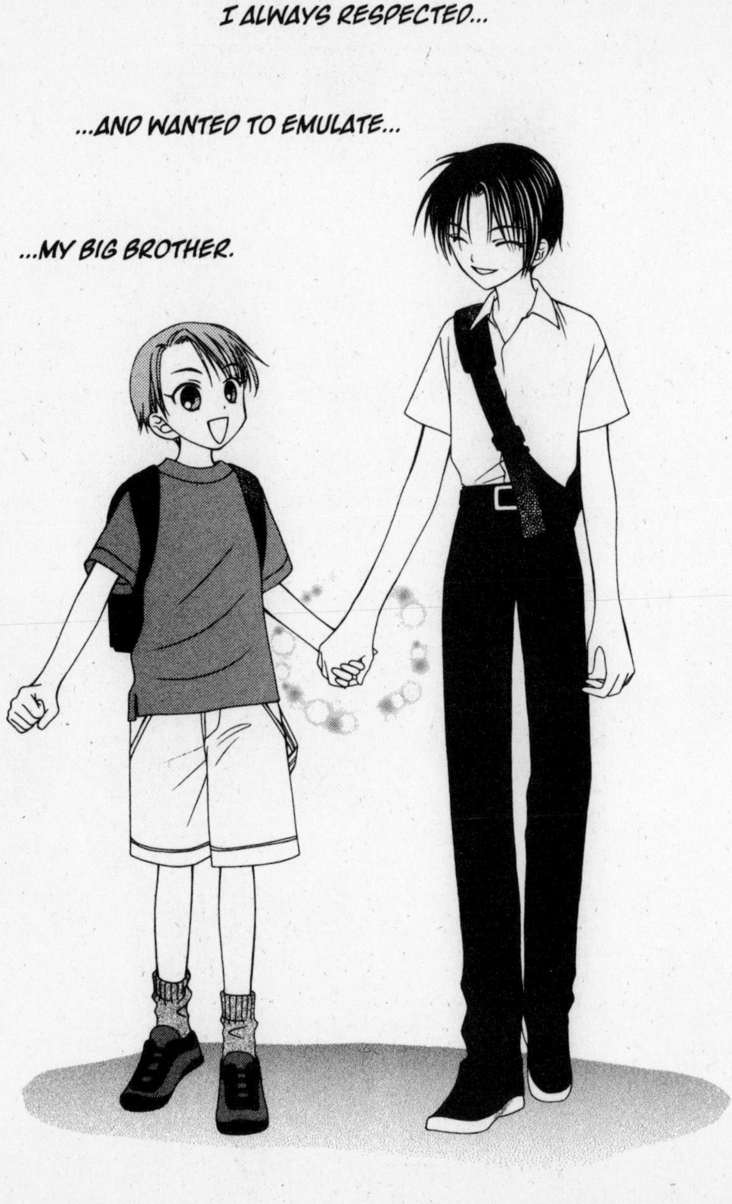
I ALWAYS RESPECTED...
...AND WANTED TO EMULATE...
...MY BIG BROTHER.

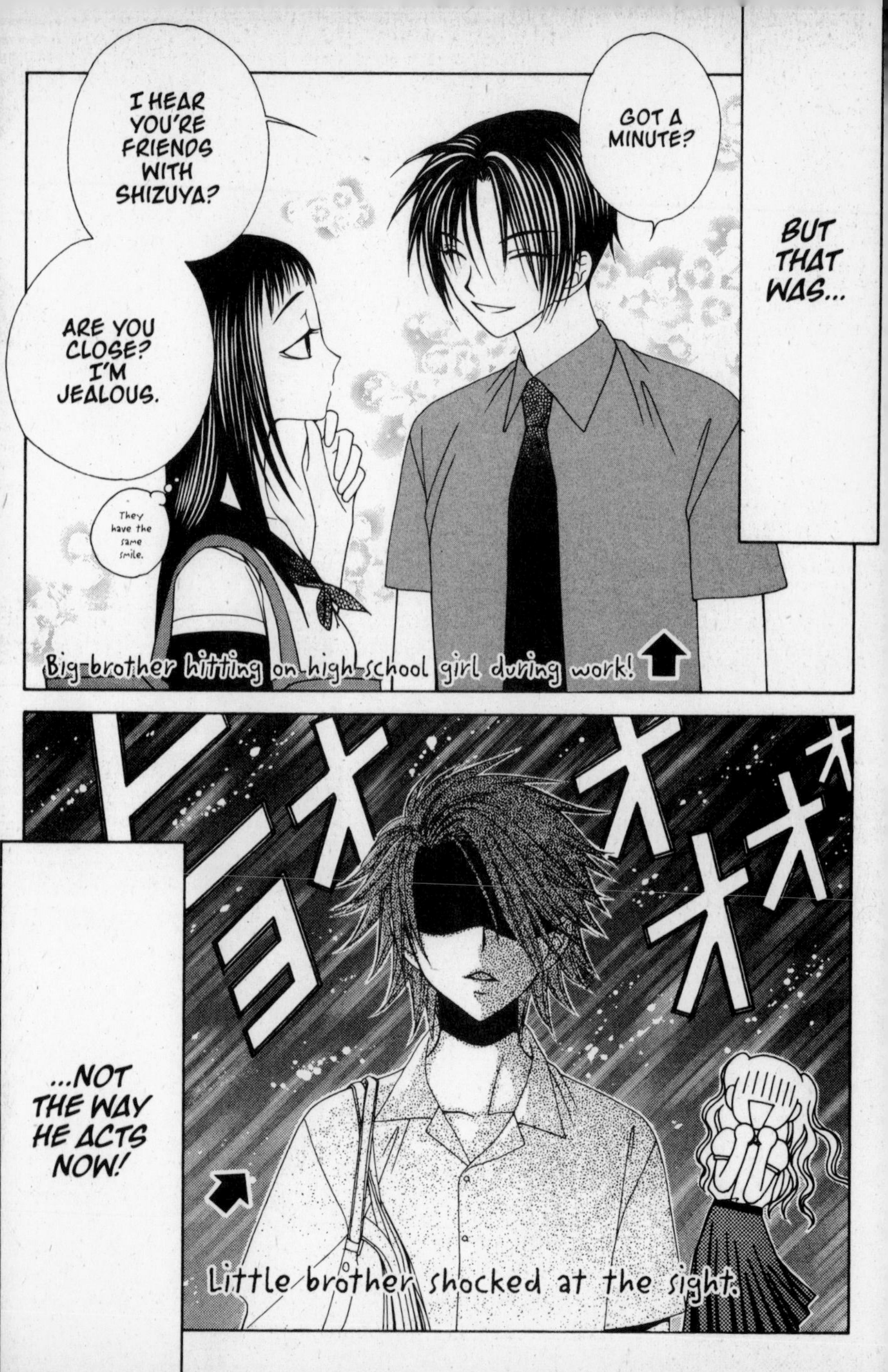
BUT THAT WAS...
GOT A MINUTE?
I HEAR YOU'RE FRIENDS WITH SHIZUYA?
ARE YOU CLOSE? I'M JEALOUS.
They have the same smile.
Big brother hitting on high school girl during work!
ドヨオオオ
...NOT THE WAY HE ACTS NOW!
Little brother shocked at the sight.

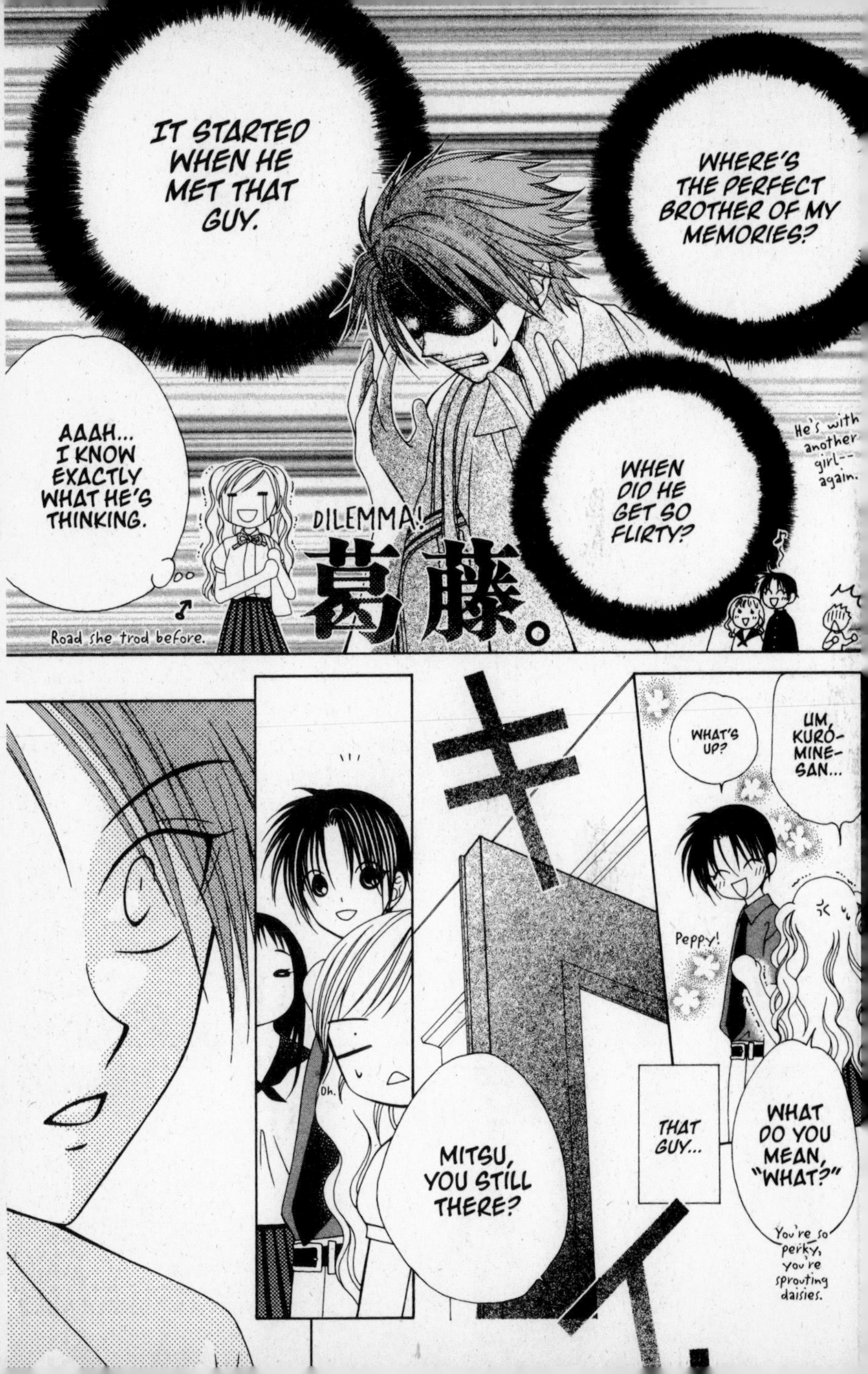
WHERE'S THE PERFECT BROTHER OF MY MEMORIES?
IT STARTED WHEN HE MET THAT GUY.
He's with another girl--again.
WHEN DID HE GET SO FLIRTY?
DILEMMA!
葛藤。
AAAH... I KNOW EXACTLY WHAT HE'S THINKING.
Road she trod before.
UM, KURO-MINE-SAN...
WHAT'S UP?
Peppy!
WHAT DO YOU MEAN, "WHAT?"
You're so perky, you're sprouting daisies.
THAT GUY...
キ
イ
MITSU, YOU STILL THERE?
Oh.

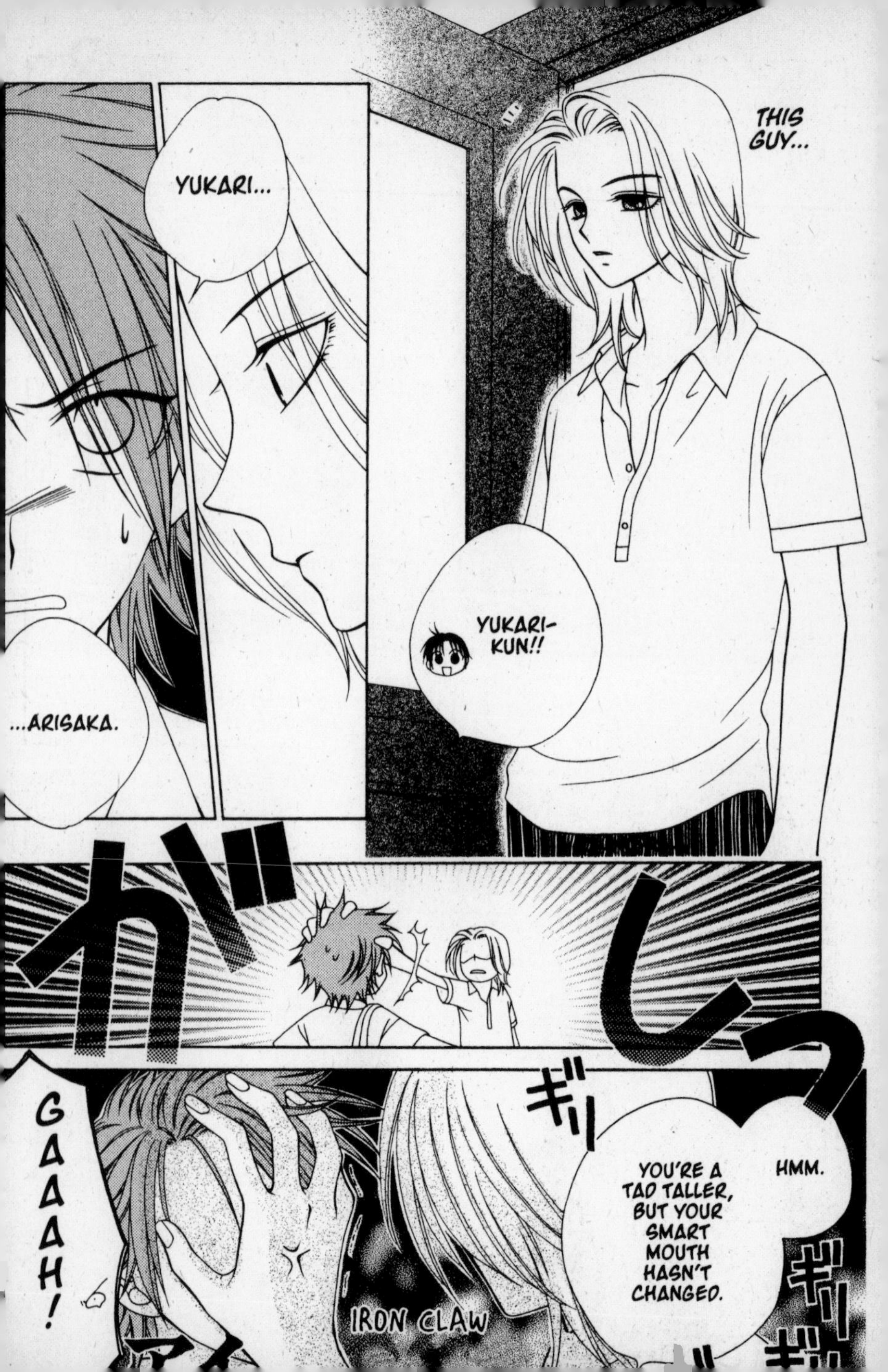
THIS GUY...
YUKARI-KUN!!
YUKARI...
...ARISAKA.
がしっ
ギリ
HMM.
YOU'RE A TAD TALLER, BUT YOUR SMART MOUTH HASN'T CHANGED.
ギリギリ
IRON CLAW
GAAAAH!

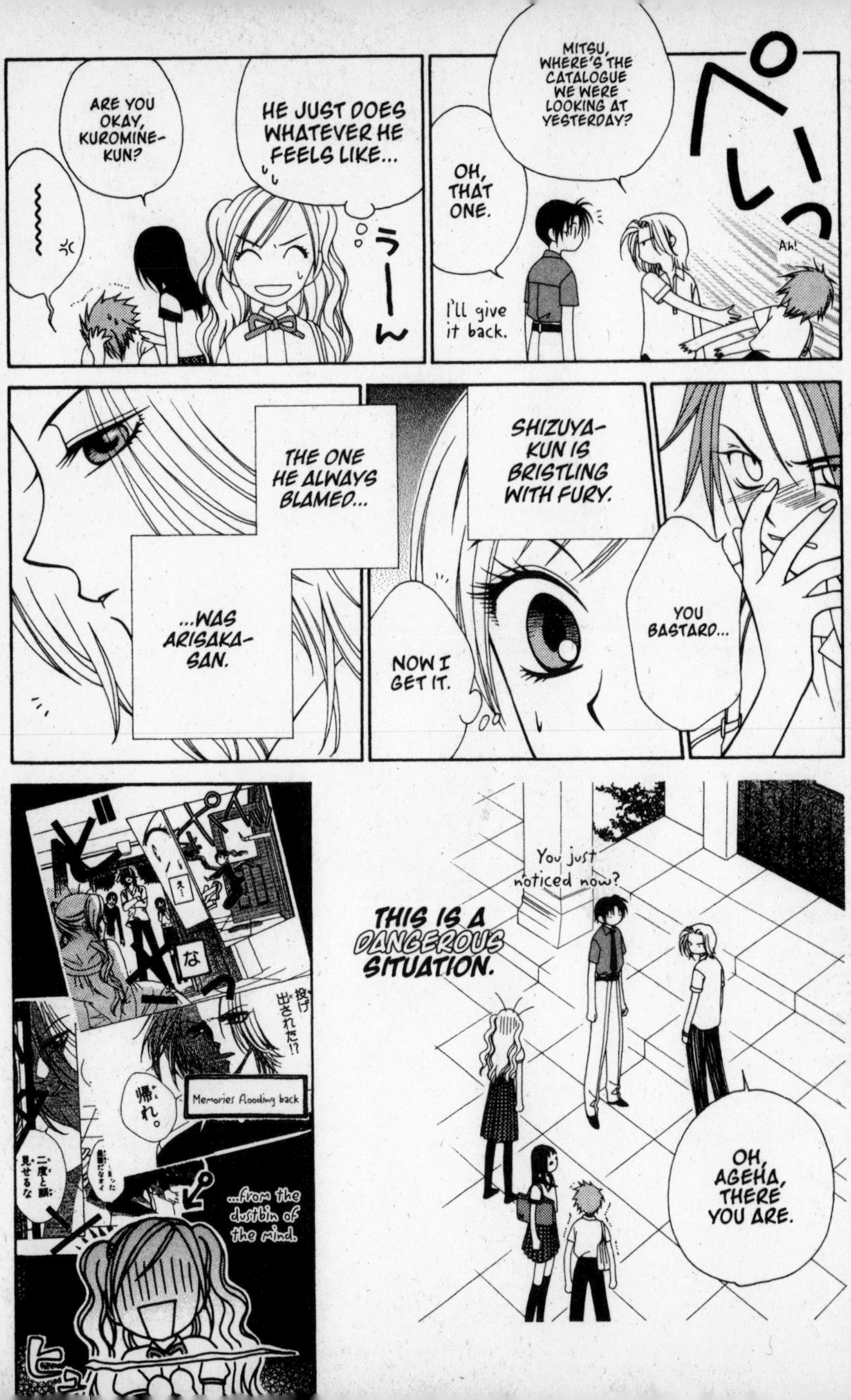

ペーいっ
Ah!
MITSU, WHERE'S THE CATALOGUE WE WERE LOOKING AT YESTERDAY?
OH, THAT ONE.
I'll give it back.
HE JUST DOES WHATEVER HE FEELS LIKE...
うーん
ARE YOU OKAY, KUROMINE-KUN?
~~~~
YOU BASTARD...
SHIZUYA-KUN IS BRISTLING WITH FURY.
NOW I GET IT.
THE ONE HE ALWAYS BLAMED...
...WAS ARISAKA-SAN.
OH, AGEHA, THERE YOU ARE.
You just noticed now?
THIS IS A DANGEROUS SITUATION.
Memories flooding back
投げ出された!?
帰れ。
二度と顔見せるな
...from the dustbin of the mind.
~~~~

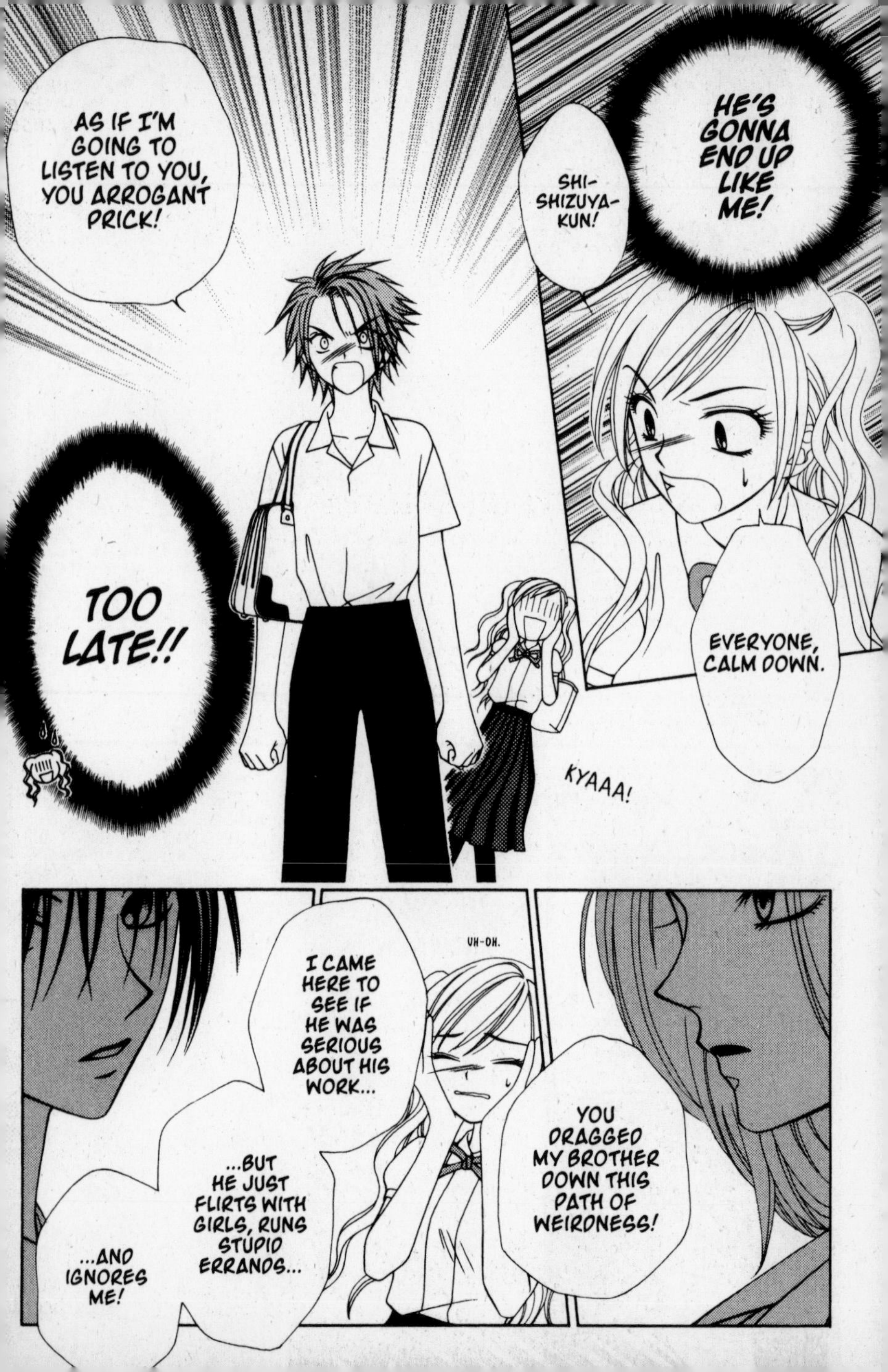
HE'S GONNA END UP LIKE ME!
SHI-SHIZUYA-KUN!
EVERYONE, CALM DOWN.
AS IF I'M GOING TO LISTEN TO YOU, YOU ARROGANT PRICK!
TOO LATE!!
KYAAA!
YOU DRAGGED MY BROTHER DOWN THIS PATH OF WEIRDNESS!
UH-OH.
I CAME HERE TO SEE IF HE WAS SERIOUS ABOUT HIS WORK...
...BUT HE JUST FLIRTS WITH GIRLS, RUNS STUPID ERRANDS...
...AND IGNORES ME!

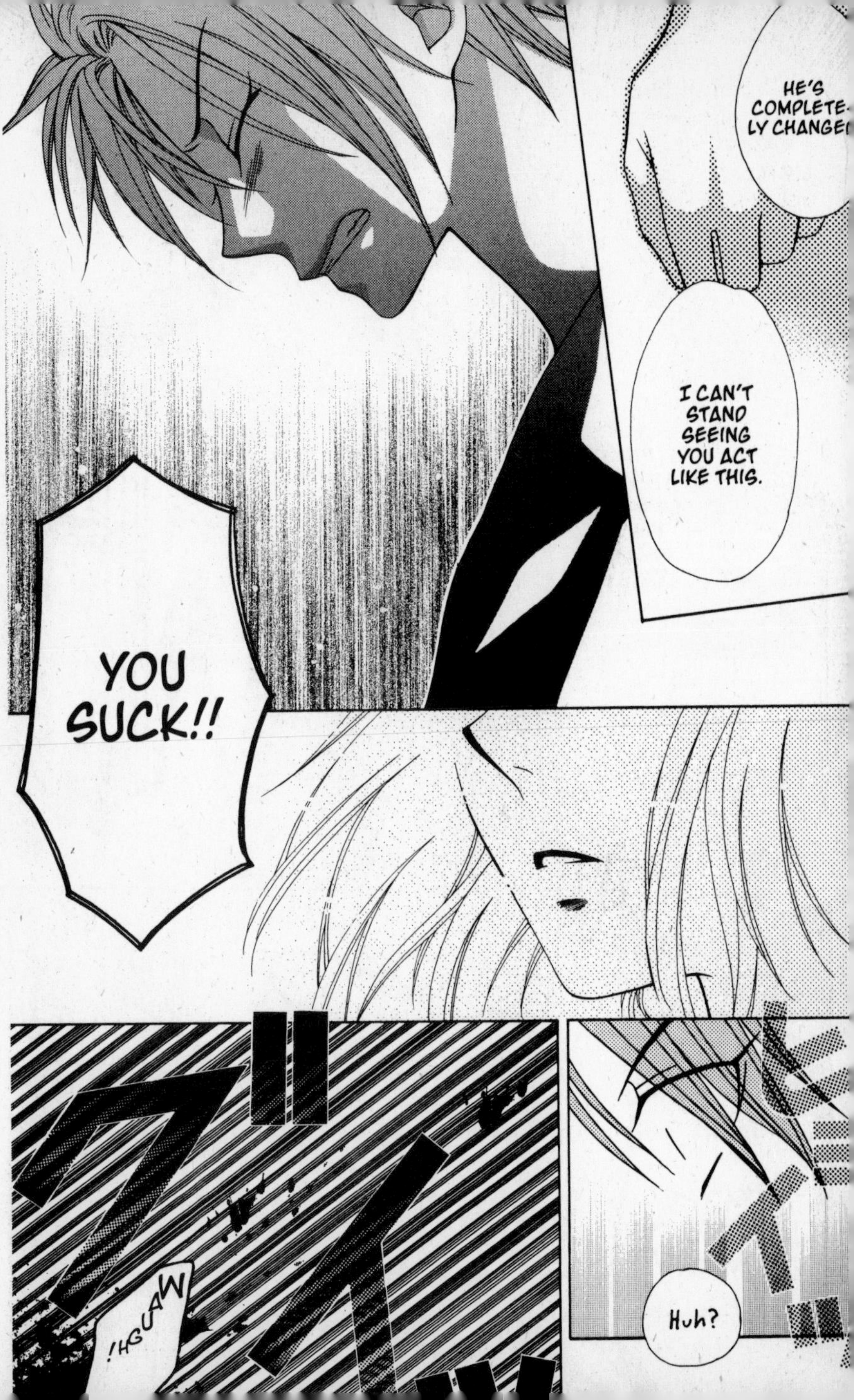
HE'S COMPLETE-LY CHANGE
I CAN'T STAND SEEING YOU ACT LIKE THIS.
YOU SUCK!!
Huh?
WAUGH!

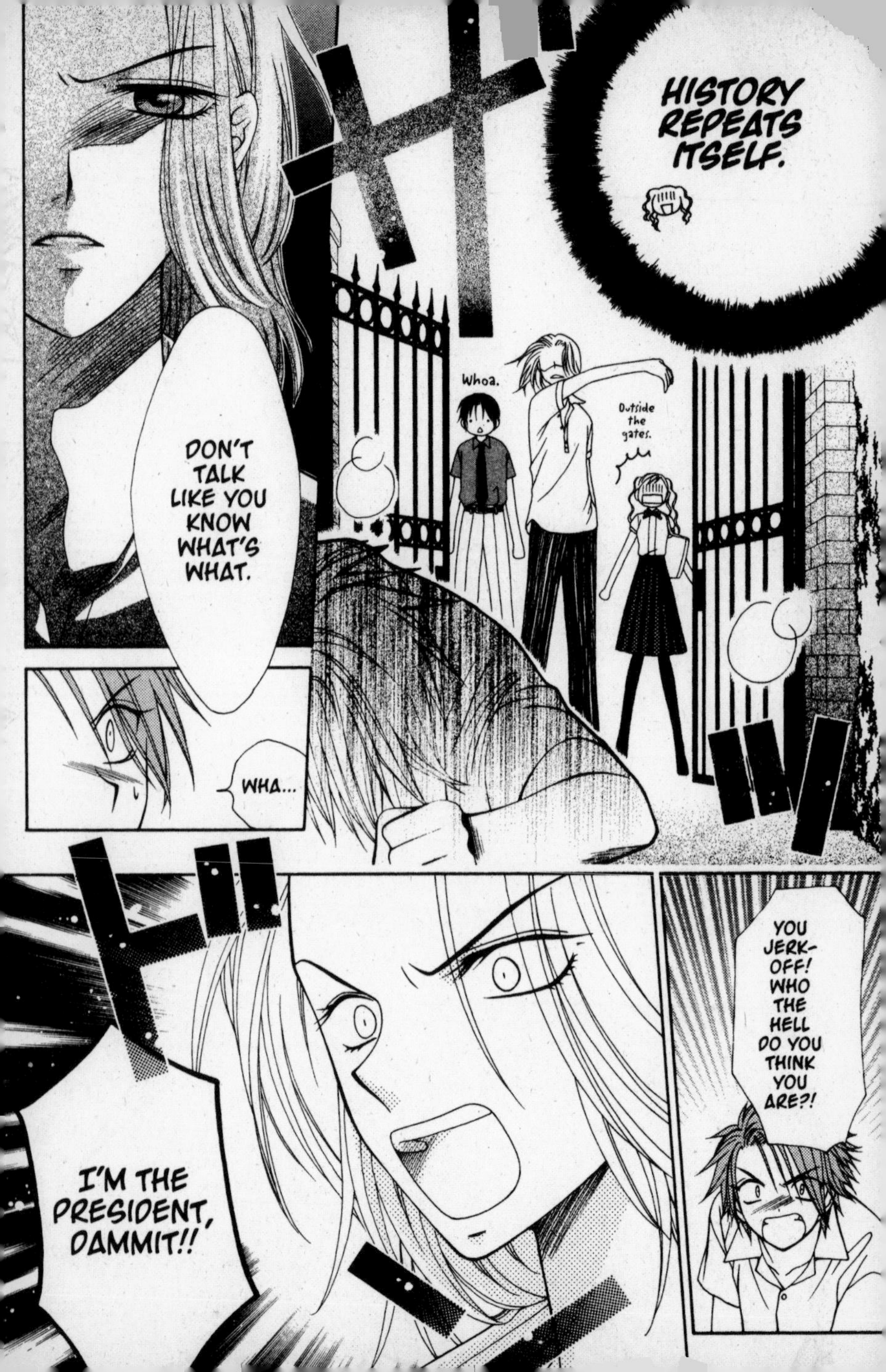
HISTORY REPEATS ITSELF.
Outside the gates.
Whoa.
DON'T TALK LIKE YOU KNOW WHAT'S WHAT.
WHA...
YOU JERK-OFF! WHO THE HELL DO YOU THINK YOU ARE?!
I'M THE PRESIDENT, DAMMIT!!

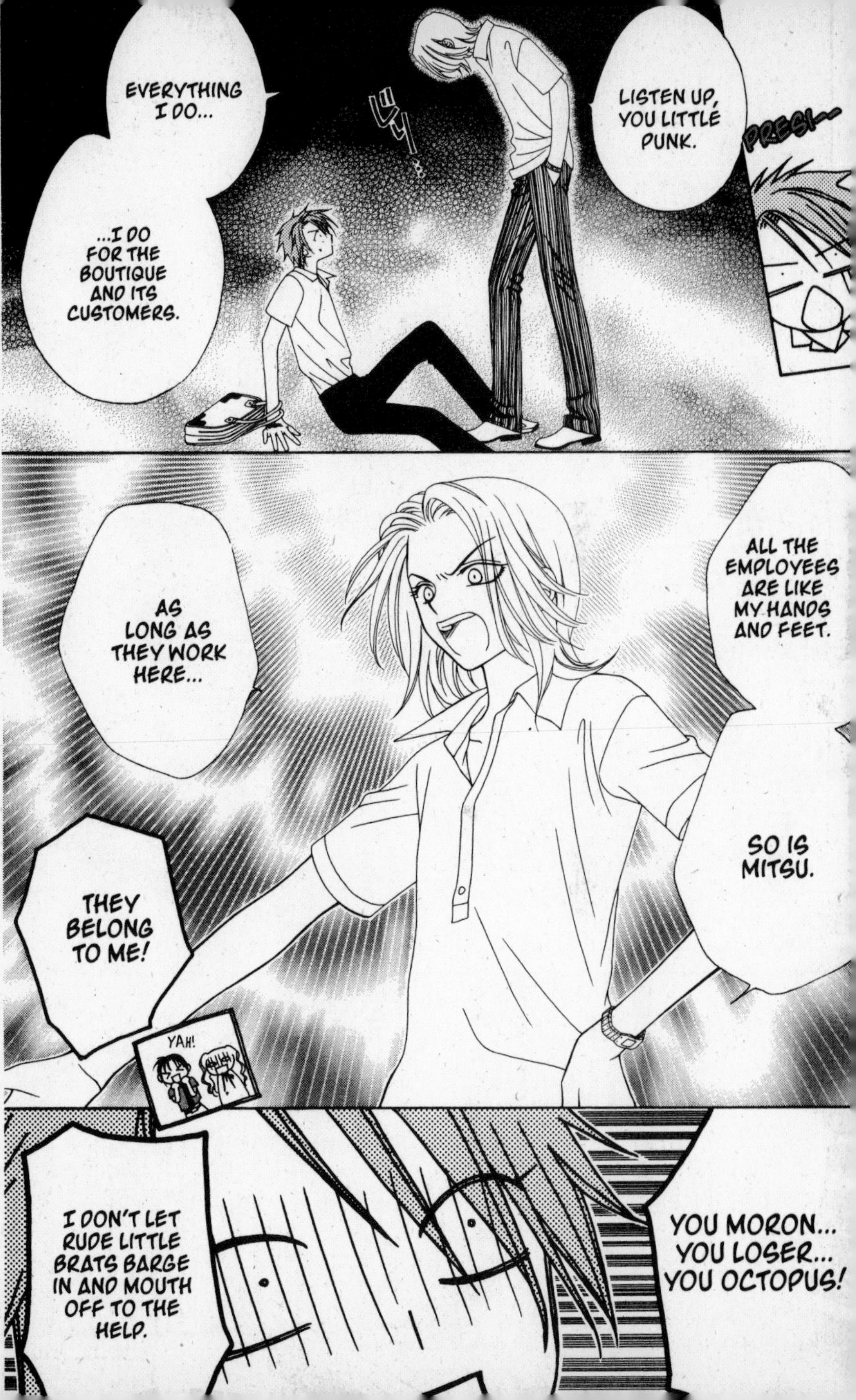
PRESI--
LISTEN UP, YOU LITTLE PUNK.
EVERYTHING I DO...
...I DO FOR THE BOUTIQUE AND ITS CUSTOMERS.
ALL THE EMPLOYEES ARE LIKE MY HANDS AND FEET.
SO IS MITSU.
AS LONG AS THEY WORK HERE...
THEY BELONG TO ME!
YAH!
YOU MORON... YOU LOSER... YOU OCTOPUS!
I DON'T LET RUDE LITTLE BRATS BARGE IN AND MOUTH OFF TO THE HELP.

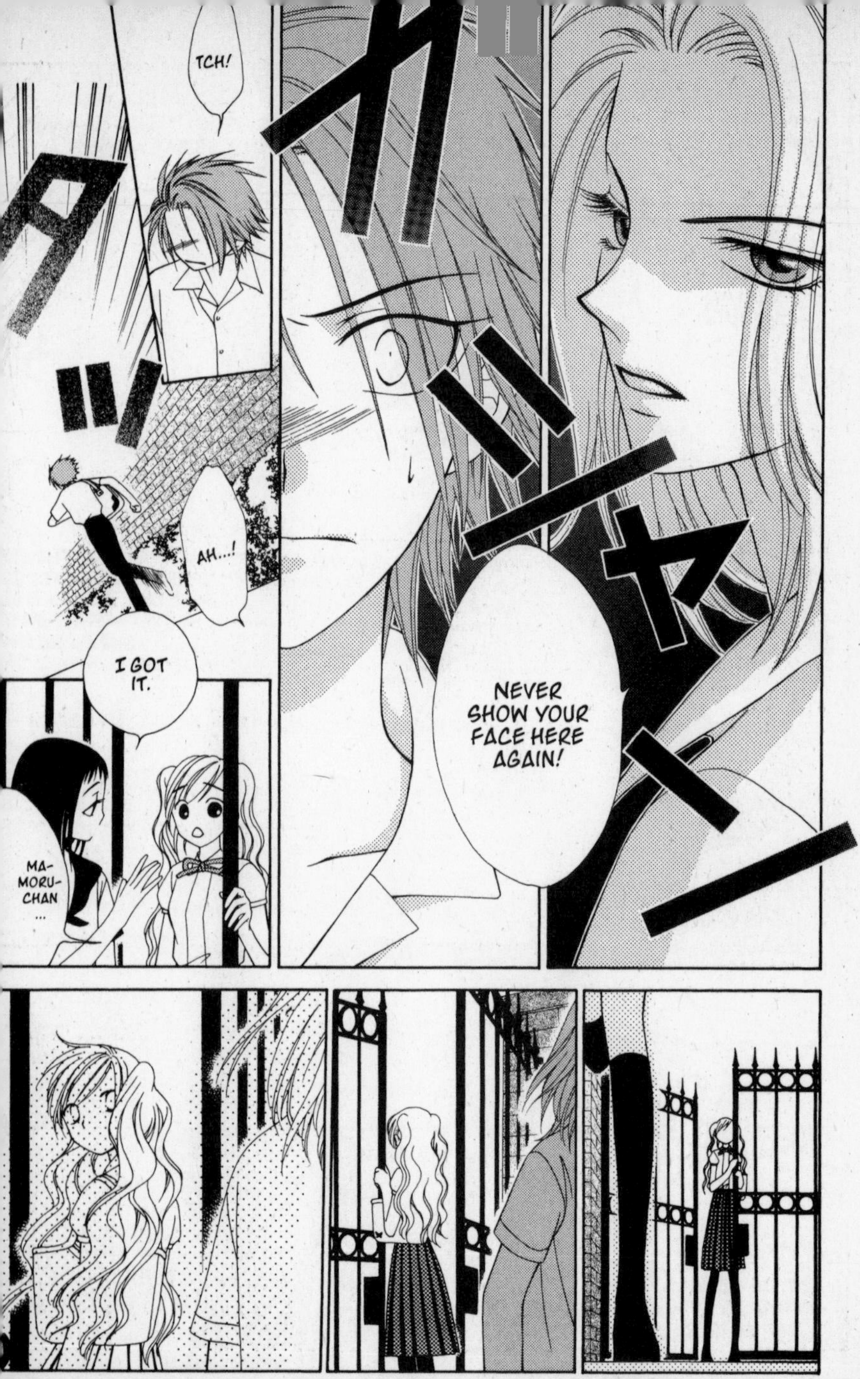
NEVER SHOW YOUR FACE HERE AGAIN!
TCH!
AH...!
I GOT IT.
MA-MORU-CHAN ...

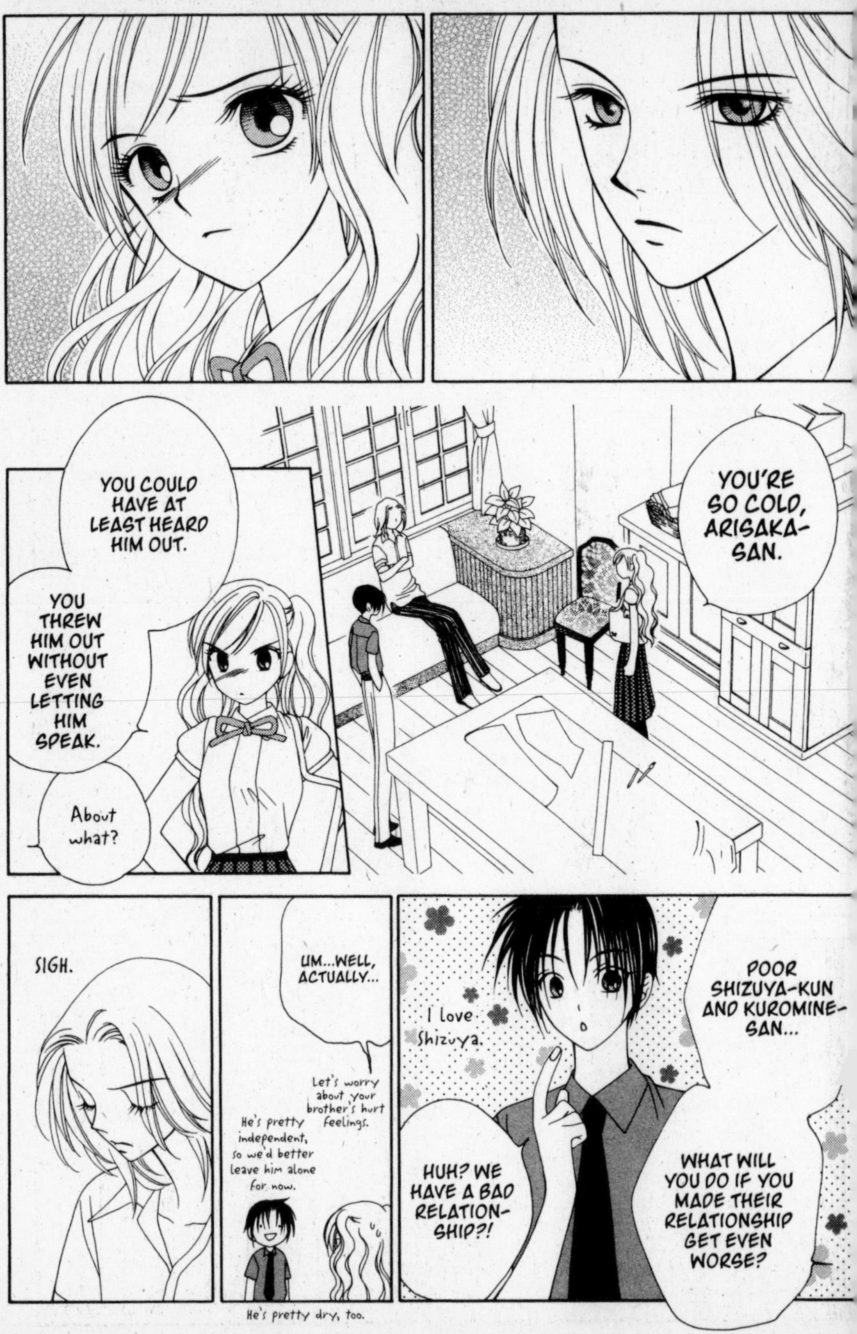
YOU'RE SO COLD, ARISAKA-SAN.
YOU COULD HAVE AT LEAST HEARD HIM OUT.
YOU THREW HIM OUT WITHOUT EVEN LETTING HIM SPEAK.
About what?
POOR SHIZUYA-KUN AND KUROMINE-SAN...
I love Shizuya.
WHAT WILL YOU DO IF YOU MADE THEIR RELATIONSHIP GET EVEN WORSE?
HUH? WE HAVE A BAD RELATIONSHIP?!
UM...WELL, ACTUALLY...
Let's worry about your brother's hurt feelings.
He's pretty independent, so we'd better leave him alone for now.
SIGH.
He's pretty dry, too.

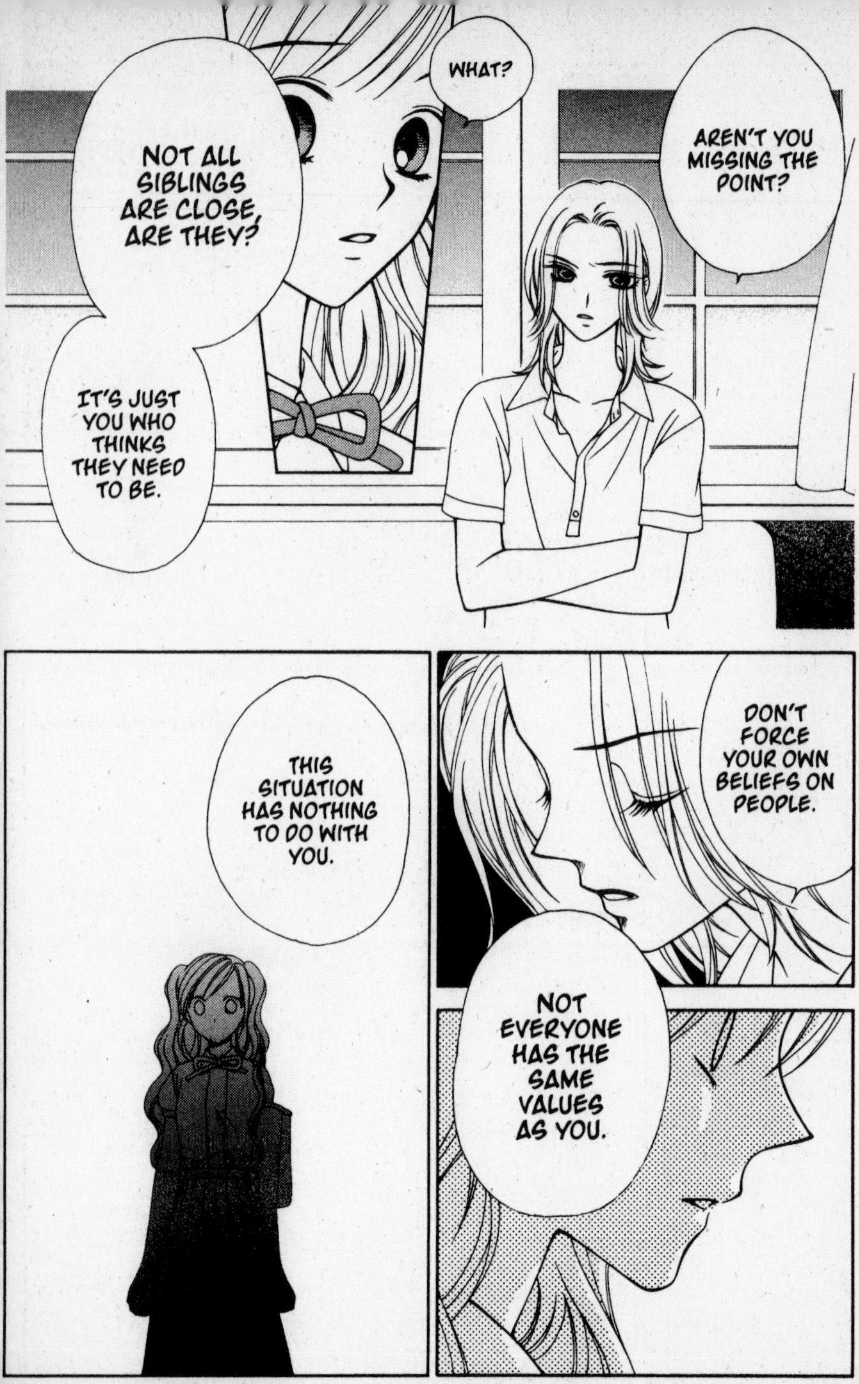
AREN'T YOU MISSING THE POINT?
WHAT?
NOT ALL SIBLINGS ARE CLOSE, ARE THEY?
IT'S JUST YOU WHO THINKS THEY NEED TO BE.
DON'T FORCE YOUR OWN BELIEFS ON PEOPLE.
NOT EVERYONE HAS THE SAME VALUES AS YOU.
THIS SITUATION HAS NOTHING TO DO WITH YOU.

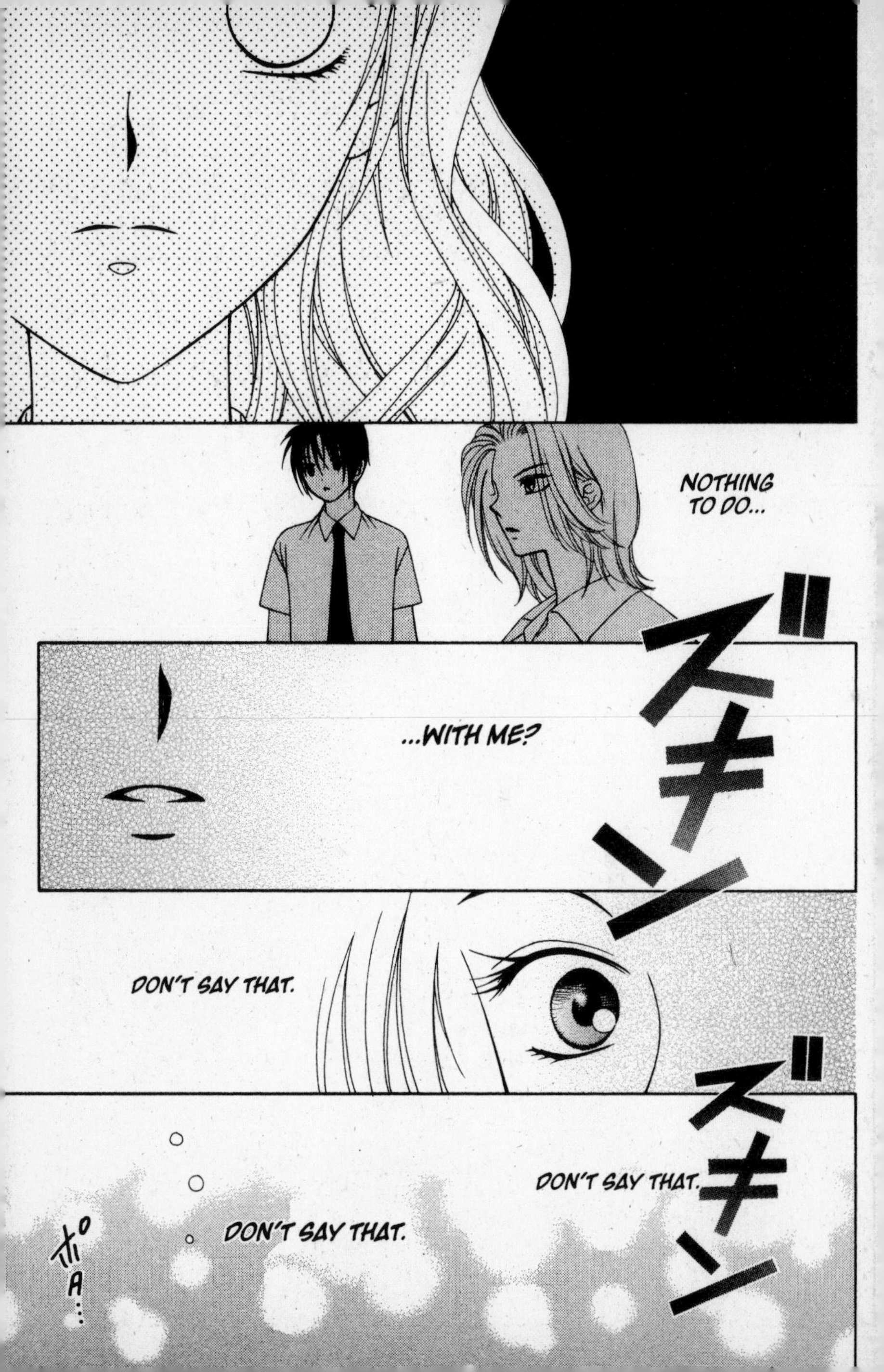
NOTHING TO DO...
ズキン
...WITH ME?
DON'T SAY THAT.
ズキン
DON'T SAY THAT.
DON'T SAY THAT.
ポ A...

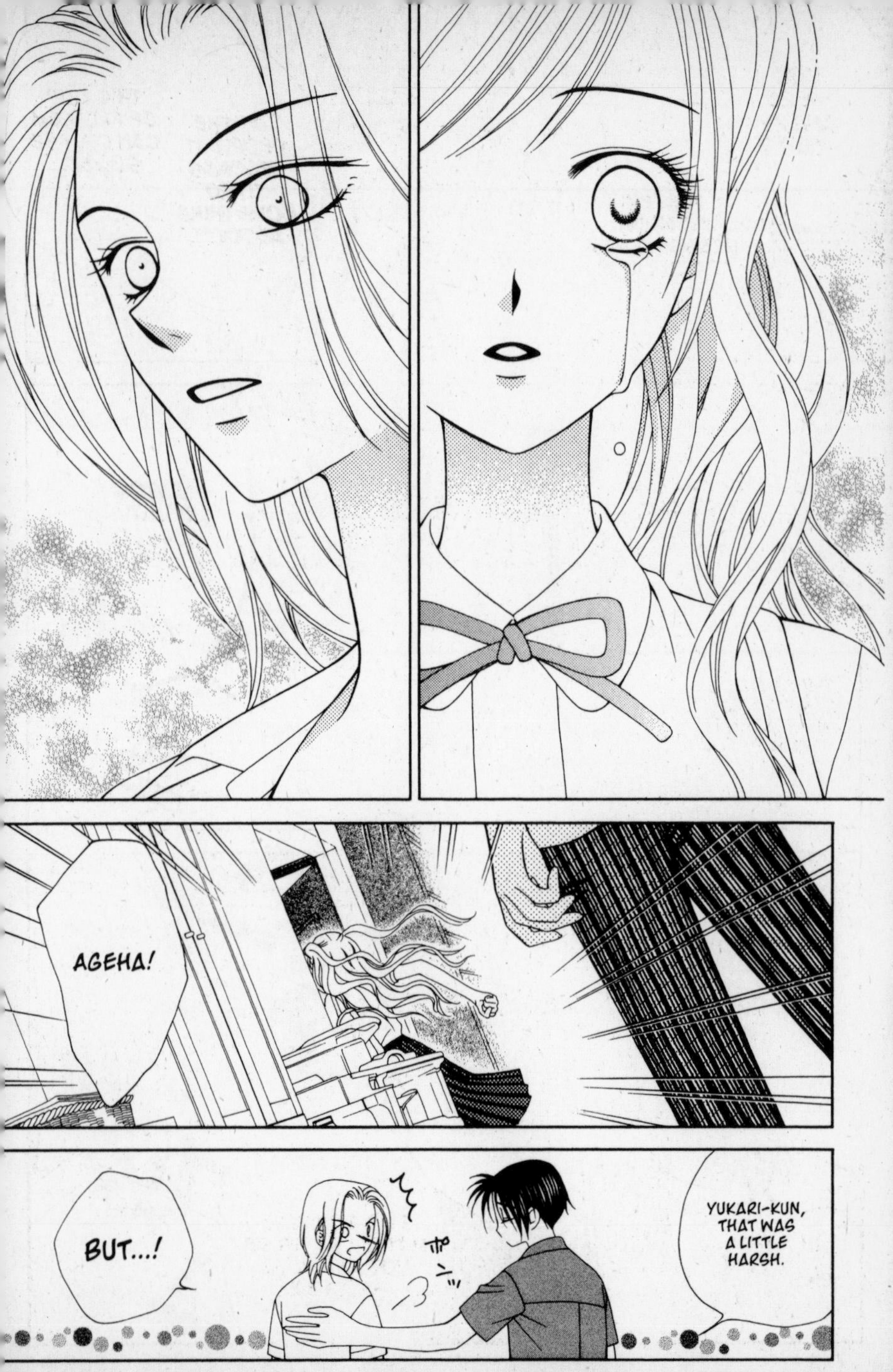
AGEHA!
YUKARI-KUN, THAT WAS A LITTLE HARSH.
BUT...!

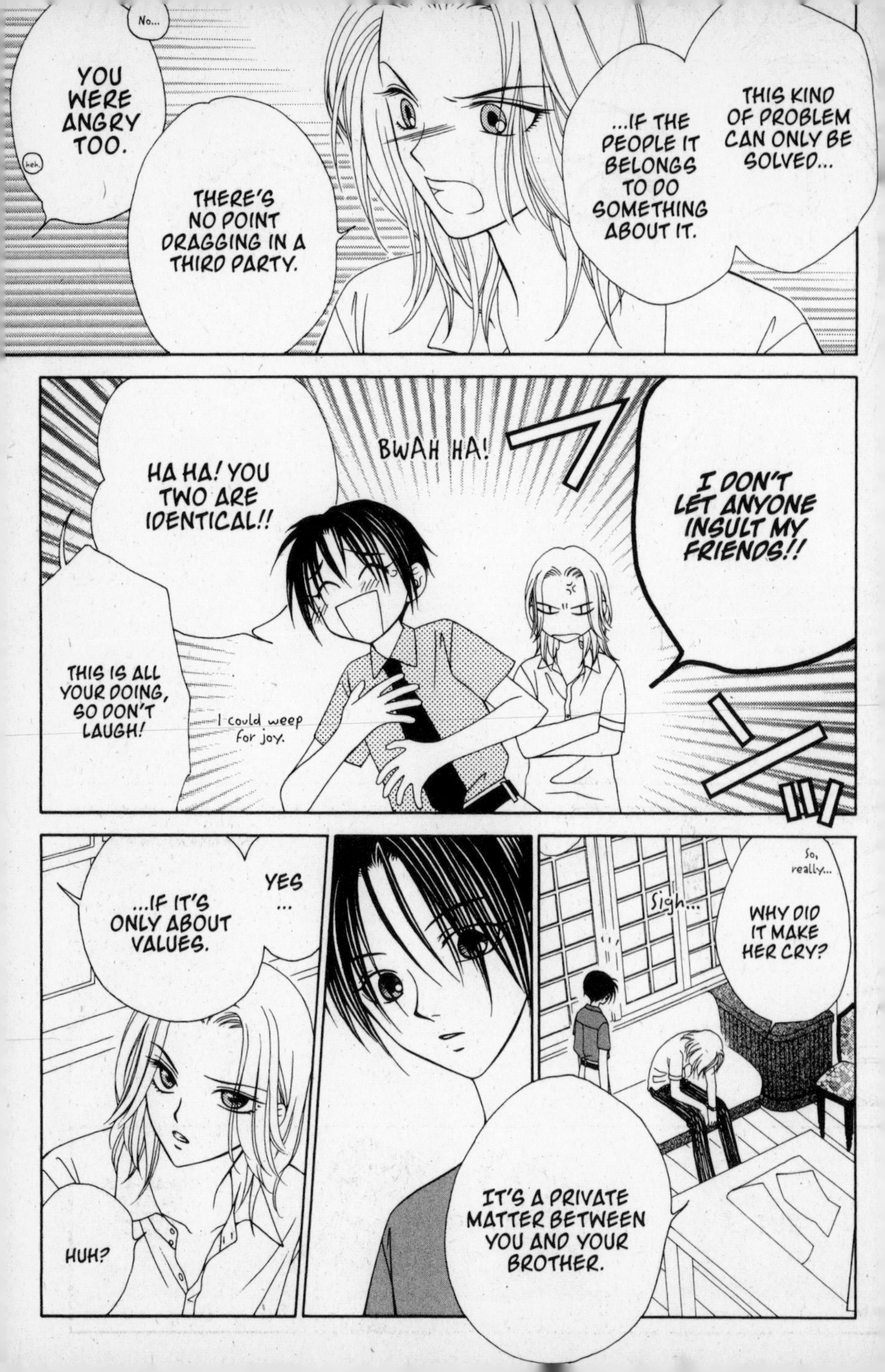
THIS KIND OF PROBLEM CAN ONLY BE SOLVED...
...IF THE PEOPLE IT BELONGS TO DO SOMETHING ABOUT IT.
THERE'S NO POINT DRAGGING IN A THIRD PARTY.
No...
YOU WERE ANGRY TOO.
heh.
I DON'T LET ANYONE INSULT MY FRIENDS!!
BWAH HA!
HA HA! YOU TWO ARE IDENTICAL!!
I could weep for joy.
THIS IS ALL YOUR DOING, SO DON'T LAUGH!
So, really...
WHY DID IT MAKE HER CRY?
Sigh...
IT'S A PRIVATE MATTER BETWEEN YOU AND YOUR BROTHER.
YES...
...IF IT'S ONLY ABOUT VALUES.
HUH?

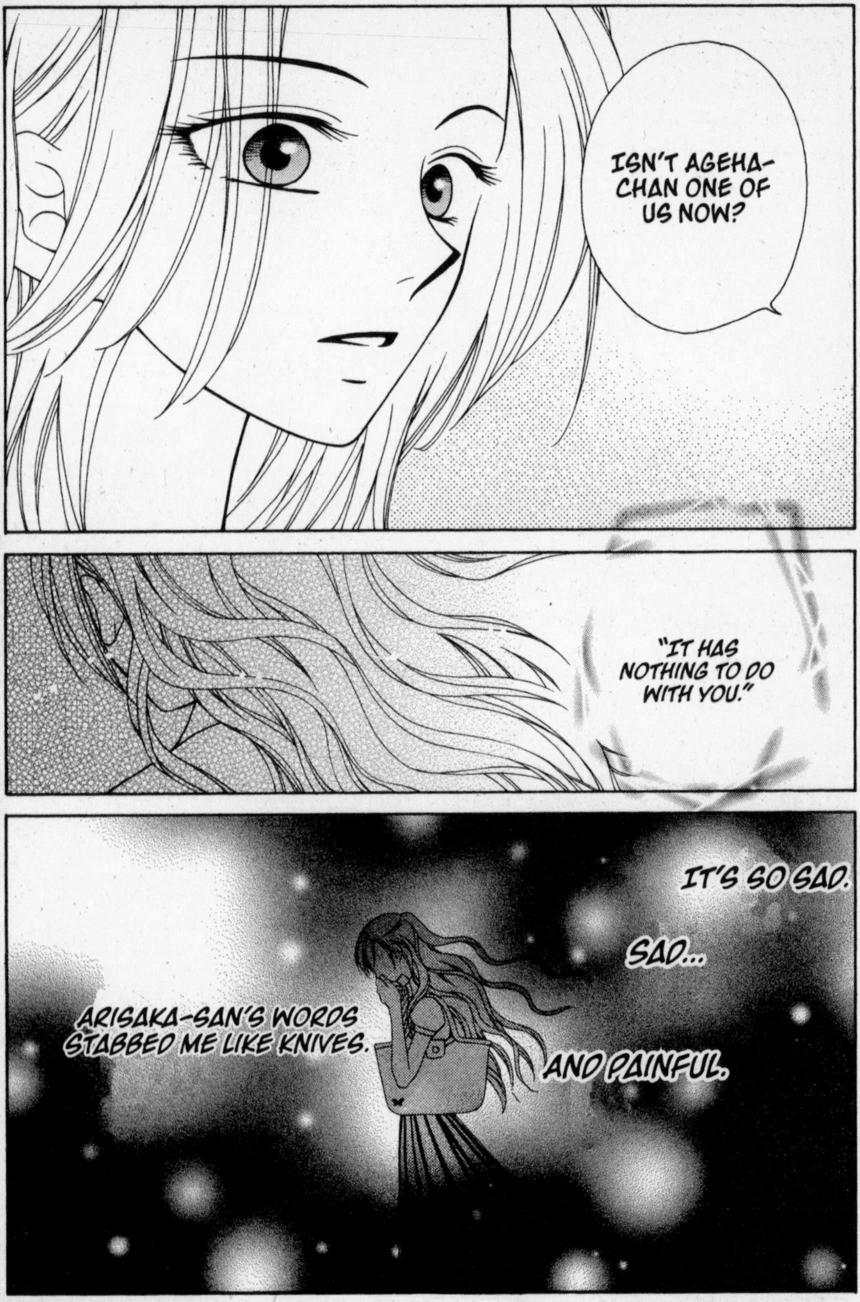
ISN'T AGEHA-CHAN ONE OF US NOW?
"IT HAS NOTHING TO DO WITH YOU."
IT'S SO SAD.
SAD...
AND PAINFUL.
ARISAKA-SAN'S WORDS STABBED ME LIKE KNIVES.

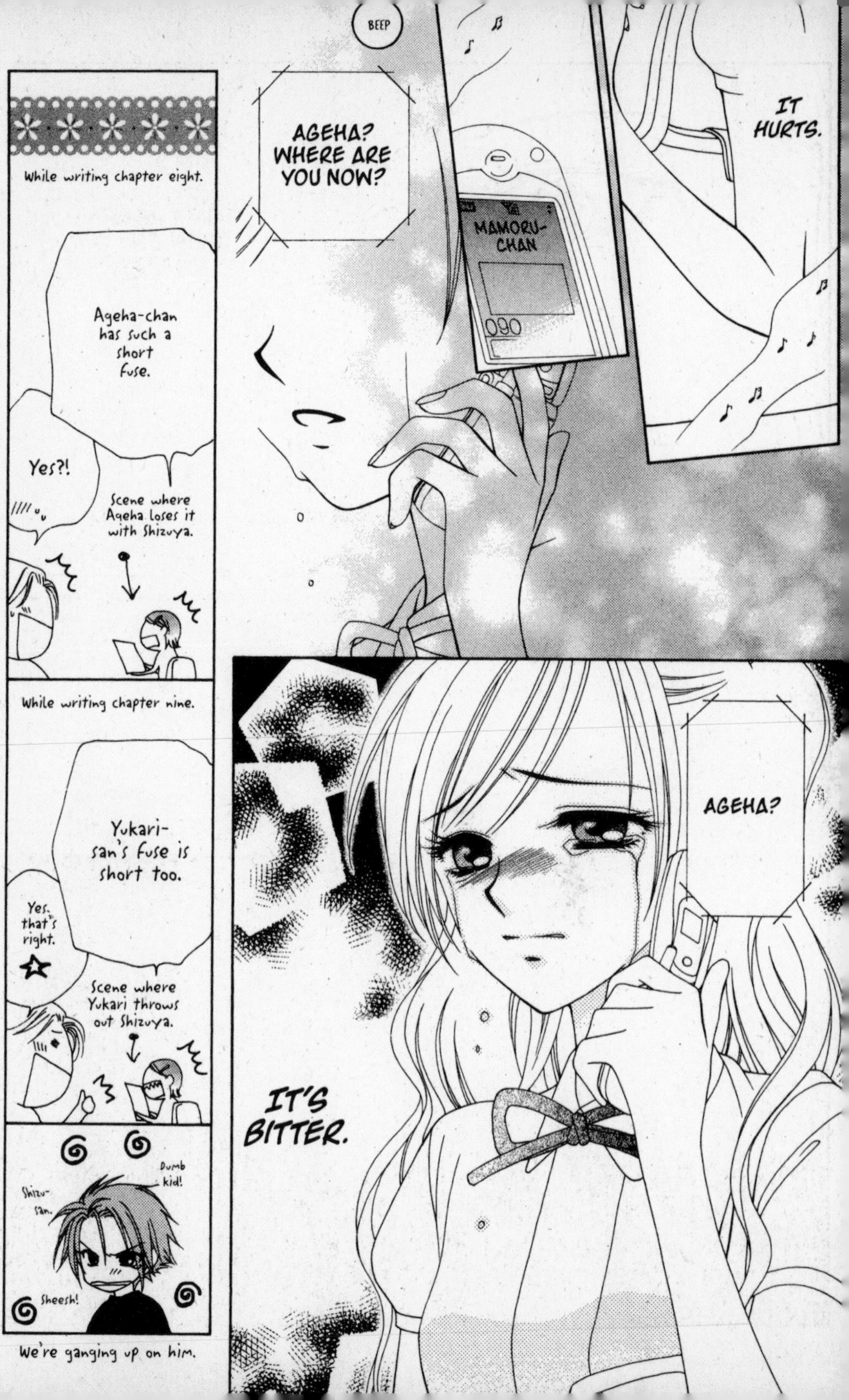
BEEP
IT HURTS.
AGEHA? WHERE ARE YOU NOW?
MAMORU-CHAN
090
AGEHA?
IT'S BITTER.
While writing chapter eight.
Ageha-chan has such a short fuse.
Yes?!
Scene where Ageha loses it with Shizuya.
While writing chapter nine.
Yukari-san's fuse is short too.
Yes. that's right.
Scene where Yukari throws out Shizuya.
Dumb kid!
Shizu-san.
Sheesh!
We're ganging up on him.

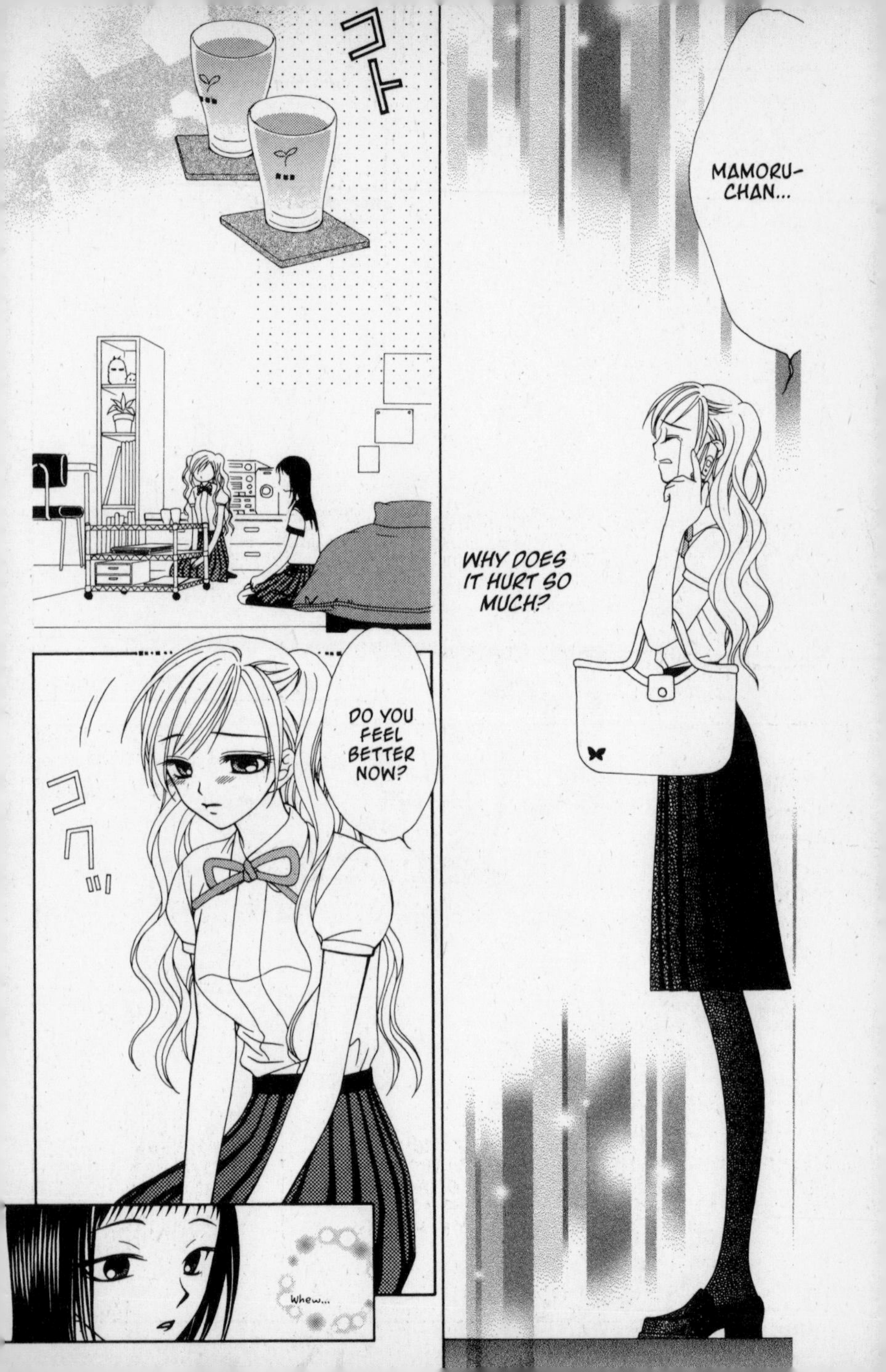
MAMORU-CHAN...
WHY DOES IT HURT SO MUCH?
コト
DO YOU FEEL BETTER NOW?
Whew...

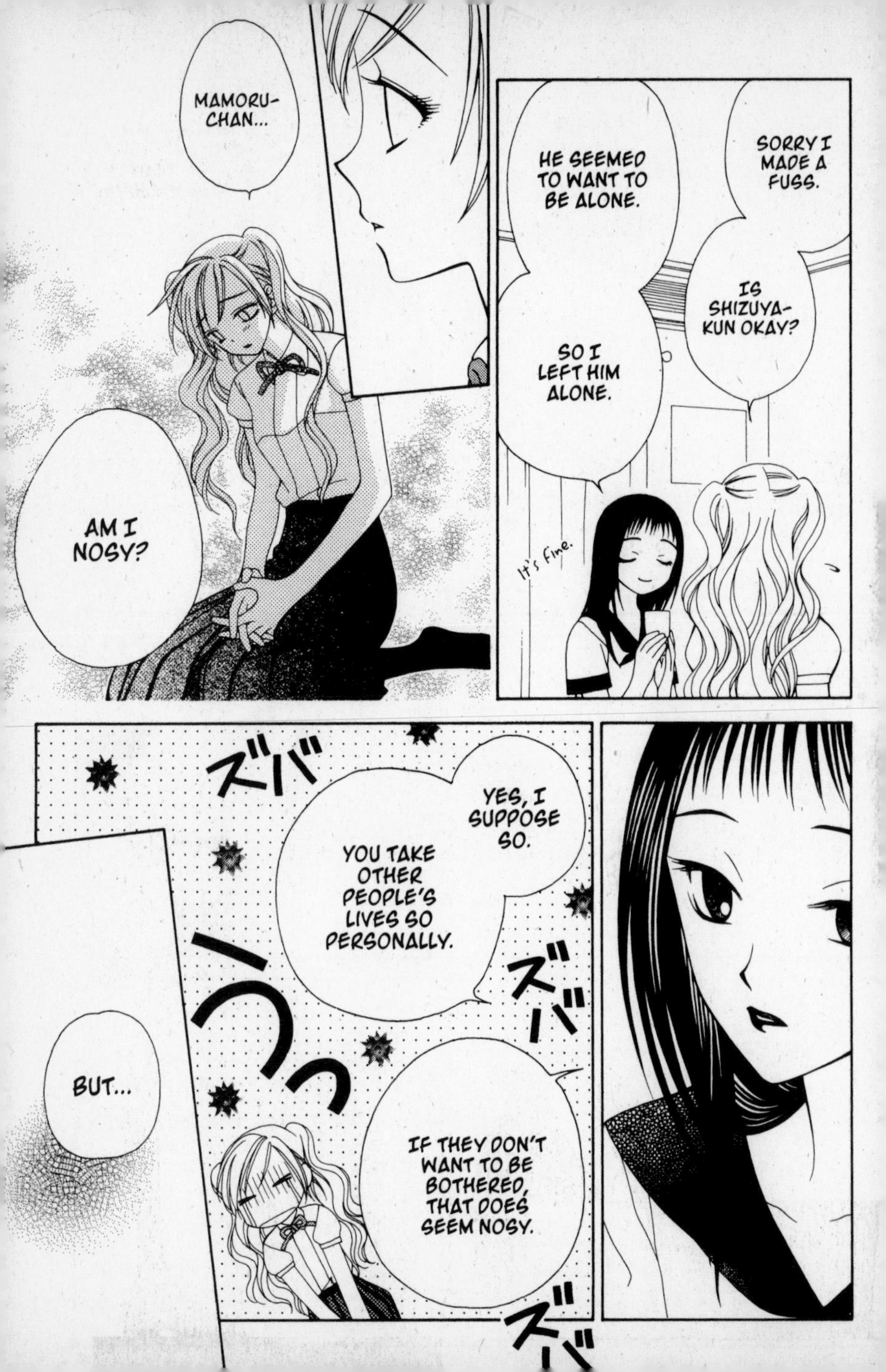
SORRY I MADE A FUSS.
IS SHIZUYA-KUN OKAY?
HE SEEMED TO WANT TO BE ALONE.
SO I LEFT HIM ALONE.
It's fine.
MAMORU-CHAN...
AM I NOSY?
ズバ
YES, I SUPPOSE SO.
YOU TAKE OTHER PEOPLE'S LIVES SO PERSONALLY.
ズバ
IF THEY DON'T WANT TO BE BOTHERED, THAT DOES SEEM NOSY.
ズバ
BUT...

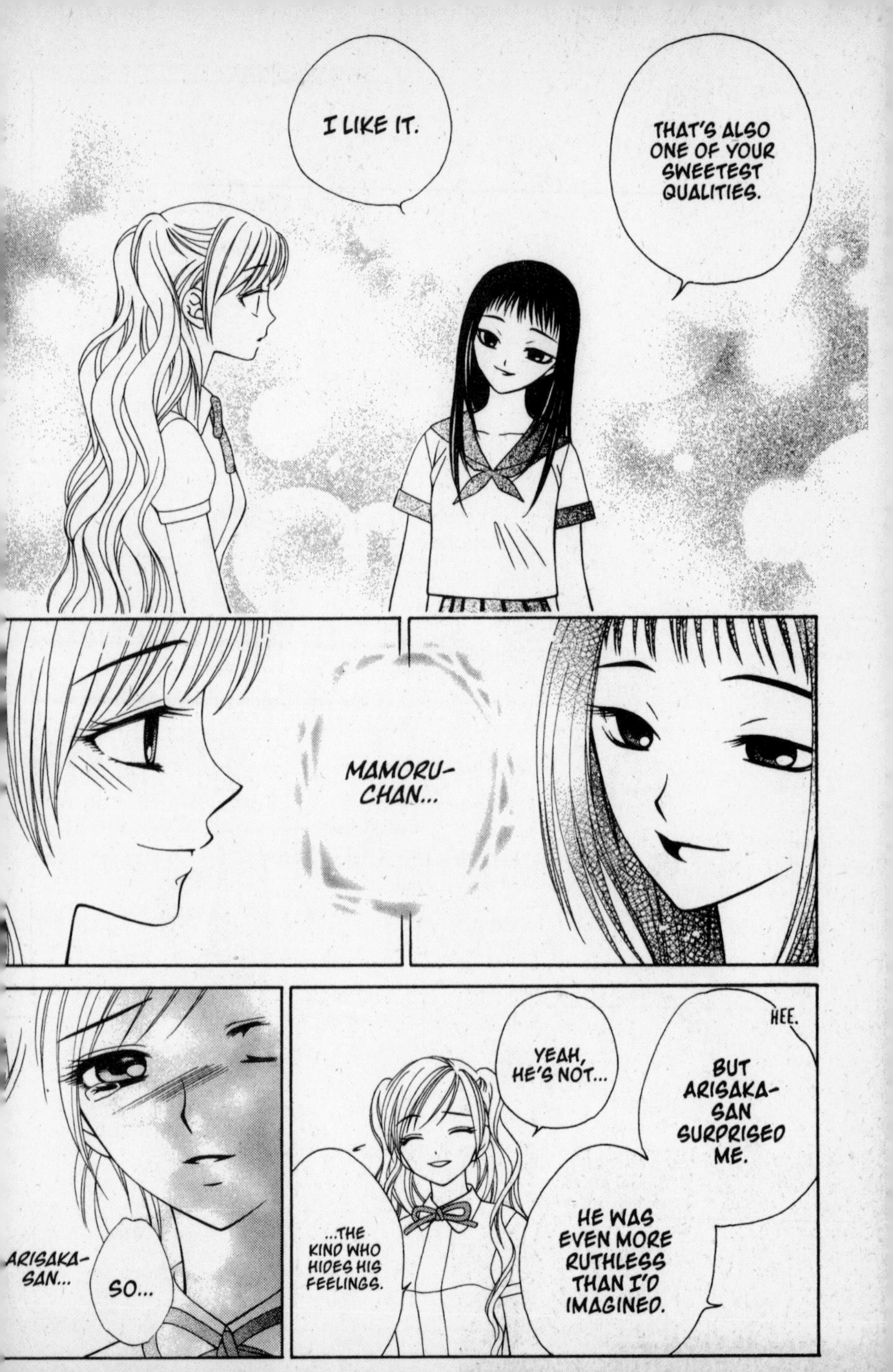
THAT'S ALSO ONE OF YOUR SWEETEST QUALITIES.
I LIKE IT.
MAMORU-CHAN...
HEE.
BUT ARISAKA-SAN SURPRISED ME.
HE WAS EVEN MORE RUTHLESS THAN I'D IMAGINED.
YEAH, HE'S NOT...
...THE KIND WHO HIDES HIS FEELINGS.
SO...
ARISAKA-SAN...

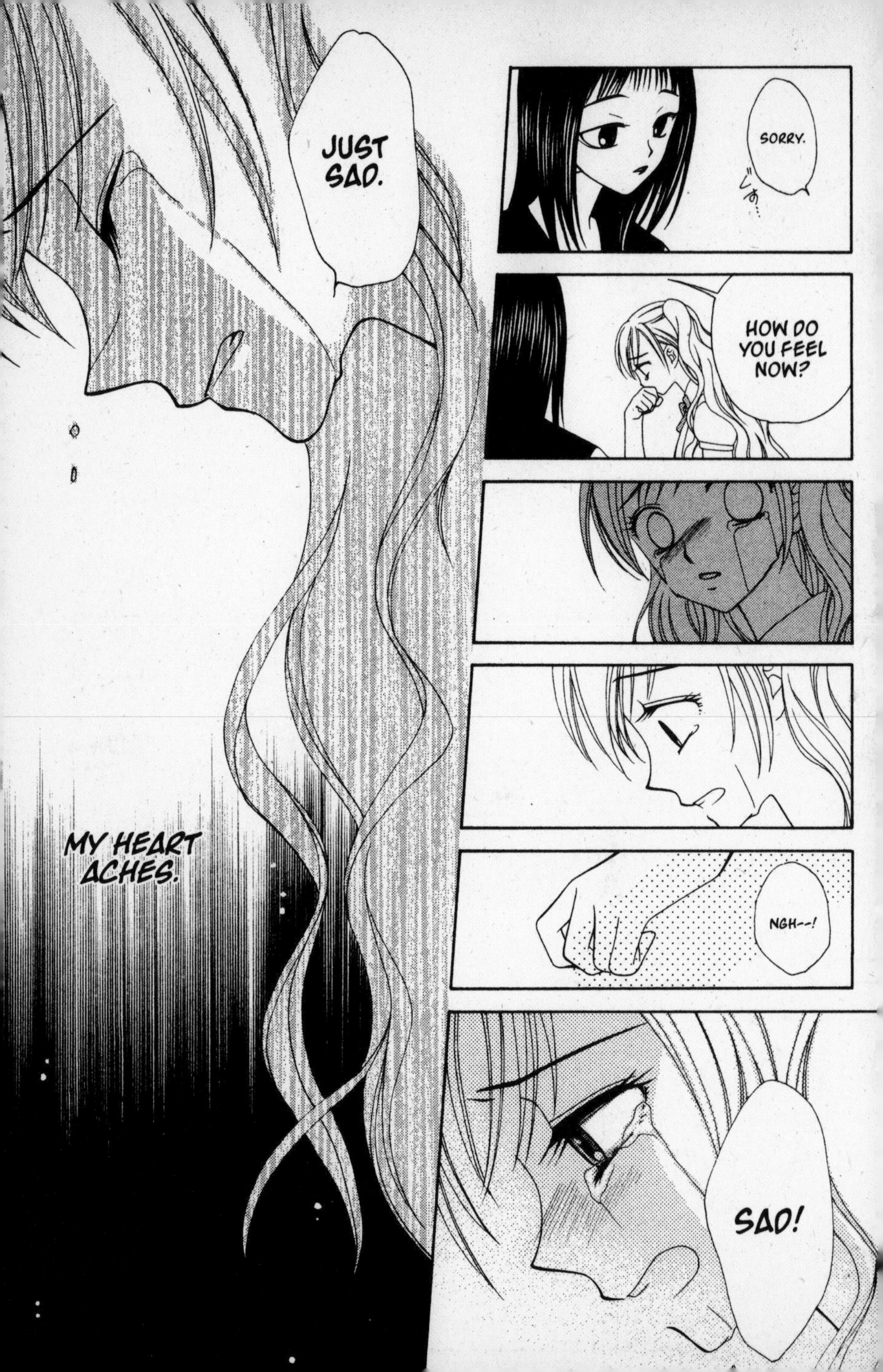
SORRY.
じわ…
HOW DO YOU FEEL NOW?
NGH--!
SAD!
JUST SAD.
MY HEART ACHES.

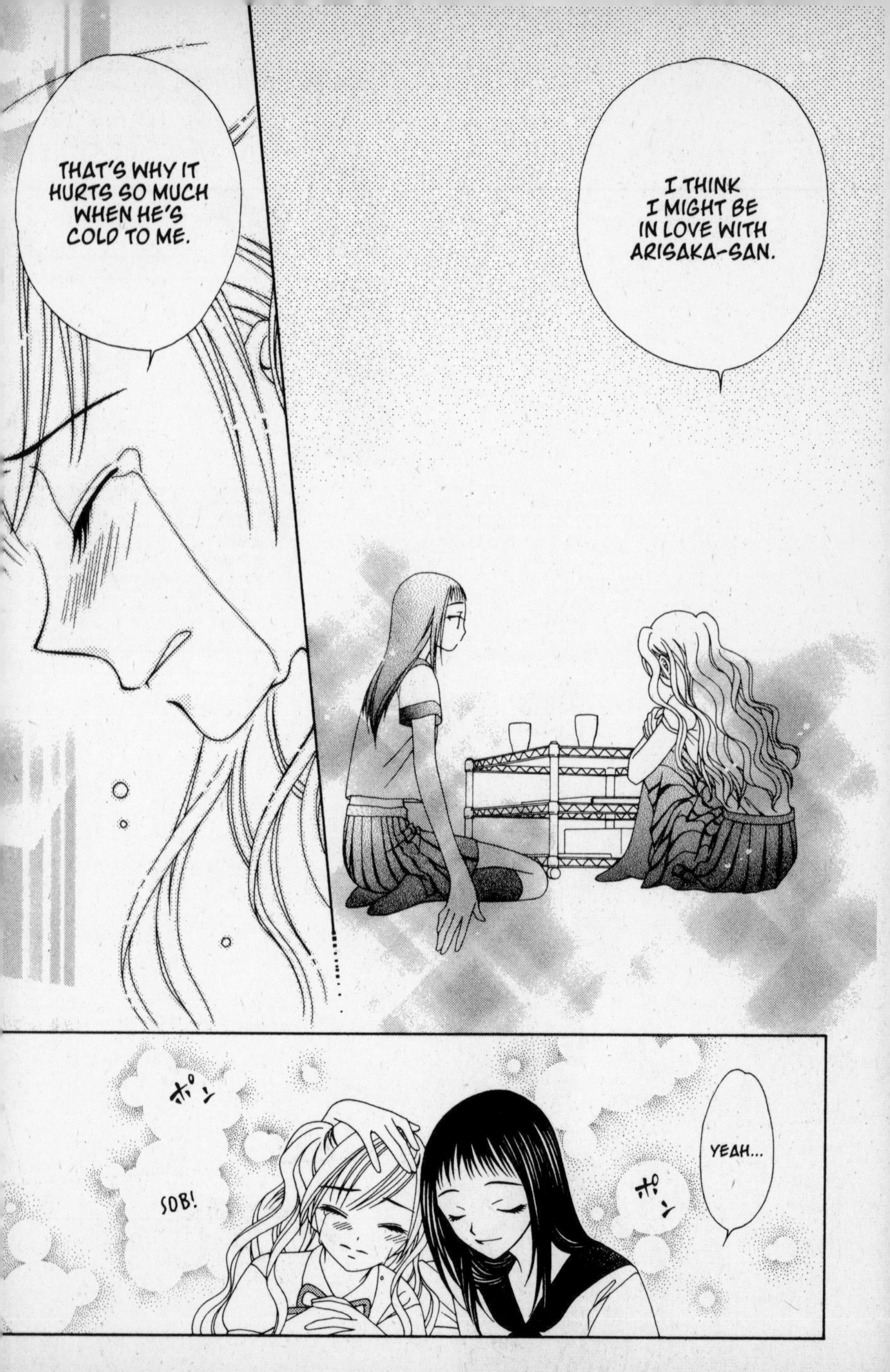
I THINK I MIGHT BE IN LOVE WITH ARISAKA-SAN.
THAT'S WHY IT HURTS SO MUCH WHEN HE'S COLD TO ME.
YEAH...
ポン
SOB!
ポン

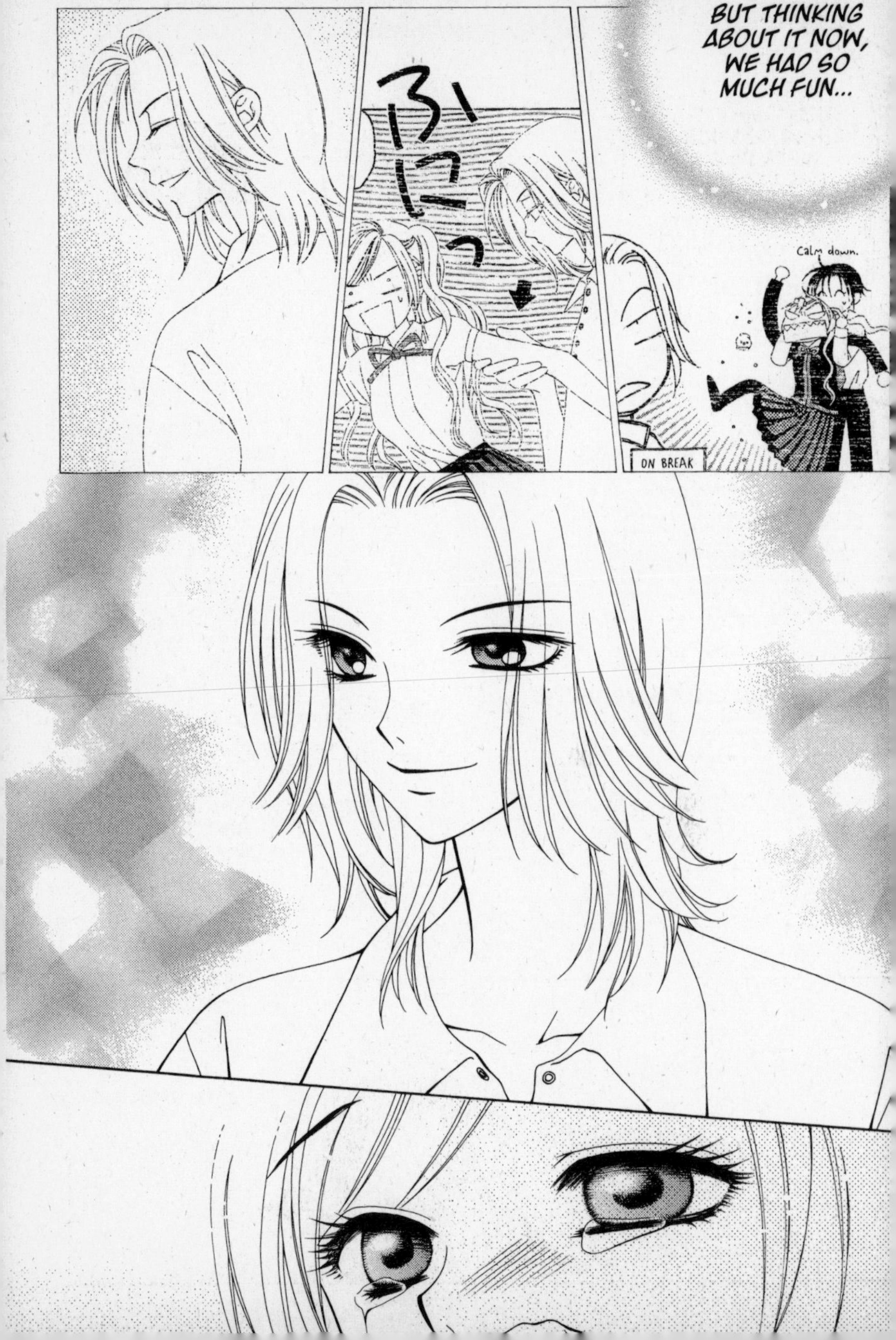
BUT THINKING ABOUT IT NOW, WE HAD SO MUCH FUN...
Calm down.
ON BREAK
ふにーっ

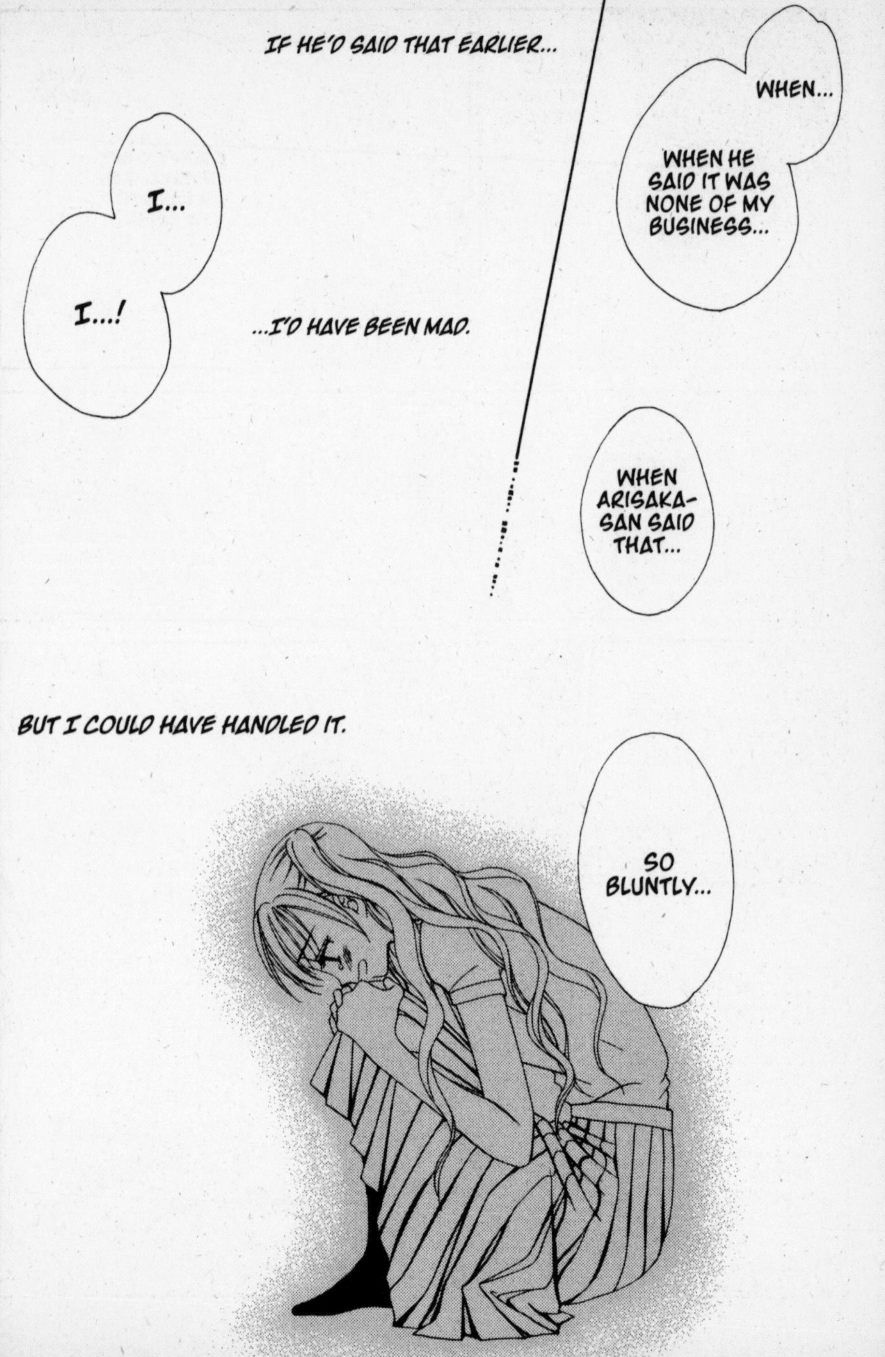
WHEN...
WHEN HE SAID IT WAS NONE OF MY BUSINESS...
WHEN ARISAKA-SAN SAID THAT...
IF HE'D SAID THAT EARLIER...
...I'D HAVE BEEN MAD.
I...
I...!
SO BLUNTLY...
BUT I COULD HAVE HANDLED IT.

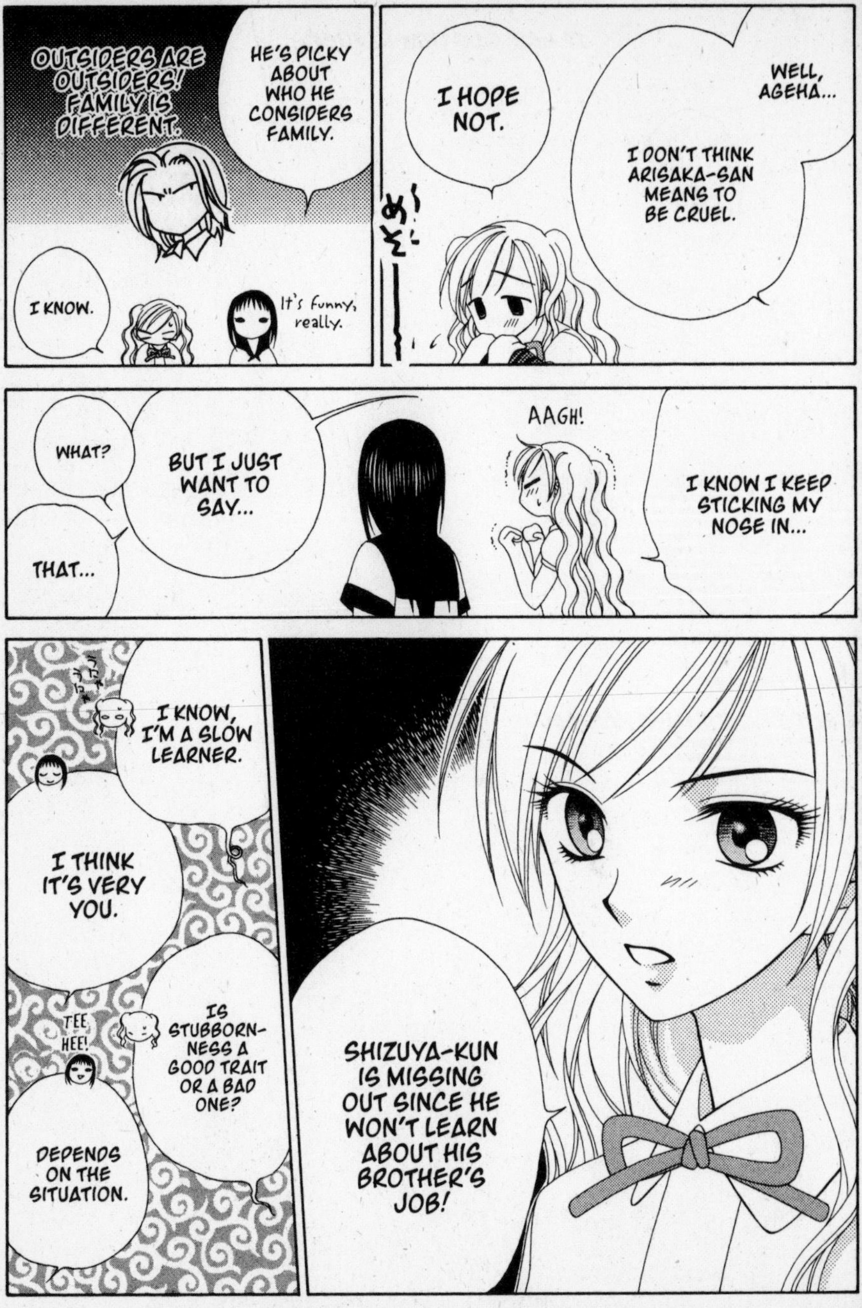
WELL, AGEHA...
I DON'T THINK ARISAKA-SAN MEANS TO BE CRUEL.
I HOPE NOT.
HE'S PICKY ABOUT WHO HE CONSIDERS FAMILY.
OUTSIDERS ARE OUTSIDERS! FAMILY IS DIFFERENT.
It's funny, really.
I KNOW.
I KNOW I KEEP STICKING MY NOSE IN...
AAGH!
BUT I JUST WANT TO SAY...
WHAT?
THAT...
SHIZUYA-KUN IS MISSING OUT SINCE HE WON'T LEARN ABOUT HIS BROTHER'S JOB!
I KNOW, I'M A SLOW LEARNER.
I THINK IT'S VERY YOU.
IS STUBBORNNESS A GOOD TRAIT OR A BAD ONE?
TEE HEE!
DEPENDS ON THE SITUATION.

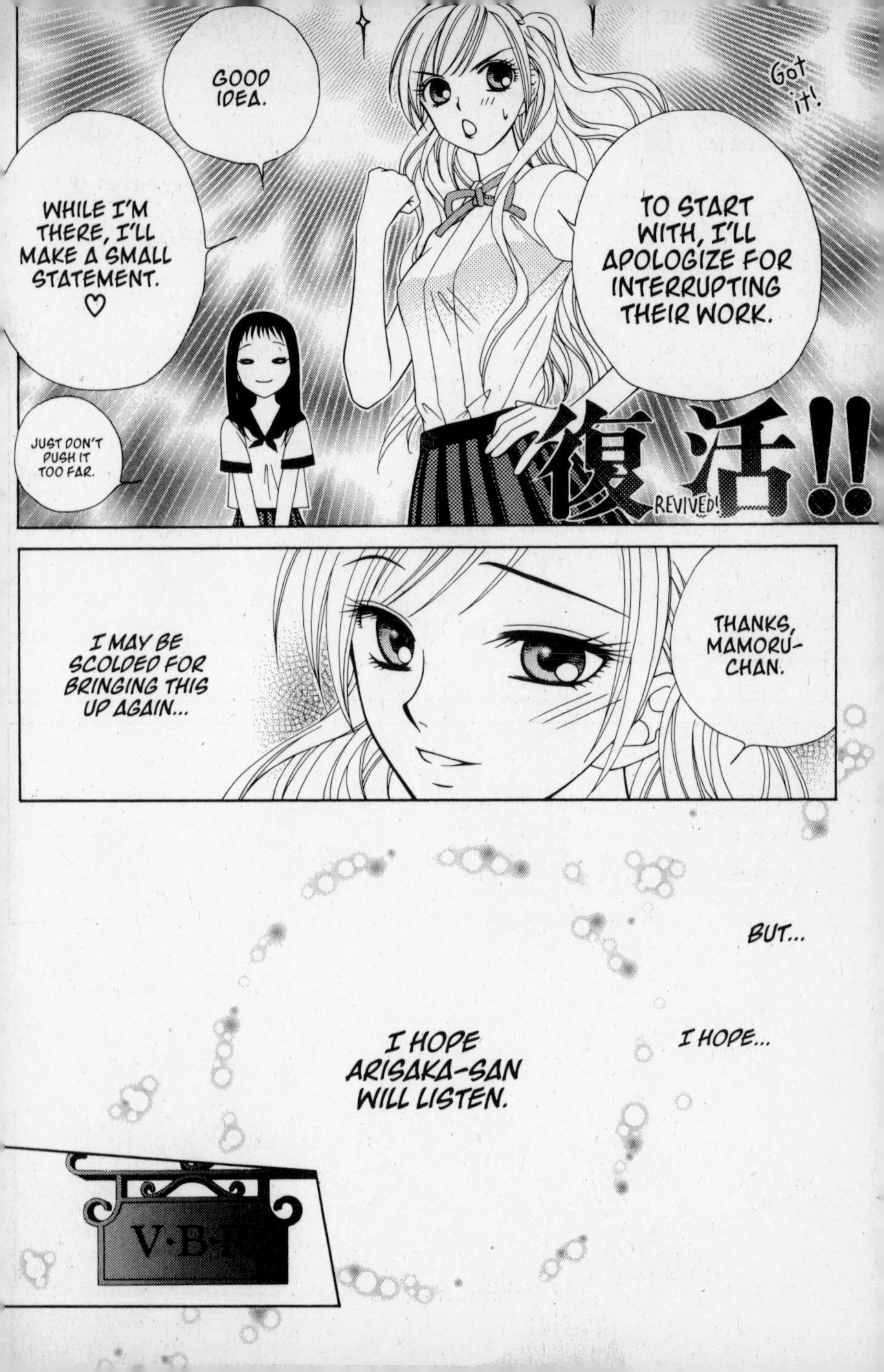

Got it!
TO START WITH, I'LL APOLOGIZE FOR INTERRUPTING THEIR WORK.
GOOD IDEA.
WHILE I'M THERE, I'LL MAKE A SMALL STATEMENT. ♡
復活!!
REVIVED!
JUST DON'T PUSH IT TOO FAR.
THANKS, MAMORU-CHAN.
I MAY BE SCOLDED FOR BRINGING THIS UP AGAIN...
BUT...
I HOPE...
I HOPE ARISAKA-SAN WILL LISTEN.

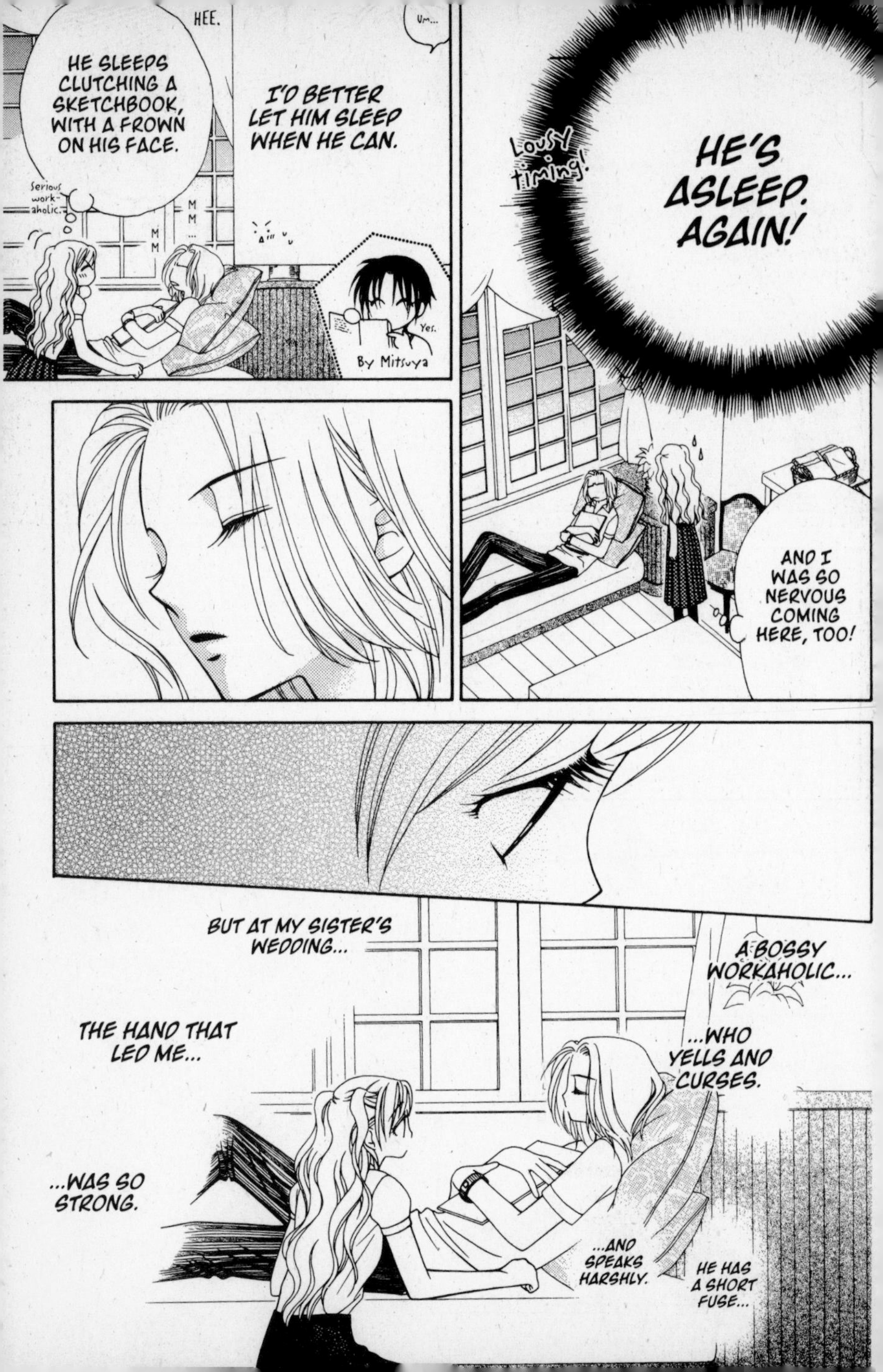
Lousy timing!
HE'S ASLEEP. AGAIN!
AND I WAS SO NERVOUS COMING HERE, TOO!
Um...
HEE.
HE SLEEPS CLUTCHING A SKETCHBOOK, WITH A FROWN ON HIS FACE.
Serious workaholic.
MMMM...
I'D BETTER LET HIM SLEEP WHEN HE CAN.
Yes.
By Mitsuya
A BOSSY WORKAHOLIC...
...WHO YELLS AND CURSES.
HE HAS A SHORT FUSE...
...AND SPEAKS HARSHLY.
BUT AT MY SISTER'S WEDDING...
THE HAND THAT LED ME...
...WAS SO STRONG.

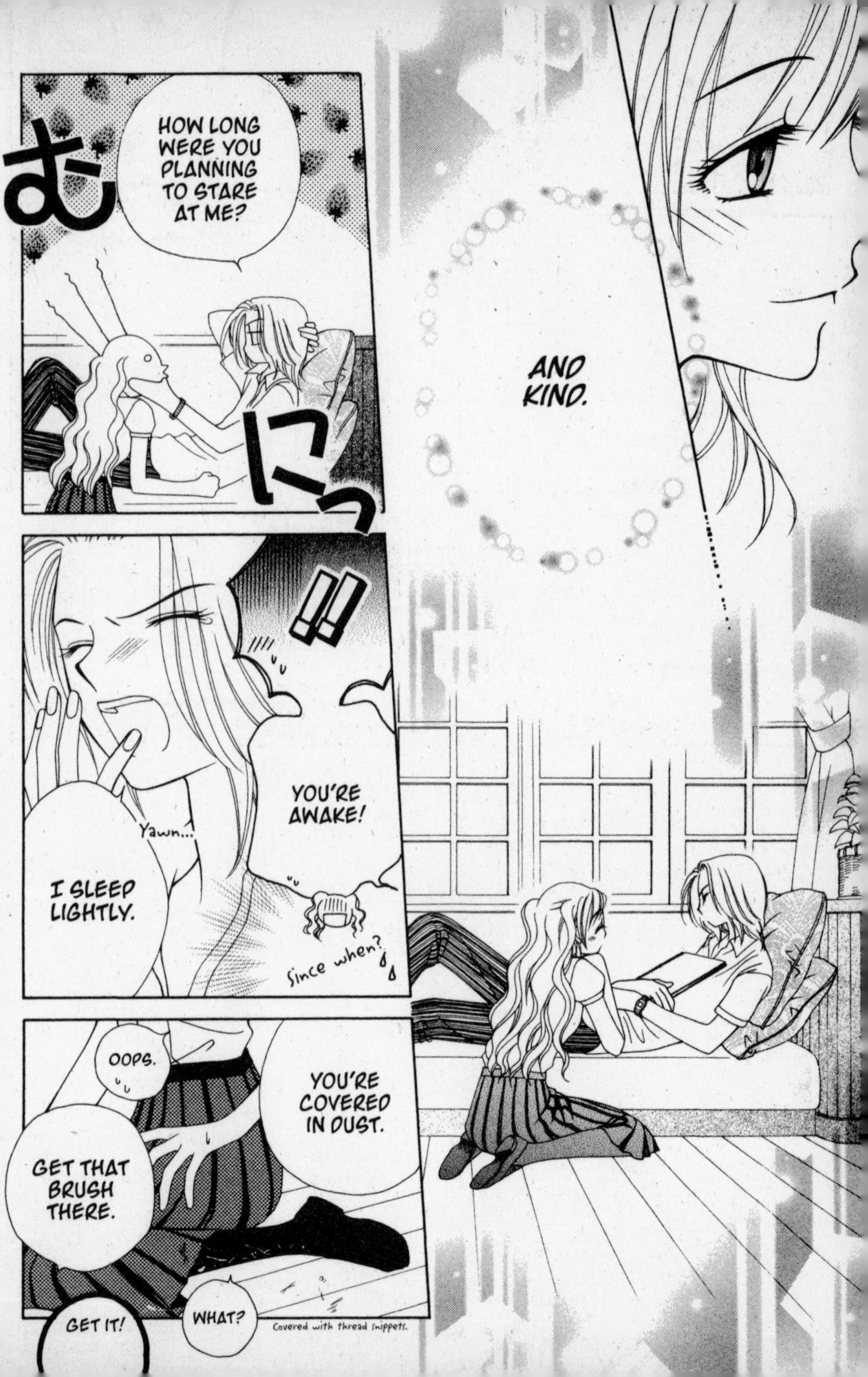
AND KIND.
む
HOW LONG WERE YOU PLANNING TO STARE AT ME?
にっ
!!
YOU'RE AWAKE!
Since when?
Yawn...
I SLEEP LIGHTLY.
YOU'RE COVERED IN DUST.
OOPS.
GET THAT BRUSH THERE.
WHAT?
GET IT!
Covered with thread snippets.

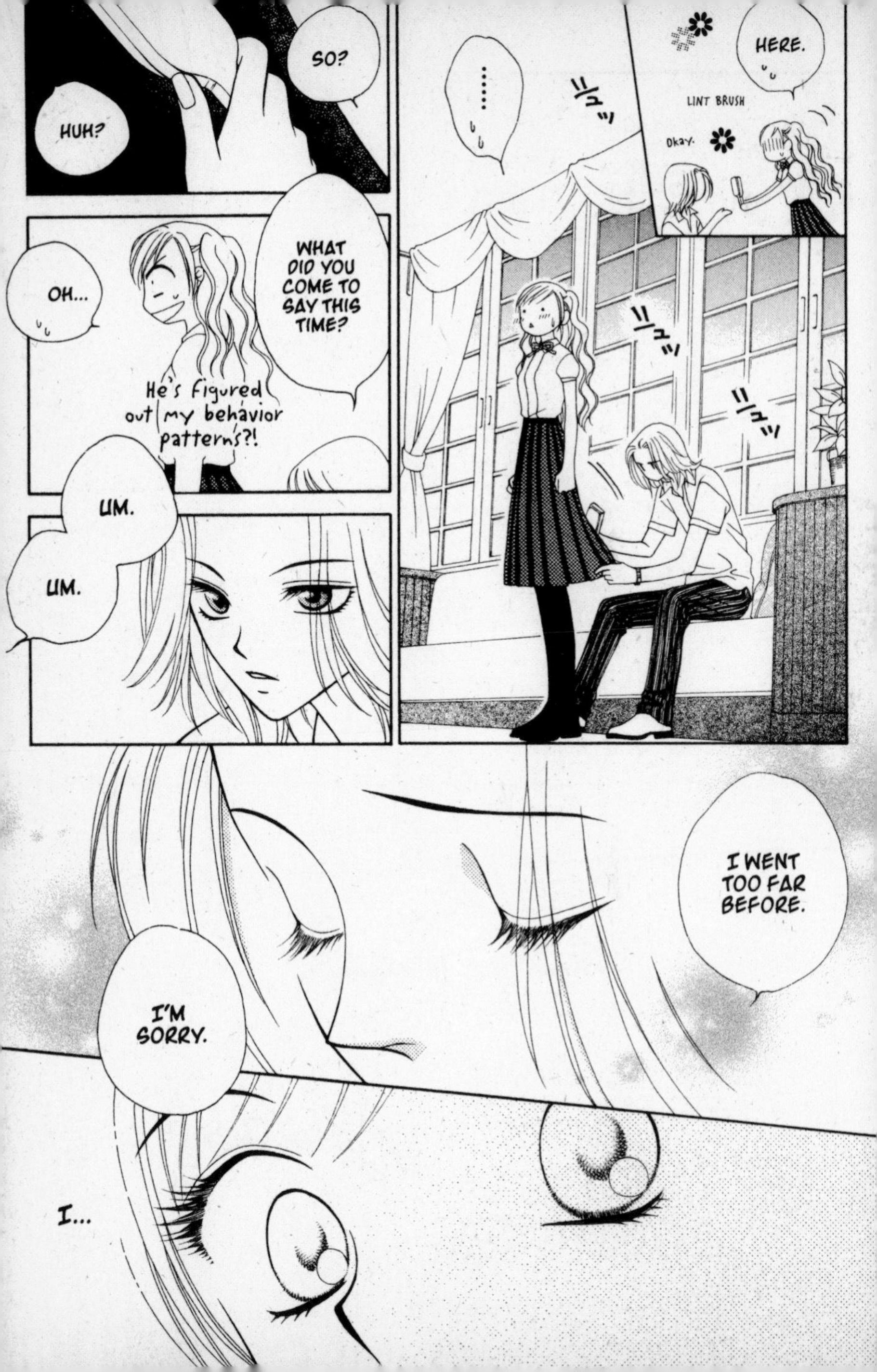
HERE.
LINT BRUSH
Okay.
......
SO?
HUH?
WHAT DID YOU COME TO SAY THIS TIME?
OH...
He's figured out my behavior patterns?!
UM.
UM.
I WENT TOO FAR BEFORE.
I'M SORRY.
I...

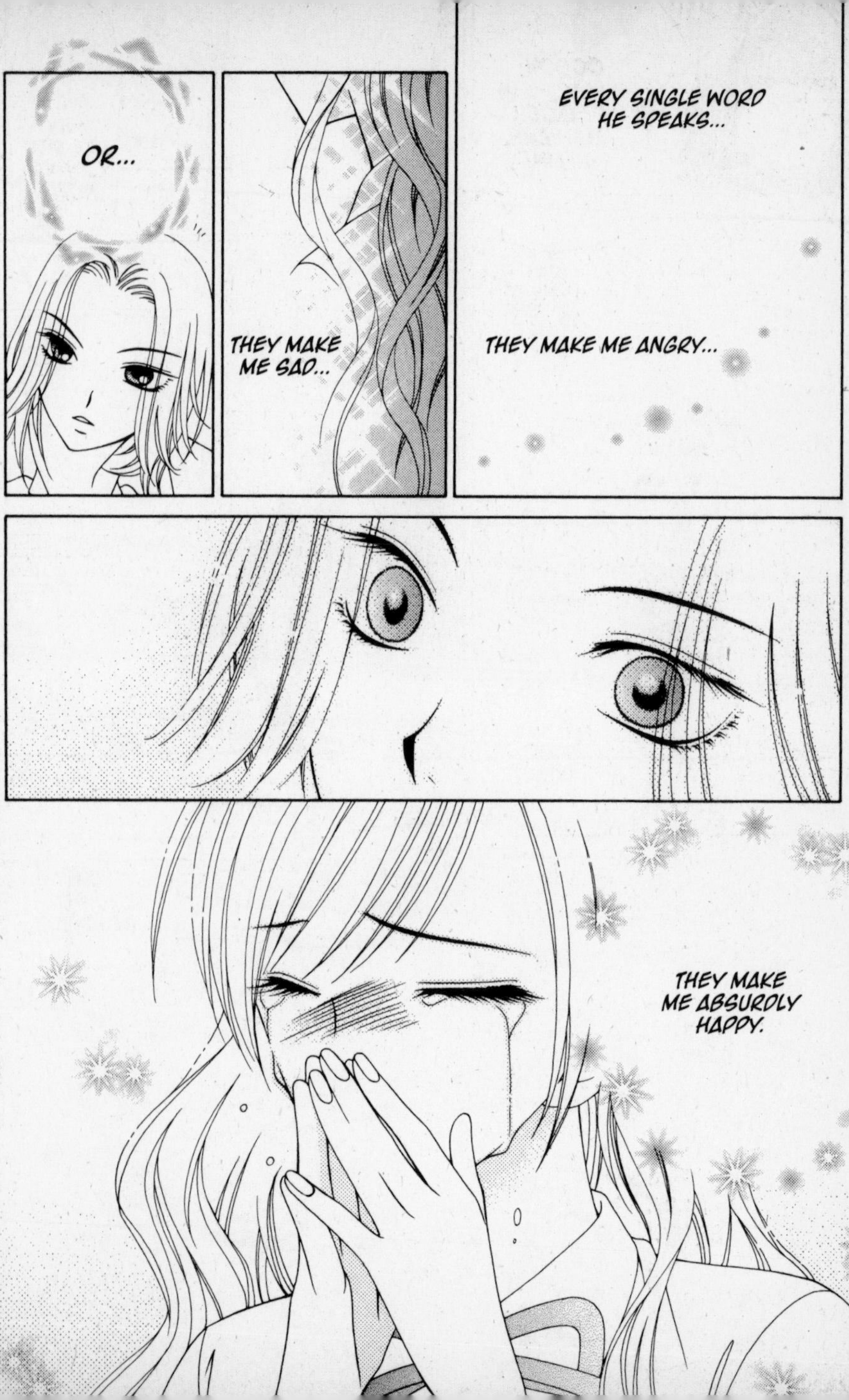
EVERY SINGLE WORD HE SPEAKS...
THEY MAKE ME ANGRY...
THEY MAKE ME SAD...
OR...
THEY MAKE ME ABSURDLY HAPPY.

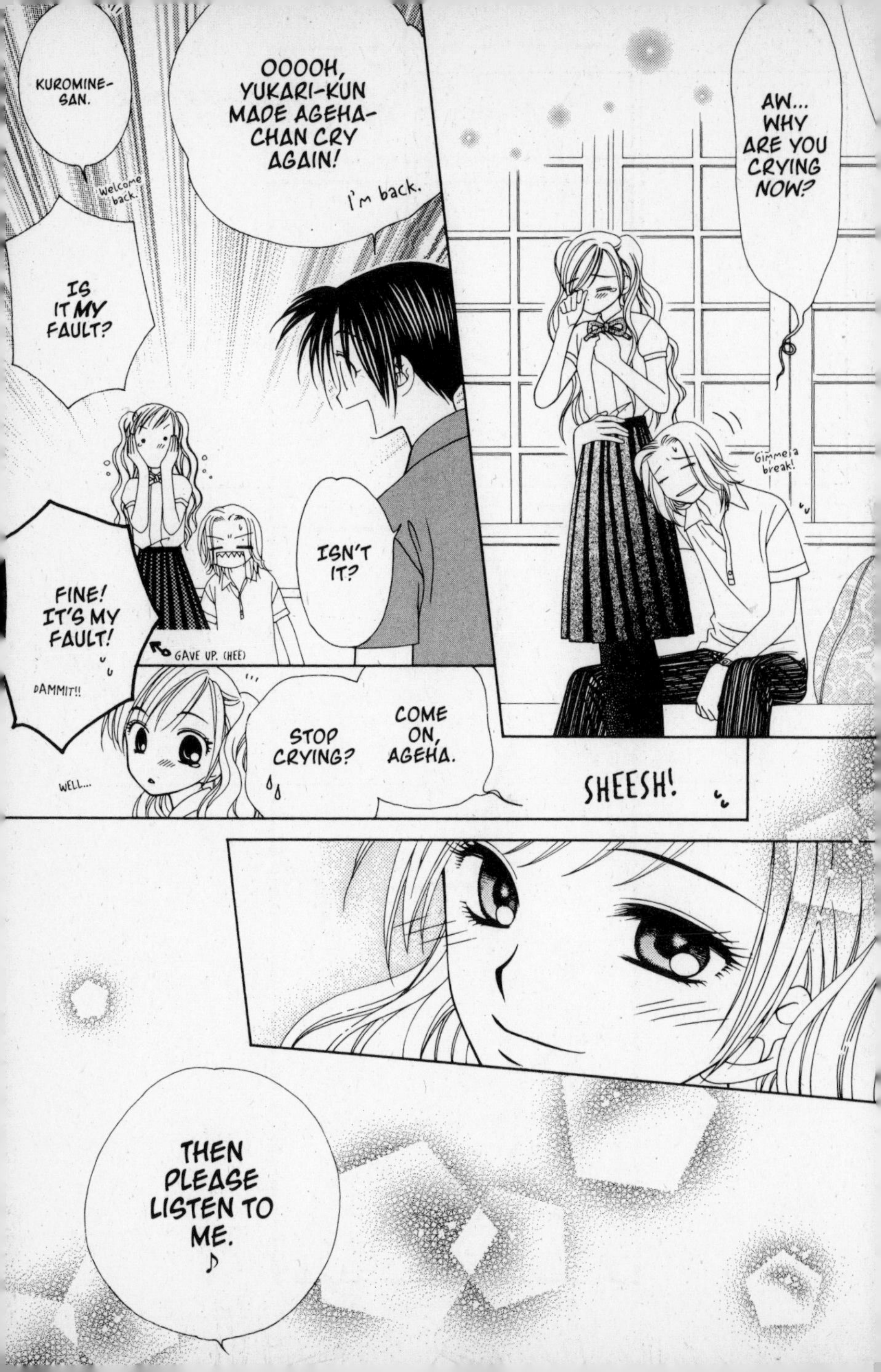
AW... WHY ARE YOU CRYING NOW?
Gimme a break!
I'm back.
OOOOH, YUKARI-KUN MADE AGEHA-CHAN CRY AGAIN!
Welcome back.
KUROMINE-SAN.
IS IT MY FAULT?
ISN'T IT?
GAVE UP. (HEE)
FINE! IT'S MY FAULT!
DAMMIT!!
SHEESH!
COME ON, AGEHA.
STOP CRYING?
WELL...
THEN PLEASE LISTEN TO ME. ♪

Instructions to V • ⑧

Velvet

The first panel on the last page of chapter ten...

My assistant's reaction was...

↑

The page right before this page...

Work time!

Yukari-san's committing sexual harassment!!

What?!

Is that not okay?

Oh, that's true.

His arm is around her hip!!

I received letters from fans as well.

He's allowed. (heh!)

HEY!

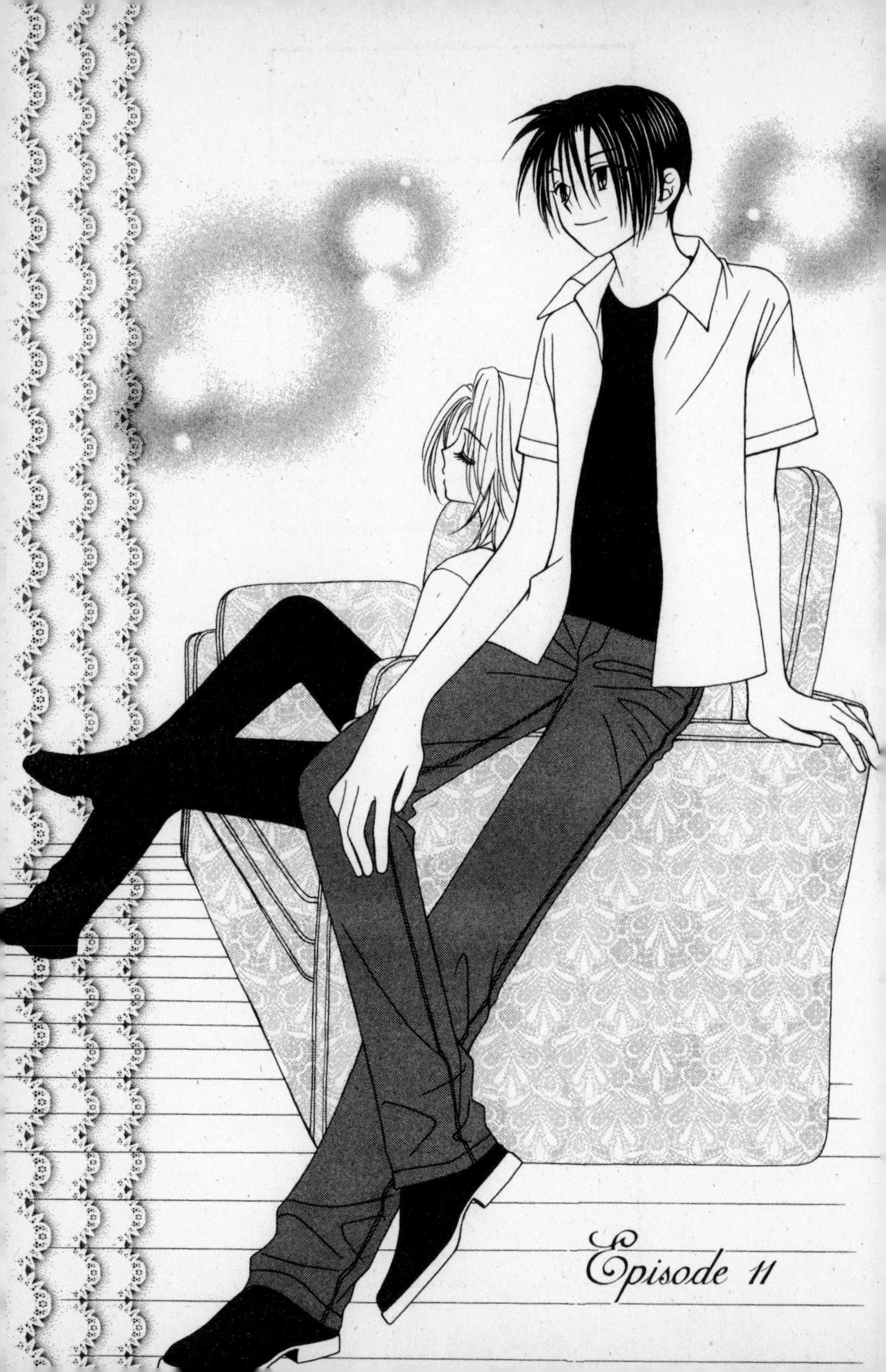
Episode 11

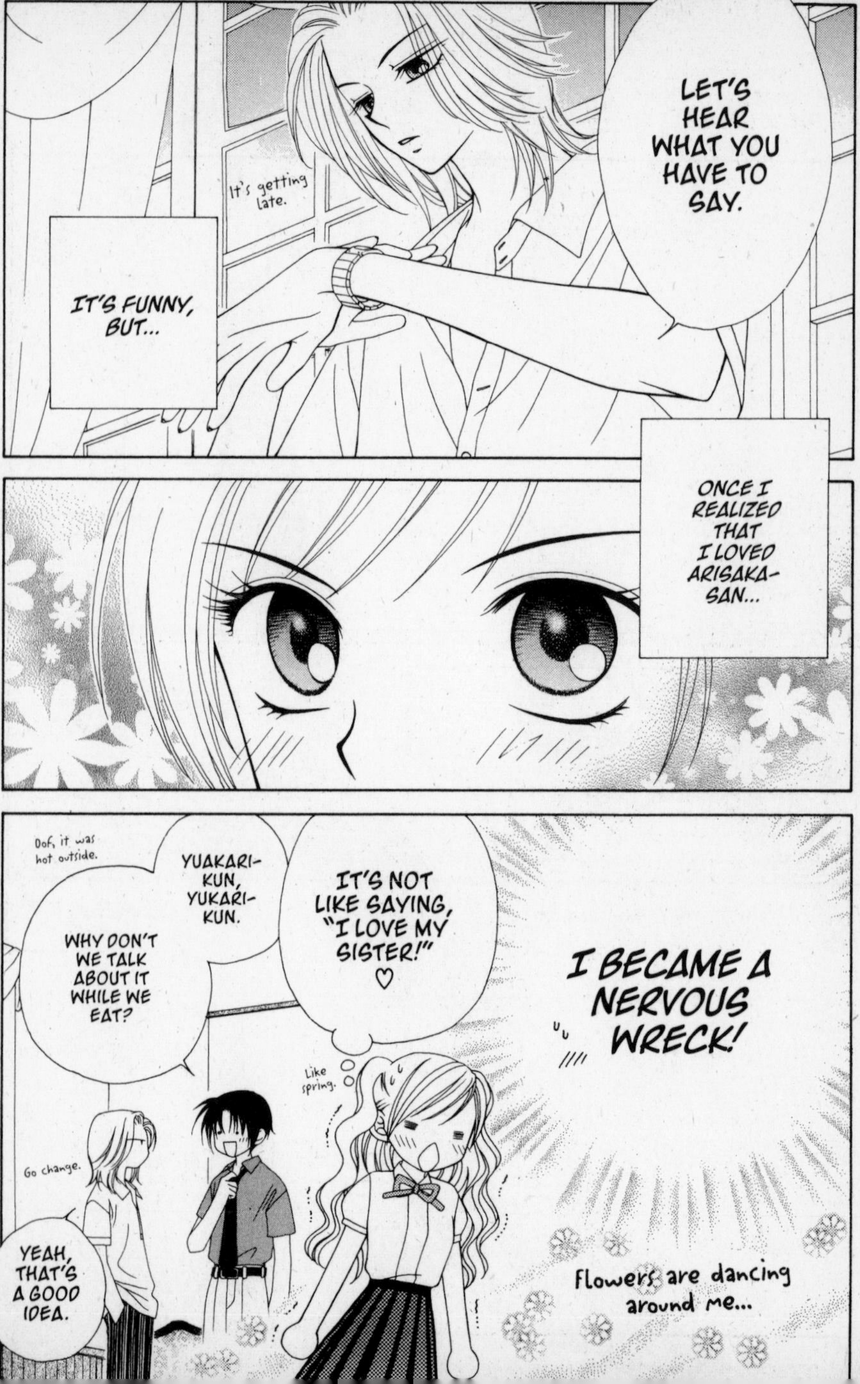
LET'S HEAR WHAT YOU HAVE TO SAY.
It's getting late.
IT'S FUNNY, BUT...
ONCE I REALIZED THAT I LOVED ARISAKA-SAN...
I BECAME A NERVOUS WRECK!
Flowers are dancing around me...
IT'S NOT LIKE SAYING, "I LOVE MY SISTER!" ♡
Like spring.
YUAKARI-KUN, YUKARI-KUN.
WHY DON'T WE TALK ABOUT IT WHILE WE EAT?
Oof, it was hot outside.
Go change.
YEAH, THAT'S A GOOD IDEA.

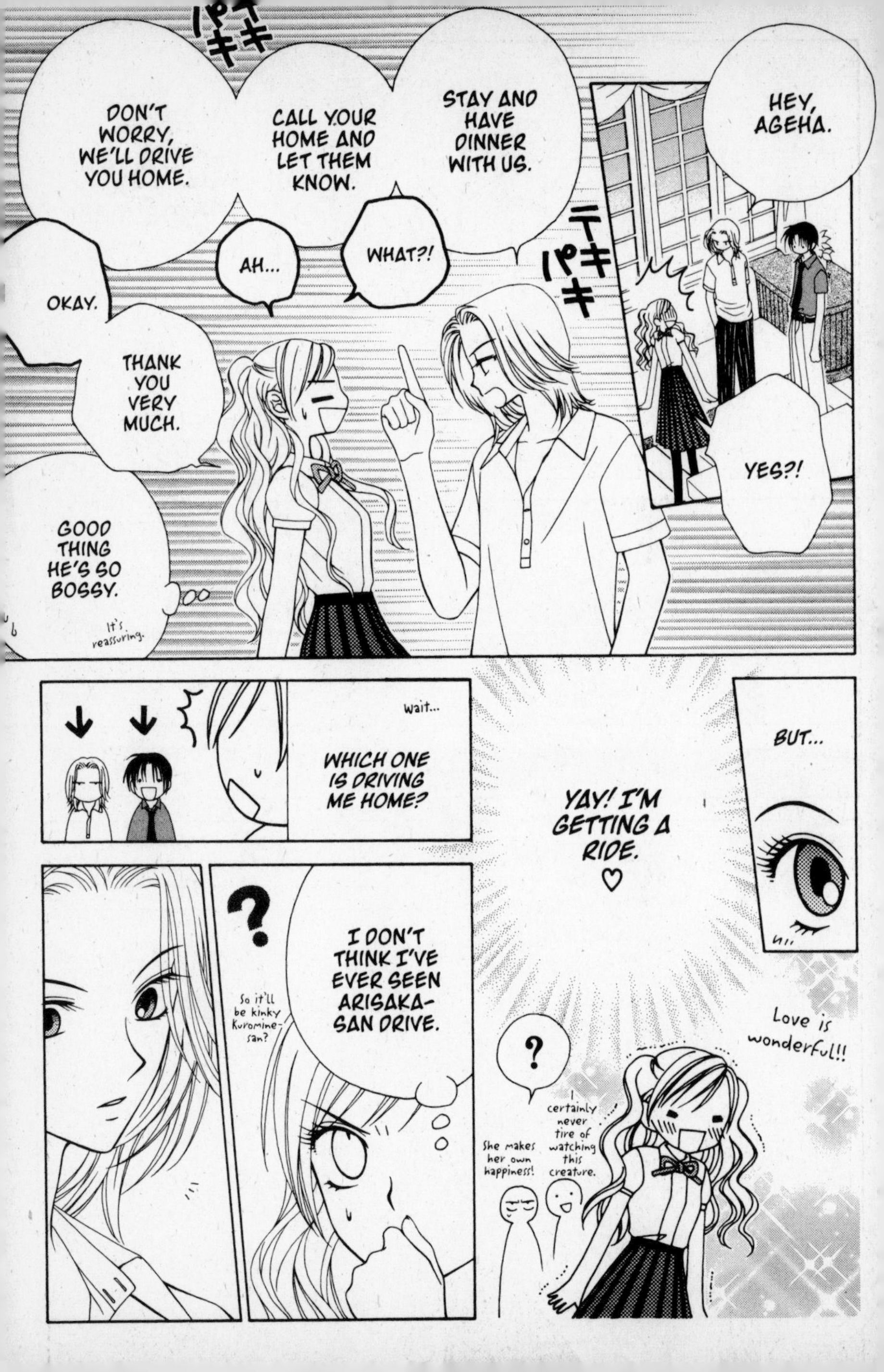
HEY, AGEHA.
テキパキ
YES?!
STAY AND HAVE DINNER WITH US.
CALL YOUR HOME AND LET THEM KNOW.
DON'T WORRY, WE'LL DRIVE YOU HOME.
WHAT?!
AH...
OKAY.
THANK YOU VERY MUCH.
GOOD THING HE'S SO BOSSY.
It's reassuring.
BUT...
YAY! I'M GETTING A RIDE. ♡
wait...
WHICH ONE IS DRIVING ME HOME?
Love is wonderful!!
?
I certainly never tire of watching this creature.
She makes her own happiness!
I DON'T THINK I'VE EVER SEEN ARISAKA-SAN DRIVE.
So it'll be kinky Kuromine-san?
?

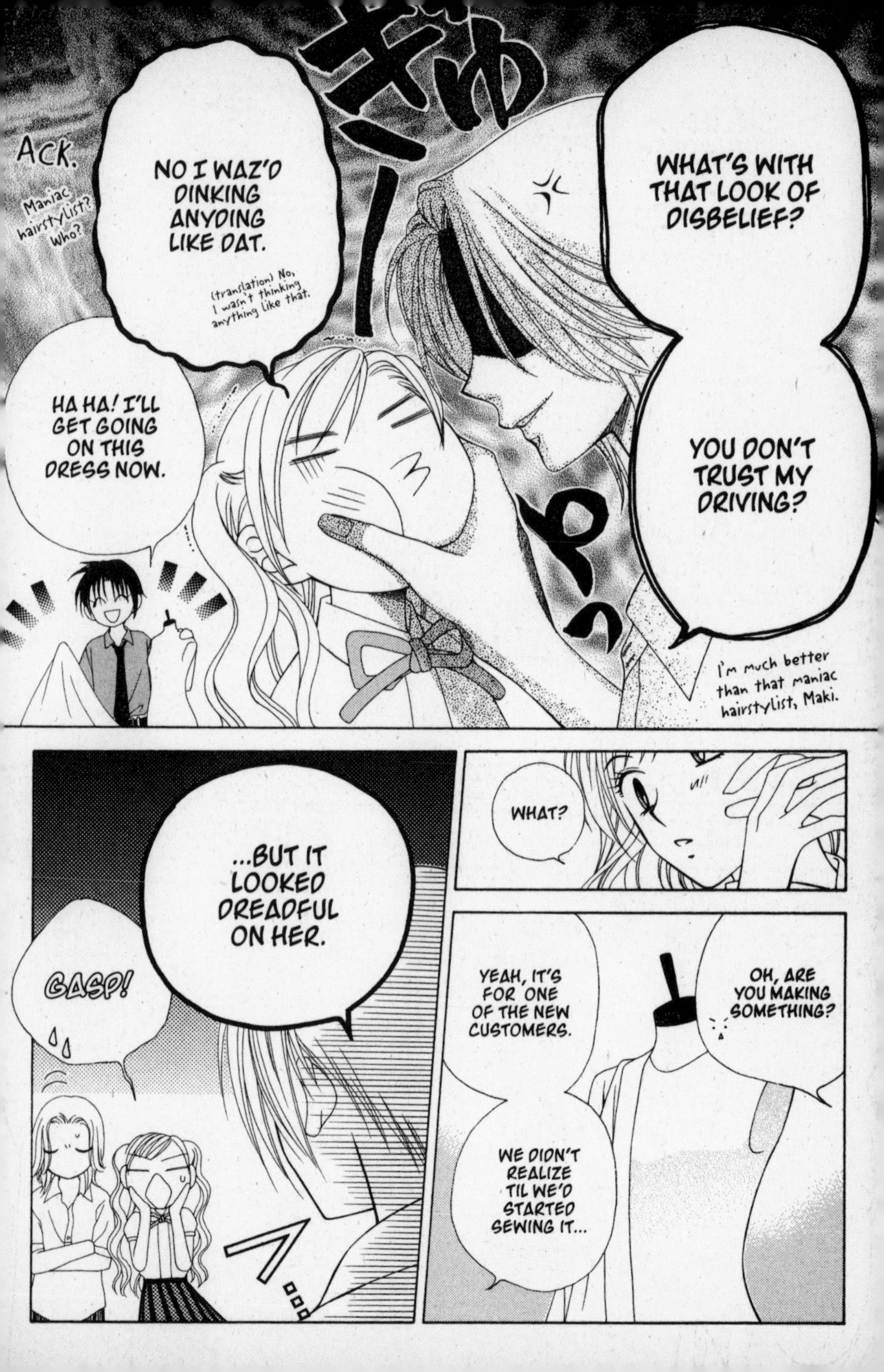
ぎゅー
WHAT'S WITH THAT LOOK OF DISBELIEF?
YOU DON'T TRUST MY DRIVING?
I'm much better than that maniac hairstylist, Maki.
NO I WAZ'D DINKING ANYDING LIKE DAT.
(translation) No, I wasn't thinking anything like that.
ACK.
Maniac hairstylist? Who?
HA HA! I'LL GET GOING ON THIS DRESS NOW.
WHAT?
OH, ARE YOU MAKING SOMETHING?
YEAH, IT'S FOR ONE OF THE NEW CUSTOMERS.
WE DIDN'T REALIZE TIL WE'D STARTED SEWING IT...
...BUT IT LOOKED DREADFUL ON HER.
GASP!

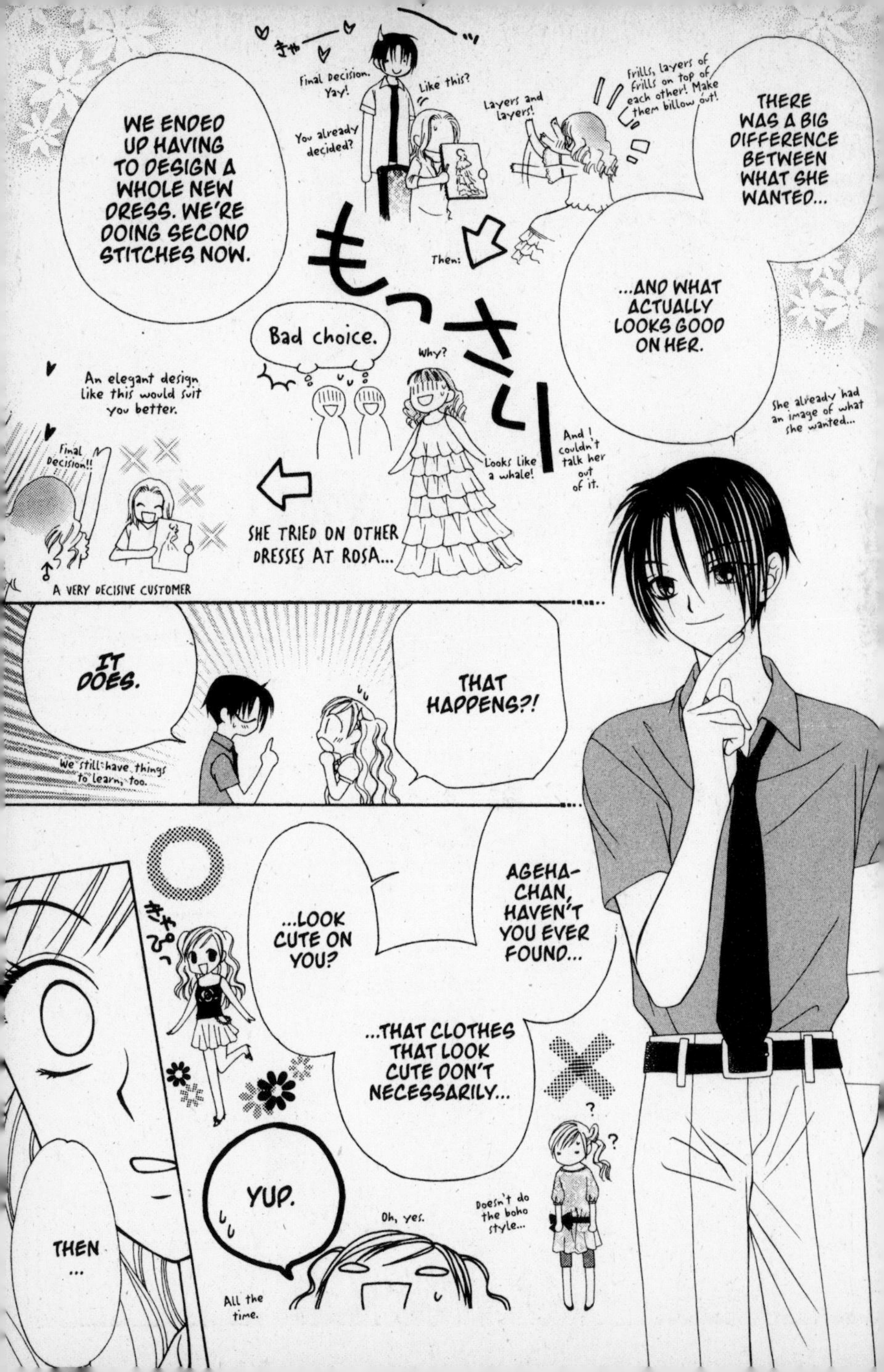

THERE WAS A BIG DIFFERENCE BETWEEN WHAT SHE WANTED...
...AND WHAT ACTUALLY LOOKS GOOD ON HER.
She already had an image of what she wanted...
Frills, layers of frills on top of each other! Make them billow out!
Layers and layers!
Like this?
Final Decision. Yay!
You already decided?
Then:
もっさり
And I couldn't talk her out of it.
Looks like a whale!
Why?
Bad choice.
SHE TRIED ON OTHER DRESSES AT ROSA...
An elegant design like this would suit you better.
Final Decision!!
A VERY DECISIVE CUSTOMER
WE ENDED UP HAVING TO DESIGN A WHOLE NEW DRESS. WE'RE DOING SECOND STITCHES NOW.
AGEHA-CHAN, HAVEN'T YOU EVER FOUND...
...THAT CLOTHES THAT LOOK CUTE DON'T NECESSARILY...
...LOOK CUTE ON YOU?
Doesn't do the boho style...
THAT HAPPENS?!
IT DOES.
We still have things to learn, too.
YUP.
Oh, yes.
All the time.
THEN...

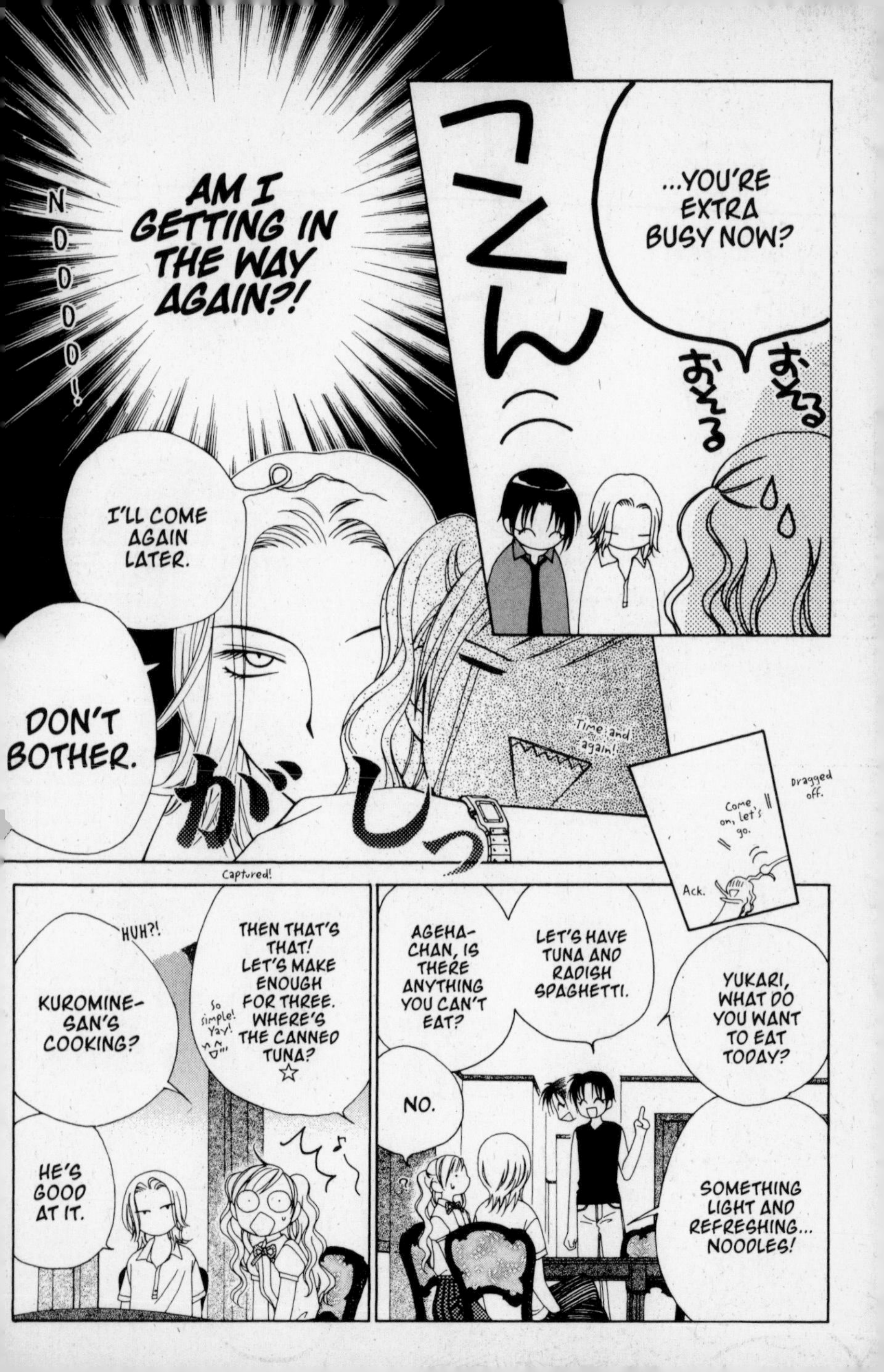
...YOU'RE EXTRA BUSY NOW?
おそる おそる
こくん
AM I GETTING IN THE WAY AGAIN?!
NOOOOO!
I'LL COME AGAIN LATER.
DON'T BOTHER.
Time and again!
がしっ
Captured!
Dragged off.
Come on, let's go.
Ack.
YUKARI, WHAT DO YOU WANT TO EAT TODAY?
SOMETHING LIGHT AND REFRESHING... NOODLES!
LET'S HAVE TUNA AND RADISH SPAGHETTI.
AGEHA-CHAN, IS THERE ANYTHING YOU CAN'T EAT?
NO.
THEN THAT'S THAT! LET'S MAKE ENOUGH FOR THREE. WHERE'S THE CANNED TUNA? ☆
So simple! Yay!
HUH?!
KUROMINE-SAN'S COOKING?
HE'S GOOD AT IT.

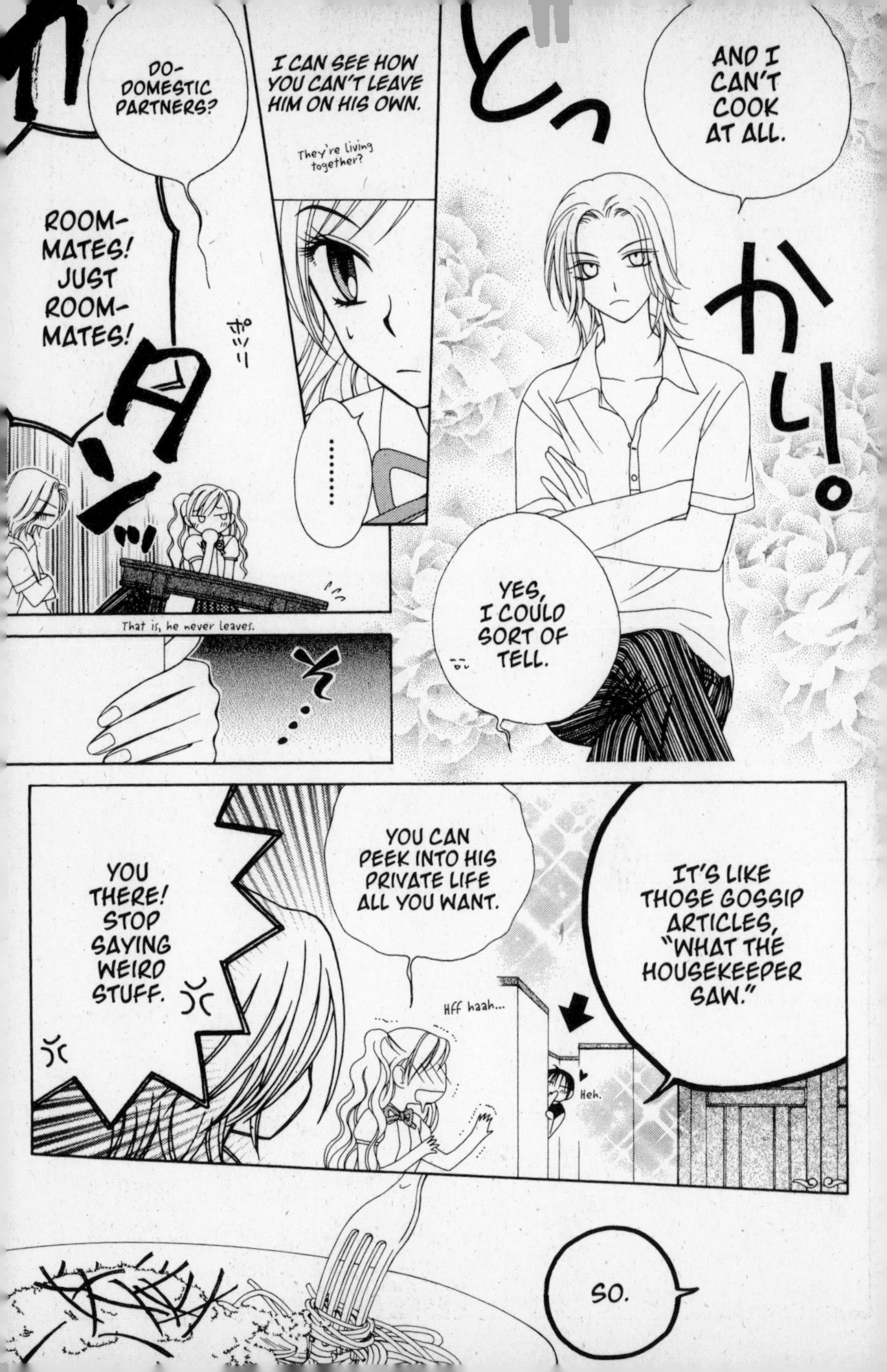
AND I CAN'T COOK AT ALL.
YES, I COULD SORT OF TELL.
I CAN SEE HOW YOU CAN'T LEAVE HIM ON HIS OWN.
They're living together?
......
DO-DOMESTIC PARTNERS?
ROOM-MATES! JUST ROOM-MATES!
That is, he never leaves.
IT'S LIKE THOSE GOSSIP ARTICLES, "WHAT THE HOUSEKEEPER SAW."
YOU CAN PEEK INTO HIS PRIVATE LIFE ALL YOU WANT.
Heh.
Hff haah...
YOU THERE! STOP SAYING WEIRD STUFF.
SO.

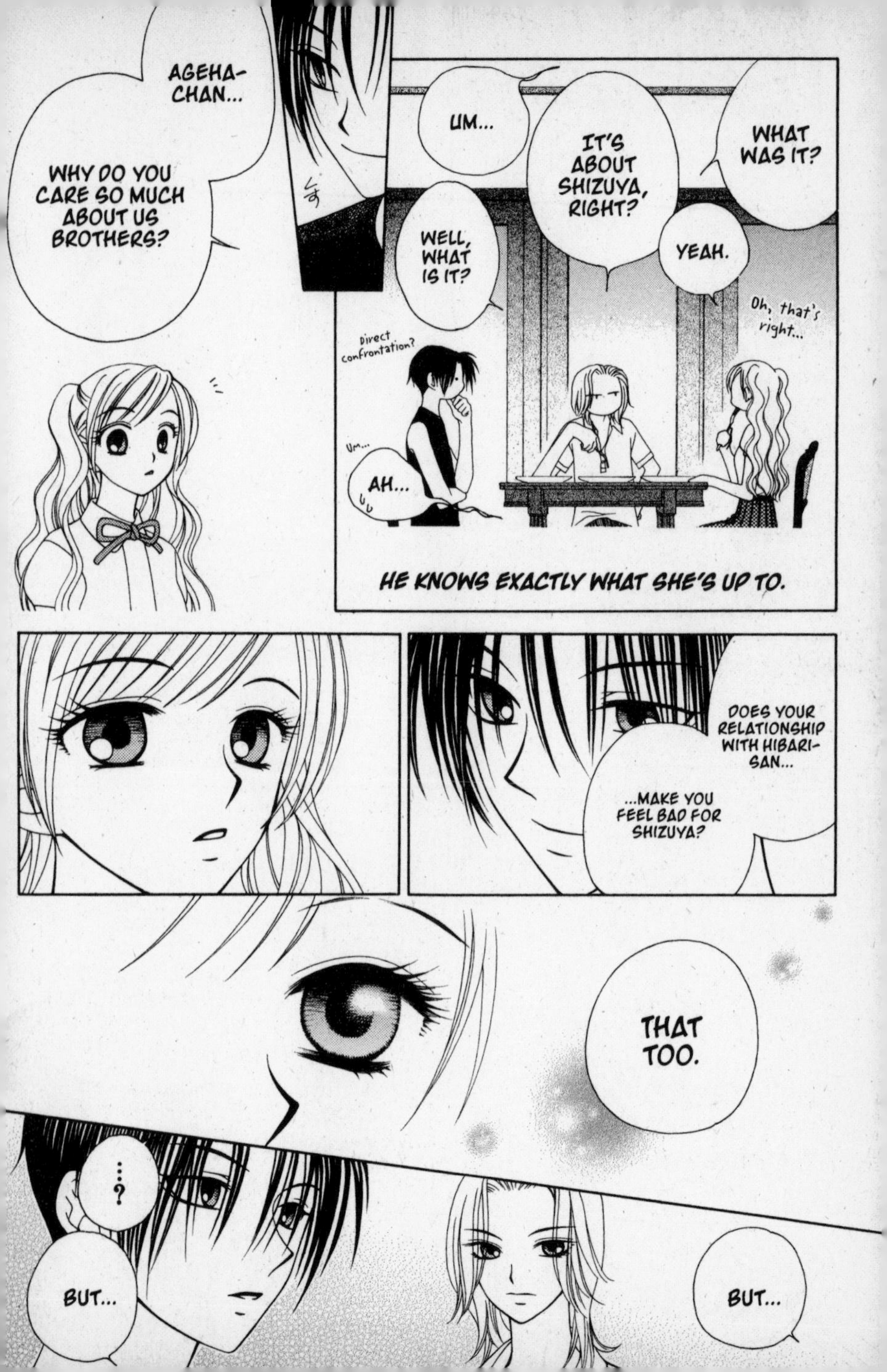
WHAT WAS IT?
IT'S ABOUT SHIZUYA, RIGHT?
UM...
YEAH.
WELL, WHAT IS IT?
Oh, that's right...
Direct confrontation?
Um...
AH...
HE KNOWS EXACTLY WHAT SHE'S UP TO.
AGEHA-CHAN...
くす
WHY DO YOU CARE SO MUCH ABOUT US BROTHERS?
DOES YOUR RELATIONSHIP WITH HIBARI-SAN...
...MAKE YOU FEEL BAD FOR SHIZUYA?
THAT TOO.
BUT...
...?
BUT...

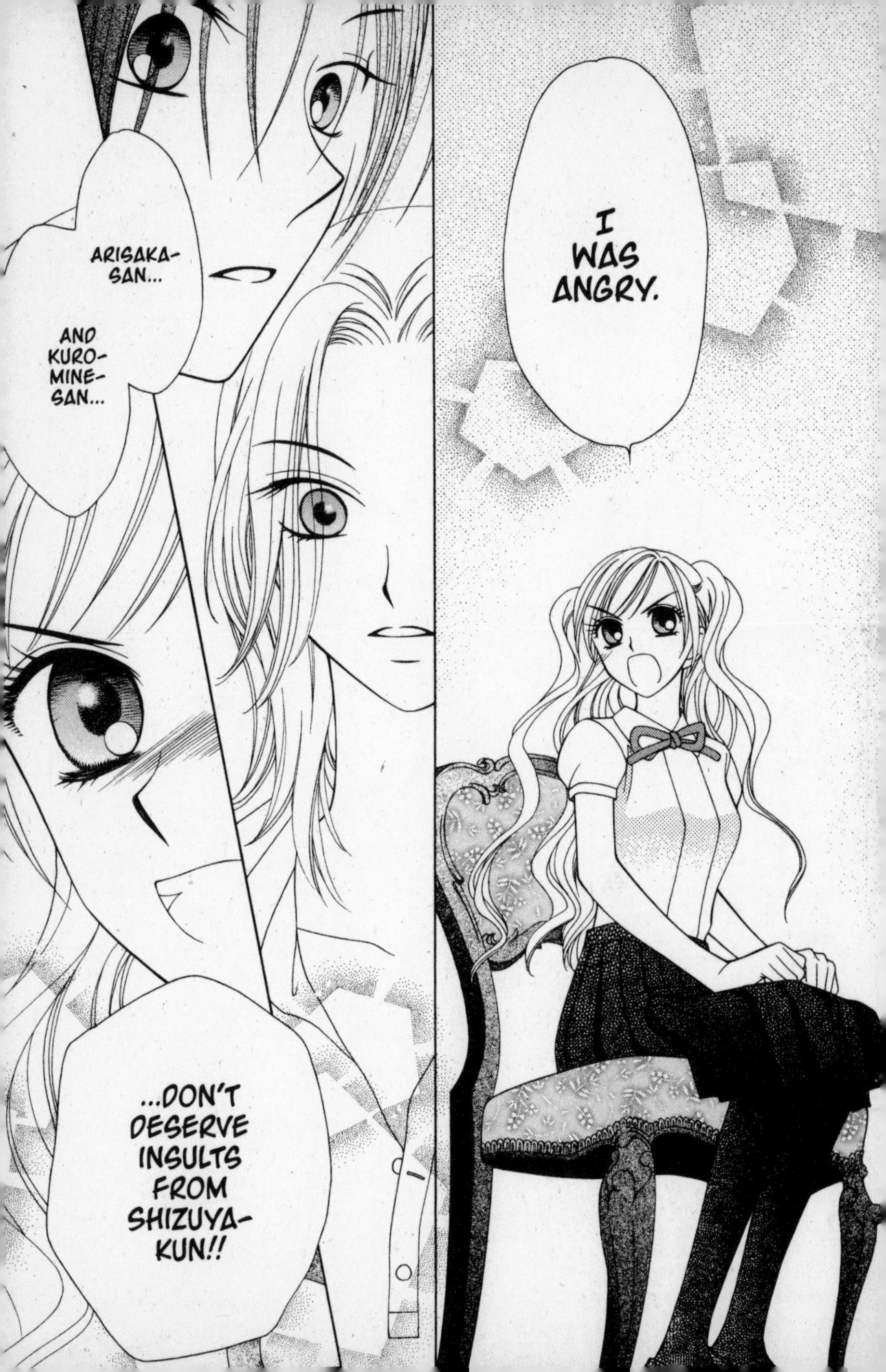
I WAS ANGRY.
ARISAKA-SAN...
AND KUROMINE-SAN...
...DON'T DESERVE INSULTS FROM SHIZUYA-KUN!!

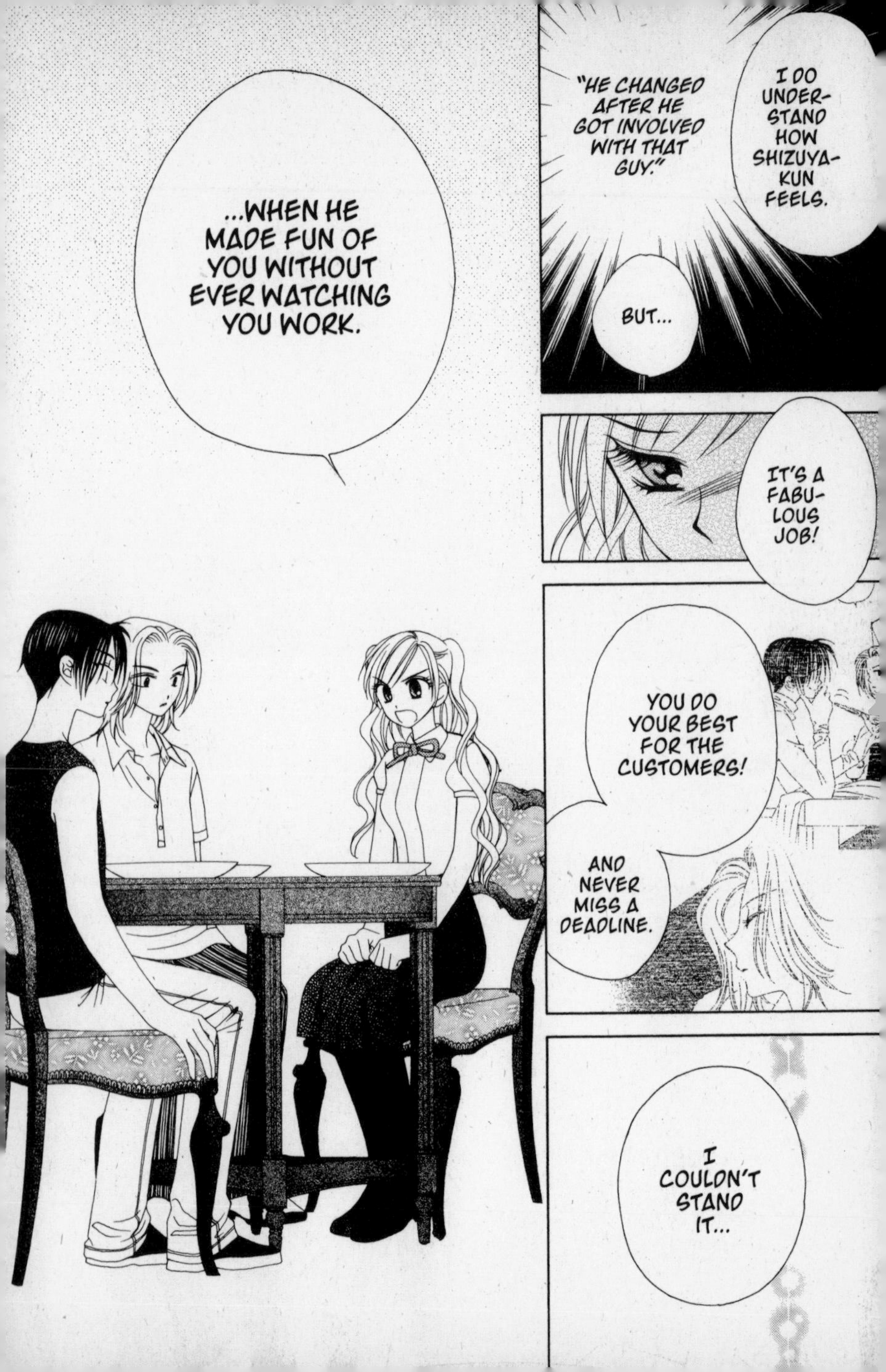
I DO UNDER-STAND HOW SHIZUYA-KUN FEELS.
"HE CHANGED AFTER HE GOT INVOLVED WITH THAT GUY."
BUT...
IT'S A FABU-LOUS JOB!
YOU DO YOUR BEST FOR THE CUSTOMERS!
AND NEVER MISS A DEADLINE.
I COULDN'T STAND IT...
...WHEN HE MADE FUN OF YOU WITHOUT EVER WATCHING YOU WORK.

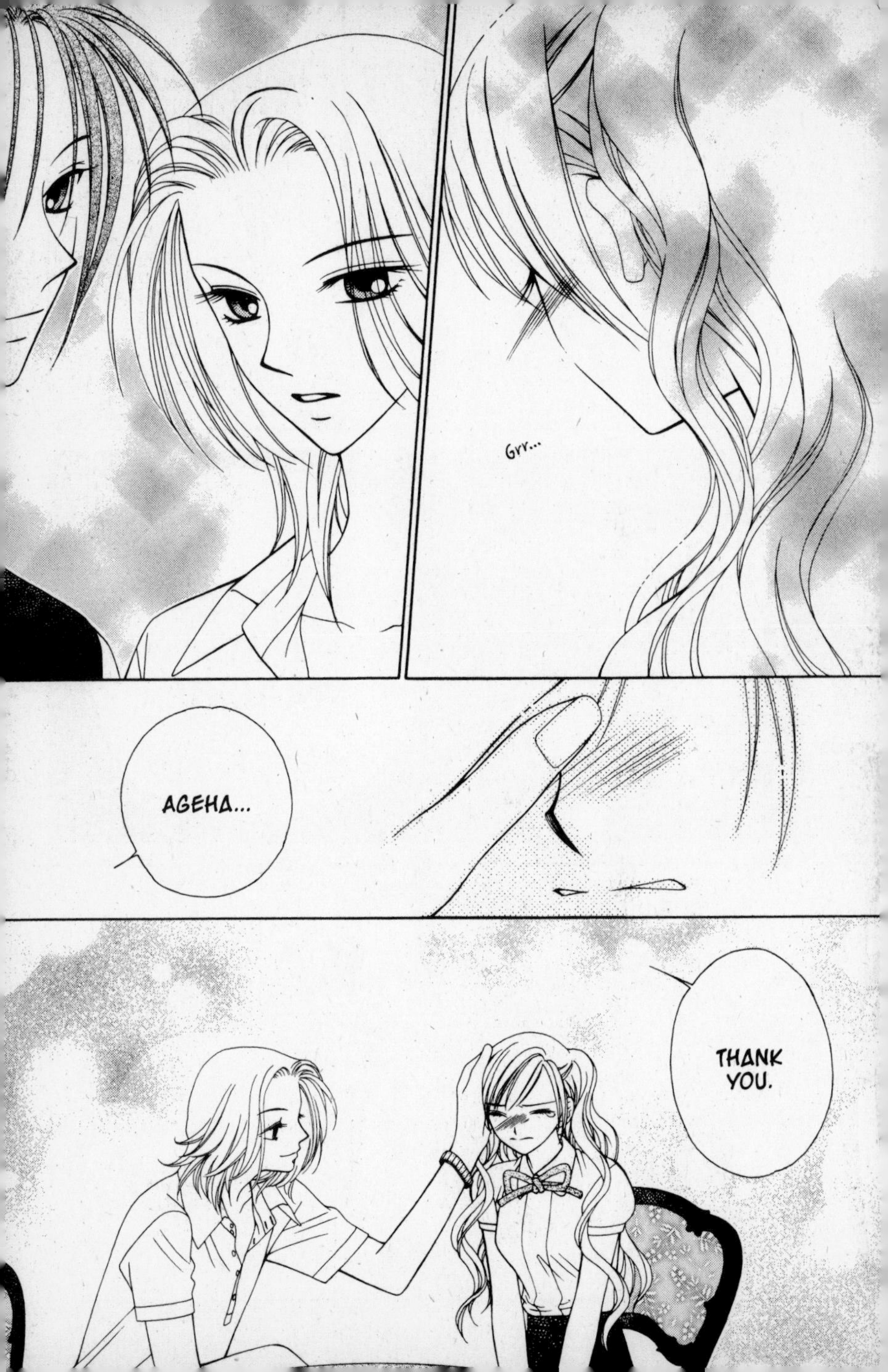
Grr...
AGEHA...
THANK YOU.

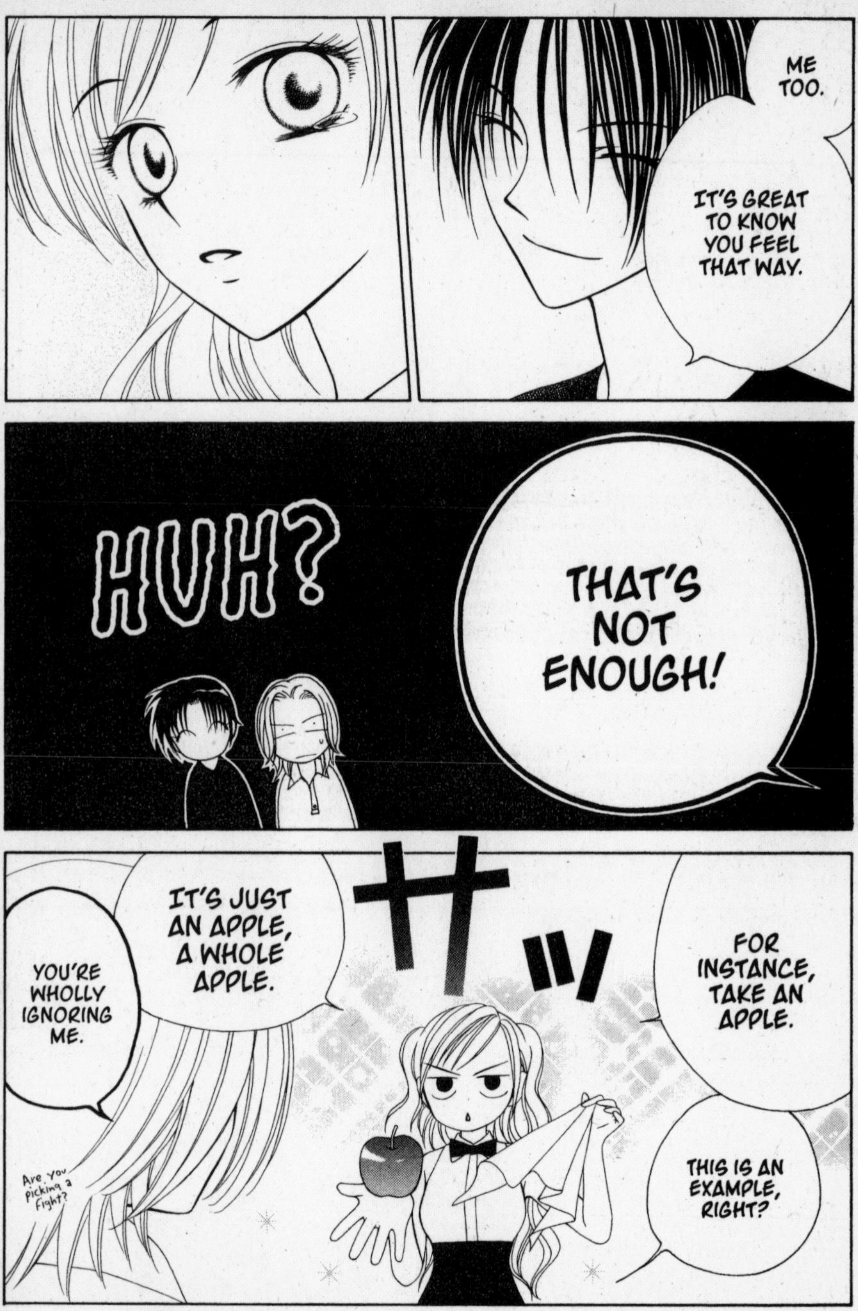
ME TOO.
IT'S GREAT TO KNOW YOU FEEL THAT WAY.
THAT'S NOT ENOUGH!
HUH?
FOR INSTANCE, TAKE AN APPLE.
THIS IS AN EXAMPLE, RIGHT?
IT'S JUST AN APPLE, A WHOLE APPLE.
YOU'RE WHOLLY IGNORING ME.
Are you picking a fight?

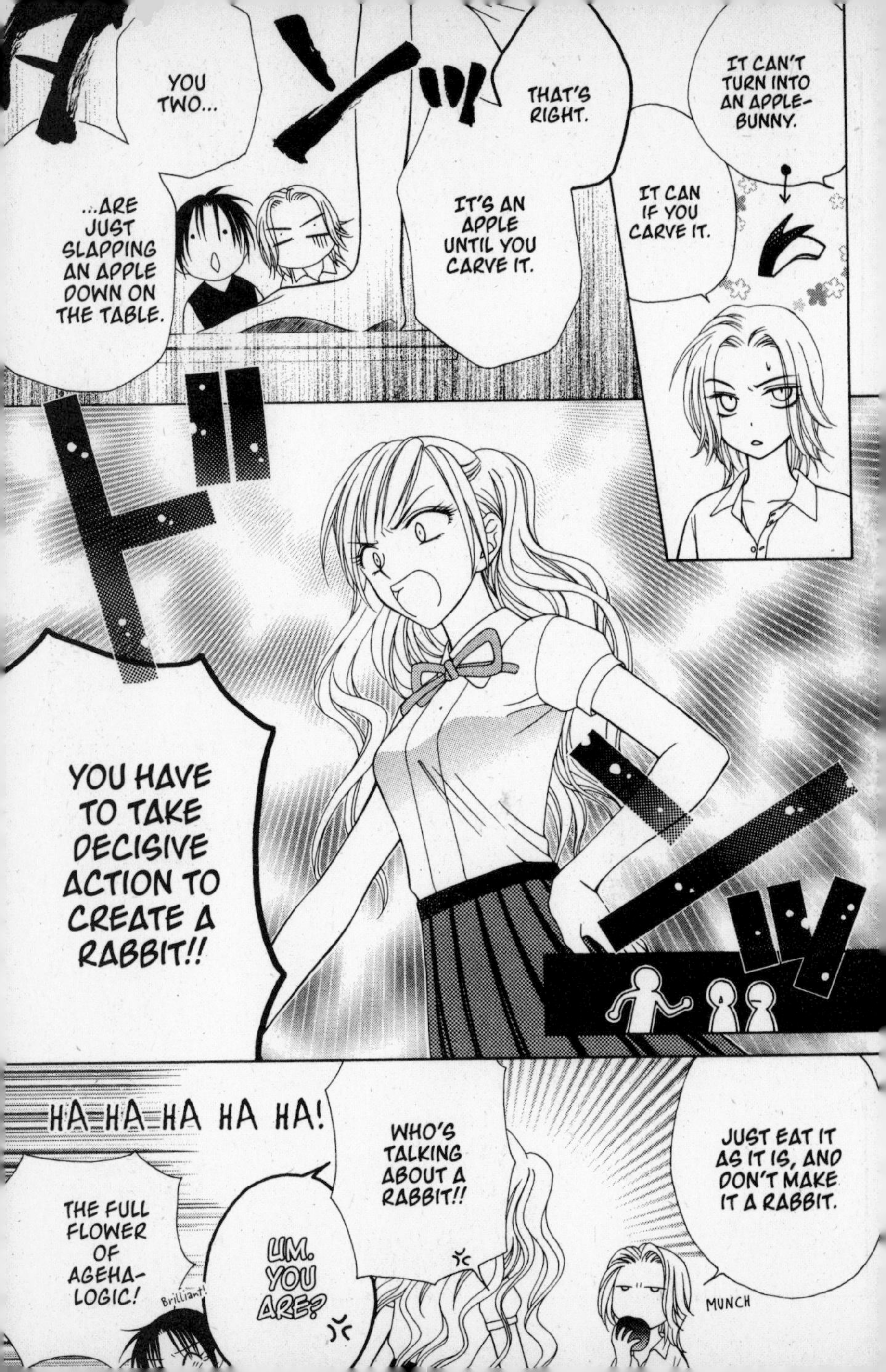
IT CAN'T TURN INTO AN APPLE-BUNNY.
IT CAN IF YOU CARVE IT.
THAT'S RIGHT.
IT'S AN APPLE UNTIL YOU CARVE IT.
YOU TWO...
...ARE JUST SLAPPING AN APPLE DOWN ON THE TABLE.
YOU HAVE TO TAKE DECISIVE ACTION TO CREATE A RABBIT!!
JUST EAT IT AS IT IS, AND DON'T MAKE IT A RABBIT.
MUNCH
WHO'S TALKING ABOUT A RABBIT!!
UM. YOU ARE?
HA HA HA HA HA HA!
THE FULL FLOWER OF AGEHA-LOGIC!
Brilliant!

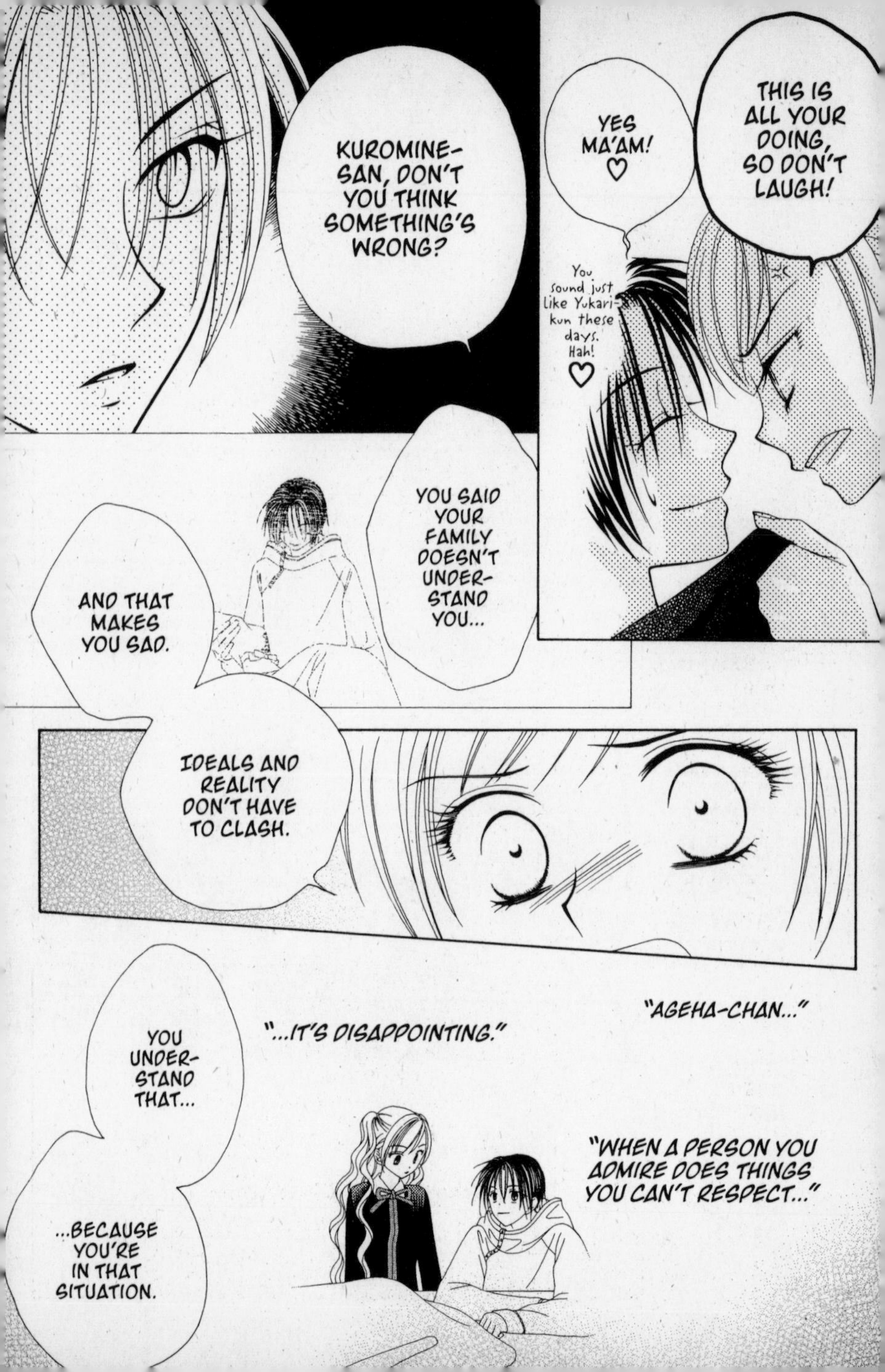
THIS IS ALL YOUR DOING, SO DON'T LAUGH!
YES MA'AM! ♡
You sound just like Yukari-kun these days. Hah! ♡
KUROMINE-SAN, DON'T YOU THINK SOMETHING'S WRONG?
YOU SAID YOUR FAMILY DOESN'T UNDER-STAND YOU...
AND THAT MAKES YOU SAD.
IDEALS AND REALITY DON'T HAVE TO CLASH.
"AGEHA-CHAN..."
"WHEN A PERSON YOU ADMIRE DOES THINGS YOU CAN'T RESPECT..."
"...IT'S DISAPPOINTING."
YOU UNDER-STAND THAT...
...BECAUSE YOU'RE IN THAT SITUATION.

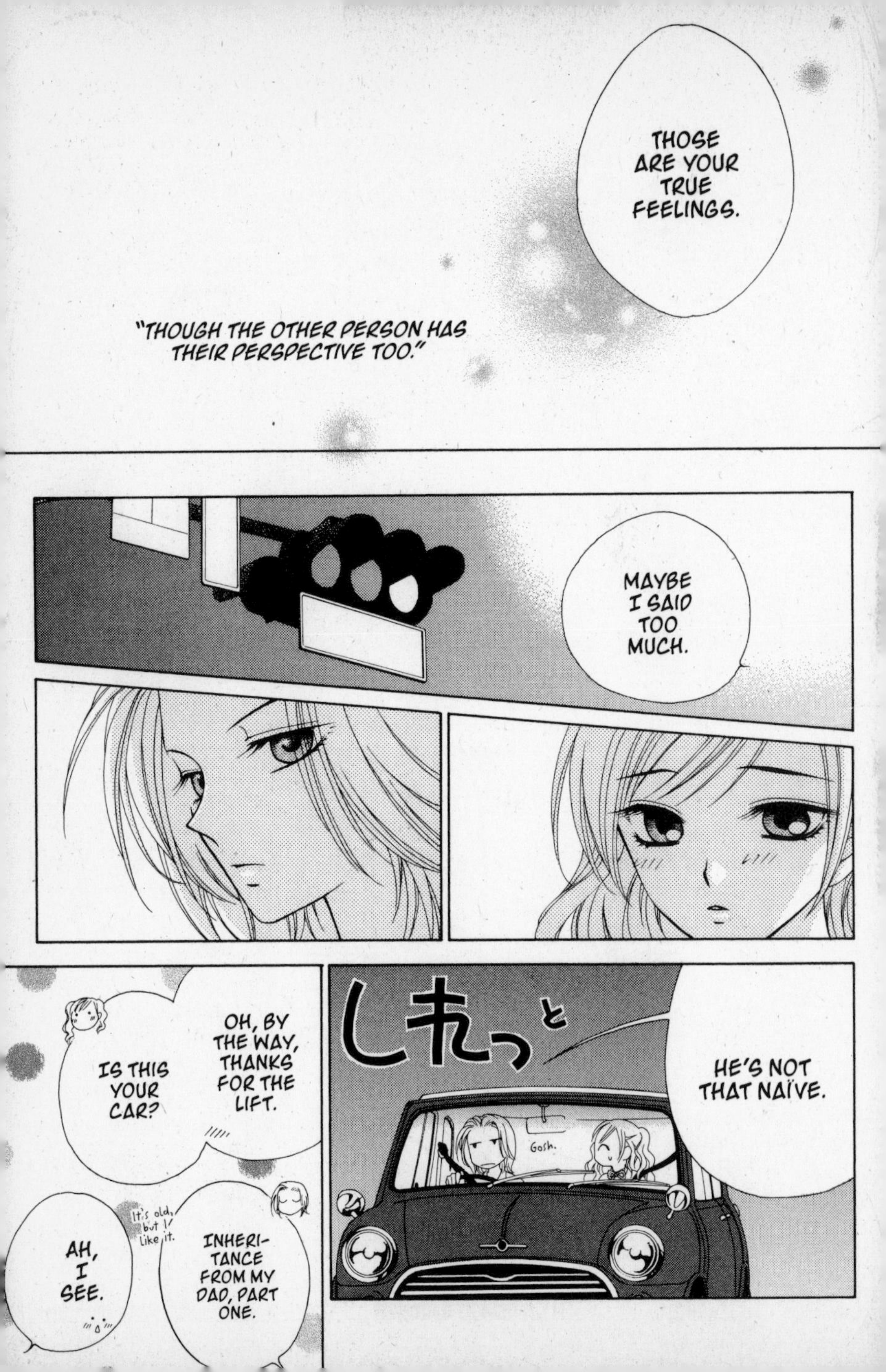
THOSE ARE YOUR TRUE FEELINGS.
"THOUGH THE OTHER PERSON HAS THEIR PERSPECTIVE TOO."
MAYBE I SAID TOO MUCH.
HE'S NOT THAT NAÏVE.
しれっと
Gosh.
OH, BY THE WAY, THANKS FOR THE LIFT.
IS THIS YOUR CAR?
INHERI-TANCE FROM MY DAD, PART ONE.
It's old, but I like it.
AH, I SEE.

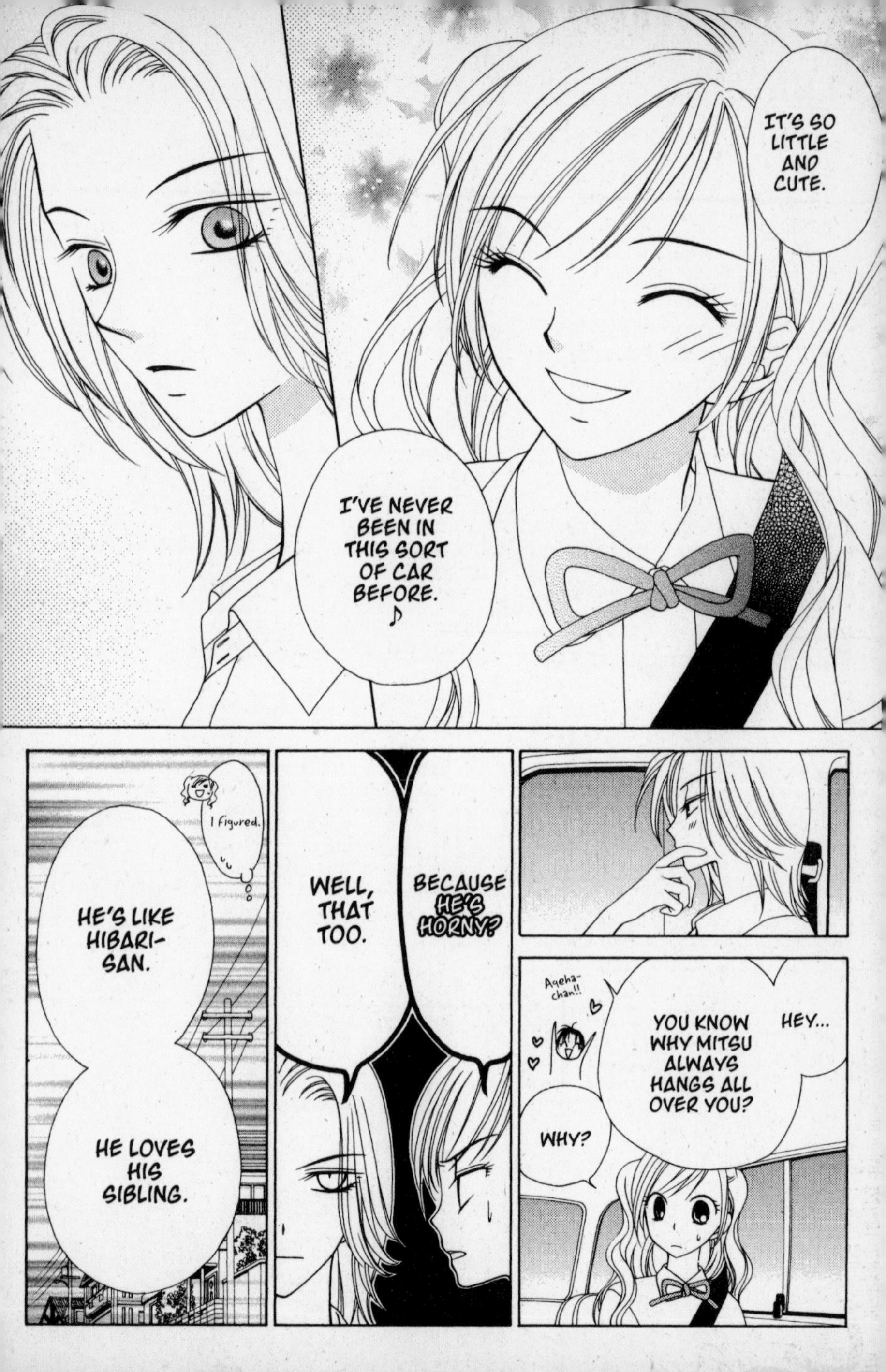
IT'S SO LITTLE AND CUTE.
I'VE NEVER BEEN IN THIS SORT OF CAR BEFORE. ♪
HEY...
YOU KNOW WHY MITSU ALWAYS HANGS ALL OVER YOU?
Ageha-chan!!
WHY?
BECAUSE HE'S HORNY?
WELL, THAT TOO.
HE'S LIKE HIBARI-SAN.
I figured.
HE LOVES HIS SIBLING.

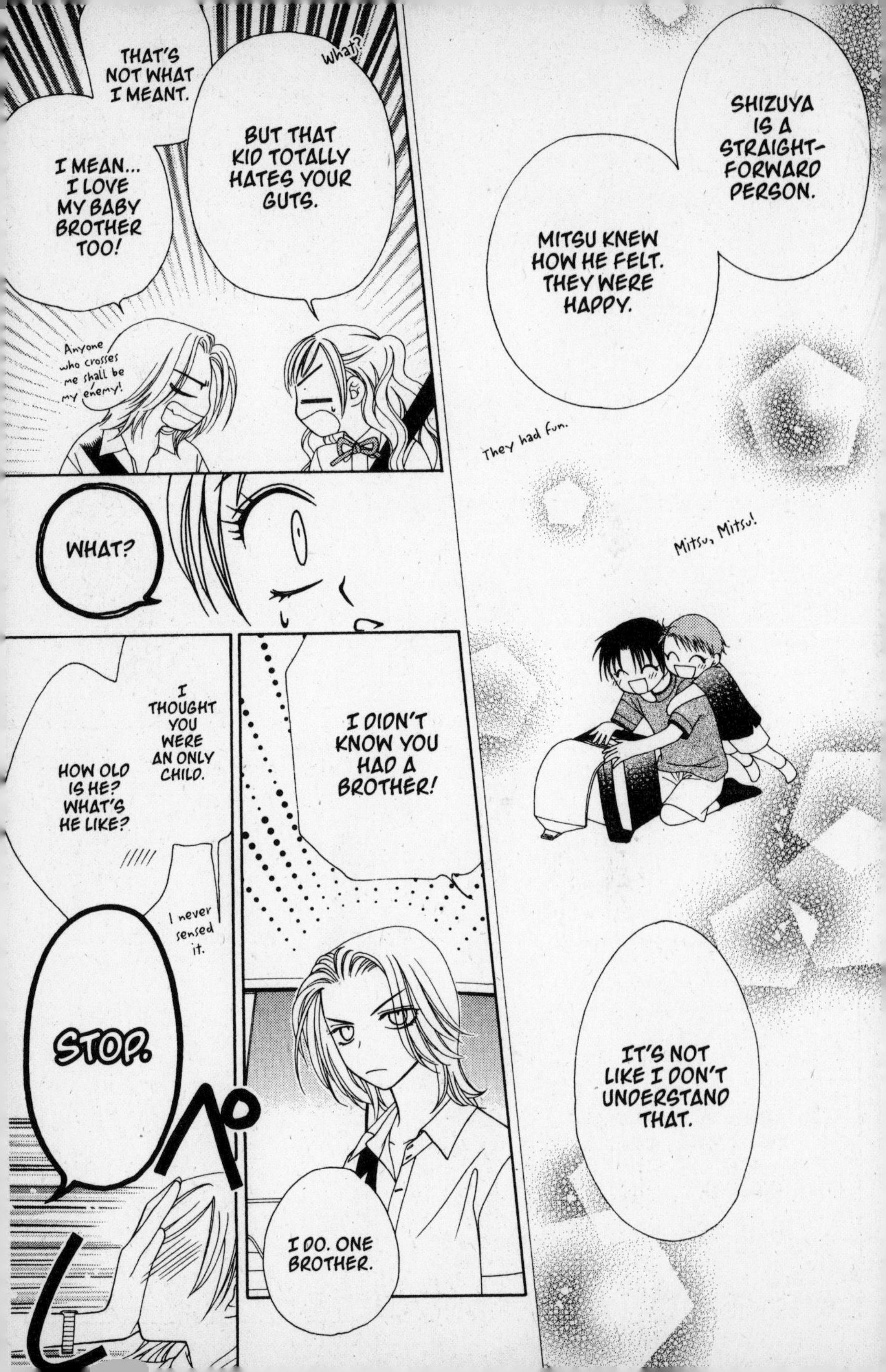
SHIZUYA IS A STRAIGHT-FORWARD PERSON.
MITSU KNEW HOW HE FELT. THEY WERE HAPPY.
They had fun.
Mitsu, Mitsu!
IT'S NOT LIKE I DON'T UNDERSTAND THAT.
What?
BUT THAT KID TOTALLY HATES YOUR GUTS.
THAT'S NOT WHAT I MEANT.
I MEAN... I LOVE MY BABY BROTHER TOO!
Anyone who crosses me shall be my enemy!
WHAT?
I DIDN'T KNOW YOU HAD A BROTHER!
I DO. ONE BROTHER.
I THOUGHT YOU WERE AN ONLY CHILD.
HOW OLD IS HE? WHAT'S HE LIKE?
I never sensed it.
STOP.

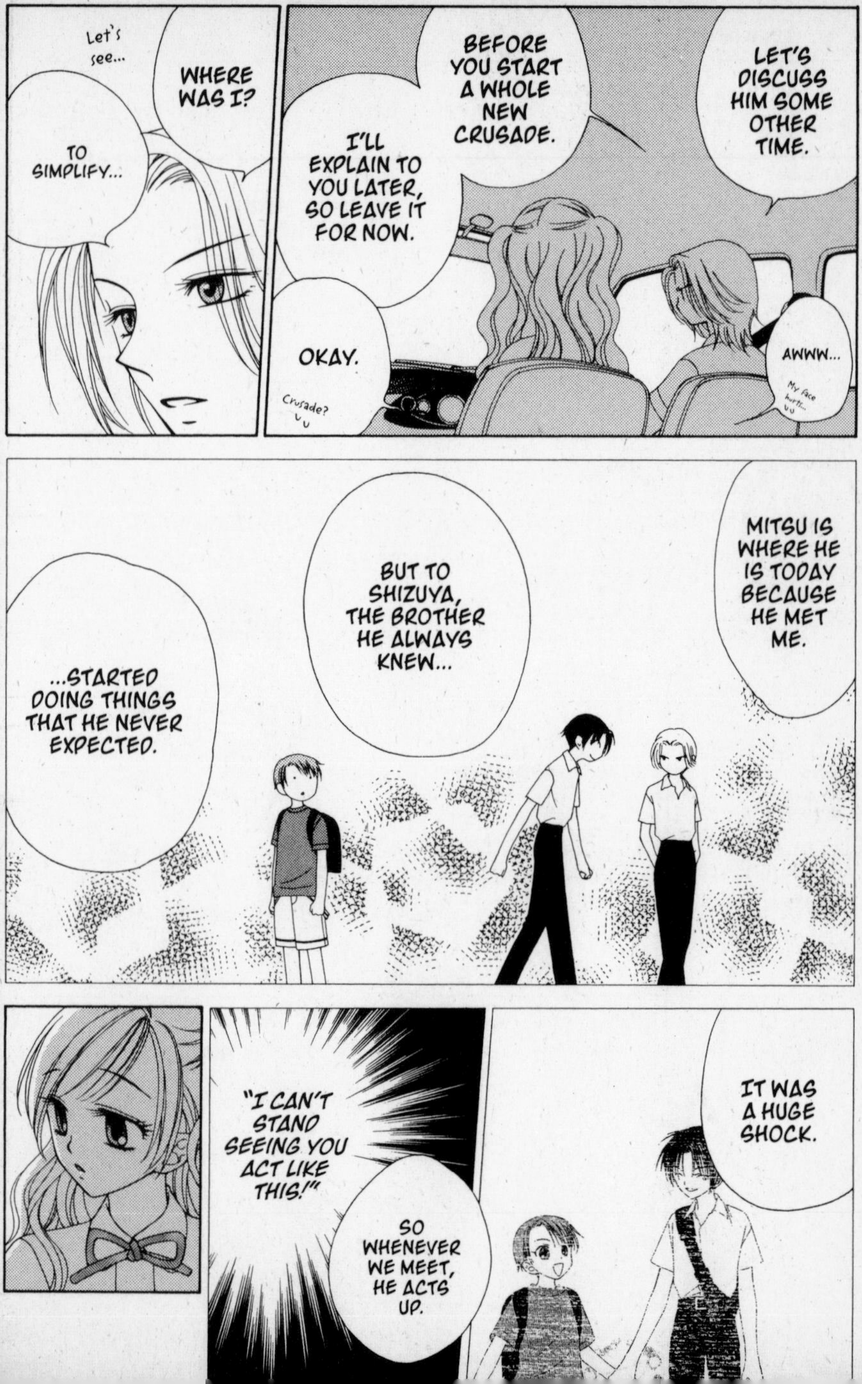
LET'S DISCUSS HIM SOME OTHER TIME.
BEFORE YOU START A WHOLE NEW CRUSADE.
AWWW...
My face hurts...
I'LL EXPLAIN TO YOU LATER, SO LEAVE IT FOR NOW.
OKAY.
Crusade?
WHERE WAS I?
Let's see...
TO SIMPLIFY...
MITSU IS WHERE HE IS TODAY BECAUSE HE MET ME.
BUT TO SHIZUYA, THE BROTHER HE ALWAYS KNEW...
...STARTED DOING THINGS THAT HE NEVER EXPECTED.
IT WAS A HUGE SHOCK.
SO WHENEVER WE MEET, HE ACTS UP.
"I CAN'T STAND SEEING YOU ACT LIKE THIS!"

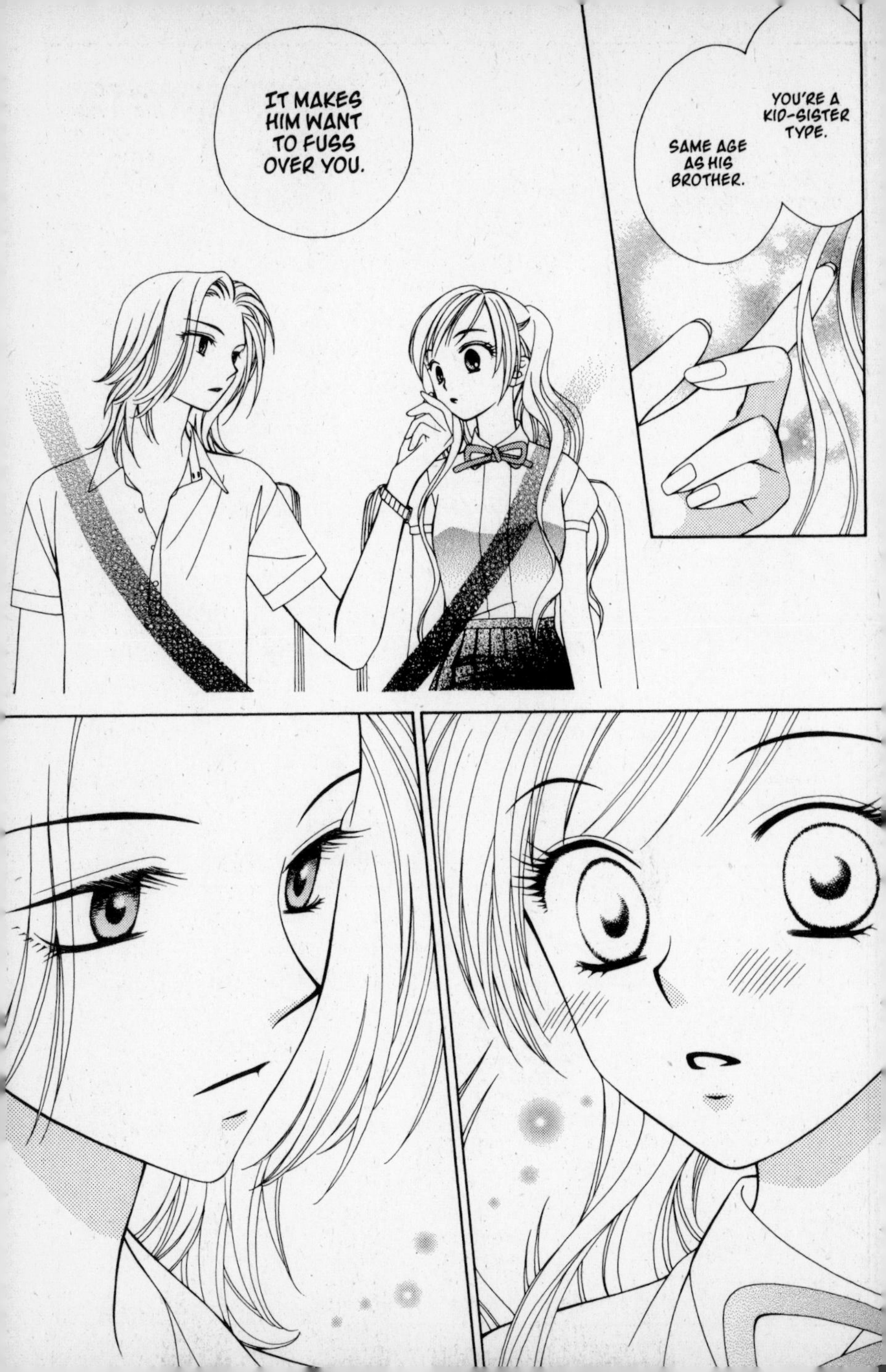
YOU'RE A KID-SISTER TYPE.
SAME AGE AS HIS BROTHER.
IT MAKES HIM WANT TO FUSS OVER YOU.

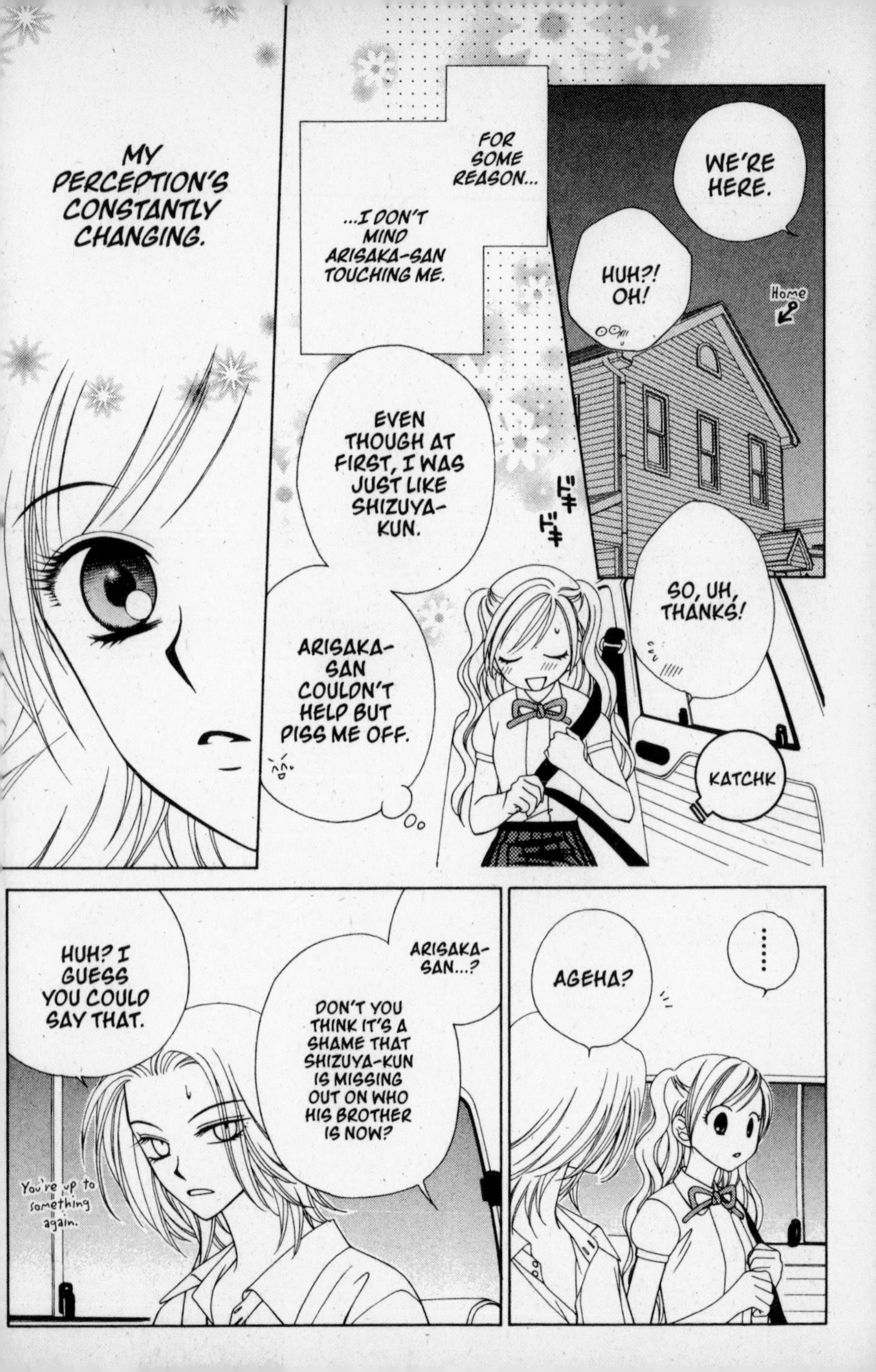
WE'RE HERE.
HUH?! OH!
Home
ドキ
ドキ
SO, UH, THANKS!
KATCHK
FOR SOME REASON...
...I DON'T MIND ARISAKA-SAN TOUCHING ME.
EVEN THOUGH AT FIRST, I WAS JUST LIKE SHIZUYA-KUN.
ARISAKA-SAN COULDN'T HELP BUT PISS ME OFF.
MY PERCEPTION'S CONSTANTLY CHANGING.
......
AGEHA?
ARISAKA-SAN...?
DON'T YOU THINK IT'S A SHAME THAT SHIZUYA-KUN IS MISSING OUT ON WHO HIS BROTHER IS NOW?
HUH? I GUESS YOU COULD SAY THAT.
You're up to something again.

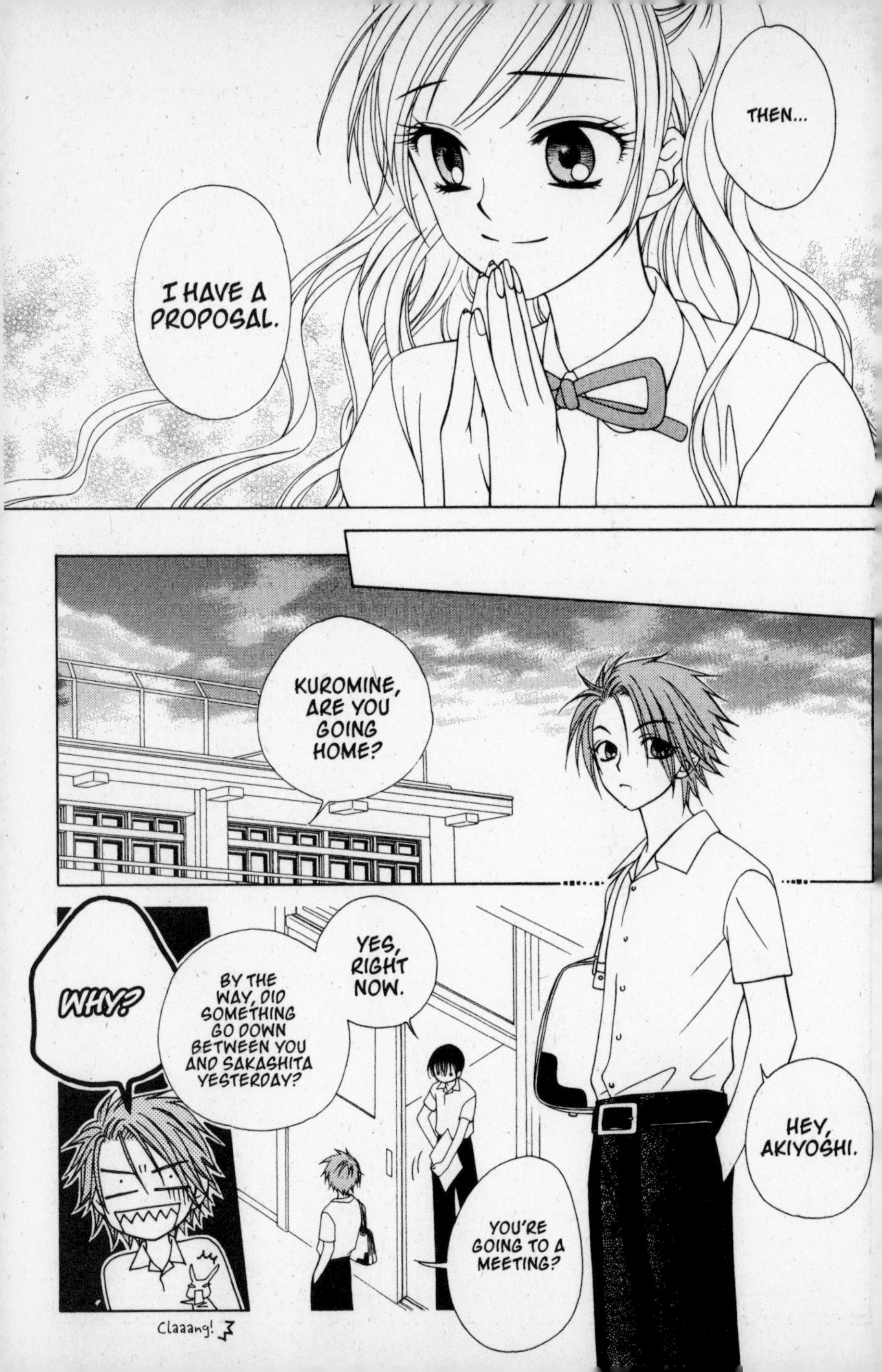
THEN...
I HAVE A PROPOSAL.
KUROMINE, ARE YOU GOING HOME?
HEY, AKIYOSHI.
YOU'RE GOING TO A MEETING?
YES, RIGHT NOW.
BY THE WAY, DID SOMETHING GO DOWN BETWEEN YOU AND SAKASHITA YESTERDAY?
WHY?
Claaang!

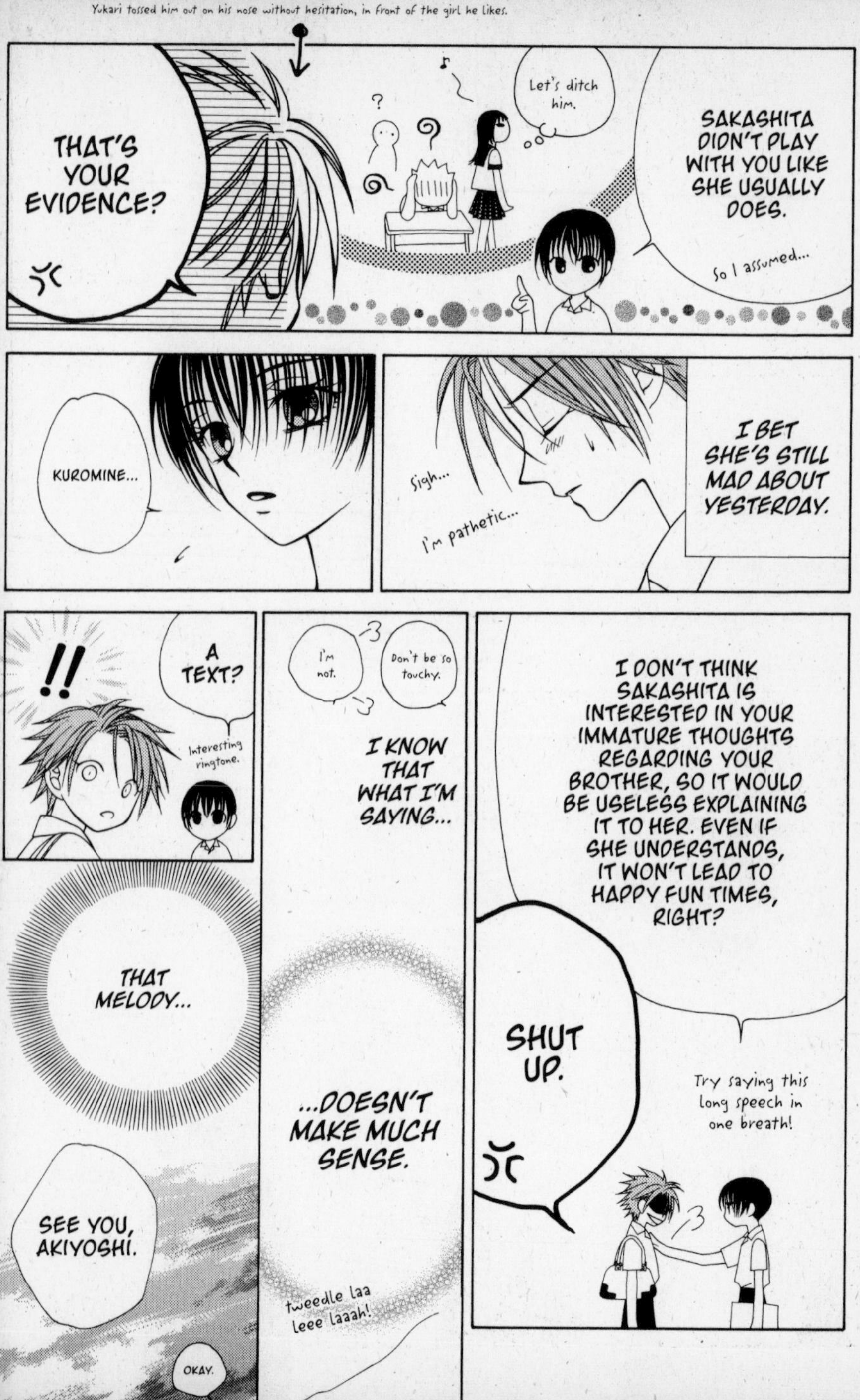
Yukari tossed him out on his nose without hesitation, in front of the girl he likes.
SAKASHITA DIDN'T PLAY WITH YOU LIKE SHE USUALLY DOES.
So I assumed...
Let's ditch him.
THAT'S YOUR EVIDENCE?
I BET SHE'S STILL MAD ABOUT YESTERDAY.
Sigh...
I'm pathetic...
KUROMINE...
I DON'T THINK SAKASHITA IS INTERESTED IN YOUR IMMATURE THOUGHTS REGARDING YOUR BROTHER, SO IT WOULD BE USELESS EXPLAINING IT TO HER. EVEN IF SHE UNDERSTANDS, IT WON'T LEAD TO HAPPY FUN TIMES, RIGHT?
SHUT UP.
Try saying this long speech in one breath!
Don't be so touchy.
I'm not.
I KNOW THAT WHAT I'M SAYING...
...DOESN'T MAKE MUCH SENSE.
tweedle laa leee laaah!
A TEXT?
!!
Interesting ringtone.
THAT MELODY...
SEE YOU, AKIYOSHI.
OKAY.

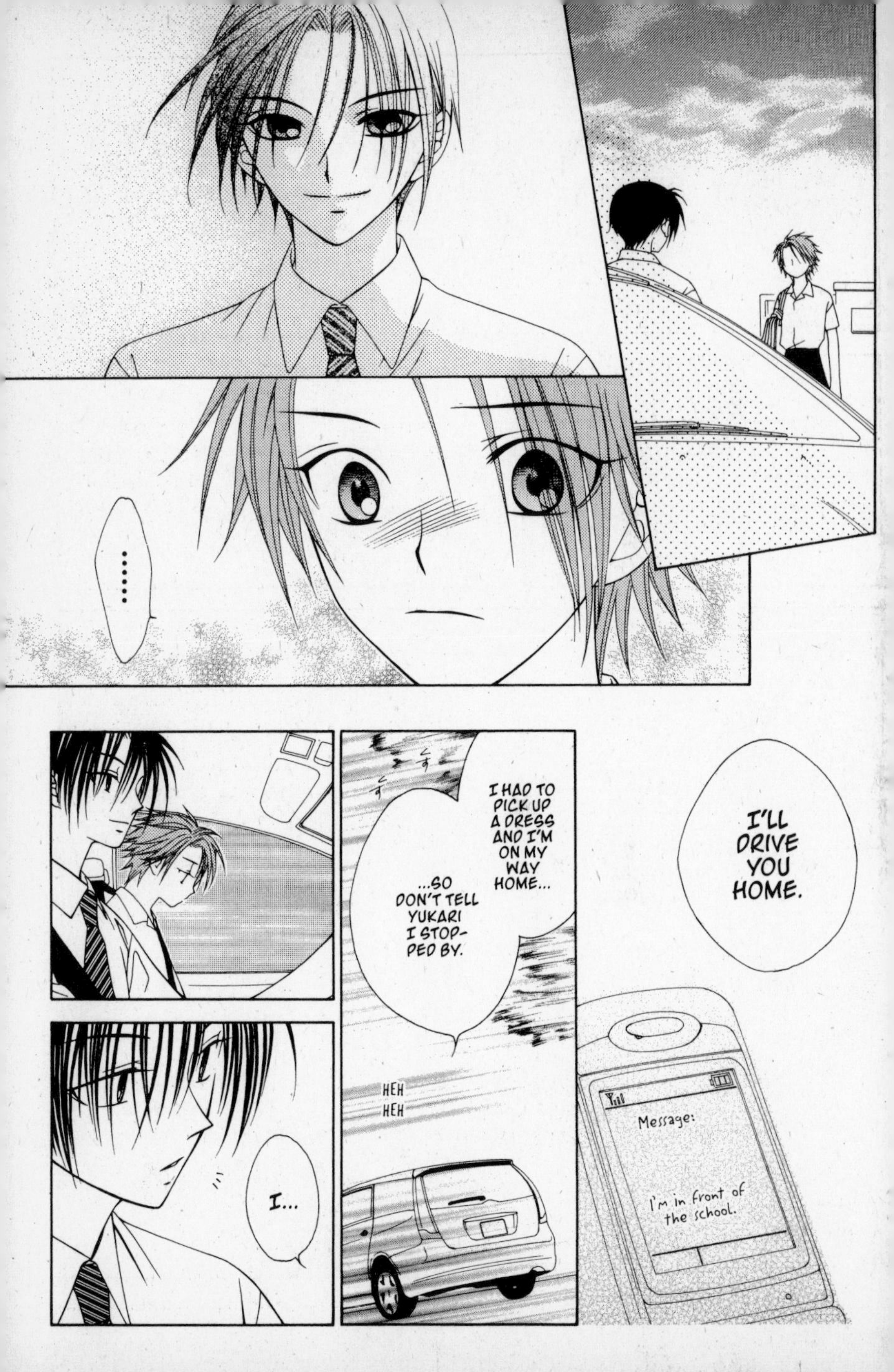
......
I'LL DRIVE YOU HOME.
Message:
I'm in front of the school.
I HAD TO PICK UP A DRESS AND I'M ON MY WAY HOME...
...SO DON'T TELL YUKARI I STOP-PED BY.
HEH HEH
I...

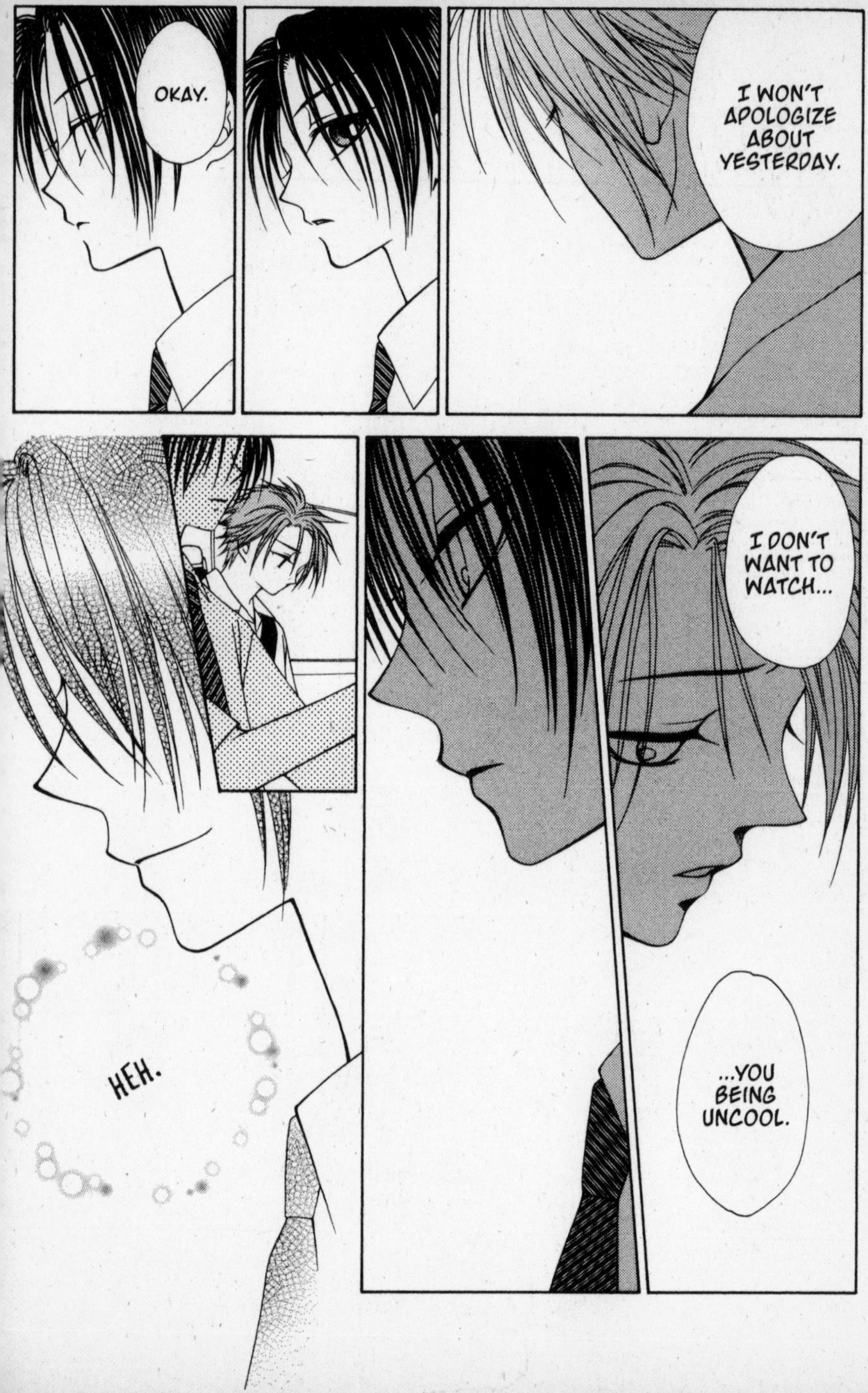
I WON'T APOLOGIZE ABOUT YESTERDAY.
OKAY.
I DON'T WANT TO WATCH...
...YOU BEING UNCOOL.
HEH.

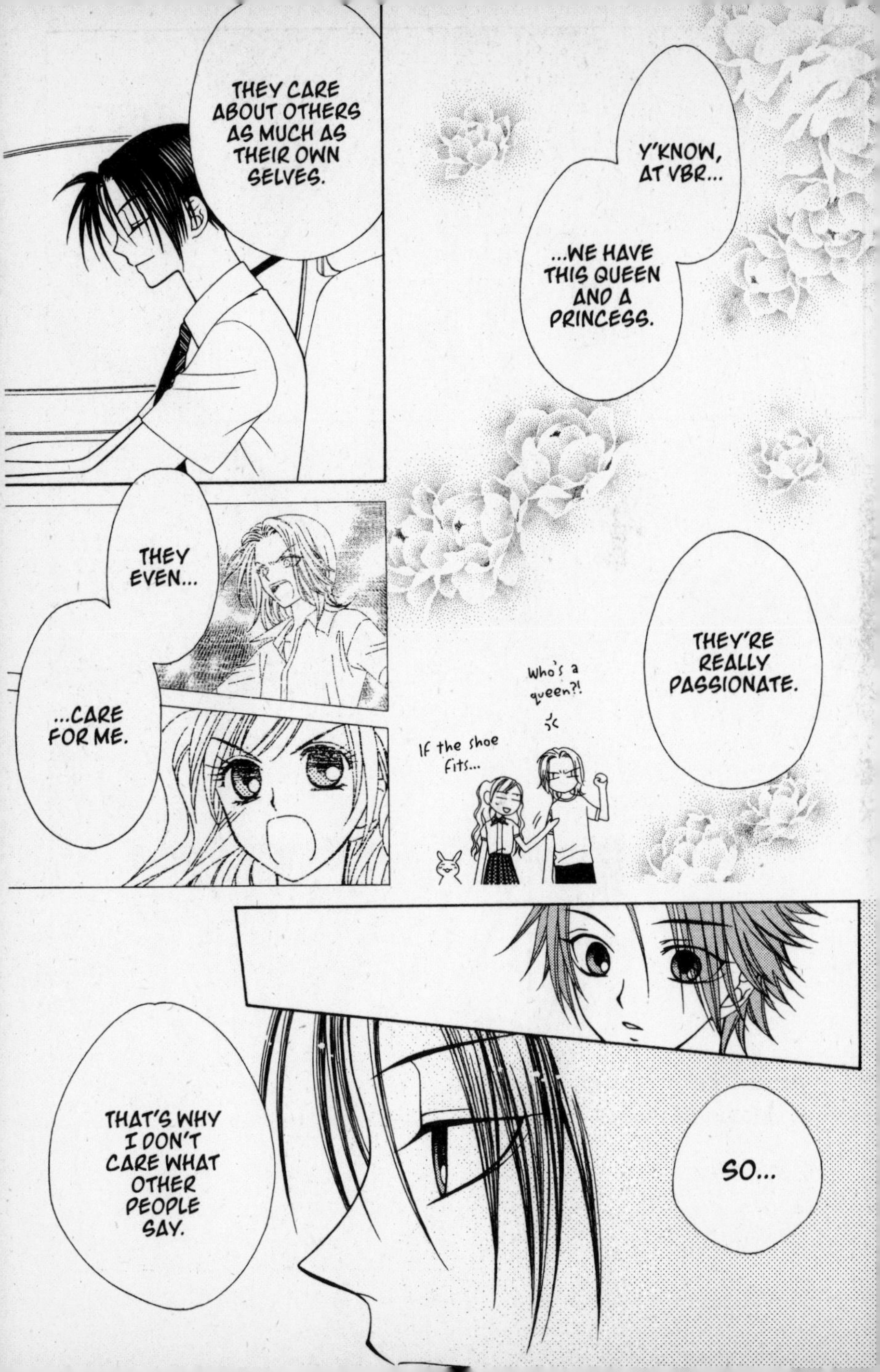
Y'KNOW, AT VBR...
...WE HAVE THIS QUEEN AND A PRINCESS.
THEY'RE REALLY PASSIONATE.
Who's a queen?!
If the shoe fits...
THEY CARE ABOUT OTHERS AS MUCH AS THEIR OWN SELVES.
THEY EVEN...
...CARE FOR ME.
SO...
THAT'S WHY I DON'T CARE WHAT OTHER PEOPLE SAY.

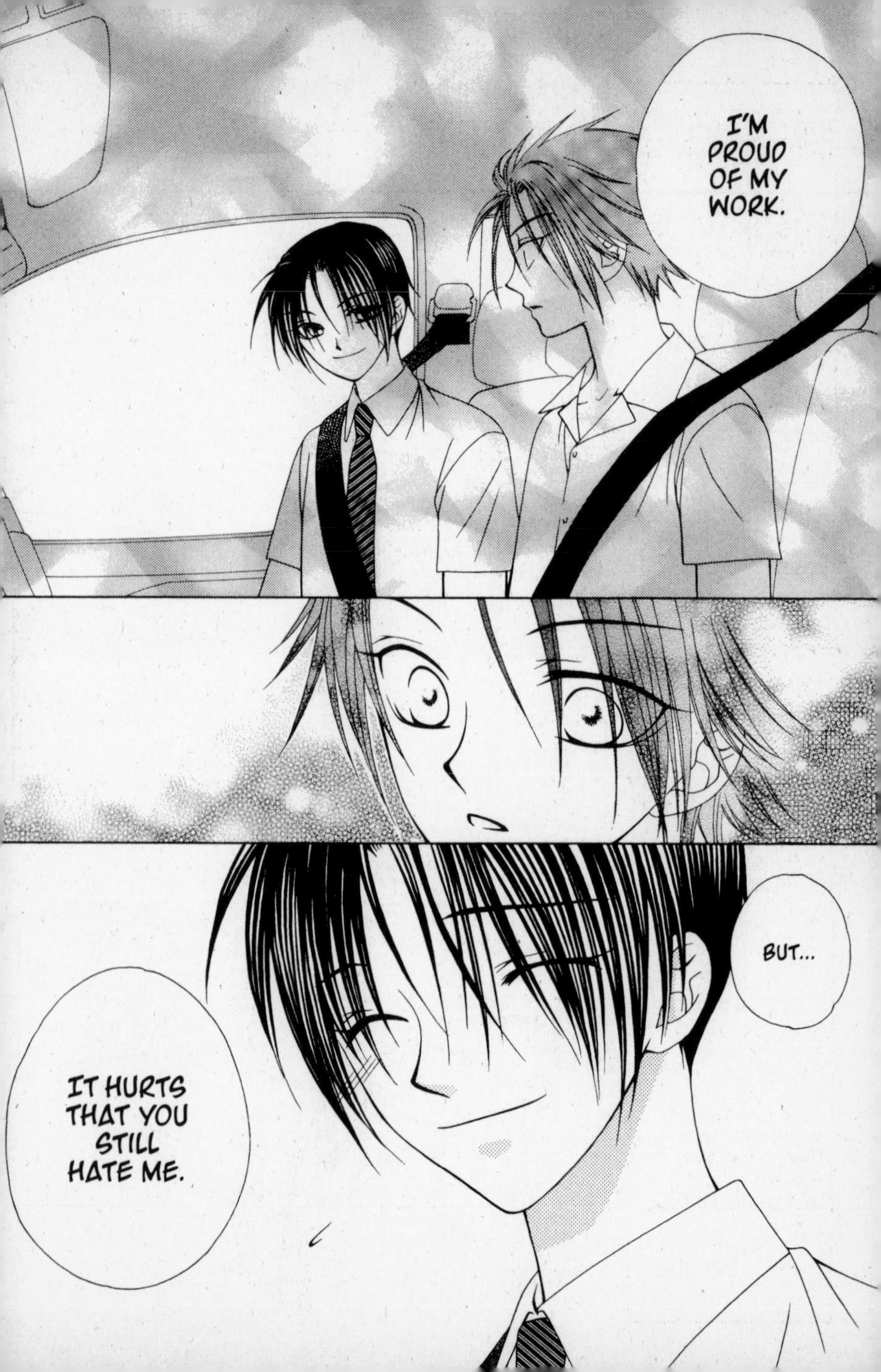
I'M PROUD OF MY WORK.
BUT...
IT HURTS THAT YOU STILL HATE ME.

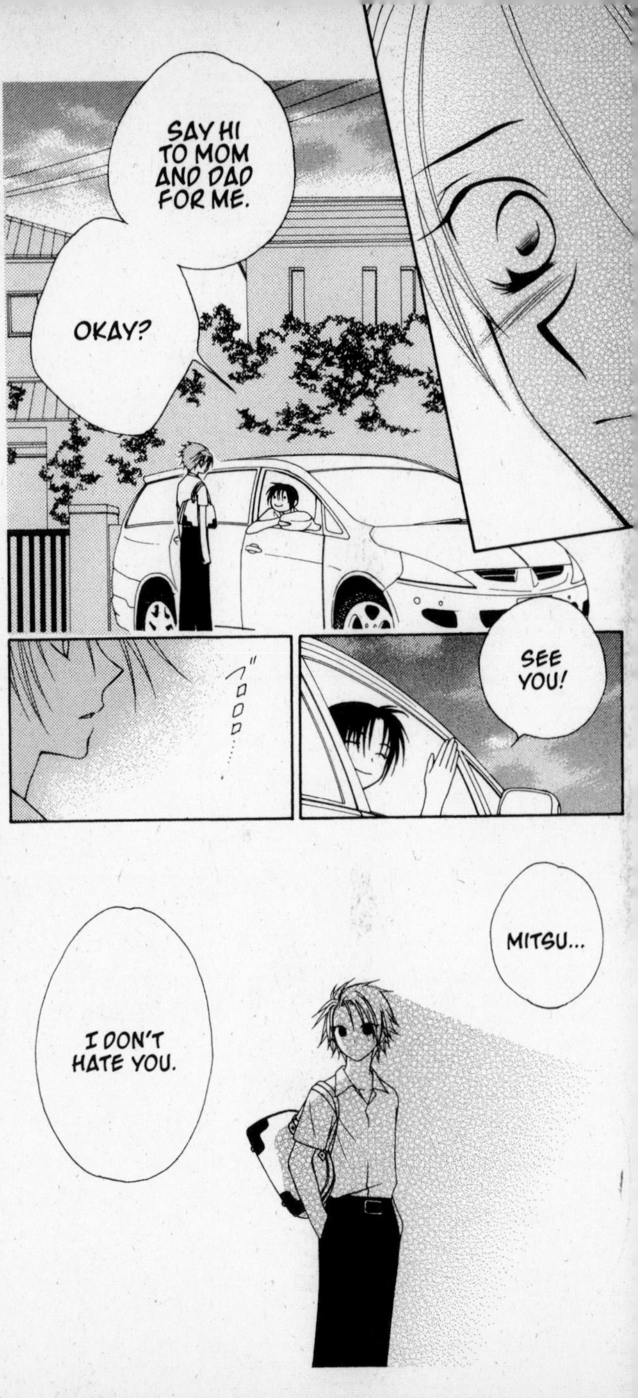
SAY HI TO MOM AND DAD FOR ME.
OKAY?
SEE YOU!
MITSU...
I DON'T HATE YOU.

This is the last side bar. Thank you so much for reading this far!♡

Thanks to all of you who helped me, and to all of you who read this book.

Page187: The assistants' reaction when they saw Mitsu await Shizuya in front of the school:

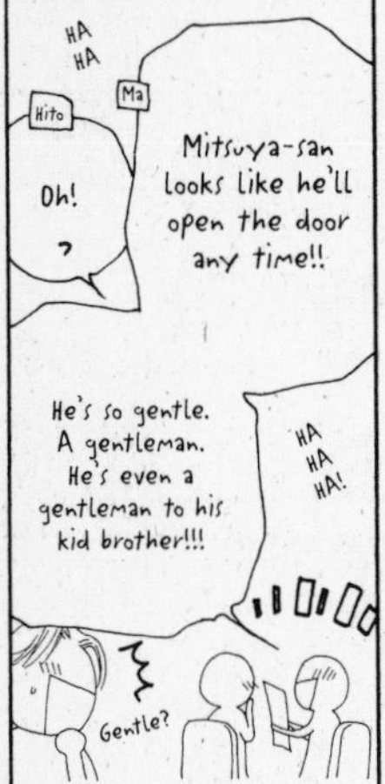
HA HA
Hito
Ma
Oh!
?
Mitsuya-san looks like he'll open the door any time!!
He's so gentle. A gentleman. He's even a gentleman to his kid brother!!!
HA HA HA!
Gentle?

It made me laugh out loud.

This is the end of Volume 2, but hope you'll write me letters about it.

Attn: Banri Hidaka
C/o TOKYOPOP Inc.
5900 Wilshire Blvd.
Suite 2000
Los Angeles, CA 90036

I look forward to them!

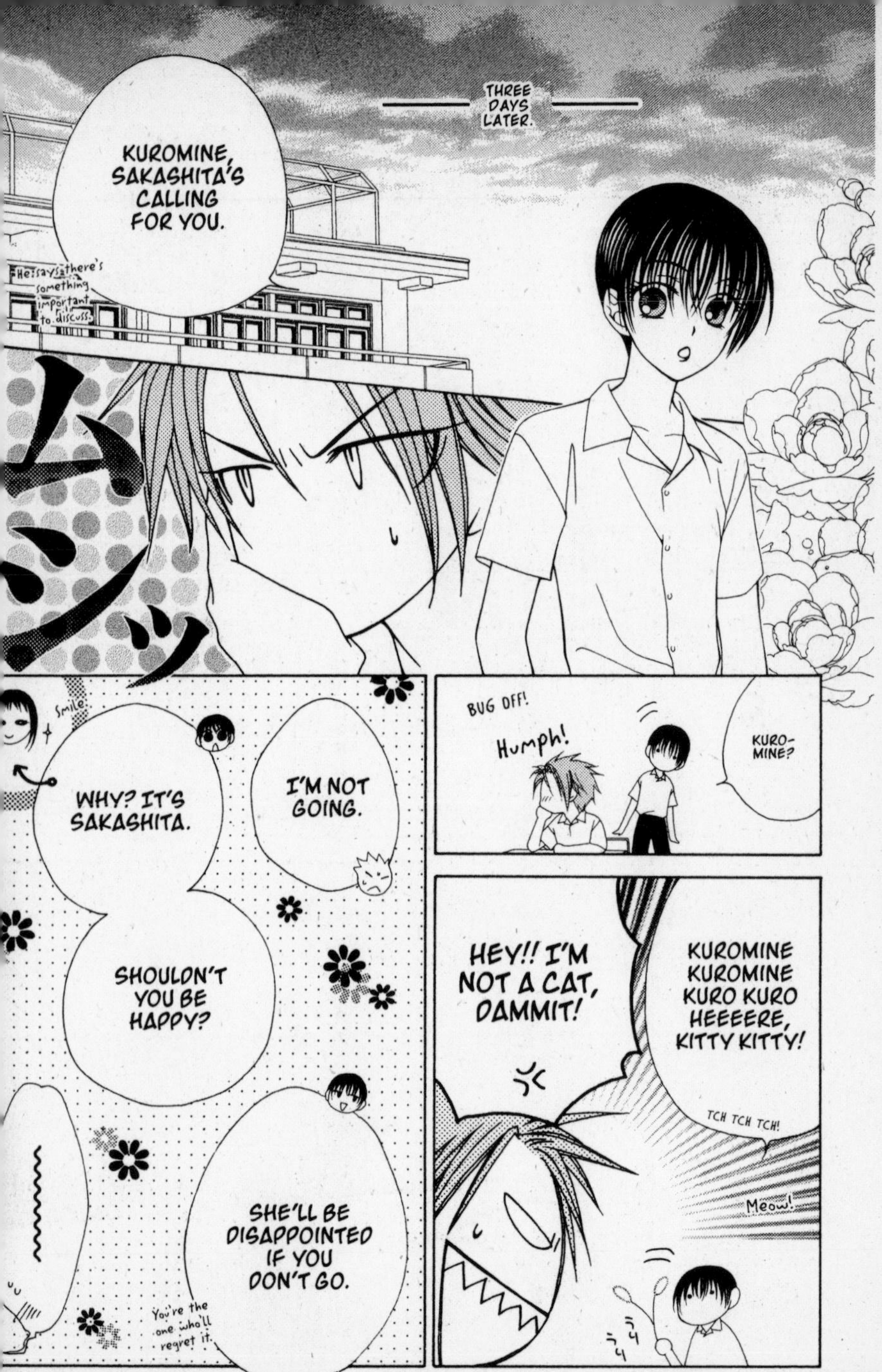
THREE DAYS LATER.
KUROMINE, SAKASHITA'S CALLING FOR YOU.
He says there's something important to discuss.
ムシッ
KURO-MINE?
BUG OFF!
Humph!
KUROMINE KUROMINE KURO KURO HEEEERE, KITTY KITTY!
TCH TCH TCH!
Meow!
HEY!! I'M NOT A CAT, DAMMIT!
I'M NOT GOING.
WHY? IT'S SAKASHITA.
Smile.
SHOULDN'T YOU BE HAPPY?
SHE'LL BE DISAPPOINTED IF YOU DON'T GO.
You're the one who'll regret it.

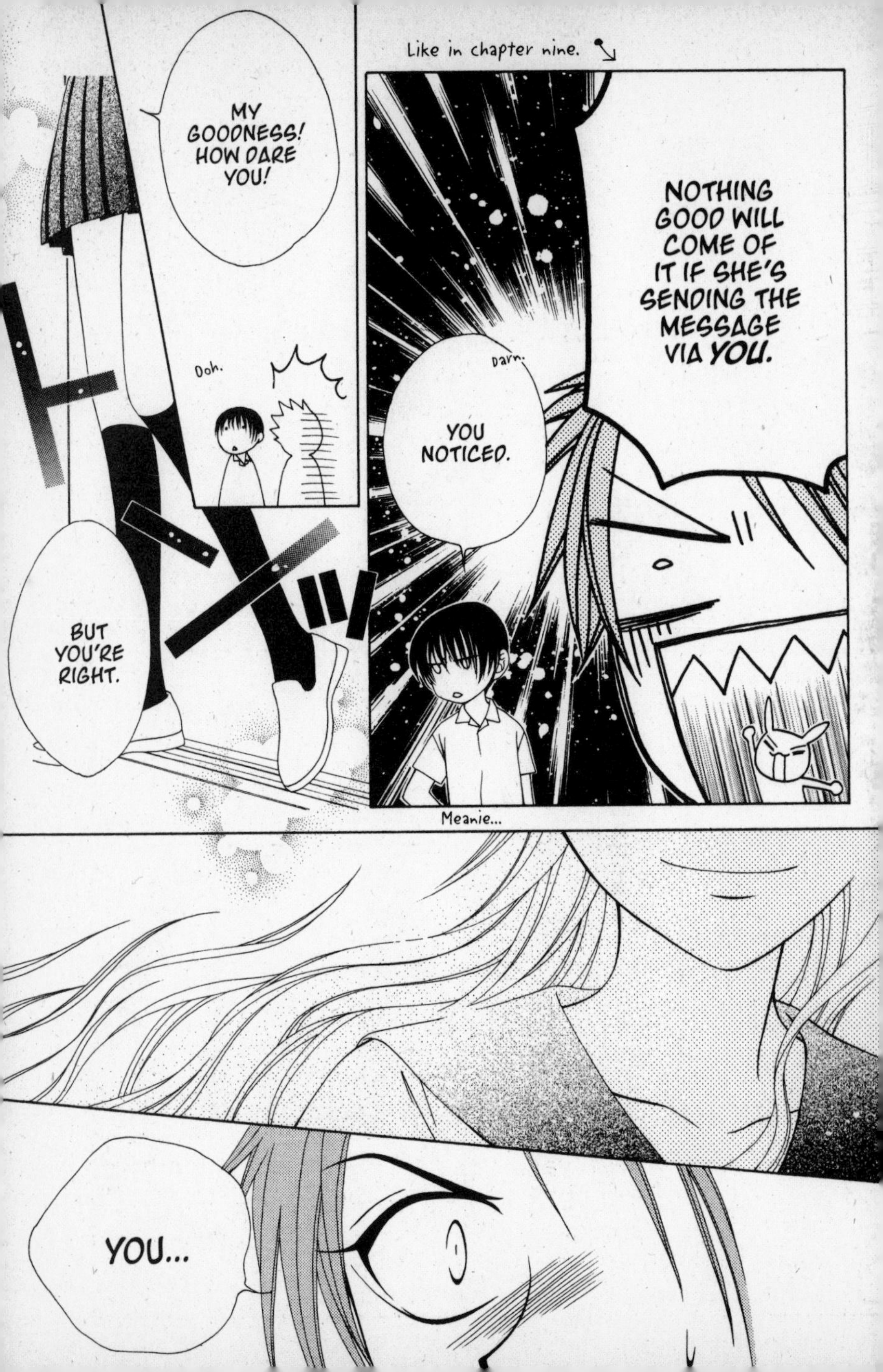

Like in chapter nine.
NOTHING GOOD WILL COME OF IT IF SHE'S SENDING THE MESSAGE VIA YOU.
Darn.
YOU NOTICED.
Meanie...
MY GOODNESS! HOW DARE YOU!
Ooh.
BUT YOU'RE RIGHT.
YOU...

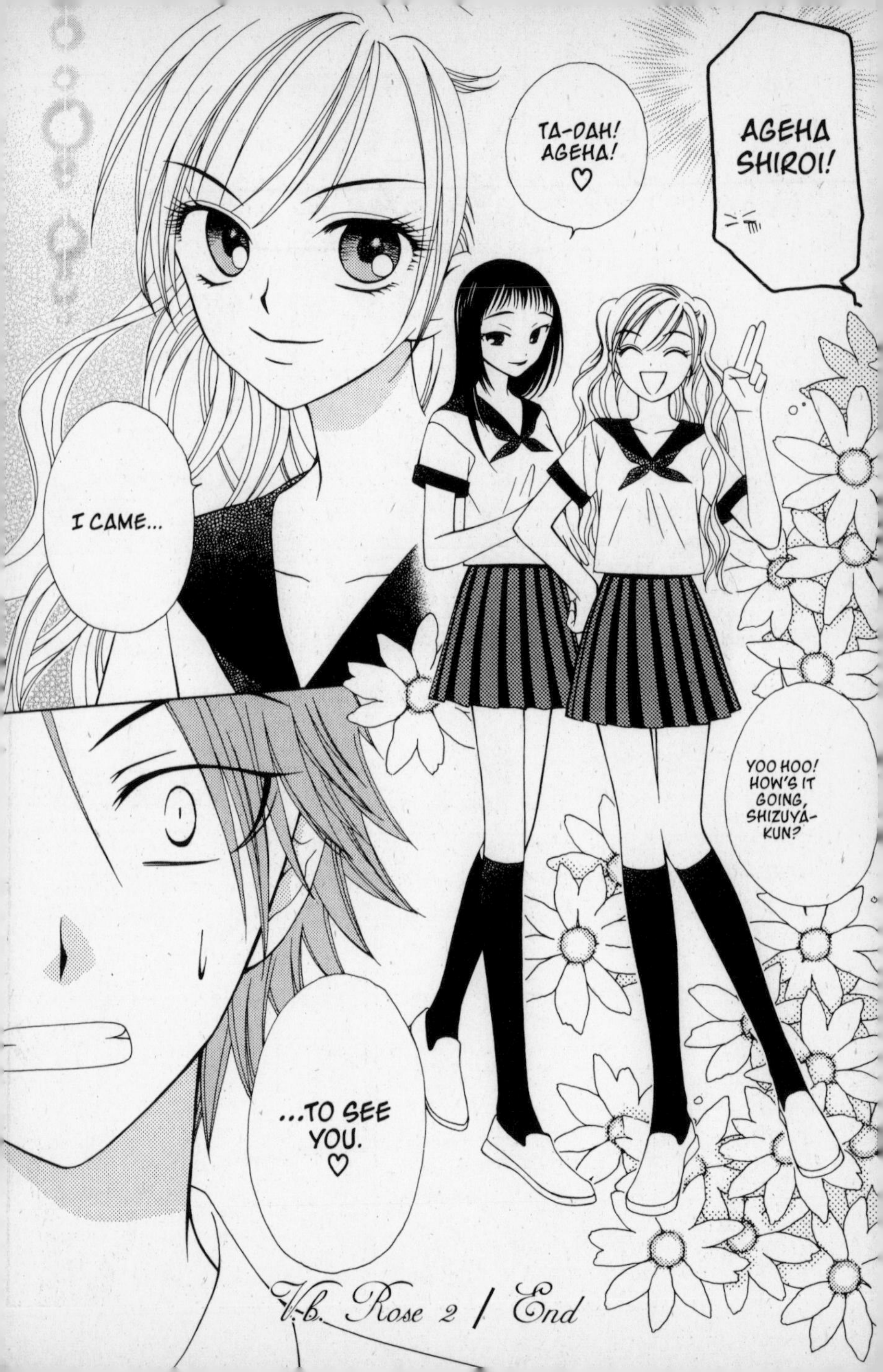
AGEHA SHIROI!
TA-DAH! AGEHA! ♡
I CAME...
YOO HOO! HOW'S IT GOING, SHIZUYA-KUN?
...TO SEE YOU. ♡
V.B. Rose 2 / End

Banri Hidaka's Everyday Heaven!

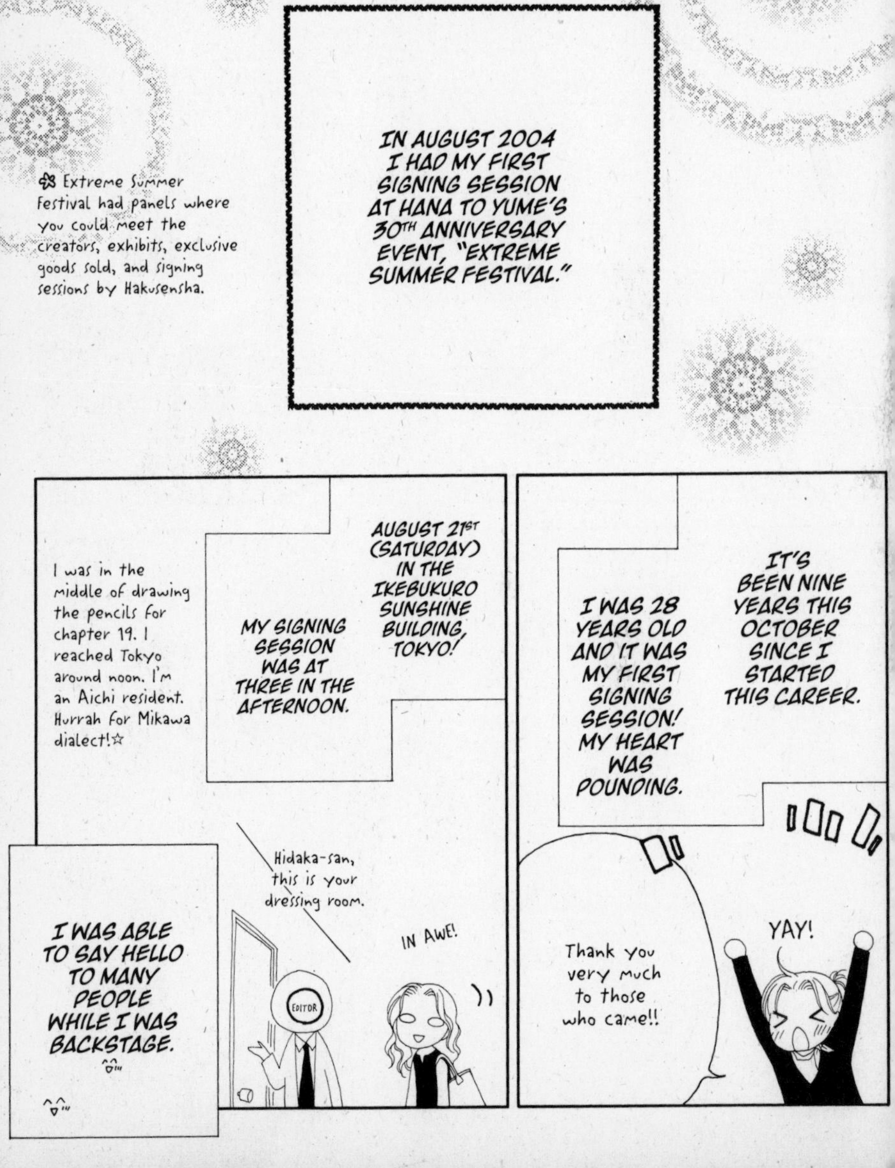

IN AUGUST 2004 I HAD MY FIRST SIGNING SESSION AT HANA TO YUME'S 30TH ANNIVERSARY EVENT, "EXTREME SUMMER FESTIVAL."
✿ Extreme Summer Festival had panels where you could meet the creators, exhibits, exclusive goods sold, and signing sessions by Hakusensha.
IT'S BEEN NINE YEARS THIS OCTOBER SINCE I STARTED THIS CAREER.
I WAS 28 YEARS OLD AND IT WAS MY FIRST SIGNING SESSION! MY HEART WAS POUNDING.
YAY!
Thank you very much to those who came!!
AUGUST 21ST (SATURDAY) IN THE IKEBUKURO SUNSHINE BUILDING, TOKYO!
MY SIGNING SESSION WAS AT THREE IN THE AFTERNOON.
I was in the middle of drawing the pencils for chapter 19. I reached Tokyo around noon. I'm an Aichi resident. Hurrah for Mikawa dialect!☆
Hidaka-san, this is your dressing room.
EDITOR
IN AWE!
I WAS ABLE TO SAY HELLO TO MANY PEOPLE WHILE I WAS BACKSTAGE.

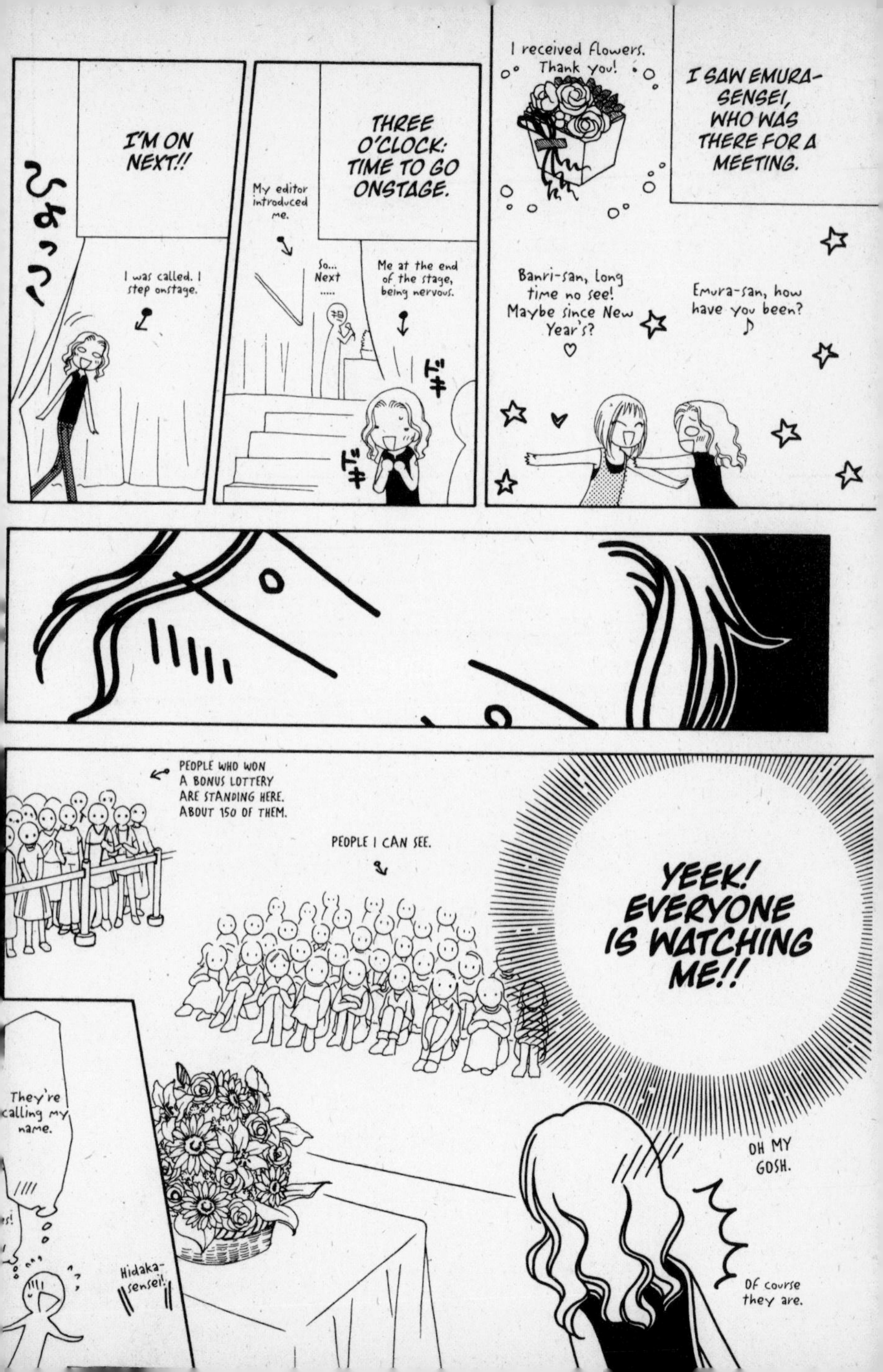

I SAW EMURA-SENSEI, WHO WAS THERE FOR A MEETING.
I received flowers. Thank you!
Emura-san, how have you been? ♪
Banri-san, long time no see! Maybe since New Year's? ♡
THREE O'CLOCK: TIME TO GO ONSTAGE.
Me at the end of the stage, being nervous.
ドキ
ドキ
So... Next .....
My editor introduced me.
I'M ON NEXT!!
ひょっこ
I was called. I step onstage.
YEEK! EVERYONE IS WATCHING ME!!
PEOPLE I CAN SEE.
PEOPLE WHO WON A BONUS LOTTERY ARE STANDING HERE. ABOUT 150 OF THEM.
OH MY GOSH.
Of course they are.
Hidaka-sensei!
They're calling my name.

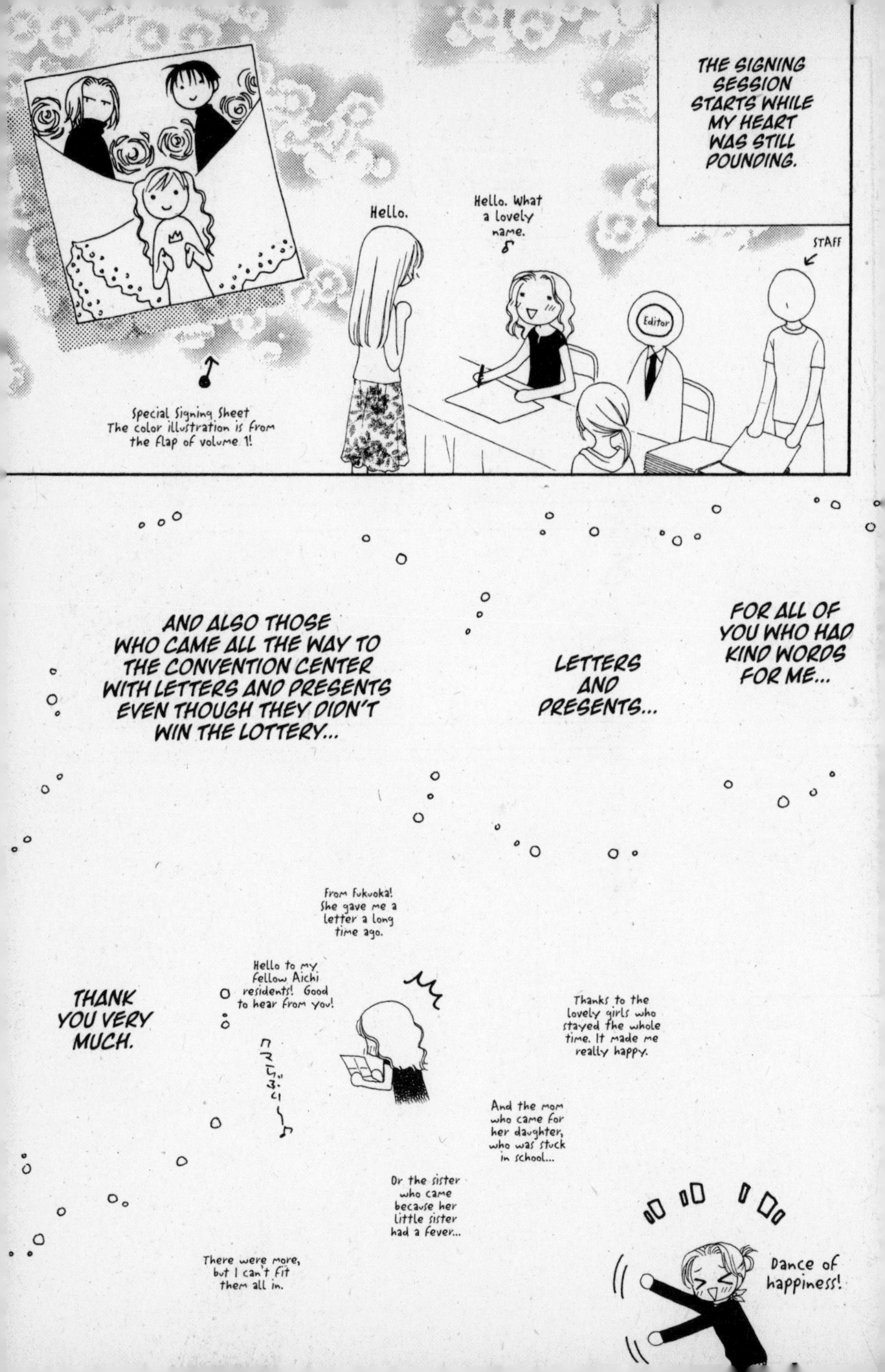
THE SIGNING SESSION STARTS WHILE MY HEART WAS STILL POUNDING.
STAFF
Hello. What a lovely name.
Editor
Hello.
Special Signing Sheet
The color illustration is from the flap of volume 1!
FOR ALL OF YOU WHO HAD KIND WORDS FOR ME...
LETTERS AND PRESENTS...
AND ALSO THOSE WHO CAME ALL THE WAY TO THE CONVENTION CENTER WITH LETTERS AND PRESENTS EVEN THOUGH THEY DIDN'T WIN THE LOTTERY...
Thanks to the lovely girls who stayed the whole time. It made me really happy.
From Fukuoka! She gave me a letter a long time ago.
Hello to my fellow Aichi residents! Good to hear from you!
THANK YOU VERY MUCH.
And the mom who came for her daughter, who was stuck in school...
Or the sister who came because her little sister had a fever...
Dance of happiness!
There were more, but I can't fit them all in.

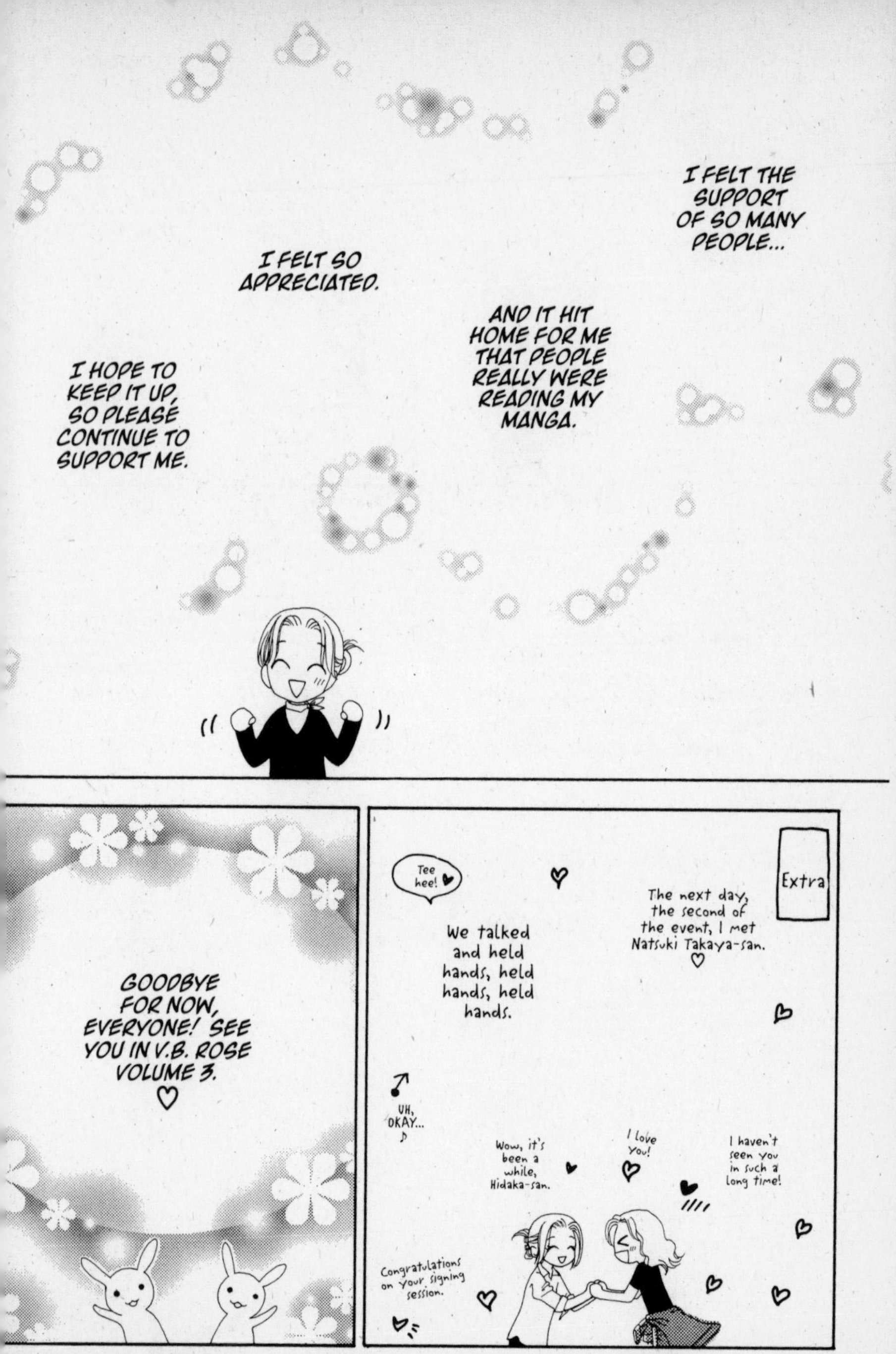
I FELT THE SUPPORT OF SO MANY PEOPLE...
I FELT SO APPRECIATED.
AND IT HIT HOME FOR ME THAT PEOPLE REALLY WERE READING MY MANGA.
I HOPE TO KEEP IT UP, SO PLEASE CONTINUE TO SUPPORT ME.
Extra
The next day, the second of the event, I met Natsuki Takaya-san. ♡
We talked and held hands, held hands, held hands.
Tee hee! ♥
I haven't seen you in such a long time!
I love you! ♡
Wow, it's been a while, Hidaka-san.
UH, OKAY... ♪
Congratulations on your signing session.
GOODBYE FOR NOW, EVERYONE! SEE YOU IN V.B. ROSE VOLUME 3. ♡

In the Next Volume of

V.B. Rose

Ageha's meddling may yet reunite the Kuromine siblings, but her presence at V.B. Rose is getting increasingly complicated! Her skills as an assistant are growing, much to the joy of all concerned, but her feelings for Yukari are growing as well. And others are starting to take notice. Can she balance her desire to know more about her prickly boss with her tendency to interfere?

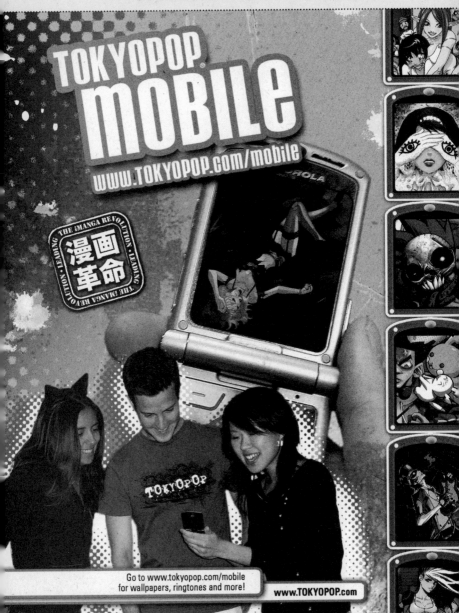

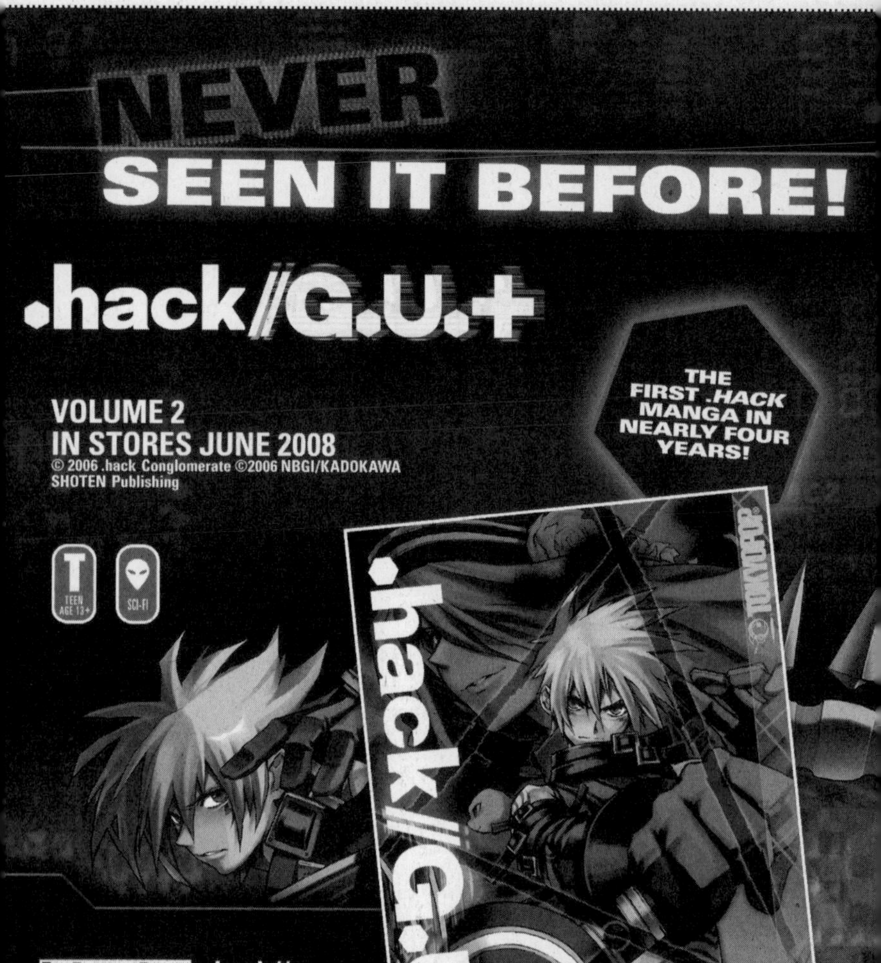
NEVER
SEEN IT BEFORE!
.hack//G.U.+
VOLUME 2
IN STORES JUNE 2008
© 2006 .hack Conglomerate ©2006 NBGI/KADOKAWA SHOTEN Publishing
THE FIRST .HACK MANGA IN NEARLY FOUR YEARS!
T TEEN AGE 13+
SCI-FI
TOKYOPOP
.hack//G.U.+
2
Story by Tatsuya Hamazaki // Art By Yuzuka Morita
.hack// AI buster
.hack//
AI buster
Volumes 1-2
© 2002 Tatsuya Hamazaki / KADOKAWA SHOTEN

STOP!

This is the back of the book.
You wouldn't want to spoil a great ending!

This book is printed "manga-style," in the authentic Japanese right-to-left format. Since none of the artwork has been flipped or altered, readers get to experience the story just as the creator intended. You've been asking for it, so TOKYOPOP® delivered: authentic, hot-off-the-press, and far more fun!

DIRECTIONS

If this is your first time reading manga-style, here's a quick guide to help you understand how it works.

It's easy... just start in the top right panel and follow the numbers. Have fun, and look for more 100% authentic manga from TOKYOPOP®!